A COMMENTARY

ON

The Gospel According to Luke

BY

H. LEO BOLES

GOSPEL ADVOCATE COMPANY

Nashville, Tenn.

1991

Complete Set ISBN 0-89225-000-3
This Volume ISBN 0-89225-003-8
Paperback   ISBN 0-89225-435-1

PREFACE

Some time ago a plan was formed by interested brethren to give to the public a complete commentary on the New Testament; the author was assigned the task of writing in separate volumes commentaries on Matthew and Luke. The volume on Matthew was given to the public in 1936, and the favorable reception that it has received has been a source of inspiration to the author in preparing the volume on Luke. More than two years of preparation have been given to the present volume; time was taken to examine and study closely and fully, in the light of many commentators, every word and sentence in the book of Luke. The bibliography shows the wide range of commentators and scholars that have been studied.

Only one brief commentary on Luke has been written by anyone of the Restoration Movement. J. S. Lamar, in 1877, published his "Commentary on Luke." It is now sixty-one years old; it is a small volume, but has many merits. There is a need for a new commentary on Luke; it is hoped that this may fill that need and be a large contribution to the literature of Biblical knowledge.

The author has studiously and scrupulously refrained from consulting his "Commentary on Matthew" on the parallel passages found in Luke. He wished this volume to be an original and independent treatment of those parallel passages; he wished to be free from any bias in thought or language from any of his former comments, and to give a full and fresh study to these parallel passages. He has kept in mind the common people, and has prepared this volume on Luke with the view of helping the average Bible reader to come to a fuller knowledge of divine thought as expressed by the Holy Spirit through Luke. Greek words, when used, have been given an English spelling so that the average person can understand them. Technicality has been avoided.

The language and style used are those of the classroom instructor, and are free from ornate expressions and embellishments that adorn expression of thought. The author has had

more than twenty-five years' experience as a teacher of the
Bible in college, more than thirty years' experience as a
preacher of the gospel and writer for the religious press; he
has written Sunday school lessons for adults for ten years;
hence out of this long and wide experience as teacher of the
Bible and preacher of the gospel have come many of the comments to be found in this volume.

The plan or outline of this book is simple. It is divided
into sections which are recognized by scholars as natural divisions of the Gospel According to Luke; these sections are divided into smaller sections, according to the natural composition of Luke; and the smaller sections are divided into para-
graphs for easy and clear comprehension. The traditional division into chapters and verses has been disregarded, as these
divisions were made for easy reference, and not for comprehension. The American Standard Version has been used as
the text and all quotations are made from that version.

This volume is offered to the public with a prayer that it
may prove a rich blessing to all who reverently and devoutly
study its contents.

H. LEO BOLES.

Nashville, Tennessee, January 1, 1940.

OUTLINE OF THE GOSPEL ACCORDING TO LUKE

PREFACE OF THE GOSPEL
1 : 1-4

SECTION ONE
BIRTH OF JOHN THE BAPTIST; BIRTH AND
CHILDHOOD OF JESUS
1 : 5 to 2 : 52

SECTION TWO
THE PREPARATION; BEGINNING OF CHRIST'S
PUBLIC MINISTRY
3 : 1 to 4 : 13

SECTION THREE
THE MINISTRY OF JESUS IN GALILEE
4 : 14 to 9 : 50

SECTION FOUR
THE MINISTRY OF JESUS IN PEREA; JOURNEYS
TOWARD JERUSALEM
9 : 51 to 19 : 28

SECTION FIVE
THE MINISTRY OF JESUS IN JERUSALEM; LAST
DAYS OF PUBLIC TEACHING
19 : 29 to 21 : 38

SECTION SIX
BETRAYAL; ARREST; TRIALS; CRUCIFIXION
OF JESUS
22 : 1 to 23 : 56

SECTION SEVEN
RESURRECTION; COMMISSION; ASCENSION
OF JESUS
24 : 1-53

CONTENTS

SECTION FOUR

THE MINISTRY OF JESUS IN PEREA; JOURNEYS TOWARD JERUSALEM (9: 51 to 19: 28)

INTRODUCTION

The name "Luke" is an abbreviated form of "Lucanus," or "Lucilius." It should not be confused with "Lucius," mentioned in Acts 13: 1, neither should it be confused with "Lucas," as "Lucas" is not an abbreviated form of "Lucanus"; "Lucas" is not found in classical literature, but "Lucanus" is frequently found there. Luke is mentioned by name only three times in the Bible (Col. 4: 14; 2 Tim. 4: 11; Phile. 24), and these instances are all found in the writings of Paul. Luke has not mentioned his name either in his gospel narrative or Acts of the Apostles. However, there are other scriptures which clearly refer to Luke without mentioning his name. He was faithful in giving the history of our Lord and in narrating the chief acts of the apostles in establishing the church and giving a history of the early conversions, yet he has allowed all knowledge of himself to remain in oblivion. There is no use to speculate about his reasons for this.

KNOWLEDGE OF THE WRITER

It seems clear from the writings of Eusebius and others that Luke was of Grecian origin; he was born and reared at Antioch in Syria. All the certain knowledge that we have of the personal history of Luke is found in Acts of the Apostles and in Paul's prison letters. He first appears in history as a companion of Paul. Some think that he was a proselyte to the Jewish religion, and that he became an early disciple of Jesus during his personal ministry. We know, however, that he was not an eyewitness of the personal ministry of Christ, nor of the many events which he described in his narrative; he makes this clear in his preface to his gospel. (Luke 1: 2.) We do not know when he was converted to Christ. We learn that he was "a physician," and that he was an evangelist, but little else can be said of him. There have been many legends and theories about him, but no authentic and satisfactory evidences have been produced to verify them. Luke nowhere avows his authorship in the gospel or Acts of the Apostles. In each of the thirteen Pauline epistles, Paul declares himself to be the author; so also James, Peter, and Jude avow their authorship of the letters which bear their respective names. John likewise declares himself to be the author of Revelation (Rev. 1: 4), but John does not so declare himself in his epistles. Neither writer of the gospels, the Acts, and Hebrews declares the authorship.

LUKE, A COMPANION OF PAUL

The first mention that we have of Luke is that he is an evangelist and a companion of Paul. He joined Paul at Troas on his second missionary tour. (Acts 16: 10, 11.) He continued with Paul and his company on his tour to Philippi (Acts 16: 11, 12) and there remained with him (Acts 16: 12, 13, 15-17) until he departed from Philippi, but Luke did not leave Philippi with Paul. We can trace his journey and association with Paul by his use of the pronoun "we"; he uses the pronoun "they" when he is not associated with Paul and his company. In Acts 17: 1, Luke resumes the history of Paul's journey, and speaks in the third person, which shows that he was not one of the party. He again appears in history as the companion of Paul from Philippi (Acts 20: 6) on Paul's return to Asia; he continues his travels with Paul from place to place, spending a week among the disciples at Tyre and a longer time (some days) with them at Caesarea as guests of Philip the evangelist (Acts 20: 13-15; 21: 1-18). They left Caesarea and went to Jerusalem, accompanied with other disciples from Caesarea.

Paul was arrested at Jerusalem and put in prison; a little later he was sent to Caesarea where he remained two years; then he was sent as a prisoner to Rome, and Luke accompanied him on his tempestuous voyage to Rome. (Acts 27: 1; 28: 2, 11-16.) In all of these references Luke says nothing of himself except as the companion of Paul on this voyage to Rome. The "we" necessarily implies companionship and may possibly represent a diary kept at that time. There is no doubt but that the "we" sections are by the same author as the rest of the book of Acts; hence we know that Luke was Paul's companion during the period represented by the "we" sections of Acts. If Luke be "the brother whose praise in the gospel . . . through all the churches" (2 Cor. 8: 18), we find him acting with Titus as one of the brethren for the collection and custody of the contributions for the poor saints at Jerusalem. It seems clear that he was with Paul in both of Paul's imprisonments and trials at Rome (Col. 4: 14; 2 Tim. 4: 11).

THE BOOK OF LUKE

Luke, being a Greek, wrote in the Greek language. Neither the place nor time of his writing this book can be ascertained. Some have compared Luke's writings with those of Paul, and have found more than 200 expressions or phrases common to both. It is thought that Luke wrote for Greek readers. There are about fifty words not found elsewhere in the New Testament in the Gospel According to Luke and Acts of the Apostles. Luke differs from Matthew and Mark in that his sentence structures are more elaborate and his style of composition more finished. The total number of Greek words used by Matthew, Mark, and Luke exclusive of proper names, is about 2,400; of this number Mark uses about 1,200 different words, Matthew about 1,500, and Luke nearly 1,800. The Gospel According to Matthew in Greek (Revised Text, Oxford, 1881) contains 18,370 words; Mark, 10,981; and Luke, 19,496 words. The number of different Greek words used by Matthew, but not found in Mark or Luke, is 243; the number used by Mark, but not found in Matthew or Luke, is 174; while the number used by Luke, but not found in Matthew or Mark, is 614. This shows the fullness of the vocabulary of Luke, which is particularly seen in a greater number of words from the classic Greek.

Paul represents Luke as his fellow worker and "the beloved physician." (Col. 4: 14.) It is clear from Paul's statement in Col. 4: 11 where he names his "fellow-workers" "of the circumcision," or Jews, that Luke was not "of the circumcision," as he was with Paul at that time. (Col. 4: 14.) There is a striking similarity in the writings of Luke and Paul. Paul and Luke used frequently words that express the universality of gospel salvation; for example, "grace, favor" occur eight times in the Gospel According to Luke, and sixteen times in Acts of the Apostles; Paul uses this word ninety-five times; Luke uses the Greek word for "mercy" six times; and Paul uses it ten times. They agree in their report of the institution of the Lord's Supper, both giving "This cup is the new covenant in my blood," for "this is my blood of the covenant," and both add "in remembrance of me." There are many other instances of parallelism of thought and expression that may be cited. Luke's style is clear and picturesque. When he describes events on the authority of others, his manner is purely historical; but when he is narrating events which have come under his own observation, he treats them in the minute and circumstantial style of an eyewitness. His language is rhythmical and his vocabulary rich and well selected.

The books of Matthew, Mark, and Luke have been called the "Synoptics." Luke's record is the fullest of the four writers of the gospel. Matthew uses 1,071 verses; Mark, 678; Luke, 1,151; and John, 879. Different theories have been advanced as to which of the gospels was written first. One theory is that Matthew wrote first, and that Mark copied from Matthew, and then Luke copied somewhat from both the others; another is that Matthew wrote first, then Luke, and lastly, Mark; another theory is that Mark wrote first, then Luke and Matthew; another is that Mark wrote first, then Matthew, and then Luke. Still another theory is that Luke wrote first, then Mark, and lastly, Matthew; and then another theory is that Luke wrote first, next Matthew, and lastly, Mark. It will be observed that these theories must be largely destructive of one another. It does not matter which wrote first, as all wrote as they were guided by the Holy Spirit. (2 Tim. 3: 16, 17.)

A COMMENTARY ON THE GOSPEL
ACCORDING TO LUKE

PREFACE OF THE GOSPEL
1: 1-4

1 Forasmuch as many have taken in hand to draw up a narrative concerning those matters which have been [1]fulfilled among us, 2 even as they deliv-

[1]Or, *fully established*

---

1 **Forasmuch as many**—Luke introduces his narrative of the earthly life of Jesus by giving in his preface a reason for his writing it. "Many" had written accounts of the ministry of Jesus; the preaching of the apostles related the history of the earthly life of Jesus, and those who heard them prepared an account for the benefit of others. The "many" does not include Matthew and Mark, although Matthew was an apostle and an eyewitness, and Mark probably drew his material from what he learned from Peter. John's gospel was not written at this time, and it is not probable that Luke had seen the accounts of Matthew and Mark. Those who had written these accounts to which Luke here refers were uninspired; hence the necessity of Luke's giving an inspired and accurate account.

have taken in hand to draw up a narrative—The failure of those referred to by Luke and their partial account imposed the necessity on Luke to give a complete record. However, some think that nothing more is meant here by Luke than the simple undertaking of the task before him without any reference to the incomplete work of others. The motive of others was to give to the world the story of Jesus; hence they had drawn "up a narrative concerning those matters which have been fulfilled among us." Luke purposes to give to the world a complete history of the facts of the Christian faith; he designs to substitute an inspired account in the place of those accounts written by the "many" to which he here refers.

2 **even as they delivered them unto us,**—All the first witnesses of these things were apostles, disciples, and others;

ered them unto us, who from the beginning were eyewitnesses and ministers
of the word, 3 it seemed good to me also, having traced the course of all

Luke is a sure witness because he gives a true account of the
facts of the gospel as the whole company of the apostles declared them. Luke begins his account with the conception of
John the Baptist; but the disciples were eyewitnesses only
from the beginning of the ministry of Jesus, when he was
about thirty years old; the other information Luke gleaned
from the testimony of those persons who were acquainted
with the facts, and guided by the Holy Spirit recorded them.
"Eyewitnesses" were those who had seen the events as they
occurred, and were the apostles and other disciples of Jesus;
they had not been witnesses of the birth and childhood of
John and Jesus. These witnesses are referred to as "ministers
of the word"; some take "word" here in the sense of eternal
word (John 1: 1-3), but this specific and peculiar use of the
term is used only by John. The gospel is often called the
"word" (Luke 5: 1; Acts 6: 2). It seems clear from this that
Luke was not a disciple from the beginning.

3 it seemed good to me also,—Here Luke gives his reason
for writing; his course is natural. From these motives he
thought best to write, since he had a perfect knowledge of
these things. He had "traced the course of all things accurately from the first"; that is, he had checked on all of the
things of which he writes from those who had been eyewitnesses. Luke, guided by the Holy Spirit, was incited to write
on this subject because he had peculiar qualifications and fa-
cilities for the task; he had the perfect knowledge of all the
things relating to his narrative. "All things" refer to all
things of importance, such as Luke deemed by the Holy Spirit
essential to his narrative; he had traced all these accounts
"accurately from the first" and was prepared to give them in
the order that he follows in his narrative. The word "accurately" gives the emphasis to what he states as being perfectly
reliable; these are given by Luke "in order"; that is, they are
arranged in his account in their proper connection; he does
not mean here that he is going to relate everything in his gospel in chronological order.

things accurately from the first, to write unto thee in order, most excellent Theophilus; 4 that thou mightest know the certainty concerning the ²things ³wherein thou wast instructed.

²Gr. *words*
³Or, *which thou wast taught by word of mouth*

most excellent Theophilus;—Luke writes to "Theophilus." It is a matter which has not been determined whether Theophilus was the name of an individual, or whether the name is used to denote all "lovers of God" or "friends of God." The name signifies "a lover of God" or a "friend of God." This name was common for persons at that time; some commentators have interpreted this name to mean all who have dedicated themselves as lovers of God and beloved of him; others think that Theophilus was a pupil of Luke, and that Luke intended through him to give to the world this narrative of Jesus. The epithet "most excellent" seems to restrict the name to an individual, as it is applied to Festus and Felix. (Acts 24: 23; 26: 25.)

4 that thou mightest know the certainty concerning the things—This again expresses Luke's purpose of writing this narrative; it was that Theophilus and by implication all others would inform themselves in regard to the origin of these facts and principles on which Christianity was based. This implies that the other accounts referred to in verses 1 and 2 were imperfect narratives, and that no one could get an accurate and connected view of Christ's life and ministry. Theophilus as a Christian disciple had already received some instruction in divine things; naturally this instruction would follow the order of a connected narrative. He was to be "instructed" in all the things recorded by Luke. The original from which "instructed" comes means "catechised," which means to instruct by word of mouth; this is the term used also of Apollos (Acts 18: 25) and the Jews addressed by Paul (Rom. 2: 18) as the representative of the church. This passage shows the insufficiency of oral instruction, and it also shows the habit of the early church, to teach systematically out of these narratives. The Holy Spirit thus through Luke made an inspired history for all to read and study.

SECTION ONE

BIRTH OF JOHN THE BAPTIST; BIRTH AND CHILDHOOD OF JESUS
1 : 5 to 2 : 52

1. THE BIRTH OF JOHN THE BAPTIST FORETOLD
1 : 5-25

5 There was in the days of Herod, king of Judæa, a certain priest named Zacharias, of the course of Abijah: and he had a wife of the daughters of

---

5 There was in the days of Herod,—This entire chapter is found in Luke only, and is therefore the only record which we have of these events connected with the birth of John and of Jesus. This Herod, king of Judea, is commonly distinguished as "Herod the Great." Luke properly begins with this verse, as the preceding verses constitute what we call the "Preface." Matthew uses similar language with respect to Herod. (Matt. 2: 1.) Luke recognizes events as being marked by the life or times of some principal man. (Luke 4: 25, 27.) Judea was a province under the Roman government at this time, and had been for some years. It is probable that the birth of John occurred near the end of the reign of Herod. The title "king of Judaea" had been decreed to Herod by the Roman senate on the recommendations of Antony and Octavius.

a certain priest named Zacharias, of the course of Abijah: —Luke wastes no words in getting to his subject; he describes minutely the parents of John . "The course of Abijah" was the eighth course. (1 Chron. 24: 1-10.) David divided the priests into twenty-four classes for their convenience in ministering in the tabernacle worship "as the duty of every day required." (2 Chron. 8: 14.) Each course, from this circumstance, seems to have been called a "daily" course, though the period of its service lasted a week. Abijah received the eighth of the twenty-four classes into which David divided the priests; the head of a course was called the "chief priests."

Zacharias had "a wife of the daughters of Aaron, and her name was Elisabeth." Elisabeth was a descendant of Aaron and of the priestly tribe; it was a Levitical law that no priest

Aaron, and her name was Elisabeth. 6 And they were both righteous before God, walking in all the commandments and ordinances of the Lord blameless. 7 And they had no child, because that Elisabeth was barren, and they both were *now* ⁴well stricken in years.

⁴Gr. *advanced in their days*

---

should marry out of his tribe. (Num. 36: 7, 8.) John the Baptist was of the tribe of Levi on both sides; his father Zacharias was a priest and his mother Elisabeth of the priestly family; Luke is careful to show that both the father and mother were of the priestly line.

6 **And they were both righteous before God,**—Here Luke speaks of the character and circumstances in life of these parents of John. "They were both righteous." This describes their personal character; they were pious and humble before God; "righteous" refers to what is just and right in the sight of the law rather than to goodness and benevolence of disposition, although the two qualities were combined in Zacharias. They walked "in all the commandments and ordinances of the Lord blameless." This expresses the habitual daily conduct, including moral precepts and ceremonial rites. Perhaps Luke means to express extraordinary piety, rather than absolute perfection. Such parents are usually chosen of God to be eminently honored and blessed; they were both obedient to the will of God as contained in the Old Testament scripture; they were truly and sincerely living in accordance to the law of Moses; they were blameless according to the imperfect system under which they lived.

7 **And they had no child,**—Zacharias and Elisabeth were both very old, "well stricken in years"; it seemed from the course of nature that it was impossible for them to have children. "Elisabeth was barren"; many of the Old Testament characters were barren. Sarah, Rebecca, Rachel, and Hannah were barren; it was accounted a disgrace among the ancients for a wife to be barren; not that their barrenness was the effect of sin, but ordained rather by man as a failure to fill the mission that God intended. The wife of Aaron was named Elisabeth (Elisheba), as was the wife of Zacharias. (Ex. 6: 23.) Some claim that Zacharias could not have been over

8 Now it came to pass, while he executed the priest's office before God in the order of his course, 9 according to the custom of the priest's office, his lot was to enter into the ⁵temple of the Lord and burn incense. 10 And the whole multitude of the people were praying without at the hour of incense.

⁵Or, *sanctuary*

---

fifty years old, as the duties of the priest's office could not be performed beyond that age. "Well stricken in years" does not necessarily mean that he was bowed down and wrinkled with age; it is quite likely that Elisabeth was near the same age of her husband, and if after many years of married life they were childless, their prospects of having children must have been hopeless.

8, 9 Now it came to pass, while he executed the priest's office—Zacharias was faithful in performing the duties which pertained to his course; he ministered with others of the course or family of Abijah. One of the priests burned incense, another changed the showbread on the Sabbath day, and another took charge of the fire on the altar for burnt offerings; in this way their labors were appointed and a more responsible discharge of the various services secured from each individual. Each of the twenty-four courses served in rotation, but those belonging to a course cast lots each day for the service they were respectively to perform. At this time the course to which Zacharias belonged was serving in the sanctuary, and it fell to him by lot to burn incense, which was the most honorable service, and could be performed only once on the same day by any priest, although incense was offered twice each day, at the morning and evening sacrifice. (Ex. 30: 7, 8.)

10 And the whole multitude of the people were praying—The people assembled in the courts which surrounded the holy place, and while the priests were within burning incense, the people out in the court were engaged in silent prayer. One of the two priests, whose lot it was to offer incense, brought fire from off the altar of burnt offering to the altar of incense, and then left the other priest there alone, who, on a signal from the priest presiding at the sacrifice, kindled the incense. Reference is had in Rev. 8: 3, 4 to this service, and the prayers of God's people, which were symbolically said to

11 And there appeared unto him an angel of the Lord standing on the right side of the altar of incense. 12 And Zacharias was troubled when he saw *him*, and fear fell upon him. 13 But the angel said unto him, Fear not,

---

ascend upon the smoke of the incense. Since the people assembled for silent prayer at the time of the burning of incense, that hour has been called the hour of prayer. (Acts 3: 1.) This hour was at the evening sacrifices which began about three o'clock.

11 **And there appeared unto him an angel of the Lord**— While Zacharias was attending to the duties of burning incense the angel Gabriel appeared to him; we do not know the length of time that was spent in burning incense, but it is thought that the angel appeared near the end of his service in the sanctuary. This was no uncommon thing, as there are numerous accounts of divine messengers in the Old Testament. (Gen. 19: 1; 32: 1, 2.) This angel represented Jehovah; it is an awful thought for weak sinful man, even at his best, to be brought face to face with a spiritual being; the mortal terrors of one's own sin and their punishment are enough to frighten one. This angel appeared "standing on the right side of the altar of incense." The altar of incense stood near the veil in the holy place by the ark of the testimony which was separated from the altar by the veil. It was made of acacia wood, overlaid with gold; the length and breadth of it were one cubit and the height two cubits; on the four corners were golden horns and a crown or scroll work of gold ran around the top. The priest placed upon it the censer of burning incense.

12, 13 **And Zacharias was troubled when he saw him,**—A pious man learned from the Old Testament scriptures (Judges 13: 6, 21, 22), as well as from his own heart, to fear to look upon the celestial beings; the sudden and unusual appearance of the angel terrified or affrighted Zacharias. The angel knew the condition of Zacharias and hastened to reassure him with the usual form of encouragement "fear not" (Dan. 10: 12, 19; Rev. 1: 17). As Zacharias had given up all hope of a son, this must not be referred to prayer offered at this time, when the angel said "thy supplication is heard." It is not probable that

Zacharias: because thy supplication is heard, and thy wife Elisabeth shall bear thee a son, and thou shalt call his name John. 14 And thou shalt have joy and gladness; and many shall rejoice at his birth. 15 For he shall be great in the sight of the Lord, and he shall drink no wine nor ⁶strong drink;

⁶Gr. *sikera.*

Zacharias was praying at this time for a son, so the angel referred to the petitions which he and his wife Elisabeth had often made. They had doubtless oftentimes mourned that their prayer was not heard and answered; but now while Zacharias had ceased to pray for a son, he had not done this from a rebellious spirit, but in cheerful acquiescence to the divine will, and hence his mind was in a proper state to receive the blessing. "Thy wife Elisabeth shall bear thee a son"; this shows the special object of their prayers; the angel was more specific than just announcing that Zacharias should have a son; he even told him what to name the son; "thou shalt call his name John." These names of divine appointment were usually symbolical of some blessing or grace accompanying them, of which they were the pledge. "John" signifies "given" or "bestowed graciously of God." This name was very appropriate, since the child was given, both as denoting God's gracious answer to the prayer of Zacharias and the office of John who was to be the forerunner of the Savior of man.

14 **And thou shalt have joy and gladness;**—The Greek here is highly intensive; it means literally that there should be a "leaping for joy." This is not to be referred to the simple fact that a child was born to him so unexpectedly, but to John's piety and evident possession of the divine favor, which would fill his father's heart with emotions of joy. Not only should the parents of this promised child "leap for joy," but "many shall rejoice at his birth." The joy of Zacharias was to be shared by many others; this joy reached its culminating point when thousands flocked to John's ministry from all parts of the land. (Matt. 3: 5.) There should be rejoicing because John would herald the long-expected Messiah.

15 **For he shall be great in the sight of the Lord,**—There was a literal fulfillment of this promise, for Jesus said: "Ver-

and he shall be filled with the Holy Spirit, even from his mother's womb.
16 And Many of the children of Israel shall he turn unto the Lord their God.

---

ily I say unto you, Among them that are born of women there hath not arisen a greater than John the Baptist." (Matt. 11: 11.) This means that among men born up to that time there had been no one so highly favored of God. John's greatness consisted in his privilege of announcing the immediate coming of the Messiah, and the gracious zeal and eloquence with which he did it. (John 10: 41.) John was to be great "in the sight of the Lord," not so much in the sight of men; Zacharias is here cautioned against supposing that his son's greatness would consist in worldly honor or wealth. "He shall drink no wine nor strong drink"; he was to be bound with the Nazirite vow. (Num. 6: 1-20.) Samson was also bound with this vow. (Judges 13: 2-5.) Wine was the fermented juice of grapes, and God saw fit to restrict the Nazirite and not permit him to drink wine; by such signs all the Jews recognized a man of God, and listened to him with reverence. (Matt. 21: 32.) Furthermore, John should "be filled with the Holy Spirit, even from his mother's womb." This is given as the reason why he was to be a Nazirite from his very birth. In the life of a Nazirite, there appears consecrated the strict legal character which John, the close and crowning stone, as it were, of the old dispensation, was called to exhibit.

16 **And many of the children of Israel shall he turn**—John's success is here predicted. "The children of Israel" means the descendants of Jacob, called also Israel. (Gen. 32: 28.) John was a prophet to the Jews only; he did not preach to the Gentiles. We are not told how many were converted under his preaching, but that the number was great is evident, not only from this verse, but from Matt. 3: 5, 6; Mark 1: 5; Luke 3: 7, and other scriptures, where John's ministry and baptism are referred to. His work is described as turning the people "unto the Lord their God." Their sins had separated them from God, and by repentance and obedience, they were brought back to him; John instructed and persuaded the people to do this. Jehovah, in a peculiar sense, was the God of Israel; theirs were "the adoption, and the glory, and the cove-

17 And he shall [7]go before his face in the spirit and power of Elijah, to turn the hearts of the fathers to the children, and the disobedient to *walk* in the wisdom of the just; to make ready for the Lord a people prepared *for him.* 18 And Zacharias said unto the angel, Whereby shall I know this? for

[7]Some ancient authorities read *come nigh before his face*

nants, and the giving of the law, and the service of God, and the promises; whose are the fathers, and of whom is Christ as concerning the flesh, who is over all, God blessed for ever." (Rom. 9: 4, 5.)

17 **And he shall go before his face**—John was to go before Christ as a herald precedes a king. The Christ for whom the people waited was soon to come, and this child should anticipate his coming only by a little; these words perhaps refer to Mal. 4: 5, 6. John should go before Christ like one sent forward by an eastern king to prepare the way and make ready suitable places of reception. He should go "in the spirit and power of Elijah." He should have the zeal and energy of the spirit of Elijah, and should inculcate the universal principles of peace, and get the people ready for the coming of the Messiah. The many points of resemblance between John and Elijah are interesting; it should be noted that the angel here quoted scripture. The angels announced "and on earth peace among men in whom he is well pleased" (Luke 2: 14) as a characteristic of Christ's coming; in John's mission this peace was announced. The account of John's first preaching to the Jews indicated that all ranks and parties felt, for a time, an inclination to lay aside their differences, and unite to await the Messiah. With the power and spirit of Elijah, John would "turn the hearts of the fathers to the children"; this corresponds to the prophecy of Malachi. In turning the hearts of the fathers to the children, he would move them to holy prayer and endeavor for their salvation. Furthermore he would cause "the disobedient to walk in the wisdom of the just." This would bring men back from the waywardness of their folly and rebellion against God to the true wisdom of seeking the Lord in penitence and prayer. This is summed up in stating that John would "make ready for the Lord a people prepared for him."

I am an old man, and my wife [8]well stricken in years. 19 And the angel answering said unto him, I am Gabriel, that stand in the presence of God; and I was sent to speak unto thee, and to bring thee these good tidings. 20 And behold, thou shalt be silent and not able to speak, until the day that these things shall come to pass, because thou believedst not my words, which

[8]Gr. *advanced in her days*

18 **And Zacharias said unto the angel,**—Zacharias, though smitten with great fear, being assured of the angel not to fear, was pleased to hear all that the angel had said to him. He asked the angel, "Whereby shall I know this?" He wanted to know that the words of the angel were true. A similar question was proposed by Abraham (Gen. 15: 8; Judges 6: 17); Hezekiah asked for a sign (Isa. 38: 22). In the case of Zacharias there was so little faith in the message of the angel that the sign of the fulfillment of the promise was also a punishment of his unbelief. Zacharias gave two reasons showing, as he thought, that it would be impossible to fulfill the promise; he said: "I am an old man," and his second reason was "my wife well stricken in years." He was not like faithful Abraham who "wavered not through unbelief, but waxed strong through faith." (Rom. 4: 18-22. See also Gen. 17: 1, 17; Heb. 11: 12.) Zacharias, being a priest, should have believed on the testimony of the angel.

19 **And the angel answering said unto him,**—In reply to Zacharias' question and in answering his two reasons proposed, the angel said: "I am Gabriel, that stand in the presence of God." This should have been enough for the bewildered and doubting Zacharias. The angel condescended to inform Zacharias of his name and angelic dignity. "Gabriel" means "man of God"; he was an archangel sent on a special mission. A Jewish priest should know at once that this name carried with it the authority and presence of God. (Dan. 8: 16; 9: 21.) He is represented as the chief archangel, ministering to the infant Messiah. The name "Gabriel" is made up of two Hebrew words, signifying "the man of God." He stood "in the presence of God" as a dignitary may stand in the presence of a monarch. Our high priest is said "now to appear before the face of God for us." (Heb. 9: 24.)

shall be fulfilled in their season. 21 And the people were waiting for Zacharias, and they marvelled ¹while he tarried in the ²temple. 22 And when he came out, he could not speak unto them: and they perceived that he had

¹Or, *at his tarrying*
²Or, *sanctuary*

---

20 **And behold, thou shalt be silent**—The word in the Greek may also signify "deaf"; because Zacharias believed not the words of the angel, he should be deaf and should not be able to speak. The angel even told him that he should not be able to speak "until the day that these things shall come to pass"; it was the eighth day after the birth of the child that the punishment of his unbelief was remitted, and the power of speech again restored to him. The sentence was pronounced upon Zacharias in terms of severe and expressive fullness. It is specifically declared that unbelief was the cause of his punishment, but we should not lose sight of the love with which his punishment was tempered in that it was a gracious sign of the due fulfillment to the promise. The angel further declared that all that had been promised him would "be fulfilled in their season." Every event promised, such as the birth, naming, education, and mission of the child, would all occur in orderly succession, and in exact accordance with the prediction made by the angel.

21 **And the people were waiting for Zacharias,**—The priest did not usually tarry long within the holy place, lest the people, whose representative he was, should be alarmed with the apprehension that divine vengeance had overtaken him for some failure in the discharge of his priestly duty. "They marvelled while he tarried in the temple"; they were wondering and anxious about him, for they knew that it was an awful thing to minister before God. Very likely their mode of conducting their service was so regular and exact that any variation was remarkable. They began to reason among themselves as to the cause of his delay. We do not know how long the interview lasted with the angel; we have no means of knowing; it was probably of short duration, but was longer than others had remained in the sanctuary. This gives a reason for believing that the angel appeared at the close of the

seen a vision in the ²temple: and he continued making signs unto them, and remained dumb. 23 And it came to pass, when the days of his ministration were fulfilled, he departed unto his house.

period of the ministry of Zacharias this day, and the conversation with the angel delayed the time and caused the people to be anxious about him; the people had assembled for prayer.

22 And when he came out, he could not speak unto them: —The people saw at once when Zacharias came out that he had seen a vision; they judged this to be the explanation of his delay, and then of his disturbed looks and his unusual silence when he came out. He was unable to dismiss them with the common benediction, so he "continued making signs unto them, and remained dumb." He made signs to inform them that something extraordinary had occurred, and to dismiss them to their homes. Prophecy had been silent now about four hundred years, and now the priesthood had become dumb as a sign of the approaching end of the Levitical ordinances.

23 And it came to pass, when the days of his ministration— The term "days" used here means the period of time that Zacharias served; they were the days of the week of the course or lot of the priests of Abijah. The priests during their term of service did not enter their own houses, but remained continually in the enclosures of the sacred hill. At the end of their weeks they returned home; Zacharias could not leave, though he had seen an angel; for the angel had not brought him permission to violate the duties of his office. It is supposed that Zacharias lived in the priestly city of Hebron. The priests were divided into twenty-four courses, and a course came to the sanctuary and ministered for a period of time, usually one or two weeks; but even one course or set was so numerous that it was necessary to make a selection out of it of those who should perform the most solemn parts of the service; this was done by lot. It fell to the lot of Zacharias to burn incense, and this is probably the first time that he had had this exalted duty. What a favored lot he drew at this time!

24 And after these days Elisabeth his wife conceived; and she hid herself five months, saying, 25 Thus hath the Lord done unto me in the days wherein he looked *upon me,* to take away my reproach among men.

24, 25 **And after these days Elisabeth his wife conceived;—** The event here spoken of took place soon after the return of Zacharias to his house. After her conception Elisabeth "hid herself five months." She did this for purposes of modesty and constant devotion; she desired probably to await the certain signs of the facts; she withdrew herself wholly from the sight of others, choosing her own place of concealment. Her sense of delicacy may have been heightened in this instance by her age which would subject her to more than usual notice and remark. Again she had been instructed that the child was to be a Nazirite, and Elisabeth wanted to keep herself within the limitations of a Nazirite; she could do this by voluntarily secluding herself; Elisabeth said that the Lord had thus taken away "my reproach among men." The hopes of a Messiah to be born of a woman increased in the minds of the Jewish women the natural desire for children. (Psalm 113: 9.) Jewish women thought it peculiarly a reproach to be barren; barrenness was in those times also considered as a deep privation of a great blessing.

2. THE ANNUNCIATION TO MARY
1 : 26-38

26 Now in the sixth month the angel Gabriel was sent from God unto a city of Galilee, named Nazareth, 27 to a virgin betrothed to a man whose name was Joseph, of the house of David; and the virgin's name was Mary.

26, 27 **Now in the sixth month the angel Gabriel**—In this verse we learn the comparative age of Jesus and John; the place of the residence of Joseph and Mary give some light on Matt. 2: 23. Reckoning from the time of Elisabeth's conception it was six months before the angel Gabriel made his appearance to Mary. John was about six months old when Jesus was born. The angel Gabriel was sent from God to Nazareth, a city of Galilee. Palestine was divided into three divisions—Judea in the south, Samaria in the center, and Galilee in the north. Many have thought that this was about December of our calendar; however, there is no evidence as to the

28 And he came in unto her, and said, Hail, thou that are ³highly favored,
the Lord *is* with thee.⁴ 29 But she was greatly troubled at the saying, and
cast in her mind what manner of salutation this might be. 30 And the angel
said unto her, Fear not, Mary: for thou hast found ⁵favor with God. 31 And

---

³Or, *endued with grace*
⁴Many ancient authorities add *blessed* art *thou among women* See ver 42
⁵Or, *grace*

---

exact time of year when Jesus was born; if he were born in
December the angel came to Mary sometime in April. Mary
is described as "a virgin betrothed to a man whose name was
Joseph, of the house of David." The tribe of King David was
Judah, and Joseph was a direct descendant of the house of
David. Some make the phrase "of the house of David" refer
to Mary instead of to Joseph. Mary was "betrothed" to Joseph; she was engaged to Joseph; this was a sacred agree-
ment between them. Mary was "a virgin." Isaiah had prophesied that a virgin should become the mother of the Messiah. (Isa. 7 : 14.)

28, 29 **And he came in unto her, and said,**—The angel Gabriel came to Mary and said: "Hail, thou that art highly favored, the Lord is with thee." This was the salutation with
which the angel greeted Mary; he came into her dwelling or
the apartment where she then was. "Hail" is a salutation of
honor in Greek and corresponds to the Hebrew form "peace
be unto you." (Luke 24: 36.) The angel sought to encourage as well as honor Mary. He addressed her as one "highly
favored" of God; this means the spiritual blessings already bestowed upon Mary and includes those which would be conferred upon her. She is pronounced as one who is honored by
Jehovah. Mary was somewhat troubled as to "what manner
of salutation this might be."

30-33 **And the angel said unto her, Fear not, Mary:**—In tenderness and assurance the angel Gabriel told her to "fear
not"; the angel had declared to Zacharias that his prayers
were to be answered, but to Mary "thou hast found favor with
God." This was not from any personal worthiness on her
part, or any immaculacy of moral character, but from the
abundant grace of God bestowed upon her as upon all others
who earnestly seek divine favor and guidance. Special refer-

behold, thou shalt conceive in thy womb, and bring forth a son, and shalt call
his name JESUS. 32 He shall be great, and shall be called the Son of the
Most High: and the Lord God shall give unto him the throne of his father
David: 33 and he shall reign over the house of Jacob ᵃfor ever; and of his

ᵃGr. *unto the ages*

ence is made to the great blessing which was about to be conferred upon her in being the mother of the promised Messiah.
Mary was about to receive and enjoy a blessing long reserved
in store for her.

thou shalt conceive in thy womb,—This strange announcement to Mary carried with it an astonishment. She did not
understand how all of this would come to pass to her, a lowly
maiden of Nazareth. The promise was that she should "bring
forth a son," and the instruction was that she should "call his
name JESUS." "Jesus" means "Saviour"; this was because he
should "save his people from their sins." The angel continued to emphasize the character of this Son; "he shall be great,
and shall be called the Son of the Most High." This does
not refer to temporal greatness, but to the glory and power
to which he was to be exalted. He should be universally
acknowledged as the "Son of the Most High." This is a
special and definite name as Jesus, Christ, Messiah, and
Lord are given to him. "The Son of the Most High" was
evidently a Messianic title, like "Son of the Blessed." (Mark
14: 61.) The promise was made that he should be given
"the throne of his father David." This promise of authority
and dominion was made primarily and in the lowest sense to
Solomon (2 Sam. 7: 12, 13), who was thus the type of Christ;
in its higher and spiritual sense, it was prophetically made to
the Messiah, who, according to the flesh, was to spring from
David (Rom. 1: 3). It should be noted that Mary, though not
actually married, had no difficulty in understanding this angelic
message arising from family descent. This shows that she
was herself, as many claim, a descendant of David, and fully
aware of this distinguished honor, a fact which throws much
light on the genealogy of our Lord as given a little later by
Luke. (Luke 3: 23-38.)

he shall reign over the house of Jacob for ever;—This verse
and the word "throne" in verse 32 are to be understood as rep-

kingdom there shall be no end. 34 And Mary said unto the angel, How
shall this be, seeing I know not a man? 35 And the angel answered and said

---

resenting a spiritual dominion. "The house of Jacob" means
the Israelitish nation, which, in the Messianic times, was to
embrace all who were partakers of the faith of Abraham,
whether they were Jews or Gentiles. (Gal. 3 : 7.) There was
to be no end to his kingdom; other kingdoms, like the four
spoken of in Dan. 7 : 14, should end, but this one would never
cease from being a spiritual kingdom till he should surrender
the redeemed saints to God the Father. (1 Cor. 15 : 28; Heb.
2 : 8, 9.) It could not have been true as a promise to David in
a temporal sense, for his kingdom and throne did cease. This
kingdom, over which the promised Messiah should reign, extended beyond all generations and could not be limited by political boundaries. Christ will never cease to be King of his
people; he will ever be adored as the Lamb of God that was
slain to redeem his people from endless death.

34 **And Mary said unto the angel,**—Mary did not understand; nothing of the kind had ever occurred, even as nothing
of the kind has ever since occurred; the words of Mary are
not those of unbelief, but the outpouring of a childlike spirit,
seeking for light on a subjct so manifestly dark and mysterious. The words of the angel replied that the conception
should take place immediately, and as she was yet unmarried,
she saw not how the promise could be fulfilled. Zacharias
was punished for his doubtful attitude toward the message of
Gabriel; his was that unbelief; Mary's one of inquiry, directed
in a childlike spirit which is not to be blamed.

35 **And the angel answered**—The miraculous conception of
this child Jesus is here assigned as the reason for his being
called the Son of God; viewed on the side of his human nature
and relations, this cannot be misunderstood. As Christ was
the Son of the Father and begotten of him (John 1 : 14), this
must be understood as the divine influence or energy exerted
through the agency of the Holy Spirit. The Holy Spirit did
not create the world, but only moved upon the chaotic mass,
bringing order out of confusion, so Christ was not begotten of

unto her, The Holy Spirit shall come upon thee, and the power of the Most
High shall overshadow thee: wherefore also [7]the holy thing which is begotten [8]shall be called the Son of God. 36 And behold, Elisabeth thy kinswoman,
she also hath conceived a son in her old age; and this is the sixth month

[7]Or, *that which is to be born shall be called holy, the Son of God*
[8]Some ancient authorities insert *of thee*

the Holy Spirit, although the energy and influence of the
Spirit was instrumentally employed in the conception of
Mary. This is further emphasized by the statement that "the
Holy Spirit shall come upon thee, and the power of the Most
High shall overshadow thee." The figure used here is borrowed from a cloud; as the shadow of a cloud rests upon and
circumfuses the top of a hill or mountain, so the divine influence was to be exerted and rest upon Mary for the production
of the intended effect. This figure or imagery implies nothing
gross or material, but simply the operation of the divine energy in the conception of Christ.

wherefore also the holy thing which is begotten—It is emphatically declared here that Jesus was called the "Son of
God" because in his human nature he was begotten of God,
and sustained a relation to God such as no one else has ever
borne. "The holy thing," the neuter gender is here used in
accordance with general usage, which withholds the idea of
sex from an infant, until it is indicated by name or otherwise.
It simply means in the original Greek "thy holy offspring."
Christ is the Son of God only in his relation to the redemption
of man; he is his "Son" only in that he was born of a woman.
He existed with God in eternity and was not the "Son of God"
before he came in the flesh; he was "in the beginning" a member of the "Godhead"; but since he came in the flesh, suffered,
died, and was raised from the dead, he is spoken of as "the
Son" of God. His divinity and deity are from eternity.

36-38 And behold, Elisabeth thy kinswoman,—The angel
continued his conversation with Mary and informed her of the
condition of Elisabeth. We do not know how closely Mary
and Elisabeth were related; she is represented here as "thy
kinswoman," which does not express the degree of blood relation. Many think that the relation was on the mother's side,
as Elisabeth was of the tribe of Levi (verse 5), and Mary was

with her that [9]was called barren. 37 For no word from God shall be void of
power. 38 And Mary said, Behold, the [10]handmaid of the Lord; be it unto
me according to thy word. And the angel departed from her.

[9]Or, *is*
[10]Gr. *bondmaid*

of the tribe of Judah; the genealogy was always reckoned on
the paternal side. The angel informed Mary that Elisabeth
had "conceived a son in her old age," and that "this is the
sixth month with her that was called barren." Elisabeth's
home was in the mountains of Judea, probably at Hebron, and
Mary's home was at Nazareth in Galilee, far north from Elisabeth. The mode of communication was not as easy as it is
now, and although it had been six months since Elisabeth conceived, Mary, though a kinswoman of Elisabeth, had not
learned of it. In this way the mother of the forerunner of
Christ and the mother of Christ are brought together by the
same angel.

For no word from God shall be void—This is the great and
crowning reason why Mary was to be assured of the accom-
plishment of all the things which had been spoken by the
angel; although it was apparently so contrary to the natural
course of events, yet Mary was to believe that nothing was
impossible with God. This should strengthen her faith and
prepare her for the great event; with God nothing shall ever
be, nothing can ever be impossible. It is the glory of God
that, when he wills, he does things impossible to human agen-
cies. Mary's soul bowed in sweet confidence and submission
to this divinely revealed purpose; she said "be it unto me according to thy word."

3. THE VISIT OF MARY TO ELISABETH
1: 39-56

39 And Mary arose in these days and went into the hill country with

39, 40 And Mary arose in these days and went—It seems
that Mary did not delay; since the angel had informed her
with respect to Elisabeth, she "arose" and went "with haste";
we do not know the significance of "these days" as to the definite time. Some think that Joseph had been informed of

haste, into a city of Judah; 40 and entered into the house of Zacharias and saluted Elisabeth. 41 And it came to pass when Elisabeth heard the saluta-

---

Mary's condition before her visit to Elisabeth, which might have happened in three or four weeks from the time of her pregnancy; since a betrothed virgin could not travel, whereas, after Joseph had taken her home (Matt. 1 : 24), she could with propriety visit her kinswoman as here related. Others think that Joseph did not discover Mary's condition until the fourth or fifth month of her pregnancy, and therefore her visit to Elisabeth was before Joseph discovered her condition. It seems that it was the sixth month after Elisabeth's conception that the annunciation took place, and as Mary stayed with Elisabeth about three months (verse 56), after which time, as is evident from verse 57, John was born, Mary must have left Nazareth almost immediately after the visit of the angel, and no space is therefore found for the three or four weeks, which some think intervened before she left Nazareth for the hill country.That she left very soon after the annunciation is evident also from the haste with which she prosecuted her journey. When she arrived in the hill country of Judea she entered "into the house of Zacharias and saluted Elisabeth." There were various forms of salutations among the ancient Hebrews, such as "be thou blessed of Jehovah," "the blessings of Jehovah be upon thee," "may God be with thee," "may peace be yours." (Judges 19: 20; Ruth 2: 4; 1 Sam. 25: 26; 2 Sam. 20: 9.) We do not know which salutation Mary used.

41-45 **And it came to pass, when Elisabeth heard**—When Elisabeth heard the salutation spoken by Mary, "the babe leaped in her womb"; such a movement often accompanies sudden excitement, yet the reference to it by Luke, and the words of Elisabeth, show that it was to be attributed to a secret and powerful spiritual influence. The verb in the Greek is used to denote the leaping and frisking for joy of young animals, and denotes here something more than the natural movements of the unborn child; this gives weight to the words she uttered in reply to Mary's salutation. "Elisabeth was filled with the Holy Spirit," which shows that her words

tion of Mary, the babe leaped in her womb; and Elisabeth was filled with
the Holy Spirit; 42 and she lifted up her voice with a loud cry, and said,
Blessed *art* thou among women, and blessed *is* the fruit of thy womb. 43
And whence is this to me, that the mother of my Lord should come unto

were inspired, and gives the cause of the sudden motion mentioned; as a pious and just woman, she expressed her joy at
the great favor which was done to her youthful kinswoman,
and prophesied concerning her. So far as the record shows
Mary had only saluted her and had as yet told her nothing;
hence Elisabeth learned of Mary's condition by inspiration.

and she lifted up her voice with a loud cry,—Here follows
the inspired utterances of Elisabeth. "Lifted up her voice
with a loud cry" shows that she was excited to great transport
of mind by the Holy Spirit with which she was filled. She
began her utterance by saying, "Blessed art thou among
women"; this was not an ordinary salutation, but one in the
very words employed by the angel Gabriel (verse 28), of
whose appearance to Mary Elisabeth was probably yet ignorant; it was a salutation prompted by the Holy Spirit and was
calculated to encourage Mary in her condition. Furthermore
she said: "Blessed is the fruit of thy womb." Here again Elisabeth must have been enlightened by the influence of the
Holy Spirit, for she had no knowledge as yet of Mary's conception; by the Holy Spirit Elisabeth blessed Mary and her
unborn child. Some think that this implies nothing but the
superiority of the age of Elisabeth over Mary; however, it
must imply much else. It was natural for the age of Elisabeth
to bless her young friend.

And whence is this to me,—Here Elisabeth uses the language of humility; she expressed her wonder that she had
been considered worthy of such a visit from Mary; she inquired: "Whence is this to me, that the mother of my Lord
should come unto me?" This seems to be the first one to
speak of Jesus as "my Lord"; later it became a common title
among the disciples of Jesus. Such utterances made of an unborn child can be attributed only to the inspiration of the
Holy Spirit, and were the words spoken by Elisabeth who was
filled with the Spirit. Elisabeth reveals to Mary that, "when

me? 44 For behold, when the voice of thy salutation came into mine ears,
the babe leaped in my womb for joy. 45 And blessed *is* she that [11]believed;
for there shall be a fulfilment of the things which have been spoken to her
from the Lord. 46 And Mary said,
    My soul doth magnify the Lord,

[11]Or, *believed that there shall be*

---

the voice of thy salutation came into mine ears, the babe
leaped in my womb for joy." This explains why Elisabeth
knew that Mary was to be the mother of the long-expected
Messiah. While this knowledge of Elisabeth was the result of
divine revelation she, under the influence of the Spirit, refers
to it as the effect that Mary's salutation had upon her unborn
child.

And blessed is she that believed ;—Elisabeth, by inspiration,
recognized that Mary had from the first believed, and was unlike Zacharias, who at that time was still smitten with dumbness. Her language passes from the second to the third person, and must be looked upon in the light of a prayer or invo-
cation of blessings upon Mary. Still speaking by the Holy
Spirit, Elisabeth declares that "there shall be a fulfillment of
the things which have been spoken to her from the Lord."
There is no evidence that Mary had as yet revealed to Elisabeth anything, and Elisabeth was still under the influence of
the Holy Spirit when she uttered these unusual words ; the expression, although in form indefinite, is designed to apply directly to Mary. Elisabeth recognizes that what the angel had
spoken to Mary was "from the Lord."

46-56 And Mary said, My soul doth magnify the Lord,—
Mary is now filled with the Holy Spirit and breaks forth into
expressions of joy and thankfulness ; she may not have understood the full import of her words, yet they are very significant. These verses comprise most of the recorded words of
Mary ; we have but few recorded words of the mother of Jesus
—more of them here than anywhere else. They remind one of
the ancient song of Hannah under similar circumstances. (1
Sam. 2: 1-10.) They breathe the most delightful recognition
of God's great mercy, his condescension to their humble estate, his often manifested law of moral administration to exalt

47 And my spirit hath rejoiced in God my Saviour.
48 For he hath looked upon the low estate of his [10]handmaid:
   For behold, from henceforth all generations shall call me blessed.
49 For he that is mighty hath done to me great things;
   And holy is his name.
50 And his mercy is unto generations and generations
   On them that fear him.
51 He hath showed strength with his arm;
   He hath scattered the proud [1]in the imagination of their heart.
52 He hath put down princes from *their* thrones,
   And hath exalted them of low degree.
53 The hungry he hath filled with good things;
   And the rich he hath sent empty away.
54 He hath given help to Israel his servant,
   That he might remember mercy
55 (As he spake unto our fathers)
   Toward Abraham and his seed for ever.
56 And Mary abode with her about three months, and returned unto her house.

---

[1]Or, *by*

---

the lowly and to abase the proud. Here is a celebration of his glorious fulfillment of a long extant promise to Israel of the Messiah. This speech of Mary's is put in the structure of Hebrew poetry.

my spirit hath rejoiced in God—Mary rejoiced in the fact that she was elevated from a state of earthly obscurity, but her deepest joy was in the fact that she was to bring the promised Messiah into the world. Verses 48 and 49 show the ground of Mary's praise; God had looked upon her favorably and had made her the mother of our Lord; she regarded the blessings of the Messiah's advent as reaching to the end of time; she gave utterance to great spiritual truths respecting the true glory of the Messiah's reign. She passes to a general song of praise; rising above personal blessings and losing sight of them in the divine glory and goodness of God which are revealed to her at this time.

He hath given help to Israel his servant,—In this song of praise Mary is enabled by the Holy Spirit to look back and see all the good things that Jehovah had done for Israel; she was permitted to view the future and the blessings which should come to the world through this Messiah. The language of praise and grateful remembrance of the divine help in behalf of the poor and humble now assumes a more comprehensive and general form. Jehovah had extended mercy as he had spoken unto "our fathers" and "toward Abraham and his seed for ever." God's covenant of mercy was not only made with the patriarchs, but declared to them in words of the strongest import, and confirmed with an oath. All the promises that God had made to Israel were now focusing on the babe that she would bring into the world.

4. BIRTH AND CIRCUMCISION OF JOHN
1: 57-80

57 Now Elisabeth's time was fulfilled that she should be delivered; and she brought forth a son. 58 And her neighbors and her kinsfolk heard that

---

57 **Now Elisabeth's time was fulfilled**—Luke now dismissed the history concerning Mary until her journey with Joseph to Bethlehem. (Luke 2: 1.) Mary left Elisabeth, it seems, just before the birth of John; she may have done so, wishing to avoid the excitement of the occasion, and the observation of such an assemblage. The birth of John the Baptist was soon after Mary's departure, probably in the spring. According to the promise of Gabriel, at the proper time, a son was born to Zacharias and Elisabeth; as the prediction of the angel was fulfilled in this particular, so we may expect every prophecy concerning John to be fulfilled.

58, 59 **And her neighbors and her kinsfolk heard**—When the kinspeople heard that Elisabeth had brought forth a son, they were ready to congratulate her on being blessed even in her old age; very likely they were more enthusiastic since hope had been lost in her becoming a mother. "They rejoiced with her"; it was a happy occasion for Elisabeth and her neighbors and kinspeople with her; thus early began to be fulfilled the prediction of the angel as recorded in verse 14. There was a similar rejoicing at the birth of Obed. (Ruth 4: 14-17.) "And it came to pass on the eighth day, that they came to circumcise the child." According to the patriarchal custom and the Mosaic law the male child was to be circumcised on the eighth day. (Gen. 17: 12; Lev. 12: 3.) If the eighth day came on the Sabbath, the rite was not postponed. (John 7: 22, 23.) According to the Jewish traditional law, ten persons

the Lord had magnified his mercy towards her; and they rejoiced with her.
59 And it came to pass on the eighth day, that they came to circumcise the
child; and they would have called him Zacharias, after the name of his
father. 60 And his mother answered and said, Not so; but he shall be called

---

were required to be present as witnesses to the circumcision;
hence the presence of relatives and friends. Circumcision was
enjoined upon Abraham as a token or covenant sign, and was
to be performed upon all his male descendants and upon every
male that was admitted within the folds of the Jewish nation.
(Gen. 17: 9-14.) It was an essential condition of Jewish na-
tionality; Paul speaks of it also as "the sign of circumcision, a
seal of the righteousness of the faith which he had while he
was in uncircumcision: that he might be the father of all them
that believe." (Rom. 4: 11.) Circumcision was the attesta-
tion of Abraham's justification by faith; it became a type of
the cleansing of the heart, as Paul says "circumcision is that
of the heart, in the spirit not in the letter." (Rom. 2: 29.)
"For we are the circumcision, who worship by the Spirit of
God, and glory in Christ Jesus, and have no confidence in the
flesh." (Phil. 3: 3.)

60, 61 **And his mother answered and said, Not so;**—Evidently Zacharias had in some way communicated to Elisabeth
that his name, according to the instruction of the angel (verse
13), should be "John"; or Elisabeth had received instruction
by inspiration as to the name of her son. When the friends
persisted at his circumcision in calling him "Zacharias," Elisabeth positively refused to sanction the name Zacharias and declared that he should be called John. The custom of naming
children after some connection of the family was urged as a
ballad of objection against the name John; it was fitting that
the harbinger of the new dispensation should have a name not
found among his natural connections, as "Jesus" is not found
among our Lord's ancestors. It was a common usage then, as
in all ages, to name at least one son for the father; this law of
usage the neighbors and relatives insisted should be followed;
but the Lord had overruled it and had named him John before
his birth. "John" means "Jehovah's gift," and was a very appropriate name for this child, as he was a gift from Jehovah.

John. 61 And they said unto her, There is none of thy kindred that is called by this name. 62 And they made signs to his father, what he would have him called. 63 And he asked for a writing tablet, and wrote, saying, His name is John. And they marvelled all. 64 And his mouth was opened immediately, and his tongue *loosed,* and he spake, blessing God. 65 And fear

---

62-64 And they made signs to his father,—The neighbors and friends were surprised at Elisabeth's positive refusal to let him be called Zacharias; she had spoken with such emphasis that they thought it useless to argue with her any longer, so they "made signs to his father" and asked what his wish was; the fact that they "made signs" with the head or hands or both shows that Zacharias was deaf as well as dumb. They assumed that the father had a wish in the case, and that his wish would settle the matter. In fact, the original Greek implies that the question was so put as to demand a definite reply; more literally "they made signs as to what he is"; that is, what is his name.

And he asked for a writing tablet,—Zacharias made signs and asked for "a writing tablet" that he might give answer; he probably asked for that which he had used for nine months as a means of communicating with his wife and others. The instrument of writing then was probably a light board covered with wax and a sharp iron instrument for a pen; the iron was broad and smooth at one end for smoothing the wax and sharp at the other for writing. Zacharias wrote a simple statement—"his name is John." This means that the child had already been named and that they had nothing to do with it. The neighbors and friends all "marvelled."

And his mouth was opened immediately,—Zacharias had been smitten with dumbness from the time the angel Gabriel announced to him that he should have a son; Zacharias had asked for a sign in his unbelief that the angel had truly informed him, and the sign of his dumbness was given. Zacharias had faithfully followed the instruction of the angel and had given his son the name "John," and at that eventful moment the tongue of Zacharias was loosed, and his soul was filled with praise and his glad tongue gave it suitable expression. The naming of the child was an evidence of Zacharias'

came on all that dwelt round about them: and all these sayings were noised abroad throughout all the hill country of Judæa. 66 And all that heard them laid them up in their heart, saying, What then shall this child be? For the hand of the Lord was with him.

---

restored faith; in apprehending the full meaning of the name John, "one whom God has graciously given," he accepted in full confidence all that had been foretold. The first use of his recovered speech was not in complaint, nor in conversation with his wife or friends, but in praising or blessing God. He blessed God, not merely for himself, but for the child, and for what God was about to do for his people by the Messiah and his forerunner.

65, 66 **And fear came on all that dwelt**—"Fear" means religious awe on account of the evident display of divine power; fear has always been the first effect produced on man by the consciousness that heavenly beings are entering into nearer and unusual intercourse with man. All in the immediate neighborhood of the city of John's birth, probably Hebron, were greatly impressed by the scenes which had transpired. "All these sayings were noised abroad throughout all the hill country of Judaea"; these things were talked of everywhere and told abroad; this means the circumstances regarding John's birth became the great topic of conversation in all the hill country of Judea, but it seems that they did not reach Jerusalem. The people knew of Zacharias' affliction of dumbness; they had heard rumors of the events connected with the birth of John; now Zacharias gives his son an unusual name, which was given by the angel, and now for the first time in nearly a year he breaks his long silence. The people would remember these when John began preaching the gospel of the kingdom.

And all that heard them laid them up in their heart,—By this we are to understand that there were certain manifestations of divine favor toward the child; events which would be noticed by observers living in Hebron, but which Luke did not see fit to record. Many absurd legends were propagated in the early ages of the church concerning the period which intervenes between the births of John and Jesus and their

67 And his father Zacharias was filled with the Holy Spirit, and prophesied saying,
  68 Blessed *be* the Lord, the God of Israel;
      For he hath visited and wrought redemption for his people,
  69 And hath raised up a horn of salvation for us
      In the house of his servant David

public ministry, but we may be safe in rejecting them; if the
inspired writers had seen fit, they could have given them to
us. They observed that the hand of the Lord was with
him; the guidance, protection, and blessings of God, including
the gracious influences of the Holy Spirit, were with John.
Luke here gives a glimpse of John's early history, intimating
both the continued fulfillment of the angel's words and also
the realization of the expectations awakened among the people at his birth.

67-75 **And his father Zacharias was filled with the Holy
Spirit,**—The spirit of prophecy had ceased with Malachi, but
now, after about four hundred years, it is given again.
Zacharias was filled with the Holy Spirit, and in a strain of
sacred rapture he "prophesied." A prophet was one who was
used by God as a means of communicating his will, even
though he may not predict any future events. (Gen. 20: 7;
John 4: 19.) A prophet was God's mouthpiece to the people.
Zacharias spoke as the prophets did of old. (2 Pet. 1: 21.)
God generally chose holy men as prophets, yet sometimes he
has inspired even wicked men. (Num. 23: 5; 24: 11.)

Blessed be the Lord, the God of Israel;—The song of Zacharias is a hymn of thanksgiving and a prediction of John's
relation to Christ; it is Messianic in its character; Christ is its
theme, and it is John's glory to be forerunner of Christ. Its
structure is in the form of Hebrew poetry, and abounds in Hebrew idioms. Zacharias probably committed it to writing,
and copies of it were very likely preserved, and Luke had a
copy of it. The song consists of two parts: (1) Blessing God
for the true spiritual salvation in fulfillment of his promises.
(Verses 68-75.) (2) Presenting John as the prophet and herald
of the Messiah, the one who was to prepare the way for the
Christ. (Verses 76-79.) "Blessed be the Lord, the God of Israel." It seems natural for Zacharias to praise Jehovah; his

70 (As he spake by the mouth of his holy prophets that have been from
    old).
71 Salvation from our enemies, and from the hand of all that hate us ;
72 To show mercy towards our fathers,
    And to remember his holy covenant ;
73 The oath which he sware unto Abraham our father,

restored speech is used first in blessing God under the inspiration and guidance of the Holy Spirit. To bless God is not
only to acknowledge and proclaim his infinite and eternal
blessedness, but to render to him ascriptions of praise and
thanksgiving.

(As he spake by the mouth of his holy prophets—This
verse is parenthetical; Mary had ended her song (verse 55)
with a parenthetical statement, and Zacharias begins his with
such an expression ; he alludes to the burden of ancient prophecy ; it seems that Zacharias begins where Mary left off.
God spoke through his holy prophets. "For no prophecy ever
came by the will of man : but men spake from God, being
moved by the Holy Spirit." (2 Pet. 1: 21.) The burden of
prophecy had been the future Messiah. "For the testimony of
Jesus is the spirit of prophecy." (Rev. 19: 10.) Zacharias
refers in general to the ancient prophets and most naturally to
all who uttered predictions regarding the Christ. The first
promise of a Redeemer was made by Jehovah himself in the
garden of Eden. (Gen. 3: 15.) This was the fountainhead of
the stream of prophecy, which flowed down the ages in an
ever widening and deepening channel until it ended in the
great Redeemer.

Salvation from our enemies,—The salvation here is explanatory of and the result of the "horn of salvation for us," referred to in verse 69 : the thought in verse 69 is now taken up
after the parenthesis. This was a spiritual deliverance from
spiritual enemies, since serving God "in holiness and righteousness before him all our days" (verse 75) was to be the
result of this salvation. Zacharias may have connected this
with the deliverance from the political oppression of Herod
and the Romans, expecting national exaltation with the highest religious prosperity like that in the days of David and Sol-

74 To grant unto us that we being delivered out of the hand of our enemies
Should serve him without fear,
75 In holiness and righteousness before him all our days.
76 Yea and thou, child, shalt be called the prophet of the Most High:
For thou shalt go before the face of the Lord to make ready his ways;

omon; however it seems that he must, under the influence of the Holy Spirit, have been chiefly speaking of a salvation from the bondage of individual and national sins.

To grant unto us that we being delivered—The covenant that Jehovah made was a "holy covenant"; it was a "holy covenant" because it originated in holiness and was productive of holiness in the saved from all injustice and unrighteousness and from every imperfection. (Rom. 3: 26.) God remembered his oath for the purpose of performing or granting its fulfillment; hence he exercised mercy in remembering his holy covenant and performing his oath to grant deliverance to his people. It was of the greatest importance in the mind of Zacharias that they should serve God "without fear," and hence he makes it prominent.

76-80 **Yea and thou, child, shalt be called the prophet**—At this point the song of Zacharias begins its second part. After giving vent to his gratitude for the coming and blessing of the Messiah, Zacharias now first mentions his son, whom he addressed in language of great beauty, yet he speaks of him only as the prophet and forerunner of him whose glorious mission and salvation he was now celebrating. John was called here "the prophet of the Most High"; he was the messenger of God spoken of by Malachi. John was a prophet not only as a preacher of truth, but also as the foreteller of Christ's coming and of the vengeance that should befall the Jewish nation for its impenitence and unbelief. The preeminence of Jesus is here designated by the "Most High." John's mission is also outlined here when Zacharias said that he should "go before the face of the Lord to make ready his ways." John is likened to one going before an oriental monarch and preparing the way for him. Christ is first, John secondary; Zacharias so recognizes this relation between John and Jesus. There seems

77 To give knowledge of salvation unto his people
   In the remission of their sins,
78 Because of the [2]tender mercy of our God,
   [3]Whereby the dayspring from on high [4]shall visit us,

[2]Or, *heart of mercy*
[3]Or, *Wherein*
[4]Many ancient authorities read *hath visited us*

to be a clear reference here to the prophecies in Isa. 40: 3 and
Mal. 3: 1. The divine nature of Jesus as the Messiah is
brought to view here by the application of the name "Lord"
to him. John was to prepare the way for Jesus by pointing
out the sins of the people and leading them to repentance.

To give knowledge of salvation—This expresses the object
of John's going before Jesus to prepare his way; John
awakened in the people a conception of their need of a spiritual emancipation and of the necessity of repentance and ref-
ormation of life, and pointed to Jesus as the Lamb of God
that taketh away the sin of the world. John thus taught and
heralded the salvation which Christ was to bring, and put the
people in preparation for it. This knowledge should lead
them unto "the remission of their sins." John was to give a
knowledge of a salvation consisting in the forgiveness of sins.
Before Christ came there was not a clear understanding of
the method by which God could grant the full forgiveness of
sins, and hence the knowledge of this was the great need
of the Jews and of the world.

Because of the tender mercy of our God,—The knowledge
of the remission of sins, as well as the salvation from sin, is
through the tender mercies of God. It is also through the
tender mercy of God that Christ, man's Redeemer, should
come. "Whereby the dayspring from on high shall visit us."
Literally, "dayspring" means "the rising" of the sun, or "the
dawn of a heavenly day." We have here a reference to prophetic terms: "But unto you that fear my name shall the sun
of righteousness arise with healing in its wings; and ye shall
go forth, and gambol as calves of the stall." (Mal. 4: 2.)
This seems to compare the coming of the Christ and the dawn
of a better day to the heavenly bodies, which do not come

79 To shine upon them that sit in darkness and the shadow of death;
    To guide our feet into the way of peace.
80 And the child grew, and waxed strong in spirit, and was in the deserts
till the day of his showing unto Israel.

---

from beneath the horizon, but as it were from the very zenith.
With prophetic vision Zacharias saw the dawn already beginning and the Messiah coming.

To shine upon them—The purpose of the coming of Christ
is here given; he was to give light to the people and to illumi-
nate all who sat "in darkness and the shadow of death." The
dark, terrible, and dismal condition in which the people had
been wrought by sin was to be removed by dispelling the
darkness of spiritual death, and giving light through the
Christ. This was to be done by his guiding "our feet into the
way of peace." They were to be led by Christ into that
course of life which is attended with peace of conscience and
led to eternal peace. The gospel of Christ shows us the only
way to peace with God. The coming of Christ is like the
day-dawn that comes to the weary and benighted traveler in
the darkness of the most dismal night, and enables him to
pursue his journey in paths of peace and safety. The hymn of
Zacharias closes grandly with the boundless prospect in the
future for eternal and supernal happiness.

And the child grew,—Luke now gives us a glimpse of
John's private life, his development of both body and mind,
his preparation for his peculiar work; the conclusion is similar
to that in Luke 2: 40, 52. Some think that this marks the end
of one of those documents which Luke used under the direction of the Spirit. (Verse 3.) "The child grew" in a physical, mental, and spiritual sense; he was gradually fitted for the
great work of preaching repentance to a wicked nation. He
remained "in the deserts till the day of his showing unto Israel." "Deserts" here means sparsely-inhabited districts of
southern Palestine; the word "desert" or "wilderness" means
in the New Testament merely an unenclosed, untilled, and
thinly-inhabited district; it was applied to the mountainous
regions, to districts fitted only for pasture, and to country re-

mote from towns. John remained in "the deserts" until the time of his public manifestation, or his entrance into his public ministry, which was about thirty years of age. Some think that his parents died when he was young; he was not taught in the Jewish schools; he did not appear in the service of the temple at an age when he could have done so. (Num. 8: 24; 1 Chron. 23 : 27.)

5. THE BIRTH OF JESUS
2 : 1-20

1 Now it came to pass in those days, there went out a decree from Caesar Augustus, that all ⁵the world should be enrolled. 2 This was the first enrol-

⁵Gr. *the inhabited earth*

1. **Now it came to pass in those days,**—The first chapter closed with a brief reference to the growth, development, and private life of John; Luke now returns to a period of time a little after John's birth, and relates the birth of Jesus at Bethlehem with its attendant circumstances. Matthew's account (1: 18-24) of the angelic appearance to Joseph in a dream seems to come in between this and the preceding chapter. It is the purpose of Luke here to show how Jesus came to be born at Bethlehem, though Mary lived at Nazareth. "In those days" refers to the events recorded in chaper 1; this is his way of approaching the account of the birth of Jesus. "There went out a decree from Caesar Augustus"; this Caesar was the first Roman emperor; he was born 63 B.C. and died A.D. 14, at the age of seventy-six, after a long and prosperous reign of forty-four years; he was a nephew of the famous Julius Caesar. His title "Augustus," which means "the venerable," "the majestic," was conferred upon him by the Roman senate, and was applied to his successors. (Acts 25: 21, 25.) The title "Caesar" was assumed by him, and also applied to Roman emperors after him; in the New Testament we find it applied to Tiberius (Luke 3: 1), to Claudius (Acts 17: 7), and to Nero (Acts 25: 8; 26: 32).

that all the world should be enrolled.—"All the world" here means all the provinces of the Roman Empire which at that time embraced nearly all the civilized and known world, and

ment made when Quirinius was governor of Syria. 3 And all went to enrol

which was very commonly spoken of as "all the world." The
phrase seems to have been used sometimes in a restricted
sense; it was originally used by the Greeks to denote the land
inhabited by themselves in contrast with barbarian countries;
afterward, when the Greeks became subject to the Romans, it
was applied to the entire Roman world, and still later it was
made to include "the whole inhabited world." In the New
Testament this is the more common usage, though, in some
cases, this is conceived in the mold of the Roman Empire.
(Acts 11: 28; 19: 27.) Jesus used it in giving the commission
when he said that the gospel should be preached "in all the
world" (Matt. 24: 14); and Paul in the prediction of a general
judgment (Acts 17: 31); and one time it is used to denote
"the world to come" (Heb. 2: 5). "Enrolled" means properly
to register or enter in a list; commentators are not agreed as
to whether it refers to an enrollment for taxation, or for ascer-
taining the population, as the word may be used in either
sense.

2 **This was the first enrolment made**—From this it may be
inferred that there was another census under Quirinius, which
was indeed the case, about ten years later. The full name of
this Roman official was Publius Sulpitius Quirinius; he died
at Rome A.D. 21. "Syria" was then a Roman province, whose
boundaries are somewhat uncertain; its general boundaries
were the Euphrates on the east, the Mediterranean on the
west, Palestine on the south, and Cilicia and Mount Amanun
on the north. After the banishment of Archaelaus, A.D. 6,
Judea was added to the province of Syria by request of the
governor of Judea. According to Josephus (Antiq., 17: 13, 15;
18: 1, 1) Quirinius became governor of Syria A.D. 6, when
he took a census in Judea, which excited the opposition related
by Luke in Acts 5: 37. It appears that Luke here refers to a
census about ten years later, which was commenced during
the last days of Herod the Great, before Palestine became a
Roman province. Some think that Quirinius was twice governor, and that this enrollment came during his first term in

themselves, every one to his own city. 4 And Joseph also went up from Galilee, out of the city of Nazareth, into Judaea, to the city of David, which is called Bethlehem, because he was of the house and family of David; 5 to

---

office. There seems to be some confusion as to when this census was made; profane historians are not agreed. When such is the case, believers in the Bible take the record as found in the inspired book, and leave all conflicts and difficulties in profane records to be worked out by those who believe those records.

3-5 And all went to enrol—All the people of Palestine, and especially those of the Jews, had to go the city of their ancestors; the census was taken, in part at least, after the Jewish method; each Jew went to the headquarters of his family to be enrolled, where the ancestral records were kept; hence "Joseph also went up from Galilee, out of the city of Nazareth, into Judaea, to the city of David, which is called Bethlehem." Joseph was of the family of David, and Bethlehem was David's ancestral home. Luke's reason for mentioning this census appears to have been to show how it was that Jesus was born in Bethlehem; Caesar, prompted by God's purpose, directed the census. Each had to go "to his own city"; this was a practice that the Jews had followed for some time. Joseph "went up"; this is the usual expression in speaking of going from Galilee to the more elevated region of Jerusalem and Judea; with this physical elevation may be associated the idea of greater political, social, and spiritual privileges and standing.

"Bethlehem" signifies "house of bread"; it was fitting that the name where "the Bread of Life" was born should be called Bethlehem, or "house of bread." It was a small town about six miles south of Jerusalem, and about seventy-six miles south of Nazareth. The earliest mention that we have of it is in Gen. 35: 16-20, when Jacob was bereaved of his beloved Rachel. It is called "the city of David" because it was his birthplace and the seat of his ancestral home. (1 Sam. 16: 1.) Bethlehem was the scene of the touching story of Naomi, Ruth, and Boaz; it lay to the east of the main road from Jeru-

enrol himself with Mary, who betrothed to him, being great with child. 6
And it came to pass, while they were there, the days were fulfilled that she
should be delivered. 7 And she brought forth her firstborn son; and she

---

salem to Hebron, and was situated on a high hill. It was anciently located in the tribe of Judah (Judges 17: 9; 19: 1; 1
Sam. 17: 12), and its earliest name was Ephrath or Ephratah.

to enrol himself with Mary,—This may mean either that Joseph went up to be registered, accompanied by Mary, or that
Mary went up to be registered as well as Joseph. The Greek
can be rendered "went up with Mary," denoting merely the
fact of her accompanying him; or "to enrol himself with
Mary," implying that both their names must be registered. It
seems that Mary would not have made the trip in her condition, had she not been required to go, unless she knew the
prophecy that the Messiah should be born in Bethlehem, and
knew that her time for delivery was near at hand and that she
should be in Bethlehem at the birth of her son. We have no
way of knowing whether Mary went up to Bethlehem just in
order to fulfill the prophecy; the natural and easy way of
looking at it is that she was required by the "decree" to go to
Bethlehem and register.

6, 7 And it came to pass, while they were there,—Joseph
and Mary came the long distance from Nazareth to Bethlehem and were waiting either for the proper officer to register
them or till their own turn came to be registered. We do not
know how long they had to wait, but evidently not very long,
as they were occupying a temporary lodging place. While
they were waiting "the days were fulfilled that she should be
delivered." The child was born and Mary "brought forth her
firstborn son." The question whether Mary had other children is in itself a matter of little concern, except as the Catho-
lics have argued and decreed her perpetual virginity. That
she afterwards had other children seems to be highly probable. (Matt. 13: 55; Mark 6: 3; Luke 8: 20.) These references
seem clear enough that Mary had other children, and hence
Luke refers to Jesus as "her firstborn son"; the Greek literally
reads "her son, the firstborn."

wrapped him in swaddling clothes, and laid him in a manger, because there was no room for them in the inn.

8 And there were shepherds in the same country abiding in the field, and

---

she wrapped him in swaddling clothes,—In this verse and in verse 12 of this chapter only do we find the word "swaddling"; it is often found in medical writing. "Swaddling clothes" were bands of cloth which were wrapped around infants at their birth; the language indicates that Mary did this herself. After wrapping the babe with these bands she "laid him in a manger, because there was no room for them in the inn." Luke is the only writer that mentions his being placed in a manger. The "manger" was a hollow place for food, a feeding trough in a stable. (Isa. 1: 3.) It was sometimes spoken of as a "crib." The reason given for laying him in a manger is "because there was no room for him in the inn." "The inn" as used here implies that there was but one in the small city of Bethlehem; it was very much unlike our modern hotel. It was probably but little more than a large enclosure where the traveler might sleep, stable his beasts, and deposit his goods, furnishing his own bed and food. Such inns were common in the East. Sometimes there were separate stables for cattle in the rear under a shed running all along behind the walls; some supposed that it was in one of these rear stables that Joseph and Mary were compelled to lodge on that eventful night. It was perfectly natural after finding no lodging place within the inn, to have found it in one of the stables or outhouses.

8, 9 And there were shepherds in the same country—Shepherds were common among the Jews; one of their chief occupations was that of herding sheep, goats, and cattle; the business was an honorable and humble calling. Biblical literature is enriched by figures of speech taken from the occupation of shepherds. The patriarchs, Abraham, Isaac, Jacob, and his twelve sons were shepherds; David was a shepherd, as were some of the prophets. The calling and office of shepherds have been highly honored; Christ styled himself "the good shepherd" (John 10: 11), and he is called "the great shepherd of the sheep" (Heb. 13: 20), and the "Lamb of God" (John 1:

keeping ¹watch by night over their flock. 9 And an angel of the Lord stood
by them, and the glory of the Lord shone round about them: and they were

¹Or, *night-watches*

29.) The region near Bethlehem was a fertile country and a
fine pasture land. These shepherds were "abiding in the field,
and keeping watch by night over their flock." They were
"abiding" in the field; that is, they were remaining or living in
the open field, after the custom of shepherds. Some think
that these shepherds were living in the tower "Migdal Eder"
which means "tower of the flock," or "a watchtower," which
was not far from Jerusalem; it is claimed that this tower was
built for herdsmen in watching and guarding their flocks.
The prophet Micah mentions this tower and Bethlehem with
Messianic expectation. (Mic. 4: 8; 5: 2.) The shepherds do
not appear to have been in this tower at this time. They were
probably on one of the neighboring hills, where shepherds and
flocks frequently remained.

keeping watch by night—Literally this means that they were
keeping watches of the night over their flocks; that is, they
were taking their turns at the several nights' watches. The
night was at this time divided into four watches. (Matt. 14:
25.) The Jews first divided the night into three "watches," a
"watch" being a period of the night spent by soldiers, in keeping awake, to guard against enemies, or to prevent the escape
of prisoners; finally it came to mean any division of the night.
The Roman custom was to divide the night into four
"watches"; these watches began at six, nine, twelve, and three
o'clock.

And an angel of the Lord stood by them,—"An angel" came
to the shepherds and "stood by them"; the angel appeared in
a visible form standing by them; the meaning is that the
angel appeared suddenly and unexpectedly. (Luke 24: 4;
Acts 23: 11.) The surpassing brightness of the angel was
such that "the glory of the Lord shone round about them";
this usually accompanied the presence of angels. (Ex. 24: 16;
Num. 14: 10; Matt. 17: 5). The shepherds were overshadowed and surrounded with the divine effulgence. The effect

sore afraid. 10 And the angel said unto them, Be not afraid; for behold, I bring you good tidings of great joy which shall be to all the people: 11 for there is born to you this day in the city of David a Saviour, who is ²Christ

²Or, *Anointed Lord*

upon them was that they "were sore afraid." Literally this means that "they feared with a great fear." There was a glory attending the angel beyond anything that Zacharias or Mary had seen; the supernatural and the holy produced an awe in them that is common to one who sees a representative of Jehovah. (Ex. 20: 19; 33: 20; Judges 13: 22; Matt. 17: 6.)

10-14 **And the angel said unto them,**—The angel knew that they were "sore afraid," and assured them that they should not be disturbed; "be not afraid" were the assuring words of the angel. They should not be frightened, for the angel was a messenger, not of bad, but of good tidings; hence there was no need of cringing fear. "I bring you good tidings of great joy which shall be to all the people." The Greek when taken strictly literal means "I evangelize to you a great joy." An angel is the first to announce to the world that the Messiah had actually come. The good tidings would not only bring great joy to the shepherds, but to the whole people, and especially to all Israel who were expecting the Messiah. The shepherds later made known the good tidings to others; while the message is limited here, the blessings of it are general.

for there is born to you this day in the city of David a Saviour,—The city of David was Bethlehem, David's native city and Christ's promised birthplace. (Mic. 5: 2; Matt. 2: 5, 6.) "A Saviour" means one who is to save; he was called Jesus, which means Savior, "who is Christ the Lord." Jesus saves men from the power and penalty of sin; "Christ" is the official name of Jesus and is the Greek for "anointed," and corresponds with the Hebrew "Messiah." It was common for the Jews to apply this name to the expected deliverer. (Psalm 2: 2; Dan. 9: 24, 25; John 1: 41; 4: 25.) He was the anointed Prophet, Priest, and King of spiritual Israel, or the kingdom of God. "Lord" means "ruler or governor"; the Jews thought the name Jehovah too sacred to pronounce and substituted for

the Lord. 12 And this *is* the sign unto you: Ye shall find a babe wrapped in swaddling clothes, and lying in a manger. 13 And suddenly there was with the angel a multitude of the heavenly host praising God, and saying,
   14 Glory to God in the highest,
   And on earth ³peace among ⁴men in whom he is well pleased. 15

³Many ancient authorities read *peace, good pleasure among men*
⁴Gr. *men of good pleasure*

it in their oral reading a term which the Greek translators of the Old Testament rendered by this word "Lord." Sarah called Abraham "lord" (Gen. 18: 12); Joseph is called "lord" of the country (Gen. 42: 33) and is addressed by his brethren as "my lord" (Gen. 42: 10). This term is applied to God also. (Gen. 18: 27; Ex. 4: 10.) In the New Testament it is a name for God. (Matt. 1: 20, 22, 24; 2: 15; Acts 11: 16; 12: 11, 17.)

And this is the sign unto you:—As in the case of Mary (Luke 1: 36), the sign is promised where none was asked; God anticipated their necessity; they were to be witnesses and proclaimers of the wonderful event; hence they are qualified by divine guidance in bearing this witness. The sign that was given them was that they should "find a babe wrapped in swaddling clothes, and lying in a manger." There would be but one babe so poorly provided for in Bethlehem; the angel did not tell them everything, but left something for faith to supply. They were to believe the angel, and were to follow the instruction which they received; they believed, went, and *found*. This babe would be found "lying in a manger"; the fact that it would be wrapped in swaddling clothes was not the sign, for that was common—all newborn babes were wrapped in swaddling clothes; but the fact that this babe would be found in a manger was the sign to the shepherds. This lowly birth and all of its surroundings were in keeping with him who was to be the "man of sorrows," "the friend of the poor," and without even a place to lay his head; his lowly condition was adapted to dispel any fears which these humble shepherds might have in approaching a newborn king and excite their sympathy for one so great in nature and yet so humble in earthly estate.

And suddenly there was with the angel a multitude—Only one angel appeared to the shepherds and announced to them

the birth of Jesus; but "suddenly," just as the angel had finished speaking, "a multitude of the heavenly host" appeared.
There was a celestial army which came swiftly to impress the
message which the angel had delivered.   Some have thought
that the "heavenly host" was present while the angel was talking to the shepherd, but the context seems to imply otherwise.
A host of angels is represented in the Old Testament as forming the bodyguard of Deity.   (Psalm 103: 21; Dan. 7: 10.)
The glory of the Lord (verse 9) was the first token to the
shepherds of the divine presence; next the angelic hosts which
appeared praising God emphasized God's presence.   These angels or "army of angels" were "praising God" by saying
"Glory to God in the highest, and on earth peace among men
in whom he is well pleased."   This praise was a proclamation
of the newborn king and the confirmation of the glorious tidings to the shepherds, and through them to all men.   Angels
shouted for joy at creation (Job 38: 7), ministered at the giving of the law (Deut. 33: 2; Acts 7: 53; Gal. 3: 19) and now,
with more reason than ever, exult at the advent of the Savior.
Their message is confirmed by the proclamation of peace; the
"Prince of Peace" is born, and he brings peace to all who accept him.

   Chronology of the birth of Christ.—The exact day and year
of the birth of Jesus cannot be ascertained with certainty.   The
"Christian era" should properly begin with the year Jesus was
born; that was the intention of the one who arranged our present calendar.   By the "Christian era" is meant the system
upon which calendars are constructed, and by which historical
events are now dated in practically all the civilized world.
Dionysius Exiguus, an abbot of Rome, in the year A.D. 532,
arranged the scheme of counting dates from the birth of
Jesus.   He calculated that the year of Jesus' birth was 753
from the founding of Rome.   It has long been admitted that
Dionysius made an error of at least four years.   Jesus was
born before the death of Herod the Great (Matt. 2: 1, 19),
which took place about the year of Rome 753; this is definitely fixed by an eclipse of the moon which is mentioned as
occurring a little before the death of Herod; this eclipse, by

And it came to pass, when the angels went away from them into heaven, the shepherds said one to another, Let us now go even unto Bethlehem, and see this ⁵thing that is come to pass, which the Lord hath made known unto us. 16 And they came with haste, and found both Mary and Joseph, and the babe

⁵Or, *saying*

astronomical calculation, took place in the year of Rome 753, or four years before our common era; but Jesus was born somewhat earlier. The error Dionysius Exiguus made was not discovered until many years afterwards, and no attempt has been made to correct the error.

15 **And it came to pass, when the angels went away**—It seems that immediately upon the departure of the angels the shepherds resolved to go to Bethlehem; the angels "went away from them into heaven" which was their abiding place, and the shepherds, while under the holy influence of the sacred scene, said: "Let us now go even unto Bethlehem." The expression indicates that they were a little distance from the city, and it may imply that Bethlehem was not their home. At any rate, they determined to go and "see this thing that is come to pass." The words of the shepherds are not those of doubt, but of belief and obedience; they were assured that what the angel had told them was true, and they wanted to see this wonderful babe of Bethlehem. We have no evidence that the angel commanded them to go, but the angel told them where they would find the babe, and this carried with it the force of commanding them. They were anxious to see the one who had been expected for so long a time.

16, 17 **And they came with haste,**—We may judge that they did not delay after the angel left them, for they "came with haste" to Bethlehem. They came before the night was over, leaving their flocks to the care of providence, showing how strong their faith was. When they arrived they found everything as the angel had described; they found "both Mary and Joseph, and the babe lying in the manger." How they found the Messianic babe is not told us; we need not suppose, with some, that the stable belonged to these shepherds, nor, with others, that the angel gave them minute directions regarding it. We only know that their faith was strong enough and

lying in the manger. 17 And when they saw it, they made known concerning
the saying which was spoken to them about this child. 18 And all that heard
it wondered at the things which were spoken unto them by the shepherds.
19 But Mary kept all these °sayings, pondering them in her heart. 20 And

°Or, *things*

their desire great enough to cause them to search and find the
babe. "Mary and Joseph" were found with and protecting the
babe; Mary is mentioned first as chief in honor; both Mary
and Joseph may have been humiliated by the humble surroundings, but they were comforted and cheered by the unexpected visit of these shepherds, and the news that the heavenly hosts were rejoicing over the birth of the Savior.

And when they saw it,—When the shepherds saw the child
and Mary and Joseph, they knew that the angel had described
accurately the babe, and that the Messiah had come. The
shepherds were satisfied with the sign which the angel gave
them and their faith strengthened in the divine arrangement
which had been revealed to them. The shepherds not only
told Mary and Joseph what the angel had announced and
what "the heavenly host" had sung with respect to the child,
but they "made known concerning the saying which was spoken to them about this child" to all who would believe them.
They gave a full account of the scene as it had occurred. It
seems that it was not intended that the report of the birth of
Jesus should then be spread abroad, like that of John, in "all
the hill country of Judaea."

18-20 **And all that heard it wondered**—The effect of this
glorious intelligence upon all those that heard caused them to
wonder; they were amazed, astonished at hearing so strange
an account, for they had not looked for the Messiah to come
in such a humble way; they could not reconcile these humble
circumstances with their conception of the coming of the Messiah. While others were wondering in amazement about
these things, "Mary kept all these sayings, pondering them in
her heart." Mary laid them up in her mind and compared the
things which the shepherds had told her with what the angel
had announced to her when he first visited her. The silent
pondering of Mary contrasts strongly with the wonder of

the shepherds returned, glorifying and praising God for all the things that
they had heard and seen, even as it was spoken unto them.

those mentioned in the preceding verse. They may have soon
forgotten many of the incidents, but Mary kept all of them in
her heart. It is noticeable that Joseph is not now mentioned,
but he doubtless participated in Mary's feelings and hopes.

And the shepherds returned, glorifying and praising God—
The shepherds returned to their flocks; the wonderful revelation did not withdraw them from their common duties, but
rather caused a joyful attention to them. They glorified and
praised God; like the angelic host, they give glory to God, assured that they had seen the fulfillment of the angel's prediction and that the child was indeed the Messiah. It is probable
that Mary and Joseph related to the shepherds some things
regarding the babe, and that this also confirmed the faith of
the shepherds. Luke says that they glorified and praised God
for "all the things that they had heard and seen, even as it
was spoken unto them." This could include what they had
learned from Mary and Joseph. Luke's account of the birth
of Jesus bears upon every line the evidence of simple, honest
truth in striking contrast to the imaginary legends of the spu-
rious accounts given by others. Uninspired men would have
written differently about the birth of the Son of God, but
God's word comes in the majesty of simple truth.

6. THE CIRCUMCISION AND PRESENTATION OF JESUS
2: 21-40

21 And when eight days were fulfilled for circumcising him, his name
was called JESUS, which was so called by the angel before he was conceived in the womb.

21 **And when eight days were fulfilled**—The law required
that the first-born male be dedicated to Jehovah. (Lev. 12:
1-8.) This was to be done on the eighth day, or when the
child was eight days old; these days were required for the
preparation of the ceremony of circumcision; at this time the
child officially received its name. The angel at the annunciation had told Mary that she should call "his name Jesus."

22 And when the days of their purification [7]according to the law of Moses
were fulfilled, they brought him up to Jerusalem, to present him to the Lord
23 (as it is written in the law of the Lord, [8]Every male that openeth the

[7]Lev. 12.2-6
[8]Ex. 13.2, 12

(Matt. 1: 21; Luke 1: 31.) The construction in the Greek is
such that the naming of Jesus is made the principal subject,
and the rite of circumcision being alluded to, merely denotes
the time and occasion of the bestowal of that name; hence,
Mary was faithful to the instruction of the angel and named
him Jesus. Luke is very specific about this name, and says
that it was given to the child "before he was conceived in the
womb."

22-24 **And when the days of their purification**—The mother
of a child was unclean for forty days after the birth of a son,
and for eighty days after the birth of a daughter; the time for
a son was forty days from his birth, or thirty-three days after
the circumcision. When the days were fulfilled for the purification, "they brought him up to Jerusalem, to present him to
the Lord." Women on errands commonly rode to the temple
on oxen; they did this because the body of an ox was so large
that it increased the space between the woman and the ground
to prevent any chance of further defilement from passing over
any unclean thing on the road.

(as it is written in the law of the Lord,—The word "law"
occurs in this chapter five times; this is more times than in all
the rest of the Gospel of Luke. Luke emphasizes the fact that
Jesus was "born of a woman, born under the law" (Gal. 4: 4),
and accordingly he elaborates the details of the fulfillment of
the law by the parents of both John and Jesus. There are different expressions for the law of Moses; it is called "law of
Moses," "the law of the Lord," and "the law." (Neh. 8: 1, 3,
7, 8, 14, 18; Mark 7: 10.) From the day when the first born of
Egypt had been smitten by the destroying angel, the first born
of Israel among the male were consecrated to the Lord.
(Num. 3: 13.) However, God ordained and accepted, as a
substitute for the first born, the tribe of Levi, which was set
apart for his special service. (Num. 3: 12.) But as the num-

womb shall be called holy to the Lord), 24 and to offer a sacrifice according
to that which is said in the law of the Lord, [9]A pair of turtledoves, or two
young pigeons. 25 And behold, there was a man in Jerusalem, whose name
was Simeon; and this man was righteous and devout, looking for the conso-

[9]Lev. 12.8; 5.11

ber of the first born exceeded that of the tribe, a redemption
price of five shekels was to be paid to the priests (Num. 3: 46,
47), which was ordained to be paid for all the first born
(Num. 18: 15, 16). This is why the first born was called
"holy."

to offer a sacrifice according to that which—This verse is
joined to verse 22, but separated by a parenthetical statement
in verse 23. The law prescribed the sacrifice to be a lamb one
year old for a burnt offering, and a young pigeon or turtle-
dove for a sin offering; but in case the poverty of the mother
forbade the offering of a lamb, two turtledoves or young pigeons were permitted as a substitute; one of these was for a
burnt offering and the other for a sin offering. (Lev. 12: 6-8.)
The fact that Mary offered "a pair of turtledoves, or two
young pigeons" shows that she was poor, for she would not
have made the offering of the poor, if she had not been poor.
This fact also denies the legend that she was a rich heiress.
God had made provision for the poor; his service has always
been reasonable.   While the lamb for this offering would
probably cost about two dollars, the doves would cost about
sixteen cents.

25, 26 And behold, there was a man in Jerusalem,—This
man's name was Simeon; some have thought that Simeon was
the celebrated rabbi of that name, and the father of Gamaliel;
there is no evidence that this supposition is true. It was not
the design of Luke to refer to the worldly standing of Simeon, but only his religious attainments. Luke describes Simeon as being "righteous and devout." The Greek for "devout" is used only by Luke; it means circumspect or cautious;
hence Simeon was a person who took hold of things carefully;
he was cautious and careful to observe all the ordinances of
the law; he was righteous in that he kept the commandments
of the law. Simeon was one who was "looking for the conso-

lation of Israel: and the Holy Spirit was upon him. 26 And it had been
revealed unto him by the Holy Spirit, that he should not see death, before he
had seen the Lord's Christ. 27 And he came in the Spirit into the temple:
and when the parents brought in the child Jesus, that they might do concern-

---

lation of Israel." "Consolation of Israel" is the same as "hope
of Israel." (Acts 28: 20.) He was looking for the Messiah.
There was a common form of adjuration among the Jews
which said, "so may I see the consolation." Simeon was filled
with the Holy Spirit; whether he was filled just at this time
or at some previous time, we are not told.

And it had been revealed unto him—The original bears the
interpretation that it was having been revealed; that is, it
"stood" revealed while he waited for the fulfillment of the revelation. We are not informed as to what manner it was revealed to him. Some have inferred that it was revealed to
him in a dream as it was to Joseph and to the wise men
(Matt. 1: 20; 2: 12, 13, 19); but the distinct reference made
twice to the Holy Spirit would lead one to suppose that it was
made to him in a vision while he was in a state of prophetic
ecstasy. It was revealed to him "that he should not see death,
before he had seen the Lord's Christ." In Matt. 16: 28 we
have the statement, "shall in no wise taste of death, till they
see the Son of man coming in his kingdom." Taste and sight
are often put figuratively for the actual experience of a thing.
Simeon was promised that he should not die before he saw
"the Lord's Christ"; this means the Christ, the anointed of the
Lord. (Psalm 2: 2.) There is a beautiful and striking antithesis between the words "see death" and "see the Lord's
Christ."

27-32 And he came in the Spirit into the temple:—The Holy
Spirit prompted Simeon to go to the temple at this time; the
Holy Spirit moved Simeon to come to the temple at the opportune moment when Joseph and Mary brought the child
Jesus, just as the Holy Spirit brought Philip and the eunuch
together on the road to Gaza. (Acts 8: 26-31.) Simeon was
brought into the court of the women of the temple; women
were not permitted to enter the temple proper; hence we are

ing him after the custom of the law, 28 then he received him into his arms,
and blessed God, and said,
> 29 Now lettest thou thy [10]servant depart, [11]Lord,
> According to thy word, in peace;
> 30 For mine eyes have seen thy salvation,

[10]Gr. *bondservant*
[11]Gr. *Master*

---

to understand that they went into the court where women
were permitted. Here Joseph and Mary are spoken of as "the
parents" of "the child Jesus." Luke has made his record clear
that Joseph was not one of "the parents" of Jesus; he is spoken of as a "parent" of him, because he was the husband of
Mary, who was the mother of Jesus. They brought Jesus to
the temple "that they might do concerning him after the custom of the law." "After the custom" means "according to
that which was usually done"; "custom" or "to be accustomed" are used more frequently by Luke than any other writer; they are words which are common in medical writings;
hence Luke, who was a physician (Col. 4: 14), uses frequently
medical terms. Reference is here made to the payment of the
redemption price.

then he received him into his arms,—Simeon required no information in regard to the incidents attending the conception
and birth of the child; it had been revealed to him that before
his death he should see the long-expected Messiah; he had
gone to the temple by the direction of the Holy Spirit, and
when Mary entered with the babe, he recognized her child as
the promised Messiah. He then took the child and "blessed
God." His act first was one of thanksgiving; then his aged
eyes were permitted to rest on the long-expected and hope-for
Messiah; he prayed for a speedy and peaceful departure from
the toils and sorrows of life. He said: "Now lettest thou thy
servant depart, Lord, according to thy word, in peace."
Simeon regarded the sight of the promised Messiah as the
consummation of his earthly life, and hence it was to him an
assurance that his earthly labors were now about to end.

For mine eyes have seen thy salvation,—This was the
ground of his assurance: he had been permitted to see the

31 Which thou hast prepared before the face of all peoples;
32 A light for [12]revelation to the Gentiles,
   And the glory of thy people Israel.
33 And his father and his mother were marvelling at the things which

[12]Or, *the unveiling of the Gentiles*

Messiah, which was equivalent to seeing the salvation of Jehovah, for "salvation" is to be interpreted as "Saviour"; this salvation in the vision of Simeon had been prepared "before the face of all peoples." "All people" primarily include the Jews which had been scattered all over the world, and in a comprehensive sense it embraces all people of the earth. For this Savior was to be "a light for revelation to the Gentiles, and the glory of thy people Israel." "A light" is put here with the meaning of "a lamp." The Messiah was to be the Savior of the world; he was to be the moral light of the Gentiles, revealing to them the ways of God, and the true and only method of salvation through his atoning blood. The blessings of the Messiah's reign are promised here conjointly to the Jews and the Gentiles, and although Simeon spoke this under the inspiration of the Holy Spirit, there can be no doubt of the belief of such pious Israelites as Simeon and others who had studied carefully the Messianic prophecies that the Gentiles were to participate in some degree in the same blessings. There was much doubt and mystery with respect to the nature and extent of his kingdom, and it cost much effort on the part of our Lord to teach his disciples the true conception of his mission to earth. Light is promised here to the Gentiles and glory is promised to Israel; the Gentiles were regarded as in darkness and ignorance, and the Messiah would attain the true and highest glory of Israel.

33-35 **And his father and his mother**—Again we have Joseph spoken of as "his father"; this is done only in the sense that he was regarded legally as his father, since Joseph was the legal husband of Mary. God was the father of the Christ. Joseph and Mary marveled "at the things which were spoken concerning" Jesus by Simon. Although they had been prepared by the previous wonderful manifestations for the remarkable destiny of the child, yet they were doubtless very

were spoken concerning him; 34 and Simeon blessed them, and said unto
Mary his mother, Behold, this *child* is set for the falling and the rising of
many in Israel; and for a sign which is spoken against; 35 yea and a sword
shall pierce through thine own soul; that thoughts out of many hearts may

---

far from having attained to a full and just conception of the
glorious reality; they can hardly realize that the child so helpless and dependent is the manifested Messiah; hence when reminded of this by the words of the shepherds and of Simeon,
they wonder at the marvelous event almost as though they
had then heard of it for the first time.

Simeon blessed them,—While the plural is used here, the
blessing seems to be directed to Mary; some think that the
"them" includes Joseph, Mary, and the babe Jesus. In speaking to Mary, Simeon said; "Behold, this child is set for the
falling and the rising of many in Israel." He was the "falling" of some because he would be a stumbling block to many.
(Isa. 8: 14; Matt. 21: 42, 44; Acts 4: 11; Rom. 9: 33; 1 Cor. 1:
23.) He was the "rising" of many because many would be
raised up through him to life and glory. (Rom. 6: 4, 9; Eph.
2: 6.) He was also to be "a sign which is spoken against."
This expression does not voice a prophecy, but describes an
inherent characteristic of the sign, a sign of which is the character to experience contradiction from the world. In the
beginning as a babe Jesus was endangered at the hands
of Herod, and all through his earthly ministry and even on the
cross, he suffered many things and was spoken against by all
who refused to believe him.

yea and a sword shall pierce through thine own soul;—
Strictly speaking, this means a large broad sword; the original is used in the Septuagint of the sword of Goliath. (1 Sam.
17: 51.) This is a strong figure of Mary's pang when Jesus
her son was nailed to the cross, and while she stood at a distance and witnessed the dying agonies of her son. All the
manifestations of Jesus before men would have the result of
revealing many hearts; hence Simeon said "that thoughts out
of many hearts may be revealed." When Jesus stood in the
presence of men he could look into their hearts and see what
was in them; his presence became a searching test of real

be revealed. 36 And there was one Anna, a prophetess, the daughter of Phanuel, of the tribe of Asher (she was [1]of a great age, having lived with a husband seven years from her virginity, 37 and she had been a widow even unto fourscore and four years), who departed not from the temple, worshipping with fastings and supplications night and day. 38 And coming up at that very hour she gave thanks unto God, and spake of him to all them that were looking for the redemption of Jerusalem. 39 And when they had ac-

[1]Gr. *advanced in many days*

character. When Jesus came among men some hailed him with joy as one who brought the light of God from heaven to their needy, longing souls; but others hated this light, repelled it because it rebuked their evil deeds; those who refused to accept Jesus hardened their hearts and deepened their own damnation.

36-38 **and there was one Anna,**—Anna is another one of those who were prayerfully waiting with hopeful, longing expectation for the coming of the Messiah; she was guided on the present occasion by the same spirit and came at the same time that Simeon came to the temple to behold the Messiah. She was well advanced in years; she was a prophetess, "the daughter of Phanuel, of the tribe of Asher." The particularity with which her parentage and lineage is given shows that she was a person whose family as well as personal history was well known to the public. She had married in her young maidenhood, and had lived with her husband seven years; after her husband's death she lived eighty-four years, making in all ninety-one years since her marriage; on the supposition that she was twenty years old when she married, she was at this time one hundred eleven years old. She was regular in her worship, for she "departed not from the temple, worshipping with fastings and supplications night and day."

And coming up at that very hour she gave thanks—Like Simeon she gave thanks to God that her aged eyes had been spared to see the infant Messiah; she knew by the Holy Spirit that the child Jesus was the long-expected Messiah; she "spake of him to all them that were looking for the redemption of Jerusalem." Anna not only gave thanks to God, but she spoke to all others who in their hearts were waiting for the Messiah; it is not to be understood that she gave public

complished all things that were according to the law of the Lord, they returned into Galilee, to their own city Nazareth.

40 And the child grew, and waxed strong, ²filled with wisdom: and the
grace of God was upon him.

²Gr. *becoming full of wisdom*

utterance, but that she spoke to the pious ones who were with
her in the temple waiting for the Messiah. "Looking for the
redemption of Jerusalem" is equivalent to "looking for the
consolation of Israel." (Verse 25.) "Jerusalem" here stands
for the race or nation of the Jews. Anna is to be classed with
Simeon, Zacharias, and the shepherds. All of these were in a
state of prayerful expectation of the Messiah.

39 **And when they had accomplished all things**—After the
presentation of the child in the temple, Joseph and Mary returned "into Galilee, to their own city Nazareth." According
to the record given by Matthew (2: 1-12), it seems that they
returned to Bethlehem, where they were visited by the Magi,
and afterwards took their flight into Egypt (Matt. 2: 13-23).
The portion of Luke's record is parallel to Matt. 2: 22, 23, and
serves to explain what is there left out of sight, that Joseph and
Mary with the babe returned to Nazareth, because it was
"their own city." Matthew refers to this only to show that
Jesus was brought up in that despised city; Luke, whose plan
led him to speak of the previous dwelling place and condition
of Joseph and Mary, refers to Nazareth as their place of abode
before and after the birth of Jesus.

40 **And the child grew, and waxed strong,**—This shows that
Jesus had a human body and that he was capable of increasing
in wisdom and knowledge. The childhood life of Jesus followed the normal law of the race, growth of both body and
mind; the facts were peculair to him and he had the great
grace of God upon him and his wisdom was noticeable. The
Jews marked the stages of a child's development by seven different terms; the newborn babe (Isa. 9: 6); the suckling (Isa.
11: 8); the suckling beginning to ask for food (Lam. 4: 4);
the weaned child (Isa. 28: 9); the child clinging to its mother
(Jer. 40: 7); the child becoming firm and strong (Isa. 7: 14);

the youth becoming free and independent (Isa. 31 : 8). Jesus
passed through all of these stages in his human development.

7. THE BOYHOOD OF JESUS; HIS VISIT TO JERUSALEM AT AGE OF TWELVE
2 : 41-52

41 And his parents went every year to Jerusalem at the feast of the passover. 42 And when he was twelve years old, they went up after the custom

---

41 And his parents went every year—The law required all
males above the age of twelve to attend three annual feasts;
these feasts were held first where the tabernacle was pitched,
and next in Jerusalem when the temple was built. The attendance of females was not forbidden; they were left free to
attend if they wished. (1 Sam. 1 : 7, 22, 24.) The school of
Hillel made it obligatory upon women to attend the Passover.
It is not to be inferred here that Joseph and Mary went up to
no other yearly feasts than the Passover, but that upon this
feast they were in constant attendance. It seems that the fear
of the child being harmed had passed; that the Roman authorities had either forgotten about the incident of the newborn
king, or had not given much attention to it, possibly thinking
that it was a superstition of the Jews.

the feast of the passover.—The Passover was held on the
fourteenth day of month Nisan, which came some time in our
month of March. It commemorated the death angel passing
over the Israelites in Egypt and sparing the first born of the
Israelites, but destroying the first-born males of the Egyptians.
It was held annually, and was eaten with the lamb, called the
paschal lamb. (Ex. 12 : 1-48.) It had to be eaten with unleavened bread and bitter herbs; those who ate it had to be cere-
monially clean.

42-45 And when he was twelve years old,—At the age of
twelve a boy was regarded as "a son of the law," and came
under obligation to observe the ordinances of the law personally. It seems clear that this was the first time that Jesus
accompanied Joseph and Mary to the Feast of the Passover.
How little did the multitudes which filled Jerusalem on that
occasion think that the real Lamb, who was to be offered for

of the feast; 43 and when they had fulfilled the days, as they were returning, the boy Jesus tarried behind in Jerusalem; and his parents knew it not; 44 but supposing him to be in the company, they went a day's journey; and they sought for him among their kinsfolk and acquaintance: 45 and when they

---

the redemption of the world, the antitype of the lamb slain at the paschal feast, was present there! Joseph and Mary "went up after the custom of the feast" which required its celebration at Jerusalem. Before the erection of the temple the feast was kept at he place where the tabernacle was raised.

and when they had fulfilled the days,—The Passover required but one day, but the feast of unleavened bread, which immediately followed the Passover, continued for seven days. Since the Passover was the beginning of the feast of unleavened bread, the names have been used interchangeably, the Passover being applied to the feast of unleavened bread and the feast of unleavened bread to the Passover. (Ex. 12: 15, 17; 23: 15; Lev. 23: 4-8.) At the expiration of these days Joseph and Mary with their kinspeople began their journey homeward, not aware that Jesus was tarrying behind, but supposing that he was with the company made up of their neighbors and friends. These incidental circumstances show the method of travel from remote localities to the great city to attend the great feasts.

supposing him to be in the company,—This explains why they thought that Jesus was along with them; there was a great crowd of neighbors and kinspeople, and as they were traveling along engaged in religious exercises, they supposed that Jesus was along with them. Either they had committed him to some friend or relative, or they thought that he was old enough to take care of himself as they journeyed along, hence no attention was given to him until they arrived where they would spend the night. We are not to infer that Joseph and Mary were negligent with respect to Jesus. "They went a day's journey" before they discovered that the boy Jesus was not in the company. The length of "a day's journey" depended somewhat upon the distance they had to go in order to encamp where there was a supply of good water. From twenty to thirty miles is probably a fair estimate of an aver-

found him not, they returned to Jerusalem, seeking for him. 46 And it came
to pass, after three days they found him in the temple, sitting in the midst of
the ³teachers, both hearing them, and asking them questions : 47 and all that

³Or, *doctors* See ch. 5.17; Acts 5.34

age day's journey with baggage, animals, and women and
children. "A day's journey" (Num. 11: 31; 1 Kings 19: 4;
John 3: 4) was far different to a "sabbath day's journey,"
which was about three-fourths of a mile. The company
started early on their journey and usually made it a point to
stop for the night before it was dark in order to prepare their
evening meal and be ready for an early start on the morrow.

and when they found him not, they returned—They turned
back on the following morning; as they had made a day's
journey from Jerusalem, it would require another day to return to Jerusalem. It seems that they sought for him all their
way back to the city; they supposed that he had started with
the company, hence they diligently searched for him along the
way. Not finding Jesus during the entire day, nor at the
place of rest for the night, they returned to the city anxiously
seeking him.

46, 47 And it came to pass, after three days—Some have
counted the three days from the time that they arrived in Jerusalem; others think that it was three days from their separation, two days being spent in travel from and back to Jerusalem, and one day spent in searching for him in the city. It
is a little difficult to determine the exact length of time, as the
Jews were not accurate in counting time as we are today. It
seems that one day was spent in their journey, another in returning to the city, and the third day he was found in the temple. He was "in the temple," in one of the apartments of the
main building, where the Jewish doctors of the law held their
schools. He was "sitting in the midst of the teachers, both
hearing them, and asking them questions." It was the custom
for students to sit on the floor at the feet of their teachers,
who sat on raised benches of a semicircular form; Jesus was
sitting in the company of the others. The "teachers" were the
"doctors" of the law; these were the Jewish rabbis, a class of
men who after the captivity, expounded the law in the temple

heard him were amazed at his understanding and his answers. 48 And when they saw him, they were astonished; and his mother said unto him, 'Son, why hast thou thus dealt with us? behold, thy father and I sought thee sor-

'Gr. *Child*

and synagogues; they were consulted on doubtful points of the law and held public lectures and discussions wherever they could find auditors.

and all that heard him were amazed—Jesus was "both hearing them, and asking them questions." He was not "disputing" with them, but sat in their presence and asked questions of them, and answered their questions. We must think of Jesus even at the age of twelve as being humble and respectful; his questions were not those of a pert and spoiled child, but of a youthful mind, a modestly searching after truth, and seeking from the lips of age and wisdom a solution of difficulties, which he had already met in meditating upon the law of God. It was the custom in the Jewish schools for the scholars to ask questions of their teachers, and much of the books of the rabbis consisted of the answers of the rabbis to such questions. All the doctors and others who were present were "amazed at his understanding and his answers." He manifested more intelligence in asking questions and in answering their questions than the ordinary scholar; his degree of intelligence was such that all were astonished at his understanding of the law. It will be noticed here that Jesus at the age of twelve is not occupying the place of a teacher, but is sitting in the circle among the doctors and their hearers.

48-50 And when they saw him, they were astonished;— When Joseph and Mary saw Jesus engaged in this study or conversation with the rabbis, "they were astonished"; the original Greek uses a very strong verb here, which means "to strike out or drive away from"; hence the meaning is "to drive out of one's senses"; "amazed" is to throw into a "maze" or labyrinth, and is closely akin to the Greek word used here. It seems that Mary should have paused before she spake to him in the manner of reproof that she used; she should not have been so "astonished" when she remembered

rowing. 49 And he said unto them, How is it that ye sought me? knew ye
not that I must be ⁵in my Father's house? 50 And they understood not the

⁵Or, *about my Father's business* Gr. *in the things of my Father*

all the supernatural events connected with his conception,
birth, and divine protection. She said: "Son, why hast thou
thus dealt with us?" "Son" here means "child," as the original means a word which implies passive or dependent relation.
There is a rebuke in Mary's language. She adds that "thy
father and I sought thee sorrowing." Joseph was not his
father, but this shows that he had been taught to regard Joseph as his real father. Up to this time Joseph had been
called by Jesus "father," but from this time on never does he
speak of Joseph as his father, neither does Mary, henceforth,
speak of Joseph as the father of Jesus. The original means
that they had "sought" or "were seeking with sorrow." Mary
seems to be going over in mind the process of the long search
that they had made for him.

And he said unto them,—With mental anguish which
amounted to distress of body, hour after hour Joseph and
Mary had searched without success for the missing child;
hence the rebuke that Mary gave to Jesus. However, Jesus
replied: "How is that ye sought me?" This is the first recorded saying that we have of Jesus; they are spoken to his
mother. He means why have you been searching for me; the
words of Jesus do not imply a rebuke, as some have affirmed,
but are words of anxious solicitude for his mother's anxiety.
His reply has reference to the state of mental distress with
which they sought him as is shown from his next words. He
said: "Knew ye not that I must be in my Father's house?"
The word "must" here means "it is necessary" or "it be-
hooves." Jesus often used this word concerning his own appointed work, and expressed both the inevitable fulfillment of
the divine counsels and the absolute constraint of the principal duty upon himself. (Matt. 16: 21; 26: 54; Mark 8:
31; Luke 4: 43; 9: 22; 13: 33; 24: 7, 26, 46; John 3: 14;
4: 4; 12: 34.) "In my Father's house" means that he must be
doing those things of God. Mary's question was not as to
what her son had been doing, but as to where he had been;

saying which he spake unto them. 51 And he went down with them, and
came to Nazareth; and he was subject unto them: and his mother kept all
these [6]sayings in her heart.

[6]Or, *things*

Jesus answers her by asking: Where is the child to be found
but in his Father's house?

And they understood not the saying—It seems to us
strange that after the revelations that had been made to Mary
and Joseph (Matt. 1: 20; Luke 1: 32, 35) that they should
have been at a loss to understand Jesus' reply; but the years
of his infancy and childhood passing away without any striking incident, it may be that they lost sight in part of the wondrous circumstances attending his birth. They may never
have understood fully the depth of meaning, which, in the
light of the New Testament, we find no difficulty in attaching
to these declarations. It is certain that this consciousness of
Jesus as to his divine nature threw Joseph and Mary into the
profoundest reflection as to the full meaning of the words that
he uttered.

51 And he went down with them,—The geographical direction from Jerusalem to Nazareth is "down," hence Jesus went
with Joseph and Mary down to Nazareth. We do not hear
any more of Jesus until the time for his baptism; eighteen
years of silence is spent at Nazareth, as he was about thirty
years old at his baptism. We are told that "he was subject
unto them." The original in the Greek denotes "habitual,
continuous" subjection. He had been subject to them even
before this, and this is mentioned here when it might seem
that he could by this time have exempted himself from obedience to any human authority. It was a great honor to the
home of Mary to have Jesus sojourn as her son in it; no such
honor has been bestowed upon angels. We learn that Joseph
was a carpenter. (Matt. 13: 55; Mark 6: 3.) It is a very
clear inference that Jesus also learned and followed that trade.
As no further mention is made of Joseph, it is thought by
many that he died soon after the visit to Jerusalem. However
it is not strange, when we consider his relation to Jesus as
only his reputed father, that no further mention should be

52 And Jesus advanced in wisdom and [7]stature, and in [8]favor with God
and men.

[7]Or, *age*
[8]Or, *grace*

made of him by any inspired historian. "And his mother kept
all these sayings in her heart."

52 **And Jesus advanced in wisdom and stature,**—This verse
covers the eighteen years of silence in the life of Jesus; these
years intervened between his first visit to Jerusalem and the
beginning of his public ministry. During this time his mental
powers were constantly enlarging and strengthening; his
physical growth was uninterrupted by sickness or disease.
Some understand the word "stature" as to mean advanced in
wisdom as he advanced in age; however, this is not justified
by the original. "In favor with God and men" means that he
grew in divine favor, that every step of his development was
pleasing to God. Some have raised the question that if Jesus
was always pure and sinless, how could he increase in holiness, which is implied in his advancement in the divine favor.

SECTION TWO

THE PREPARATION; BEGINNING OF CHRIST'S
PUBLIC MINISTRY
3 : 1 to 4 : 13

1. THE MINISTRY OF JOHN THE BAPTIST
3 : 1-20

1 Now in the fifteenth year of the reign of Tiberius Cæsar, Pontius Pilate being governor of Judæa, and Herod being tetrarch of Galilee, and his brother Philip tetrarch of the region of Ituræa and Trachonitis, and Lysa-

---

1, 2 **Now in the fifteenth year of the reign**—Luke is a true historian; he defines very accurately the time when John began his ministry. It was the fifteenth year of the reign "of Tiberius Caesar." Luke does not refer to some one great epoch like the birth of Christ, which is followed throughout the civilized world, for then no such epoch for the world had been established. He dates from the year of the reigning Roman emperor, and adds also the name of the governor of Judea, and then the tetrarchs of the adjacent provinces, and the high priests then in office. Tiberius Caesar succeeded Augustus in A.D. 14, according to very reliable historians; his fifteenth year (and John's entrance upon his ministry) were in A.D. 29. As Jesus was six months younger than John, and about thirty years of age (verse 23) when he began his ministry, it follows that John began to preach not far from one and a half years before the baptism of Jesus.

Pontius Pilate became governor of Judea in A.D. 25 or 26. The name "tetrarch" was originally given to one who ruled a fourth part of a province; that is, one province having been divided into four parts. Pontius Pilate was a bold, heartless ruler; his first act was an outrage on the feelings of the Jews; he sent within the city of Jerusalem a body of soldiers to winter there. The Jews obtained their removal after many efforts to get them out of the holy city. Luke very aptly fixes this date as the time for the beginning of John's ministry.

Herod was tetrarch of Galilee at this time. This was Herod Antipas, son of the monster, Herod the Great; he had been left by his father as ruler of the province of Galilee.

nias tetrarch of Abilene, ²in the highpriesthood of Annas and Caiaphas, the

---

"Tetrarch" originally meant the fourth part, but came to be used to signify the part of a kingdom over which the man ruled. John the Baptist was slain by this Herod and our Savior was mocked by him; his brother Philip also received a third part of the kingdom of Herod. "Philip" was "tetrarch of the region of Ituraea and Trachonitis"; "Ituraea" was a district in the northeast of Palestine and east of the Jordan; it received its name from Jetru, one of the sons of Ishmael. (Gen. 25: 15; 1 Chron. 5: 19.) It had been subdued by Aristobulus, who compelled the people to submit to the rites of the Jews. "Trachonitis" was the region bordering upon Ituraea and east of the Jordan. The name signifies a rough mountainous country. Philip had received it on a promise to drive out the people who had dwelt there some time. "Lysanias" was "tetrarch of Abilene"; nothing is known of him; "Abilene" was named from "Ablia," which was the principal city in the region lying northwest of Damascus.

in the highpriesthood of Annas and Caiaphas,—According to the Jewish law there could be but one high priest at a time. Luke, as a historian, is not stating what should have been, but only what constituted the facts in the matter. He is taking up important names as he found them in order to fix the date of his history. He found these two men serving as high priest at that time. Caiphas was son-in-law to Annas, who was actually serving as high priest. Annas was a man of very great influence. He had been deposed as high priest, but was serving on the Sanhedrin. As Annas had been unjustly deposed by the Roman authorities, it may be that, in the opinion of the Jews, he was still termed the high priest, and a degree of power put into his hands that made him equal in authority to Caiaphas. Luke fixes the date of the beginning of the ministry of John by an emperor on one side, by a petty governor on the other, by two high priests who were serving at the time. At this date so clearly and fully defined the historian, Luke, now proceeds to narrate facts as he has collected them. It is to be remembered always that he is guided by the Holy Spirit

word of God came unto John the son of Zacharias in the wilderness. 3 And
he came into all the region round about the Jordan, preaching the baptism of

in writing his history. "The word of God came unto John the
son of Zacharias in the wilderness." Luke has now fixed definitely the time for the beginning of John's work. Like the
prophets of old, John was specially directed to utter the divine
message to the people and to baptize. (Jer. 1: 2; Ezek. 6: 1.)
This marked the beginning of John's ministry as is evident
from the whole account, not some later appearance of John
which was the cause of his imprisonment, as some have supposed. "In the wilderness" of Judea describes the barren,
hilly, and sparsely-settled region between Hebron and the
Dead Sea. The word "wilderness" or "desert" in the New
Testament denotes merely an untilled, unenclosed, and thinly-
inhabited country. The "fulness of the time" (Gal. 4: 4) has
now arrived.

3-6 **And he came into all the region**—The populous Jordan
valley was a field of labor for John the Baptist. The burden
of his message was a call upon men to repent and be baptized
as the condition of their forgiveness; hence John came
"preaching the baptism of repentance unto remission of sins."
"Preaching" means publicly announcing; as he traveled over
the country, he delivered his brief message to individuals,
families, and small companies wherever he found them, and
then afterward to great crowds who flocked to hear him.

"Baptism" is the Greek "baptisma" transferred into our language with its final letter dropped; it means literally "a
plunging and immersion." All lexicographers bear testimony
and agree to this; its figurative meaning is based on this
meaning, and always expresses an idea of immersion. (Luke
12: 50.) It is only with the literal meaning that we have here
to do. The baptism of John was a new rite; it was not
founded on the immersions of the old dispensation, under
which persons performed the ceremony of bathing or immers-
ing the whole body, not on others, but on themselves. (Lev.
15: 6; 16: 4.) The immersion of one person by another, as a
divinely appointed act, is peculiar to Christianity, and was
first introduced by John: baptism was not practiced among

repentance unto remission of sins; 4 as it is written in the book of the words
of Isaiah the prophet,
>   The voice of one crying in the wilderness,
>   Make ye ready the way of the Lord,
>   Make his paths straight,
>   5 Every valley shall be filled,
>   And every mountain and hill shall be brought low;
>   And the crooked shall become straight,
>   And the rough ways smooth;

[9]Is. 40.3 ff.

the Jews nor heathens. John himself declared that he received his commission to baptize directly from God. (John 1:
33.) Jesus intimated that the right was revealed to John from
heaven. (Luke 20: 4.) As baptism was a new rite it distinguished John's ministry from all other prophets; hence he is
called "the Baptist." (Luke 7: 20.) John's preaching is very
specifically designated as that of "baptism of repentance unto
remission of sins."

as it is written in the book of the words of Isaiah—The
preaching and baptism of John were the fulfillment of certain
prophetic conditions; Luke recognizes the authority of the
Old Testament. "The book of the words of Isaiah" means the
roll or scroll of linen, papyrus, or parchment, the ancient form
of a volume, written inside and unrolled for reading. "The
words" of Isaiah means his prophetic discourses. Isaiah
began to prophesy under the reign of Uzziah, about 759 B.C.,
and continued the prophetic office about sixty years under
Jotham, Ahaz, and Hezekiah. (Isa. 1: 1.) The predictions
here quoted are found in Isa. 40: 3-5; 52: 10. John also applies it to himself. (John 1: 23.) The figure here used is
founded on the eastern custom of sending persons to prepare
the way for the march of a king through the country. John is
described as "the voice of one crying in the wilderness," and
his message is to "make ye ready the way of the Lord, make
his paths straight." It is not John, but his preaching and mission which are made prominent here; his preaching was indeed a "voice of one crying" aloud, of short duration, but by
its great earnestness excited attention.

Every valley shall be filled,—The great oral purpose of
John's preaching was so well defined in the prophecy of him

6 And all flesh shall see the salvation of God.
7 He said therefore to the multitudes that went out to be baptized of him,

by Isaiah that Luke quotes the prophecy in full; everywhere in earnest tones, John called upon the people to prepare the way for the Greek King, leveling down the mountains, filling up the valley gorges, straightening all crooked ways, and making the rough places smooth. This is the way the royal road was prepared for the coming king. In a moral sense men must put away their sins, humble their proud spirits, and so make the way ready for the redeemer of man. All this as it stood before Isaiah's mind was to introduce the glorious reign of the Messiah by means of which "all flesh shall see the salvation of God." So remarkable and conspicuous would be the preparation and march of the King upon the straight and smooth highway that the whole human race should "see the salvation of God," which the Messiah would bring.

7-9 **He said therefore to the multitudes**—Luke now begins to record what John said to the multitudes "that went out to be baptized of him." John was a prophet, guided by the Holy Spirit, and the forerunner of the Messiah; it was his mission to get the people ready for the Messiah. The multitudes came from various quarters of the land. Matt. 3: 7 says that "many of the Pharisees and Sadducees" came to his baptism, and that John addressed them as "ye offspring of vipers, who warned you to flee from the wrath to come?" As Luke was writing for Gentiles, there was no need of his referring to these religious classes among the Jews; hence he addressed them as "ye offspring of vipers." It may be that some had come through curiosity, others were envious and jealous, and some, especially of the Sadducees, were sneering at the dangers impending in a future life; all seemed to be aroused and anxious. As John was filled with the Holy Spirit he could see at a glance their selfish and wicked motives in coming to him, and he at once addressed them as "offspring of vipers," persons both deceitful and malignant, and holding pernicious doctrines and principles. The viper was a very poisonous serpent. (Acts 28: 3-6.)

Ye offspring of vipers, who warned you to flee from the wrath to come? 8
Bring forth therefore fruits worthy of ¹repentance, and begin not to say
within yourselves, We have Abraham to our father: for I say unto you, that
God is able of these stones to raise up children unto Abraham. 9 And even
now the axe also lieth at the root of the trees: every tree therefore that

¹Or, *your repentance*

who warned you to flee—"Warned" literally means "to
show secretly"; the word implies a private or confidential hint
or reminder. (Luke 12: 5; Acts 9: 16; 20: 35.) "Who" did
not call for the names of the man or persons, but rather called
their thought to the point that someone ought to have warned
them to flee from the impending wrath of God. John had no
word for men not in earnest to escape God's wrath. It was a
Jewish maxim that no circumcised person could ever be lost,
but John warns them of a "wrath to come." The impending
wrath was to be visited upon those who rejected the kingdom
of heaven and neglected preparation. The Jews expected
troublous times in connection with the coming of the Messiah.
(Isa. 60: 12; 63: 1; Mal. 3: 1; 4: 5.) John here referred in a
prophetic way to the wrath which would come upon the Jewish nation at the destruction of Jerusalem and upon all the
wicked at the general judgment. (Matt. 24: 21, 38, 39; 1
Thess. 1: 10.)

Bring forth therefore fruits—Matthew here uses "fruit" instead of "fruits" as used by Luke. John demanded no merely
emotional and selfish fear, but such works and conduct as
would show sincerity; they were to bring fruits "worthy of repentance"; if they came professing repentance then they
should bring forth fruits in harmony with such a profession;
they should not even think that they had Abraham as their
father or they should not think that because they were descendants of Abraham they did not need repentance. The reason
assigned is that "God is able of these stones to raise up children unto Abraham."

And even now the axe also lieth at the root—"The axe laid
at the root of the tree" is a proverb that was common among
the Jews. The meaning is that the axe is ready to be applied
for use, and not only were the branches to be pruned, but
the axe was to be applied to the root of the tree. The object

bringeth not forth good fruit is hewn down, and cast into the fire. 10 And the multitudes asked him, saying, What then must we do? 11 And he answered and said unto them, He that hath two coats, let him impart to him that hath none; and he that hath food, let him do likewise. 12 And there

---

of the axe was to cut down "every tree therefore that bringeth not forth good fruit." Men are to be judged, not by their birth or their professions, but by their hearts and lives. Without delay all barren trees were to be cut down immediately and "cast into the fire." This was unquenchable fire. (Verse 17; Heb. 6: 8.) In this way John would prepare the people for the coming of Christ by awakening within them a sense of their true condition and of their spiritual need. Expecting a temporal deliverer, they would, without this, most certainly reject Jesus.

10-15 **And the multitudes asked him,**—John certainly aroused the people and stirred them to action; some of them received John's teaching and became his disciples; others were aroused to opposition. They asked: "What then must we do?" They saw that being the seed of Abraham was not sufficient and that their keeping the traditions of the law not satisfactory; hence their question, "what then must we do?" They "asked" indicates the frequent repetition of their question, so the original indicates. John's preaching moved them to press their inquiry; what are the fruits meet for repentance which they were to do, is what disturbed them. John's answer to these questions was as emphatic as was his preaching.

And he answered and said—John's first answer impressed the duties of practical life—give to those who are more destitute. "He that hath two coats, let him impart to him that hath none." A second coat no man could want if his neighbor who had none wanted his first; two coats were sometimes worn, one of them for ornamentation or luxury; in such case the one who had two coats could very well spare one to those who had none. This explains what John meant when he said: "Bring forth therefore fruits worthy of repentance." It also partially answers their question as to what they should do. Avarice and selfishness characterized at this time many of the

came also ²publicans to be baptized, and they said unto him, Teacher, what must we do? 13 And he said unto them, Extort no more than that which is appointed you. 14 And ³soldiers also asked him, saying, And we, what must we do? And he said unto them, Extort from no man by violence, neither accuse *any one* wrongfully; and be content with your wages.

---

²That is, *collectors or renters of Roman taxes*
³Gr. *soldiers on service*

Jews. (James 4: 1-4; 5: 1-6.) Furthermore, "he that hath food, let him do likewise." The "coat" and "food" represent the physical necessities of man; these should not be hoarded, but generously given to those who had need.

And there came also publicans to be baptized,—"Publicans" were collectors of Roman taxes; the Roman officials often farmed out the direct taxes and customs to capitalists on their payment of certain sums into the public treasury, hence they were called "publicans." Sometimes this sum, being greater than any one person could pay, was paid by a company; under these were "submagistri," living in the provinces; and under these again were the "portitores" or actual customhouse officers, who are referred to in the New Testament. They were often chosen from the low and wicked class of people and were so notorious for their extortions that they were habitually included in the same class with harlots and sinners.

And he said unto them, Extort no more—"Extort" means "exact"; the word is used of the exaction of legal tribute, and excessive exaction is expressed by the following words: John would hardly have commanded them to extort in any case. John does not demand that they give up their employment, but that they should be honest in the performance of their duties. If these publicans truly repented, they would indeed exhibit other fruits, but this in their case was absolutely necessary; without it there could be no true repentance.

And soldiers also asked him,—The soldiers asked the same question that the multitudes and publicans asked; hence here are three classes who have asked what they should do to "bring forth therefore fruits worthy of repentance." The "soldiers" were probably Jewish troops; for if they had been Gentiles, John would doubtless have enjoined upon them the worship of God: such worship is here taken for granted.

15 And as the people were in expectation, and all men reasoned in their hearts concerning John, whether haply he were the Christ; 16 John answered, saying unto them all, I indeed baptize you with water; but there cometh he that is mightier than I, the latchet of whose shoes I am not ⁴wor-

---

⁴Gr. *sufficient*

However, we cannot know just who they were; they could have been Jewish soldiers of the Roman province of Judea; it matters not who they were; they came under the class of bearing fruit worthy of repentance. John's answer was adapted to their sins and temptations; they were prone to indolence, violence, malice, and insubordination. Hence, John told them that they should "extort from no man by violence, neither accuse any one wrongfully; and be content with your wages." "Extort" "by violence" literally means "to shake violently," and "to vex and harass" in order to extort money for some selfish end. Neither were they to accuse "wrongfully" anyone in order to receive a bribe or a reward. They are further admonished to be "content" with their wages. "Wages" literally means something purchased to eat with bread; hired soldiers were at first paid partly in rations of meat, grain, and fruit; hence the word came to mean rations, "wages," or stipend.

15-17 **And as the people were in expectation,**—The people were anxious for John to declare himself, hence "all men reasoned in their hearts concerning John"; they were anxious to determine whether he was "the Christ." Such preaching as John did was so out of the ordinary that the people wondered as to whether he was the Messiah. John was filled with the Holy Spirit; hence his teachings were far different from those of the scribes and Pharisees. The people were anxious to know who this wonderful prophet and teacher was. When the time came John answered them and said: "I indeed baptize you with water; but there cometh he that is mightier than I." To baptize "with water" and *only* "with water" described John's work, but there would come another who was so much greater than John, as great as they thought John was, that John was not "worthy to unloose" "the latchet" of his shoes. The language used by John implies that this "Mighty One"

thy to unloose: he shall baptize you [5]in the Holy Spirit and in fire: 17 whose

[5]Or, with

was already in the midst of them. Jesus was mightier than John in his nature, office, wisdom, power, and aims. (Matt. 28: 18; John 5: 27; 10: 30, 41.) Yet none greater than John had arisen. (Matt. 11: 9-11.) "The latchet" of the shoe was a strap which fastened the sandal to the feet. The "shoes" as used here means sandals which covered only the bottom of the feet. They were taken off and laid aside on entering a house; the tying and untying the sandals was the work of the most menial servant. Yet Christ was so mighty a personage that even this work John felt himself unworthy to perform. Since John had aroused the whole Jewish nation, how great then must be the Messiah! Christ would arouse the world, his power would be felt by everyone.

he shall baptize you in the Holy Spirit and in fire:—Luke gives the same form of expression that Matthew did. (Matt. 3: 11.) The baptism "in the Holy Spirit and in fire" must not be referred to water baptism in any sense, for Christ never baptized in water, but left that to his disciples. (John 4: 2.) Neither does this baptism refer to the common influences of the Holy Spirit which are peculiar to the work of the Spirit. (John 20: 22.) It must refer to the sending of the Holy Spirit on the day of Pentecost, which was peculiarly the work of Christ. (John 16: 7; Acts 1: 5; 11: 16.) Many think that "in fire" has reference to the baptism of the Holy Spirit on the day of Pentecost, because "there appeared unto them tongues parting asunder, like as of fire; and it sat upon each one of them." (Acts 2: 3.) But this was not a baptism "in fire," for these "tongues" were not "fire," but only "like as of fire"; and these tongues only sat upon the apostles, but did not immerse them in the tongues "like as of fire." There seems to be two baptisms mentioned here that Christ would administer; one was the baptism "in the Holy Spirit," which was literally fulfilled on the day of Pentecost (Acts 2: 1-4) and at the house of Cornelius (Acts 10: 44; 11: 15-18). The baptism in the Spirit of these two groups of persons has brought blessings to

fan is in his hand, thoroughly to cleanse his threshing-floor, and to gather the wheat into his garner; but the chaff he will burn up with unquenchable fire.

18 With man other exhortations therefore preached he ⁶good tidings unto the people; 19 but Herod the tetrarch, being reproved by him for Herodias

⁶Or, *the gospel*

all mankind; the one on Pentecost brought blessings directly to the Jews, and the one at the house of Cornelius brought blessings to the Gentiles; hence the baptism in the Holy Spirit has resulted in blessings to the entire human family.

whose fan is in his hand,—The figure used here was taken from the custom of threshing grain in the East by treading it out with oxen (Deut. 25: 4), or a threshing machine was drawn over the grain (Isa. 41: 15; Amos 1: 3). The grain and chaff were mingled; in this condition both were thrown up against the wind with a shovel; the chaff was thus blown away, while the grain fell in a heap; in this way the wheat and the chaff were separated; the chaff was burned and the wheat was gathered into the garner. The figure as used by John represents the Messiah as separating the evil from the good, according to the tests of his kingdom and his gospel; the worthy are to be received into his kingdom and given a rich reward, while the unworthy are to be destroyed. There is a sharp contrast not only between the wheat and the chaff, but the destiny of the two classes. The fire that burns the wicked is "unquenchable," which means never extinguished; the doom it describes is eternal.

18-20 With many other exhortations—Luke here gives a synopsis of John's preaching by saying "with many other exhortations" he preached "good tidings unto the people." John rebuked sin, called upon the people to repent, and to manifest it by a thorough change of heart and life; proclaimed the Messiah approaching with blessings and salvation to the righteous, the believing, and judgments and destruction to the wicked, the unbelieving. In this way John prepared the way for Christ; some hearts were ready to receive him when he came. (John 1: 37, 41, 43.) The warnings and admonitions of John extended to every class of people; he made no distinc-

his brother's wife, and for all the evil things which Herod had done, 20 added this also to them all, that he shut up John in prison.

---

tion in his condemnation of sin.   Luke here gives a brief account of John's ministry, and, by way of anticipation, refers to the imprisonment of John, which occurred several months after the baptism of Jesus. (Matt. 14: 3; Mark 6: 17.)

but Herod the tetrarch, being reproved—Herod had taken "Herodias his brother's wife"; Herodias was the wife of Philip; she was the granddaughter of Herod the Great, the daughter of Aristobulus, and niece of Herod Antipas. She married Philip, a son of Herod the Great, who lived in private life, having been disinherited by his father. Herodias, preferring royalty, left Philip and married Herod Antipas, who, to make way for her, divorced his own wife, daughter of Aretas, king of Arabia, supposed to be the one mentioned by Paul in 2 Cor. 11: 32. Notwithstanding that Herodias had left her husband and married Antipas, she was "his brother's wife." (Mar 6: 17-20.) John not only reproved Herod for this one crime, but "for all the evil things which Herod had done." He condemned his revelings, his debaucheries, and his murders. According to Jewish testimony, Herod Antipas was very wicked and slew many of the wise men of Israel. In addition to all these evils, he "added this also to them all, that he shut up John in prison." It is generally understood that John was imprisoned in the fortress of Machaerus, on the eastern shore of the Dead Sea. John was imprisoned about a year after the baptism of Jesus. He remained in prison until he was beheaded; we do not know the exact time.

2. THE BAPTISM OF JESUS
3: 21, 22

21 Now it came to pass, when all the people were baptized, that, Jesus

---

21 Now it came to pass, when all the people were baptized, —There are three accounts of the baptism of Jesus (Matt. 3: 13-17; Mark 1: 9-11; Luke 3: 21, 22); Matthew's account is the fullest; he gave the conversation of John and Jesus before

also having been baptized, and praying, the heaven was opened, 22 and the Holy Spirit descended in a bodily form, as a dove, upon him, and a voice came out of heaven, Thou art my beloved Son; in thee I am well pleased.

the baptism. Matthew and Mark give the place, the river Jordan, where he was baptized; these writers also state that Jesus came from Galilee to John. Mark is specific and states that he came from Nazareth. The main points mentioned by Luke are the visible manifestation of the Holy Spirit descending upon Jesus in the form of a dove, and the voice from heaven proclaiming Jesus as the Son of God. Each of the writers records the descent of the Holy Spirit and the audible voice endorsing him as the Son of God.

"All the people were baptized" does not mean that every one in all Judea was baptized, but it means a great number. The baptism of Jesus forms the climax of John's ministry; it was the great crowning act, for he came baptizing in water that Jesus might be manifested to Israel. (John 1: 31-34.) From this time John began to decrease, but Jesus to increase; all the people were no longer gathering to hear John, but to see and hear Jesus. The disciples of Jesus were baptizing more than John. (John 4: 1, 2.) Jesus was baptized at the time when the people were baptized; some think that John's work ceased when he baptized Jesus. John had a double function; he was to get the people ready for Jesus, and then to point him out to the people. He did this soon after he baptized Jesus. (John 1: 29-34.)

22 **Thou art my beloved Son;**—The Holy Spirit came upon Jesus "in a bodily form, as a dove." There was a sudden and visible parting asunder in a portion of the sky; Jesus saw it (Mark 1: 10) and John also witnessed it (John 1: 32); we do not know whether anyone else saw this visible manifestation. This manifestation was "as a dove" or like a dove. Some understand this to mean that the Holy Spirit descended in the *manner* of a dove which descends gently and swiftly. It has been a question whether the comparison here is between the *descent* of the Holy Spirit and that of a dove, or whether the comparison is between the visable appearance of the Spirit and

the shape of a dove. Nothing is to be gained by disputing on this point. The dove was a fit emblem of the pure, gentle, and peaceful character of Jesus and his work. (Isa. 61: 1-3; Matt. 10: 16; 11: 29; 12: 19-21.) The descent of the Holy Spirit was also a token of the Messiah to John. (John 1: 33.)

There is some variation in the record given by Matthew and Luke; Mark agrees with Luke. Matthew expresses this statement in the third person—"this is my beloved Son, in whom I am well pleased"—but Mark and Luke state it in the second person—"thou art my beloved Son; in thee I am well pleased." Mark and Luke record this as God speaking to Jesus, while Matthew expresses it as God speaking to John or some other. Jesus was not only the "Son" of God, but emphatically he is "the beloved Son." The voice from heaven added "in thee I am well pleased."

3. THE GENEALOGY OF JESUS
3: 23-38

23 And Jesus himself, when he began *to teach,* was about thirty years of

23-38 **And Jesus himself, when he began to teach,**—The meaning here is that Jesus was "about thirty years of age" when he began to teach. Luke had already specified the date of the beginning of John's ministry, and now he states the age of Jesus when he began to teach. Soon after his baptism Jesus began to teach. Luke says that he was "about thirty years of age"; it is very common for Luke to use the word "about" with a specification of time. (Luke 1: 56; 9: 28; 22: 59; 23: 44; Acts 2: 41; 4: 4; 5: 36; 10: 3; 19: 7.) "About thirty" is not here a round or general number, referring to any year within two or three years of thirty, but a specific designation of time, meaning a few months below or rather above thirty. The meaning appears to be that Jesus began his ministry when he was more than thirty and less than thirty-one. This agrees with what we know of the time of our Lord's birth and baptism. Thirty was also the age when Levites entered upon their public services (Num. 4: 3, 47; 1 Chron. 23: 3), and when scribes were accustomed to enter upon their

age, being the son (as was supposed) of Joseph, the *son* of Heli, 24 the *son* of Matthat, the *son* of Levi, the *son* of Melchi, the *son* of Jannai, the *son* of Joseph, 25 the *son* of Mattathias, the *son* of Amos, the *son* of Nahum, the *son* of Esli, the *son* of Naggai, 26 the *son* of Maath, the *son* of Mattahias, the *son* of Semein, the *son* of Josech, the *son* of Joda, 27 the *son* of Joanan, the *son* of Rhesa, the *son* of Zerubbabel, the *son* of [7]Shealtiel, the *son* of Neri, 28 the *son* of Melchi, the *son* of Addi, the *son* of Cosam, the *son* of Elmadam,

---

[7]Gr. *Salathiel*

---

office as teachers. The people would not have been disposed to recognize the authority of a teacher who had not attained that age. It was God's purpose that the Messiah should not enter upon his public duties until he had arrived at the age of thirty.

being the son (as was supposed) of Joseph, the son of Heli, —It has always been regarded a very difficult task to harmonize the genealogical tables given by Matthew and Luke. Matthew's design was to trace our Lord's genealogy from Abraham down to his reputed father, Joseph, in order to furnish legal evidence to the Jews, that Jesus of Nazareth was, through his male ancestry, the lineal descendant of David and of Abraham. Luke traces his genealogy from Joseph, "as was supposed," father of Jesus, on back through David and Abraham to Adam. The difficulty seems to lie in the fact that Luke diverges from Joseph, and pursues the lineal descent of Jesus through a different series to David. How is it that Joseph is in the one case declared to be the son of Jacob and in the other the son of Heli? Many attempts have been made to answer this question; many of the attempts are not satisfactory.

If Heli was Mary's father, it is clear that Joseph was his son-in-law; the assumption that this relationship is here designated agrees with the facts of the case, or at least is not contradicted by them. The words "as was supposed," although immediately referable to the following words, "the son of Joseph," yet indicate that Luke had in mind the real parentage of Jesus, first as being the Son of God (Luke 1: 35), and then of David, through the line of his maternal ancestry, which alone was true and real. It is as though Luke intended his readers mentally to supply in the next clause the words "but

GENEALOGY OF CHRIST.
(Matthew and Luke Compared.)

ADAM

Adam to Abraham according to Genesis. Abraham to Christ according to Matthew.		Christ to Adam according to Luke.

Matthew		Luke
	Seth	Seth
	Enosh	Enos
	Kenan	Cainan
	Mahalalel	Mahalaleel
	Jared	Jared
	Enoch	Enoch
	Methuselah	Methuselah
	Lamech	Lamech
	Noah —Flood 2343 B.C.—	Noah
	Shem	Shem
	Arpachshad	Arphaxad
		Cainan
	Shelah	Shelah
	Eber	Eber
	Peleg	Peleg
	Reu	Reu
	Serug	Serug
	Nahor	Nahor
	Terah	Terah
ABRAHAM	—Call of Abraham 1917 B.C.—	ABRAHAM
Isaac		Isaac
Jacob		Jacob
Judah		Judah
Perez		Perez
Hezron		Hezron
Ram		Arni
Amminadab		Amminadab
Nahshon		Nahshon
Salmon		Salmon
Boaz		Boaz
Obed		Obed
Jesse	Jesse	
	DAVID	
Building of the Temple—Solomon		Nathan—1000 years Before Christ
Rehoboam		Mattatha
Abijah		Menna
Asa		Melea
Jehoshaphat		Eliakim
Joram		Jonam
Uzziah		Joseph
Jotham		Judas
		Symeon
Ahaz		Levi
		Matthat
Hezekiah		Jorim
		Eliezer
Manasseh		Jesus
		Er
Amon		Elmadam
		Cosam
		Addi
Josiah		Melchi
		Neri
Jechoniah		
Shealtiel	Shealtiel	
Temple destroyed 584 B.C.—ZERUBBABEL—Rebuilt by Zerubbabel 70 years		
Abiud	Rhesa	afterwards
	Joanan	
Eliakim	Joda	
	Josech	
Azor	Semein	
	Mattathias	
Sadoc	Maath	
	Naggai	
Achim	Esli	
	Nahum	
Eliud	Amos	
	Mattathias	
Eleazar	Joseph	
	Jannai	
Matthan	Melchi	
	Levi	
Jacob	Matthat	
	Heli	
Joseph	Mary	

CHRIST

the *son* of Er, 29 the *son* of Jesus, the *son* of Eliezer, the *son* of Jorim, the
son of Matthat, the *son* of Levi, 30 the *son* of Symeon, the *son* of Judas, the
son of Joseph, the *son* of Jonam, the *son* of Eliakim, 31 the *son* of Melea, the
son of Menna, the *son* of Mattatha, the *son* of Nathan, the *son* of David, 32
the *son* of Jesse, the *son* of Obed, the *son* of Boaz, the *son* of [8]Salmon, the
son of Nahshon, 33 the *son* of Amminadab, [9]the *son* of [10]Arni, the *son* of
Hezron, the *son* of Perez, the *son* of Judah, 34 the *son* of Jacob, the *son* of
Isaac, the *son* of Abraham, the *son* of Terah, the *son* of Nahor, 35 the *son* of
Serug, the *son* of Reu, the *son* of Peleg, the *son* of Eber, the *son* of Shelah,
36 the *son* of Cainan, the *son* of Arphaxad, the *son* of Shem, the *son* of
Noah, the *son* of Lamech, 37 the *son* of Methuselah, the *son* of Enoch, the *son*
of Jared, the *son* of Mahalaleel, the *son* of Cainan, 38 the *son* of Enos, the
son of Seth, the *son* of Adam, the *son* of God.

[8]Some ancient authorities write *Sala*
[9]Many ancient authorities insert *the* son *of Admin:* and one writes *Admin* for
Amminadab
[10]Some ancient authorities write *Aram*

in reality (according to the flesh) the son of Heli." If it be
asked why Luke did not openly express this idea, by putting
the name of Mary in place of Joseph, and writing, "which was
the daughter of Heli," the answer is furnished in the almost
invariable usage of the ancients, especially the Jews, to reckon
one's genealogy through the *paternal* rather than the *maternal*
line. But unless Luke, after his reference to our Lord's supposed relationship to Joseph, passed over to his real ancestry,
his genealogical table would be according to his own showing,
one that was fictitious. The complete list of names back to
Adam would rest on that of one who was only the "reputed"
father of our Lord.

It is natural to expect a genealogy somewhere in the gospels which would verify to the very letter the prediction that
Christ was to be of the seed of David and of Abraham. The
ancestry of Joseph, who was only his reputed father, would
not answer this demand. It might be adduced in the way of
legal proof to the Jew that Jesus had this mark of the Messiahship, but does not satisfy the conditions of the prophecy
that he was to be a real descendant of David. The fact that
Luke had this in mind is strengthened by the proof that he
gives in tracing the true lineage of Jesus back to David and
Abraham in his genealogical table. The fact that Luke carries his record back to Adam, who was declared to be the
"Son of God," shows clearly that it was designed to subserve

a different purpose from that of Matthew. We are forced to the conclusion that Joseph was Heli's son by the marriage of his daughter, and perhaps also by adoption, and that this genealogy of Luke was designed to furnish proof that our Lord "was born of the seed of David according to the flesh." (Rom. 1 : 3.)

4. THE TEMPTATION OF JESUS
4: 1-13

1 And Jesus, full of the Holy Spirit, returned from the Jordan, and was led in the Spirit in the wilderness 2 during forty days, being tempted of the devil. And he did eat nothing in those days: and when they were completed,

---

1, 2 And Jesus, full of the Holy Spirit,—An account of the temptation is given by Matthew (4: 1-11), Mark (1: 12, 13), and Luke. Matthew and Luke give the account more in detail; Mark makes only a brief reference to it. The third temptation with Matthew is the second with Luke. The order as given by Matthew is generally accepted as the order of occurrence. Matthew and Luke state generally that Jesus was "led in the Spirit," and Mark states that "the Spirit driveth him forth" into the wilderness. Matthew has "stone" and "bread" in the plural, while Luke has these in the singular. Some explain this as though the devil had first commanded "these stones" to be made into bread, and later only commanded one particular stone to be made into bread, and that Matthew records one of the statements of the devil and Luke records the same statement made a little later. The quotation from Deut. 8: 3 is given more fully by Matthew than by Luke, but the quotation from Psalm 91: 11, 12 is fuller in Luke than in Matthew; however the meaning is the same in both. Luke gives the language of Satan more at length than Matthew.

Jesus received the Holy Spirit at his baptism and was thus "full of the Holy Spirit." The temptation of Jesus was the last step in the preparation for his public ministry. Under the influence of the Spirit he was brought to the place of trial, and the temptation, in a large part, was the suggestion to use for selfish ends the divine powers of which he was conscious, and to forget his filial relation to his father: he was tempted

he hungered. 3 And the devil said unto him, If thou art the Son of God, command this stone that it become ¹bread. 4 And Jesus answered unto him, It is written, ²Man shall not live by bread alone. 5 And he led him

¹Or, *a loaf*
²Dt. 8.3

to rebel against God. He was "driven" or "led" into the wilderness, probably the wilderness of Jordan west of Jericho. Mark describes Jesus in the wilderness "with the wild beasts"; he remained there "during forty days." He was tempted during this time, but the full force of the temptation came with its crisis at the end of the forty days.

3, 4 **And the devil said unto him,**—Some have looked at the temptation of Jesus as being one with a threefold part; others have looked at it as being three distinct temptations. They are treated here as three temptations. The first one was to get Jesus to turn a stone or stones into bread. "If thou art the Son of God" then you have the power to make bread out of these stones. Some have looked at the clause "if thou" as expressing a doubt; however "if" seems to have the force of "since," which would express no doubt. It is claimed by some that the devil wanted Jesus to prove himself as the Son of God. The devil challenges Jesus to prove his claim to be the Son of God by a miracle; a good motive is suggested to Jesus and the sinfulness of the act is skillfully disguised by the devil. There seems to be a twofold nature to this temptation; he is tempted to satisfy his hunger and to prove himself to be the Son of God.

And Jesus answered unto him,—Jesus quoted Deut. 8: 3. These words, "it is written," are the first upon record that were spoken by Jesus after his entrance into his public ministry; hence his first words are a declaration of the authority of the scriptures. Jesus met every temptation by a quotation of scripture. Man must have bread; Jesus does not deny the place and value of "bread" in sustaining life, but he does place the emphasis on things more important. Jesus here shows his reliance on his heavenly Father, and equally shows his determination to seek no means to sustain life but such as are approved of God. To create bread out of stones contrary to

up, and showed him all the kingdoms of ³the world in a moment of time. 6
And the devil said unto him, To thee will I give all this authority, and the
glory of them: for it hath been delivered unto me; and to whomsoever I will
I give it. 7 If thou therefore wilt ⁴worship before me, it shall all be thine. 8

³Gr. *the inhabited earth*
⁴The Greek word denotes an act of reverence, whether paid to a creature, or to
the Creator (comp. marginal note on Mt. 2.2)

God's will, and in obedience to Satan, would be to die, not
live. Jesus makes no reference to his divine Sonship; he was
not called upon to prove that to Satan.

5-8 **And he led him up, and showed him all the kingdoms—**
Matthew records this temptation as the third, but Luke puts
it second. We need not speculate as to why this change is
made; no one knows, and no one now can know. We have it
as a fact that this change in the order has been made. It
seems that Luke follows the order and position of the places
—the desert, the mountain, and the temple. Here he is "led"
upon the mountain and showed "all the kingdoms of the
world in a moment of time." The word in the Greek literally
means "a mark made by a pointed instrument, a dot"; hence,
a point of time. Jesus was given a vision of the inhabited
world, "all the kingdoms of the world"; he not only saw Palestine, but also the heathen world, over which Satan exercised
spiritual dominion; from the lofty elevation the kingdoms or
tetrarchies of Palestine and adjacent regions could be seen,
and the more distant empires of the world might be suggested
by the tempter. There was something supernatural in this act
which enabled Jesus to see these in a "moment of time"; the
suddenness of the view added much to the power of the temptation. All these were promised to Jesus on the condition
that he would "worship before me." The kingdoms and the
glory of them were held before Jesus as a temptation. Many
think that these kingdoms did not belong to the devil, and
hence he could not have fulfilled his promise even if Jesus had
worshiped him. The devil here asked Jesus to transfer his al-
legiance from God to the devil; Jesus is tempted to acknowledge the supremacy and sovereignty of the devil; to do this
would be to acknowledge a falsehood, for the devil was not
supreme, neither was he a sovereign.

And Jesus answered and said unto him, It is written, Thou shalt worship the Lord thy God, and him only shalt thou serve. 9 And he led him to Jerusalem, and set him on the pinnacle of the temple, and said unto him, If thou art the Son of God, cast thyself down from hence: 10 for it is written,

> [5]He shall give his angels charge concerning thee, to guard thee:
11   and,
> On their hands they shall bear thee up,
> Lest haply thou dash thy foot against a stone.

---

[5]Gr. *wing*
[6]Ps. 91.11, 12

And Jesus answered and said unto him,—Here again Jesus quoted scripture. He said: "It is written, Thou shalt worship the Lord thy God, and him only shalt thou serve." Matthew records Jesus as saying, "Get thee hence, Satan," but Luke omits that. In righteous indignation Jesus denounced Satan as the archenemy of God his Father. In this temptation the devil threw off the mask and appeared to Jesus is his real character; hitherto Jesus had dealt with him according to his assumed character, but now he repulsed him with abhorrence. Jesus added: "Thou shalt worship the Lord thy God, and him only shalt thou serve." Here Jesus quotes Deut. 6: 13.

9-12 And he led him to Jerusalem,—This is the second temptation according to Matthew. We are not told how the devil took Jesus to Jerusalem and to the pinnacle of the temple; it may have been as the Spirit of the Lord caught away Philip. (Acts 8: 39.) Jesus permitted Satan to exercise great power over him; the language here seems to require an actual going from place to place, and yet it does not necessarily determine whether the devil did or did not transport him through the air. He brought him "to Jerusalem, and set him on the pinnacle of the temple." This was some high point of the temple building well known by the Jews at that time. The Greek word translated "temple" means literally a "winglet," and is applied to a wing-shape or pointed structure, a gable or pointed roof. The word translated "temple," both here and in Matthew, means the whole sacred enclosure or temple buildings. This time the devil said to him: "If thou art the Son of God, cast thyself down from hence." This temptation also seems to have a twofold meaning, appealing to the natural feeling and to the Messianic aspiration; since Jesus is the Son

12 And Jesus answering said unto him, It is said, [7]Thou shalt not make trial of the Lord thy God.

13 And when the devil had completed every temptation, he departed from him [8]for a season.

[7]Dt. 6.16
[8]Or, *until*

of God and is now upon the high pinnacle of the temple and can do nothing up there for the salvation of man, he is commanded to cast himself down.

And Jesus answering said unto him,—Again Jesus replied to Satan by quoting the scripture: "Thou shalt not make trial of the Lord thy God." In this application of the scripture, Jesus intimates that he must not put God on trial by exercising a presumptuous confidence or by needlessly testing his veracity. To attempt to put God to the test would show unbelief, while display of power would be opposed to humility. Jesus did not, as some have, accuse the devil of misquoting scripture; neither did he deny the promise referred to in the scripture which the devil quoted; he simply replied by giving another quotation. The quotation that Jesus here used interprets the one quoted by the devil, but does not refute that quotation. Jesus meant to say that the quotation of the devil was a scriptural quotation and applicable to himself and would be fulfilled in due time, but to throw oneself into unnecessary danger in order to "tempt" God would be a sin, and especially when it was done at the command of the devil.

13 And when the devil had completed every temptation,— This means that the devil had used every available kind of temptation; he was "tempted in all points" as we are, but "without sin." (Heb. 4: 15.) The first temptation was in the sphere of bodily appetite; Jesus was urged by Satan to transform a stone into bread; the second temptation was in the sphere of earthly ambition; it consisted in an offer of unlimited human power. The last temptation was in the sphere of intellectual curiosity; it suggested to Jesus that he should see for himself what would be the experience of one who should cast himself from a great height and then, by angel hands, be kept from harm.

"He departed from him for a season"; the devil had exhausted his power, hence "he departed from him for a season." The scene closed with Jesus victorious, and "the angels ministered unto him." (Mark 1: 13.) Jesus had triumphed, and later he taught through James: "resist the devil, and he will flee from you." (James 4: 7.) "Angels came and ministered unto him" (Matt. 4: 11) ; some think that angels brought him food, as Elijah was fed by angels after he had fasted forty days (1 Kings 19: 5.) The original from which we get "ministered" means "were ministering"; it signifies to attend as a servant; angels waited on him as human friends might have waited on one whom they found hungry, weary, lonely.

SECTION THREE

THE MINISTRY OF JESUS IN GALILEE
4 : 14 to 9 : 50

1. JESUS PREACHING AT NAZARETH
4 : 14-30

14 And Jesus returned in the power of the Spirit into Galilee: and a fame

---

We cannot determine accurately the length of his ministry in Galilee; it cannot be determined whether it began in summer or late autumn; if the feast of John 5: 1 was a Passover or there is an unknown Passover, the Galilean ministry lasted at least sixteen months, for it closed when another Passover was near. (John 6: 4.) Otherwise we should not certainly know that it lasted more than six or eight months. There is no doubt that the two subsequent periods of our Lord's ministry each lasted six months; but here we have to admit much uncertainty as to the time; after all, a determination of the time employed would be a matter of very little importance with respect to the study of this period. The immense amount of material in this period would seem to favor the idea for a length of time longer than a year. Throughout this ministry in Galilee, and the periods that will follow after, the reader may trace carefully the *progress* of the history along several lines: (1) the Savior's progressive self-manifestation; (2) the gradual training of his twelve apostles who were to carry on his teaching and work after his death; (3) the deepening and spreading hostility of the Jewish influential classes and official rulers. By constantly observing these parallel lines of progress, it will be seen that the history and teachings of our Lord exhibit a vital growth, moving on to an end by him foreseen (Luke 12: 50), when the hostility of the rulers will culminate as he before the Sanhedrin avows himself to be the Messiah, and his twelve apostles will be almost prepared to succeed him in his work.

14, 15 **And Jesus returned in the power of the Spirit**—Several months intervened between the preceding paragraph and this one; during the intervening months, Jesus was busy in

went out concerning him through all the region round about. 15 And he
taught in their synagogues, being glorified of all.
16 And he came to Nazareth, where he had been brought up: and he

---

his ministry in Judea. John (1: 15 to 3: 36) alone gives an
account of this ministry. Luke passes over in silence his ministry in Judea and gives attention to his Galilean ministry.
Jesus had left Galilee (Luke 3: 21) to be baptized of John; he
had made the two returns to Galilee, and Luke here may be
understood to make a general statement that includes both of
them. So after the marriage feast at Cana (John 1: 43; 2: 1)
and after John was cast into prison (Matt. 4: 12; John 4: 1-3),
Luke begins to relate Jesus' activities in Galilee after John's
imprisonment (Luke 3: 19, 20). Jesus "in the power of the
Spirit" came into Galilee, under the full influence of the Holy
Spirit, which descended upon him at his baptism, attended
him in the wilderness of temptation, and continued with him
in his ministry.

And he taught in their synagogues,—"Taught" in the original means "he himself taught," which verifies the favorable
report about himself in person. He was not only known by
reports of his words and acts, but in his own person and by
his teaching. All glorified him because of his teachings.
Jesus taught in the synagogues as Jewish teachers or rabbis
taught; he expounded the scriptures and instructed the people. "Synagogue" means "assembly, congregation," and is
applied both to a religious gathering having certain judicial
powers (Luke 8: 41; 12: 11; 21: 12; Acts 9: 2), and to the
place where the Jews met for their public worship on ordinary
occasions (Luke 7: 5.) There were many synagogues for the
Jews; in all cities and villages where there were at least ten
Jews, there was found a synagogue. It is said that there were
more than four hundred synagogues in Jerusalem. The Jews
met in their synagogues on the Sabbath, feast days, and afterward on the second and fifth days of the week.

16, 17 **And he came to Nazareth,**—He came to Nazareth, the
home of his childhood and youth; here he was with the people
who had known him almost from his birth. "Nazareth," according to some authorities, means "a branch," which was an

entered, as his custom was, into the synagogue on the sabbath day, and stood
up to read. 17 And there was delivered unto him ⁹the book of the prophet

⁹Or, *a roll*

appropriate name of the place where the branch should live
and grow up. (Isa. 11: 1; Zech. 3: 8; 6: 12.) Others think
that it signifies "the one guarding or guarded" from the hills
which surrounded it. New Testament writers always speak
of Nazareth as a city and never as a village. According to Josephus the population of Nazareth was above fifteen thousand; it is not mentioned in the Old Testament. It was located in lower Galilee, about seventy miles north of Jerusalem, and nearly halfway from the Jordan to the Mediterranean. "As his custom was," he went into "the synagogue on
the sabbath day, and stood up to read." This shows that
Jesus attended regularly the services in the synagogue on the
Sabbath. This appears to have been the first Sabbath after
his return to Nazareth. He "stood up to read." In the synagogue the law and the prophets were read and expounded by
the ruler of the synagogue and others; the scriptures, except
Esther, which might be read sitting, were read *standing,* while
sitting was the posture of teaching. (Matt. 5: 1; Luke 4: 20.)
When Jesus "stood up to read" he indicated as was the custom in the synagogue his desire to read, and probably the au-
dience stood while he read. According to the custom of the
Jews, seven were allowed to read every Sabbath—a priest,
two Levites, and four Israelites; the law was read first and
then the prophets.

And there was delivered unto him the book—When Jesus
stood up in the synagogue, indicating his desire to read, there
was brought to him the "book of the prophet Isaiah"; probably the law had already been read that Sabbath, and, according to custom, they were ready for the usual reading of the
prophets. Some think that he may have called for this particular book. The books of the ancients were "rolls" of parchment, papyrus, linen, or other flexible material, which were
rolled upon a stick, and upon reading were gradually rolled
around another of equal size. "And he opened the book, and

Isaiah. And he opened the [10]book, and found the place where it was written.
18 [11]The Spirit of the Lord is upon me,
    [12]Because he anointed me to preach [13]good tidings to the poor:
    He hath sent me to proclaim release to the captives,
    And recovering of sight to the blind,
    To set at liberty them that are bruised,
19 To proclaim the acceptable year of the Lord.

[10]Or, *roll*
[11]Is. 61.1 f.
[12]Or, *Wherefore*
[13]Or, *the gospel*

found the place where it was written." He unrolled the scroll; this was no accident or mere chance that he "found the place" where he wanted to read; he unrolled the volume until he found this Messianic prophecy, yet with no seeming effort or searching for it.

18-20 **The Spirit of the Lord is upon me,**—This passage is quoted from Isa. 61: 1, 2, and the clause, "to set at liberty them that are bruised," seems to be added from the Septuagint of Isa. 58: 6. The Jews generally understood this prophecy to refer to the Messiah; it was very appropriate for Jesus to read this passage in the beginning of his teachings in Nazareth; he thus appears before them, not so much as a miracle worker, as a teacher, but as the Messiah of prophecy. "The Spirit of the Lord" means that the Holy Spirit was abiding with him and hence his qualification for teaching and saving the lost. (John 3: 34.) He was anointed by the Spirit at his baptism "to preach good tidings to the poor." The time had now come for him to announce that the Messiah had come. It was customary for those who were designated to do public work to be anointed, but Jesus was anointed with the Holy Spirit, while others were anointed with the "anointing oil." The "poor" means the spiritually poor; those who are "poor in spirit." (Matt. 5: 3.) The Messiah was to release the captives, those who were in the bondage of sin. "Captives" as used here in the original meant those who were "conquered or taken in war"; hence, prisoners of war. On the first day of the year of jubilee, the priests went through the land proclaiming with sound of trumpet the blessings of the

20 And he closed the ¹⁰book and gave it back to the attendant, and sat down: and the eyes of all in the synagogue were fastened on him. 21 And he began to say unto them, To-day hath this scripture been fulfilled in your ears. 22 And all bare him witness, and wondered at the words of grace which proceeded out of his mouth: and they said, Is not this Joseph's son?

opening year. (Lev. 25 : 8-17.) Jesus here proclaims the time of his public ministry and his Messiahship.

And he closed the book,—Luke gives a very vivid picture of the manner of Jesus in the synagogue of his own village; calmly and quietly Jesus rolled up the scroll and gave it again to "the attendant" who had brought it to him; then he "sat down." He now assumed the posture of a teacher; the custom was to stand while reading and to sit while teaching. Jesus is now ready to teach. "The eyes of all in the synagogue were fastened on him." The verb or participle in the original here denotes continuous, steadfast attention. All looked intently and steadily upon him; there was something in his manner, and perhaps tone of voice, which riveted their attention on him and aroused their expectation that he was about to speak.

21 **And he began to say unto them,**—These words do not necessarily denote his first words, but they do indicate a solemn and weighty opening. "To-day hath his scripture been fulfilled in your ears." Now, at this very time, in their ears they heard the glad tidings which Jesus had announced that he was the Messiah. Since the Jews generally understood this scripture to refer to the Messiah, Jesus declares that he is a fulfillment of it; there can be no doubt but that they understood him; however, they did not believe him.

22-24 **And all bare him witness,**—All who listened to his discourse gave favorable testimony to the subject and manner of it; there was no false reasoning in it, neither were there any false or unfounded assumptions; no fallacy of argument or erroneous statement could be detected in the whole discourse; hence they "wondered at the words of grace which proceeded out of his mouth." Their wonder and admiration soon began to yield to a feeling of contempt for his pretensions, and they asked: "Is not this Joseph's son?" They

23 And he said unto them, Doubtless ye will say unto me this parable, Physician, heal thyself: whatsoever we have heard done at Capernaum, do also here in thine own country. 24 And he said, Verily I say unto you, No

---

wondered that their own townsman and one whom they had known as a workman among them should thus speak. Joseph was a man of humble circumstances; his family had occupied no distinguished place; Joseph was supposed to be the father of Jesus. Jesus had received no training from the rabbis; how could he so speak? How could he, whom they had known as a humble workman in their midst, be the Messiah? There was unbelief mingled with their admiration; they wanted more evidence.

And he said unto them,—Jesus knew their thoughts and he may have heard their question; hence he replied both to their thoughts and their question. He said: "Doubtless ye will say unto me this parable, Physician, heal thyself." This was a common proverb or adage among the Jews, and meant "pursue the course which you would have another pursue, making similar claims; give the evidence, perform the miracles, which you yourself would require of another." This meaning is reinforced by a further interpretation of their thoughts, as Jesus said they were thinking that he should have done "here in thine own country" "whatsoever we have heard done at Capernaum." Jesus had healed the nobleman's son at Capernaum. (John 4: 46-54.) Capernaum was about sixteen miles from Nazareth; the news could come in a day; Jesus had performed no miracle in Nazareth. At his second rejection he healed a few sick people. (Mark 6: 5.)

No prophet is acceptable in his own country.—Jesus here answered the desire of the people of Nazareth in wanting him to work some miracle as he had in Capernaum by giving another proverb. He states a general fact in this proverb; all other things being equal, one who has been familiar to us from early life is treated with less reverence than one who has not been thus familiar; if they honor him less, they must expect less attention. This proverb was repeated with a slight variation on his subsequent visit to Nazareth. (Matt. 13: 57.)

prophet is acceptable in his own country. 25 But of a truth I say unto you, There were many widows in Israel in the days of Elijah, when the heaven was shut up three years and six months, when there came a great famine over all the land; 26 and unto none of them was Elijah sent, but only to ¹Zarephath, in the land of Sidon, unto a woman that was a widow. 27 And there were many lepers in Israel in the time of Elisha the prophet; and none of them was cleansed, but only Naaman the Syrian. 28 And they were all filled with wrath in the synagogue, as they heard these things; 29 and they

¹Gr. *Sarepta*

Jesus does not mean that this proverb should become an infallible rule.

25-27 But of a truth I say unto you,—Here Jesus recites some Old Testament examples to show that his conduct was in harmony with that of two of their greatest prophets, who were divinely directed not to act according to the proverb, "Physician, heal thyself," and whose miraculous power was exerted on strangers, while these prophets performed their miracles on those that had need. There were many "widows in Israel in the days of Elijah," and Elijah did not visit and bless all of them. There was a famine of "three years and six months'" duration, "when there came a great famine over all the land." (1 Kings 18: 1; James 5: 17.) It stated that the third year Elijah was commanded to show himself to Ahab with the promise of rain; during this famine Elijah had sojourned with a woman of Zarephath, in the land of Sidon. In the great famine of Elijah's time (1 Kings 17: 1-9) there were hundreds of suffering widows in Israel, but Elijah was sent only to one in the heathen city of Sidon. Also "there were many lepers in Israel in the time of Elisha the prophet." Lepers were in abundance in Israel when Elisha was prophet and performing numerous miracles, but not one of them was healed except Naaman, who was not an Israelite. (2 Kings 5.)

28-30 And they were all filled with wrath in the synagogue,—That Sabbath Jesus showed those assembled in the synagogue their danger, and instead of being warned they were enraged. He could do no miracle because of their unbelief; he would go to other places as their prophets had done. The indignation of the people of Nazareth was general, and they were all filled with wrath, and "they rose up, and cast

rose up, and cast him forth out of the city, and led him unto the brow of the hill whereon their city was built, that they might throw him down headlong. 30 But he passing through the midst of them went his way.

him forth out of the city." In their wild excitement, without any reverence for the place, the day, or the occasion, they rushed upon Jesus like mad men, as they did against Stephen. (Acts 7: 57, 58.) By force they "led him unto the brow of the hill whereon their city was built." "Brow" in the original is the word used in medical language both of eyebrows and of other projections of the body. This is the only place that this word in the original is used in the New Testament. It would naturally occur to a physician, especially since the same epithets were applied to the appearance of the eyebrows in certain diseases as were applied to hills. It should be remembered that Luke was a physician. Jesus was led to this hill "that they might throw him down headlong." They meant to cast him down and kill him. This was not the usual mode of punishment among the Jews, but they sometimes did rash things. (2 Kings 9: 33; 2 Chron. 25: 12.) It was contrary to a Jewish canon to inflict punishment on the Sabbath; the people of Nazareth had become at this time a furious mob; they demonstrated the truth that a prophet was not honored among his own people.

But he passing through the midst—Some think that Jesus escaped by his composure and self-control while the confusion reigned among the crowd; others think that the majesty and divinity of Jesus so awed them that they made a way for him to pass; and still others think that he exerted some miraculous influence upon them, such as affecting their sight, rendering himself invisible or restraining them. It is true that Jesus did not work miracles merely for self-preservation, neither did his apostles; yet it seems at times that the divinity within Jesus shown forth with all-producing power. (John 8: 59; 10: 39; 18: 6.) He "went his way"; he departed from Nazareth. In this account we have an explanation of Matthew's brief allusion, "and leaving Nazareth." (Matt. 4: 13.) We see why he left Nazareth and made Capernaum his chief place of residence.

2. MIRACLES AT CAPERNAUM
4: 31-44

31 And he came down to Capernaum, a city of Galilee. And he was teaching them on the sabbath day: 32 and they were astonished at his teaching; for his word was with authority. 33 And in the synagogue there was a

---

31, 32 And he came down to Capernaum,—How Jesus escaped from the people of Nazareth we are not told, but the fact is recorded clearly that he did escape and went "down to Capernaum, a city of Galilee." Nazareth was on a high elevation, and Capernaum was on the Sea of Galilee, which was about six hundred feet lower than the Mediterranean Sea, and was much lower than Nazareth. Jesus had been at Capernaum before for a short time (John 2: 12), but now he comes to make it his place of residence. "Capernaum" was the name of a fountain and a town situated on the northwest shore of the Sea of Galilee, on the boarders of the tribes of Zebulum and Naphtali; it was on the road from Damascus to the Mediterranean. It was suited as the principal residence of Jesus during the three years of his ministry. It is called his "own city." (Matt. 9: 1.) It was also the residence of Andrew, Peter, James, and John, who were natives of Bethsaida (John 1: 44), and probably the home of Matthew.

And he was teaching them on the sabbath—Jesus preached repentance and the gospel of the kingdom of God. (Matt. 4: 17; Mark 1: 14, 15.) He availed himself of every opportunity to teach the people when they assembled for worship. His teaching had a great effect on the people, for they were "astonished at his teaching"; the reason assigned by Luke for the astonishment was "for his word was with authority." They were astonished both at what he taught and the manner in which he taught them. He never expressed a doubt; he knew the Father's will and taught that with authority. (Matt. 7: 28, 29.) Some think that reference is here made to the miracles which he wrought to witness that he was from God.

33-37 And in the synagogue there was a man,—A parallel record of the healing of "a demoniac in the synagogue" is found in Mark 1: 23-28. Luke's account is briefer than that of Mark, and with enough difference to show the independence

man, that had a spirit of an unclean demon; and he cried out with a loud voice, 34 ²Ah! what have we to do with thee, Jesus thou Nazarene? art thou come to destroy us? I know thee who thou art, the Holy One of God. 35 And Jesus rebuked him, saying, Hold thy peace, and come out of him. And when the demon had thrown him down in the midst, he came out of him,

---

²Or, *Let alone*

---

of his account. According to Mark 1: 16-22, this miracle followed the calling of the four disciples, Peter and Andrew, James and John. Jesus performed miracles as proof of his divine mission. (John 2: 22; 9: 3-5; 10: 25, 37.) The Jews expected their Messiah to work miracles. (Matt. 12: 38; Luke 11: 16; John 7: 31.) The miracles of Jesus were variously designated. When they were specially regarded as evidence of his divine mission (Luke 8: 11; John 2: 11), they were called "signs"; when they manifested his supernatural power, they were called "mighty works"; when as extraordinary phenomena, exciting astonishment or terror, they were called "wonders" (Mark 13: 22; John 4: 48; Acts 2: 22); and when viewed still more generally, as something completed, they were called "works" (John 7: 3, 21).

And Jesus rebuked him,—Jesus commanded the demon to cease bearing testimony; Jesus did not need, neither would he accept, the testimony of demons. The faith that people had in him must come from the testimony which God furnished and not from demons. Jesus commanded two things: "Hold thy peace" and "come out of him." The demon is commanded to be silent and to obey Jesus. Two distinct personalities are here recognized; the demon is treated as a person as much as the man. The personality of the demon is further shown by his crying out, convulsing the man, and coming out of him. "And when the demon had thrown him down in the midst, he came out of him, having done him no hurt." Mark records (1: 26) that "tearing him" the demon came out of the man "crying with a loud voice." Luke being himself a physician knew that this was not a case of insanity or mental hallucination; he describes the case and never hints that it was a case of insanity, but that it was a case of two distinct personalities in direct conflict with each other.

having done him no hurt. 36 And amazement came upon all, and they spake together, one with another, saying, What is ³this word? for with authority and power he commandeth the unclean spirits, and they come out. 37 And there went forth a rumor concerning him into every place of the region round about.

38 And he rose up from the synagogue, and entered into the house of Simon. And Simon's wife's mother was holden with a great fever; and they besought him for her. 39 And he stood over her, and rebuked the fever; and it left her: and immediately she rose up and ministered unto them.

³Or, *this word, that with authority . . . come out?*

And amazement came upon all,—The effect of this miracle is vididly presented by Luke; a general amazement took possession of the people which led them to discussion and to certain conclusions. "They spake together, one with another saying, What is this word?" They meant what power or authority his word carried; even the demons heard and obeyed him. Mark records them as asking: "What is this? a new teaching!" (Mark 1:27.) No one could doubt what was done. They were not ready to accept Jesus as the Messiah, and yet they could not account for such extraordinary deeds being done by him. As a result of this miracle "there went forth a rumor concerning him into every place of the region round about." This was a popular rumor concerning what he did and taught; he became a common topic of conversation among the people in Capernaum and Galilee.

38, 39 **And he rose up from the synagogue,**—Parallel records of this miracle are found in Matt. 8: 14-17 and Mark 1: 29-34. Of them Mark and Luke give about the same record. Mark tells us that this was the house of Simon and Andrew; he also records that James and John were present. This miracle was a domestic scene—a miracle in the home of his earliest disciples, and in the presence of two others. The home of Peter and Andrew was originally in Bethsaida, which was a suburb of Capernaum. This miracle must have been encouraging to his disciples. Peter's wife's mother was sick of a fever; Luke, as a physician, diagnoses the case, and says that she was "holden with a great fever." Jesus came and "stood over her, and rebuked the fever; and it left her." There was no delay; she was healed immediately and was able to minister unto them at once.

40 And when the sun was setting, all they that had any sick with divers diseases brought them unto him; and he laid his hands on every one of them, and healed them. 41 And demons also came out from many, crying out, and saying, Thou art the Son of God. And rebuking them, he suffered them not to speak, because they knew that he was the Christ.
42 And when it was day, he came out and went into a desert place: and

40, 41 **And when the sun was setting,**—Luke has recorded the two miracles of healing the demoniac and Peter's wife's mother; he now proceeds from these two particular miracles, the one public, the other private, to the statement that his miracle-working power was very largely and wonderfully exercised at that time and place. Near sunset the day became cooler, and the people brought many who were sick to Jesus. The news of his presence in the city and his wonderful cure in the synagogue had been spread until all heard about his wonderful power. Since one of his miracles was performed on the Sabbath and in the synagogue where the people had come to worship, it gave great opportunity to broadcast his power to heal. Jesus healed diseases of others, but he was never sick. He "himself took our infirmities, and bare our diseases." (Matt. 8: 17.)

And demons also came out from many,—Jesus exercised his power over the demons, and when they were cast out they came out crying and said: "Thou art the Son of God." Jesus rebuked them and would not let them bare testimony of him; Luke is clear on stating that "they knew that he was the Christ." They had supernatural wisdom and recognized Jesus as being the Son of God. Demons were not to be witnesses and messengers to proclaim the fact that Jesus was the Son of God. His own disciples were to do this, and he would furnish them all the evidence that they needed. (John 5: 32, 39, 46, 47; 20: 30, 31.) The time had not arrived for Jesus to make the full announcement that he was the Son of God, and would not permit the demons to bare such testimony.

42, 43 **And when it was day, he came out**—After healing Peter's wife's mother and many others, Jesus "went into a desert place," that is, an uninhabited and unfrequented place near Capernaum. He went there for quite meditation and prayer. (Mark 1: 35.) However, he was not permitted to

the multitudes sought after him, and came unto him, and would have stayed him, that he should not go from them. 43 But he said unto them, I must preach 'the good tidings of the kingdom of God to the other cities also: for therefore was I sent.

'Or, *the gospel*

---

remain there very long, for "the multitudes sought after him, and came unto him, and would have stayed him, that he should not go from them." From Mark's account of this it appears that Peter and his party sought and found Jesus, and reported to him that all the people were seeking him (Mark 1: 36, 37); before Jesus had time to return with Peter and his company, the multitudes searched with such diligence that they found him and attempted to prevent his going from them. At Nazareth the people drove him out of their city, but at Capernaum they seek to retain him there; what a contrast!

But he said unto them,—The reply that Jesus made showed that he had other work to do, and that the people did not understand his mission. Jesus said: "I must preach the good tidings of the kingdom of God to the other cities also." There was a moral necessity based upon the word "I must"; he must proclaim the news of the kingdom to others. Luke does not use "kingdom" so often as Matthew; "the kingdom of God" here is the same as "the kingdom of heaven" in Matt. 3: 2. "The kingdom of heaven" has special reference to its central locality, while "the kingdom of God" shows to whom the kingdom belongs. The same thing is expressed by "kingdom of Christ," or simply "kingdom." (Eph. 5: 5; Heb. 12: 28.) The kingdom, reign or administration of the Messiah is spiritual in its nature (John 18: 36; Rom. 14: 17), and is exercised over, and has its seat in, the hearts or believers (Luke 17: 21). It exists on earth (Luke 13: 18, 19, 41, 47); it extends to another state of existence (Luke 13: 43; 26: 29; Phil. 2: 10, 11); and will be fully consumated in a state of glory (Matt. 8: 11; 1 Cor. 15: 24; 2 Pet. 1: 11.) This kingdom embraces the entire mediatorial reign or government of Christ on earth and in heaven, and includes in its subjects all the redeemed. (Eph. 3: 15.)

44 And he was preaching in the synagogues of ⁵Galilee.

⁵Very many ancient authorities read *Judaea*

44 And he was preaching in the synagogues of Galilee.—Jesus continued his preaching, going throughout Galilee and meeting with the people in the synagogues; Mark adds that he also was "casting out demons." (Mark 1: 39.) This is a brief account of the first general preaching tour throughout Galilee. The many things which occurred show that in Galilee his reception among the common people was most welcome; his fame went throughout the whole country, and the enthusiasm was great.

3. THE CALLING OF THE FIRST DISCIPLES
5: 1-11

1 Now it came to pass, while the multitude pressed upon him and heard the word of God, that he was standing by the lake of Gennesaret; 2 and he

1 Now it came to pass,—Parallel accounts of this are found in Matt. 4: 18-22; Mark 1: 16-20. Some think that this portion of Luke's narrative should be placed between the thirty-first and thirty-second verses of chapter 4; Luke often departs from the regular order of events, anticipating some things and passing by others; others think that this call of Peter and his friends is different from the one recorded in Matt. 4: 18 and Mark 1: 16-20. Matthew and Mark do not record Jesus' preaching from the boat, hence some conclude that this is a different occasion; the order of events is also advanced as another reason against accepting this account as being the same as that given by Matthew and Mark. However no argument can be adduced that will justify making this account given by Luke as another one different from that recorded by Matthew and Mark. We have here a brief account of the multitude that gathered around him and heard "the word of God" as he preached from "the lake of Gennesaret." This body of water is called by four names in the Bible; it is an expansion of the river Jordan, about twelve miles long and six miles broad. It is called "sea of Galilee," "lake of Gennesaret," "sea of Chinnereth" (Num. 34: 11), "Chinneroth" (Josh. 11: 2; 1 Kings 15: 20), and "Tiberias" (John 6: 1, 21: 1).

saw two boats standing by the lake: but the fishermen had gone out of them, and were washing their nets. 3 And he entered into one of the boats, which was Simon's, and asked him to put out a little from the land. And he sat down and taught the multitudes out of the boat. 4 And when he had left speaking, he said unto Simon, Put out into the deep, and let down your nets for a draught. 5 And Simon answered and said, Master, we toiled all night,

2, 3 **and he saw two boats standing**—These boats were used for fishing. As is common Peter is made prominent; one of these boats belonged to Peter. The boats were empty at this time as the owners had "gone out of them, and were washing their nets." The servants or the hired men may have been doing this. (Mark 4: 20) It seems that they had finished their fishing and that it had been an unsuccessful night's labor. Jesus entered one of these boats and asked Peter to push it out "a little from the land." This was done that he might have a better place to teach the multitude that was pressing upon him. The boat being pushed out from the shore and anchored would give him a good pulpit from which to preach to the multitude without being pressed upon and disturbed. He "sat down and taught the multitudes out of the boat." It was usual for the teacher to sit and teach; Jesus followed this custom here as he did in preaching the Sermon on the Mount. (Matt. 5: 1.) Jesus here assumed his usual posture in teaching. (Luke 4: 20.)

4, 5 **And when he had left speaking,**—When Jesus ceased speaking to the multitude from the boat, he may have dismissed the people; it appears that he had finished his discourse with a proper ending and then began his conversation with Peter. Jesus commanded that they "put out into the deep," and when they had done this, he commanded further that they "let down your nets for a draught." Jesus addressed the others as well as Peter; he seems to have addressed the fishermen collectively. He stated why he wanted them to let down their nets; it was in order to take the fish from the water. This was a trial and test of Peter's faith. The fishermen had hung out their nets to dry, and were discouraged by their failure to catch any that night.

And Simon answered and said,—Peter is the spokesman here as he was on several other occasions. He said: "Mas-

and took nothing; but at thy word I will let down the nets. 6 And when they had done this, they inclosed a great multitude of fishes; and their nets were breaking; 7 and they beckoned unto their partners in the other boat, that they should come and help them. And they came, and filled both the

ter, we toiled all night, and took nothing." The word from which "Master" is translated is used only by Luke. (Luke 8: 24, 45; 9: 33, 49; 17: 13.) He always applies it to Jesus; he never uses "Rabbi" as does John. "Toiled" means "suffering, weariness," and indicates *exhausting* toil. Peter stood the test, for after expressing himself and telling that they had failed in their efforts during the entire night, but "at thy word I will let down the nets." "At thy word" means relying on, or on the ground only of thy word I will do as you command. Peter sacrificed his own practical knowledge as a fisherman to the authoritative word of Jesus; his faith was not great, as the sequel shows, but he had the spirit of obedience. Peter was not expecting a miracle and probably, at the best, but a small haul of fish. Peter 's act was one purely of faith.

6, 7 **And when they had done this,**—Here the entire company is included; Peter was the leader and directed the others. They cast out their nets with as much care and skill as they had done the preceding night when they had toiled without success. They enclosed such a large number of fish, "a great multitude of fishes," is the way Luke describes it, that "their nets were breaking." Portions of the net gave way, but although through the rents some fishes made their escape, yet those taken were sufficient to fill their boat and the boat of their partners to a sinking condition. Such a wondrous draught of fishes surely filled Peter and others with amazement.

and they beckoned unto their partners—It seems that Peter and Andrew, James and John were all partners. The other boat was either so far from the one in which Peter was as to be unable to be heard, or Peter was so filled with astonishment at the miracle, that "they beckoned" to their partners to come to their rescue. Some have thought that they were all so amazed that they were incapable of speaking and therefore "beckoned unto their partners." They came and filled their

boats, so that they began to sink. 8 But Simon Peter, when he saw it, fell down at Jesus' knees, saying, Depart from me; for I am a sinful man, O Lord. 9 For he was amazed, and all that were with him, at the draught of the fishes which they had taken; 10 and so were also ¹James and John, sons of Zebedee, who were partners with Simon. And Jesus said unto Simon, Fear not; from henceforth thou shalt ²catch men. 11 And when they had brought their boats to land, they left all, and followed him.

¹Or, *Jacob*
²Gr. *take alive*

boats until they "began to sink." The boats were on the point of sinking from the weight of the fishes.

8-10 But Simon Peter, when he saw it,—Peter was an impulsive man; he takes the lead in nearly everything; here he expresses his deep feeling which also expressed the feelings of others. The draught was so far beyond anything he had ever seen or heard of that he is overwhelmed with amazement and with a conviction of the superhuman power of Jesus. "Peter" means "stone"; he was so named when he was first introduced to Jesus. (John 1 : 42.) It was fitting for Luke here to speak of him as "Simon Peter" when relating this deep religious experience which was so essential to his usefulness and character as one of the foundation stones in the spiritual kingdom of Christ. When Peter saw what was done he "fell down at Jesus' knees" in homage and worshiped.

For he was amazed,—Peter and the servants who were with him were all amazed; even James and John shared in the amazement. The mention of James first here and elsewhere leads to the conclusion that he was the elder brother; John had probably before believed in Jesus as the Messiah; he was doubtless the one who went with Andrew to the dwelling place of Jesus. (John 1 : 39.) He did not at that time give up his occupation, but may have been much with Jesus. Jesus addressed Simon personally and said: "Fear not; from henceforth thou shalt catch men." James and John were partners with Peter and Andrew. The original from which we get "partners" means "fellowship" and here denotes a common interest and a very close association. "Thou shalt catch men" means literally "thou shalt be catching" men.

11 And when they had brought their boats—When these four had brought their boats to land, they forsook their nets, the ships, the fishes, their friends, hired servants, and their work, and "followed him." They showed their faith in him and their willingness to pursue their spiritual calling in his kingdom; they forsook all, not merely in form, but in heart. (2 Tim. 3: 5.) Jesus had a great work for these men in saving the lost; they were called under such surrounding circumstances that they showed their faith in following him without a moment's hesitation. The promptness with which they obeyed the call showed their willingness to sacrifice all for him.

4. JESUS CLEANSING A LEPER
5: 12-16

12 And it came to pass, while he was in one of the cities, behold, a man full of leprosy: and when he saw Jesus, he fell on his face, and besought him, saying, Lord, if thou wilt, thou canst make me clean. 13 And he stretched forth his hand, and touched him, saying, I will; be thou made

12 **And it came to pass,**—Parallel records of this healing are found in Matt. 8: 2-4 and Mark 1: 40-45. While Jesus was "in one of the cities," a man "full of leprosy" came to Jesus and "fell on his face," and said, "Lord, if thou wilt, thou canst make me clean." Among all the diseases to which human flesh is heir, leprosy is one of the worst; it is more tenacious in its grasp, most defiant of treatment, most infectious, more loathsome. Leprosy enforces almost utter seclusion from society, and from all that makes life pleasant and happy. Frequently this disease came under the notice of Jesus and his healing hand. "Leper" is derived from "Lepis," which means "a scale"; it is so called because the disease shows itself in dry, thick scales, or scabs, which are white in common leprosy. (Ex. 4: 6; Num. 12: 10; 2 Kings 5: 27.) The spots are usually about the size of a dollar. This man was "full of leprosy"; his body was thoroughly infected with the disease; the disease was in its worst form.

13 **And he stretched forth his hand,**—Jesus stretched forth his hand and touched him; it was considered a dangerous thing to touch a leper; the leper was unclean, and the one who touched him became unclean, but Jesus touched him with the healing power. When he touched him Jesus said: "I will; be

clean. And straightway the leprosy departed from him. 14 And he charged
him to tell no man: but go thy way, and show thyself to the priest, and offer
for thy cleansing, ³according as Moses commanded, for a testimony unto

³Lev. 13.49; 14.2 ff.

thou made clean." The leper had thrown himself on the
mercy of Jesus, and had faith strong enough to prostrate himself at the feet of Jesus; hence Jesus said, "I will." Some
think that Jesus violated the law of Moses when he stretched
forth his hand and touched the leper; however we may look
for an interpretation of the law in the divinity of Jesus; the
law had been given for those who were subjects to the law,
but Jesus was himself the lawgiver. The man was healed immediately; "and straightway the leprosy departed from him."
The cure was instantaneous; the leprosy, the cause of his defilement, "departed from him" at the very moment that Jesus
spoke.

14-16 **And he charged him to tell no man:**—Jesus frequently
gave this prohibition. (Mark 5: 43; 7: 36.) The reasons for
this may vary according to the circumstances. Jesus was not
wanting to create a sensation, in the enthusiams of the blessing received, the recipient often forgot or disregarded the
command not to tell what had been done. The excitement of
the people needed to be repressed so that greater good could
be done; again they did not know enough about Jesus to bear
intelligent testimony about him; sometimes it was not wise because the one who had received the blessing might be so enthusiastic that the enemies of Jesus would do harm to the one
who espoused his cause. Jesus did not wish to arouse undue
excitement (Mark 1: 45), nor would he expose himself or the
cleansed leper to the charge of violating the law. He was
commanded to show himself "to the priest, and offer" for his
"cleansing, according as Moses commanded, for a testimony
unto them." There were two stages in the ceremonial or purification of the leper (Lev. 14: 1-32); the purifying ceremonies
and offerings were united with confessions of sin and pollution, and with grateful acknowledgment of God's mercy.

them. 15 But so much the more went abroad the report concerning him: and great multitudes came together to hear, and to be healed of their infirmities. 16 But he withdrew himself in the deserts, and prayed.

But so much the more went abroad the report—Jesus had commanded the cleansed leper to "tell no man," but the report of what Jesus had done "went abroad," and "great multitudes came together to hear, and to be healed of their infirmities." The unintentional disobedience of the man who had been healed in telling about his cure caused the great multitude to come together "to hear" Jesus and "to be healed of their infirmities." Another result recorded by Mark (1: 45) was that he could no longer enter into any city, both because it had become known that he had touched a leper and the crowds and excitement might attract the suspicious notice of the authorities. Jesus was forced for a time to go into desert places. When he "withdrew himself in the deserts" he spent much time in prayer. Luke signifies in his record continuous coming together of the multitudes so that Jesus could not do his most effective work.

5. JESUS HEALING THE PALSIED MAN
5: 17-26

17 And it came to pass on one of those days, that he was teaching; and there were Pharisees and doctors of the law sitting by, who were come out of every village of Galilee and Judæa and Jerusalem: and the power of the

17 And it came to pass on one of those days,—Luke is indefinite and says that these things "came to pass on one of those days." Mark is more definite with respect to the place, as it was in Capernaum. Parallels of this account are found in Matt. 9: 2-8 and Mark 2: 1-12. Mark and Luke are much fuller than Matthew; Matthew records only the principal features of the event, while Mark and Luke give the efforts made to get the sick man into the presence of Jesus. Jesus "was teaching"; this was his mission. There were present "Pharisees and doctors of the law"; they had come "out of every village of Galilee and Judaea and Jerusalem." The "Pharisees" were a religious party or sect which originated about O150 years before Christ; their name means "separatists"; they

Lord was with him 'to heal. 18 And behold, men bring on a bed a man that was palsied: and they sought to bring him in, and to lay him before him. 19 And not finding by what *way* they might bring him in because of the multitude, they went up to the housetop, and let him down through the tiles with his couch into the midst before Jesus. 20 And seeing their faith, he said,

'Gr, *that he should heal.* Many ancient authorities read *that he should heal them*

were those who separated themselves from all impurities, as they claimed. To become a member of the Pharisaic association one had to agree to set apart all the sacred tithes and refrain from eating anything that had not been tithed. They held strictly to their oral law or traditions, attaching more importance to them than to the written law. (Matt. 15: 1-6.) Jesus often classed them with the hypocrites. "Doctors of the law" were teachers of the law. They were supposed to be men of learning and ability to expound the Jewish law; they were "law-teachers," lawyers, scribes. Distinguished hearers of the Pharisees and teachers of the law were "sitting by" in their dignity while the people stood; there seems to have been a general assembly of them from "every village of Galilee and Judaea and Jerusalem."

18-20 **And behold, men bring on a bed a man**—This man was a paralytic; he was paralyzed, having lost the power of muscular motion; he had very likely been in this condition for some time; Mark states that he was "borne of four," each holding a corner of the bed on which he lay. He was brought to the house where Jesus was. (Mark 2: 1.) They were unable to get very close to Jesus with the man on account of the multitude which filled both the house and the doorway. However, they were not to be outdone, but were determined to bring the palsied man into the presence of Jesus; so when they could not find any way to get into the presence of Jesus, "they went up to the housetop, and let him down through the tiles with his couch into the midst before Jesus." We are not told how they went "up to the housetop"; they probably went up the stairs on the outside or up a ladder; some think that they went up the stairs within an adjoining house, and passed from its roof to the roof of the house where Jesus was. The roofs of the houses were commonly flat; they removed that

Man, thy sins are forgiven thee. 21 And the scribes and the Pharisees began
to reason, saying, Who is this that speaketh blasphemies? Who can forgive
sins, but God alone? 22 But Jesus perceiving their ⁵reasonings, answered
and said unto them, ⁶Why reason ye in your hearts? 23 Which is easier, to
say, Thy sins are forgiven thee; or to say, Arise and walk? 24 But that ye

⁵Or, *questionings*
⁶Or, *What*

portion of the roof which was just above Jesus, and then they
let the man down on his bed into the presence of Jesus.
Jesus saw their faith and commended it. When Jesus saw
their faith he said: "Man, thy sins are forgiven thee." It was
encouraging for Jesus to address the sick man; he spoke in an
encouraging way. We have only two recorded occasions that
Jesus said "thy sins are forgiven"; this case and another recorded in Luke 7: 48.

21 **And the scribes and the Pharisees began to reason,—**
These were the religious leaders and they began to say
"within themselves," not aloud; the word in Mark here means
"held a dialogue with themselves." They reached the conclusion that Jesus was a blasphemer, but were not courageous
enough to accuse him of blasphemy to his face; in their reasoning they came to the conclusion that he was speaking
words of blasphemy, because no man could forgive sins except
God. Their reasoning was logical, if their premises were true.
Their argument was: "It is blasphemy for any but God to
claim to forgive sins"; this man claims the power to forgive
sins; therefore he is a blasphemer. If Jesus is not what he
claimed to be, he is a blasphemer.

22-24 **But Jesus perceivimg their reasonings,—**Jesus knew
their thoughts and answered their accusation. They must
have been greatly surprised when Jesus asked: "Why reason
ye in your hearts?" Jesus knew the hearts of men; he did not
need "that any one should bear witness concerning man; for
he himself knew what was in man." (John 2: 24, 25.) He
asked further: "Which is easier, to say, Thy sins are forgiven
thee; or to say, Arise and walk?" Again they must have been
surprised. Jesus asked them these questions, showing that he
knew what was in their hearts. The one who could say with

may know that the Son of man hath authority on earth to forgive sins (he
said unto him that was palsied), I say unto thee, Arise, and take up thy
couch, and go unto thy house. 25 And immediately he rose up before them,
and took up that whereon he lay, and departed to his house, glorifying God.

authority, arise and walk, could say with effect, thy sins are
forgiven; both were possible only for God, but impossible for
man.

But that ye may know that the Son of man hath authority
—Jesus proposes to give them evidence that they cannot
doubt, evidence that they must accept or stultify their own intelligence. To perform a miracle is as much the work of God
as to forgive sins; Jesus proposes to perform the miracle as
proof of his power to forgive sins; hence he said: "That ye
may know that the Son of man hath authority on earth to forgive sins (he said unto him that was palsied), I say unto
thee, Arise, and take up thy couch, and go unto thy house."
Jesus wrought the miracle by his own divine power; he did
not have a delegated power, but used his own power as the
Messiah. The scribes rightly understood Jesus as acting by
his own authority, and thereby claiming divine honor to himself. The "scribes" were the learned men who preserved, copied, and expounded the law and their traditions. (Ezra 7: 12;
Neh. 8: 1; Matt. 15: 1-6.) It was God in Christ manifesting
his glory, and hence a proof that Jesus could forgive sins.

25, 26 And immediately he rose up before them,—All eyes
were fixed on the paralytic and were anxiously awaiting to see
the results. If Jesus was what he claimed to be, he could heal
this man or could forgive sins; if he were not what he
claimed to be, he could do neither. Jesus calmly commanded
the sick man, not only to arise, but to take the bed or couch
upon which he lay and bear it away. The man immediately
obeyed Jesus, took up his bed, departed out of the house, "glorifying God." The man in the presence of all, not only stood
up, but showed that he was fully restored by immediately taking up his bed and departing from the house and going to his
own house, praising God as he left. The evidence of the
power of Jesus was manifested in the presence of all.

26 And amazement took hold on all, and they glorified God; and they were
filled with fear, saying, We have seen strange things to-day.

And amazement took hold on all,—The effect of the miracle
on the people was great; literally "amazement took hold on
all"; they were brought into a state of wonder, fear, and
dread. Very likely the scribes and Pharisees had never given
Jesus the credit of working a real miracle; or if they had, they
had never carried out in thought this reasoning: he who can
work a miracle must have divine power, and therefore the
right to forgive sins. Now they had both the fact and the inference to dispose of in their thought. If they had been honest minded before God, they must have come at once to the
conclusion that Jesus was really divine, and therefore the
Messiah who was to come. They had never seen or heard of
anything that could compare to what Jesus was teaching and
doing; their conclusion should have been in his favor.

6. THE CALL OF LEVI
5 : 27-32

27 And after these things he went forth, and beheld a [7]publican, named

[7]See marginal note on ch. 3.12

27 And after these things he went forth,—Parallel records
of this account are found in Matt. 9: 9-13 and Mark 2: 13-17.
This "publican," or tax collector, here called Levi and by
Mark "Levi, the son of Alphaeus," is undoubtedly the man
otherwise known as Matthew. The usual explanation of this
diversity in name, not a discrepancy, is that he had two
names, of which Levi was more used before his call, and Matthew after his call. He is the writer of the first book of the
New Testament that bears his name. It is very probable that
he had seen and heard Jesus before and was prepared to accept this call and to obey it. He was busy at the time Jesus
called him. "Matthew" in Hebrew means "the gift of God";
"Levi" means "joined," and was the name of the third son of
Jacob by Leah. Two of the ancestors of Jesus as given by
Luke bore this name. (Luke 3: 24. 29.) Matthew was "sit-

Levi, sitting at the place of toll, and said unto him, Follow me. 28 And he forsook all, and rose up and followed him.

29 And Levi made him a great feast in his house: and there was a great multitude of ʼpublicans and of others that were sitting at meat with them. 30

---

ting at the place of toll" when Jesus came by and said: "Follow me." The place of receiving custom may have been a regular customhouse or a temporary office.

28 And he forsook all,—Jesus had said: 'Follow me." He had addressed Philip, James and John, Peter and Andrew, and others in the same way. (Matt. 4: 19-21; 9: 59; John 1: 43.) To follow Christ was then as now the highest calling that one could have. The promptness and obedience of Levi is to be noted. "He forsook all, and rose up and followed him." Like Andrew and Peter (John 1: 40-42), he left everything. We are not to understand by this that he left his office without making satisfactory arrangements with the proper authorities; he did not abruptly leave his office and the funds which he had collected without proper arrangements; this would have been unfair to the Roman government.

29 And Levi made him a great feast—A record of this feast is found also in Matt. 9: 10-17 and Mark 2: 15-22. This feast gives rise to two conversations, one in regard to eating with publicans and sinners, and the other in regard to fasting. Some think that there was much time that intervened between Matthew's call and this feast, while others would put the intervening time between the discourse about eating with publicans and sinners and that about fasting. It is not probable that the feast occurred on the day that Matthew was called, but possibly soon after, and occasioned the discourse. It was proper for Matthew to give this feast as a kind of farewell meal to his business associates, and to show that he not only arranged and settled up matters, but that he still held property of his own. Matthew himself prepared and gave this reception and entertainment "in his house"; it is designated as a "great feast" because of its extensive preparation and abundant provision for a large company. Many publicans and others were present.

And [8]the Pharisees and their scribes murmured against his disciples, saying, Why do ye eat and drink with the [7]publicans and sinners? 31 And Jesus answering said unto them, They that are [9]in health have no need of a physician; but they that are sick. 32 I am not come to call the righteous but sinners to repentance.

[8]Or, *the Pharisees and the scribes among them*
[9]Gr. *sound*

---

30 **And the Pharisees and their scribes**—This does not mean merely the Pharisees and scribes who belonged to Capernaum, but those who may have belonged to the sect or party of the Pharisees. They "murmured against his disciples"; with a spirit of cowardice, they did not go to Jesus, but to his disciples. We are not to suppose that the Pharisees were present at the feast, but since it was such a large feast, their attention was called to the fact that Jesus with his disciples sat down with publicans and sinners at the feast. Matthew and Mark both give the question as aimed at Jesus: "Why eateth your Teacher with the publicans and sinners?" The fault with him implied guilt with his disciples. Persons regarded as the basest and most depraved by the self-righteous scribes and Pharisees were called "sinners." That Jesus should call Matthew, a publican, to be a disciple, and then should attend a feast with publicans, was an occasion for the scribes and Pharisees to criticize him. At another time they said: "This man receiveth sinners, and eateth with them" (Luke 15: 2.)

31, 32 **And Jesus answering said unto them,**—Jesus had either overheard the question they had asked his disciples or his disciples had told him. (Mark 2: 17.) Jesus here used a very familiar statement or proverb—"they that are in health have no need of a physician; but they that are sick." His great mission as a physician was to heal the great disease of sin; if any were really righteous, as the Pharisees imagined they were, then they did not need his healing power; the fact that these publicans and sinners were admittedly vile and wicked in the estimation of the scribes and Pharisees was proof that they were very "sick" and needed a physician. This justified the conduct of Jesus and condemned the scribes and Pharisees. Jesus then added the purpose of his mission to earth: "I am not come to call the righteous but sinners to repentance."

7. QUESTION ABOUT FASTING
5 : 33-39

33 And they said unto him, The disciples of John fast often, and make supplications; likewise also the *disciples* of the Pharisees; but thine eat and drink. 34 And Jesus said unto them, Can ye make the [10]sons of the bridechamber fast, while the bridegroom is with them? 35 But the days will come; and when the bridegroom shall be taken away from them, then will

[10]That is, *companions of the bridegroom*

33 **And they said unto him,**—Other records of this may be found in Matt. 9: 14-17 and Mark 2: 18-22. This question as recorded in Matthew was asked by the disciples of John, while Mark records that both the disciples of John and those of the Pharisees asked it; Luke represents it as being proposed by the scribes and Pharisees. Some think that the scribes and Pharisees were responsible for John's disciples joining them in asking the question. "The disciples of John fast often, and make supplications." The original for "often" as used here and in Acts 24: 26 and 1 Tim. 5: 23 means "close-packed" as a thicket, or the plumage of a bird. The language indicates what was their practice. The only fast required by the law of Moses was that of the great day of atonement. (Lev. 16: 29.) Other fasts were added after the destruction of the temple. (Zech. 7: 5; 8: 19.)

34, 35 **And Jesus said unto them,**—Jesus here makes his defense and answers the question which was asked; in his reply he presented three illustrations showing that it would be unbecoming for his disciples to fast at that time. The first illustration is taken from the familiar marriage ceremonies. He asked: "Can ye make the sons of the bridechamber fast, while the bridegroom is with them?" The friends of the bridegroom were called "sons of the bridechamber" because they had access to it during the bridal feast. (Judges 14: 10, 11.)

But the days will come;—There was no occasion for his disciples to fast while he was with them to comfort them; but the time would come when he would leave them, then they would fast and mourn. The time would arrive when the cir-

they fast in those days. 36 And he spake also a parable unto them: No man rendeth a piece from a new garment and putteth it upon an old garment; else he will rend the new, and also the piece from the new will not agree with the old. 37 And no man putteth new wine into old ⁴wine-skins; else the new wine will burst the skins, and itself will be spilled, and the skins will perish. 38 But new wine must be put into fresh wine-skins. 39 And no man having drunk old *wine* desireth new; for he saith, The old is ²good.

¹That is, *skins used as bottles*
²Many ancient authorities read *better*

cumstances would be changed and fasting would be in order then.

36 **And he spake also a parable unto them:**—The second illustration that Jesus uses in answering the question as to why his disciples did not fast is here given. It is drawn from the familiar practice of patching a garment; he points out what no one of his hearers would think of doing. Luke calls this "a parable," and he gives a fuller account of it than either Matthew or Mark. The cloth used at that time was not "shrunk"; no one would think of taking a new piece of cloth which had not been shrunk and put it upon an old garment which had been shrunk. If such should be done, "the piece from the new will not agree with the old." This thought is closely connected with the preceding thought, and is intended to enforce the same principle. If the disciples of Jesus had fasted, as did John's disciples and those of the Pharisees, they would have done that which was unsuitable to the spirit of the new dispensation.

37-39 **And no man putteth new wine into old**—The third illustration that Jesus uses is taken from the use of handling wine. These illustrations were very appropriate since garments and wine were very prominent at feasts. A "wineskin" was prepared by taking the skin off an animal and by some process fix the skin so that it would hold a liquid and using the skin as a vessel. To put "new wine" into an old wineskin would cause it to burst and the wine would be lost and the skin would be of no value. Old wineskins had been stretched to their utmost capacity; if new wine, which ferments and expands, is put into the old wineskin, it would burst the skin, and all would be lost. Jesus reminds his hearers of this which they knew to be true. "New wine must be put into fresh wine-skins" so that when the wine expands the wineskin can expand with it. This illustrates the same thought as the other two illustrations.

8. CONTROVERSY ABOUT THE SABBATH
6: 1-11

1 Now it came to pass on a ³sabbath, that he was going through the grainfields; and his disciples plucked the ears, and did eat, rubbing them in their hands. 2 But certain of the Pharisees said, Why do ye that which it is

³Many ancient authorities insert *second-first*

1 **Now it came to pass on a sabbath,**—Parallel accounts may be found in Matt: 12: 1-14 and Mark 2: 23-28 and 3: 1-6. Another ground of pharisaic opposition to Jesus is here presented; it is the supposed violation of the law of the Sabbath. The Pharisees condemned the disciples of Jesus, and he defends them because a condemnation of his disciples, when they followed his teaching, was a condemnation of Jesus. Jesus and his disciples were going through the grainfields on a Sabbath "and his disciples plucked the ears, and did eat, rubbing them in their hands." The grain was possibly wheat or barley; as they went along through the standing grain, they plucked some of the grain and ate it. The footpath which they traveled led through the field and it was easy to pluck the grain as they went along. Plucking the grain was not a violation of the rights of property; they were not accused of trespassing; they were only accused of violating the Sabbath. The grain was eaten raw.

2-5 **But certain of the Pharisees said,**—The Pharisees asked: "Why do ye that which it is not lawful to do on the sabbath day?" In Matthew and Mark this question is addressed to Jesus concerning the conduct of his disciples; the inquiry was probably repeated in various forms in order to show their pious horror at the act; it seems from a comparison of these statements of Matthew, Mark, and Luke that Jesus did not himself eat of the corn; probably his mind was

not lawful to do on the sabbath day? 3 And Jesus answering them said,
'Have ye not read even this, what David did, when he was hungry, he, and
they that were with him; 4 how he entered into the house of God, and took
and ate the showbread, and gave also to them that were with him; which it

⁴1 S. 21.6

so intent on the great object of his mission as to be insensible
to hunger at this time. We have different records of his being
hungry and fatigued when his disciples were eating and rest-
ing; sometimes they were sleeping while he spent the time in
prayer. (Matt. 26: 40, 43, 45; Mark 14: 37, 40, 41; Luke 9:
32; 22: 45.) The question is put in the form of an accusation;
it charges Jesus as being responsible for the violation of the
Sabbath.

And Jesus answering them said,—Jesus was the leader; his
disciples had done nothing that was virtually a violation of
the Sabbath, so Jesus replies to the question or accusation.
He knew that the charge was really made against him. Jesus
refers them to what David did when he was hungry. (1 Sam.
21: 1-6.) They regarded David as the faithful servant of
God; they did not condemn David for what he had done, and
yet Jesus and his disciples had done just what David had done
under similar circumstances. Jesus put the case very emphatically by asking the question. David was fleeing from Saul
and came to the tabernacle, which was located then at Nob, a
place a little north of Jerusalem. (Isa. 10: 32.) David simply
took and ate of the showbread, the bread set forth and exhibited on a table in the holy place. It consisted of twelve
loaves, which were changed every Sabbath, when the old
bread was eaten by the priests. (Lev. 24: 59.) It seems
from 1 Sam. 21: 6 that the bread had just been changed, and
hence David and his men ate it on the Sabbath. Jesus shows
by the example of David, whom all regarded as a faithful servant of God, that things which are unlawful may be done
under the law of necessity and self-preservation. Matthew
presents a second and third argument, the one derived from
the labors of the priests in the temple, the other from the
prophet Hosea (6: 6), who declares that God desires not
merely external observances, but the inward conditions of

is not lawful to eat save for the priests alone? 5 And he said unto them,
The Son of man is lord of the sabbath.
    6 And it came to pass on another sabbath, that he entered into the syna-
gogue and taught: and there was a man there, and his right hand was
withered. 7 And the scribes and the Pharisees watched him, whether he

---

kindness and love. Mark (2: 27) presents an argument not
recorded by either Matthew or Luke that the Sabbath was
designed for the good of man.

And he said unto them,—Here Jesus declares that "the Son
of man is lord of the sabbath." The final and crowning argument, growing out from the one just stated, and founded upon
the relation of the Sabbath to Christ is here given. "The Son
of man" means the Messiah is head of the human race; he
does not here deny his divinity. He is "lord of the sabbath";
since he has come in human nature to redeem man, and all
things pertaining to the human race are committed to him as
its Head, he is emphatically the Lord of the Sabbath, which
was made for the benefit of man. Jesus is indeed Lord of all
things pertaining to the kingdom of God, hence he is Lord of
the Sabbath.

    6 **And it came to pass on another sabbath,**—Luke does not
mean that this incident occurred on the following Sabbath
from that on which they plucked the grain; he is only recording what took place "on another sabbath." This time Jesus
"entered into the synagogue and taught"; as opportunity was
presented Jesus taught the people. He taught on the Sabbath
in their synagogue because they assembled for worship on
that day. This time "There was a man there, and his right
hand was withered." Luke alone mentions that it was "his
right hand" that was withered. This is a very precise way of
stating incidents; this accuracy is characteristic of Luke's profession; ancient medical writers always state whether the
right or the left member is affected. "Withered" means that
he had lost the use of that hand, that it was diseased so that
he could not use it. The "right hand" was usually the most
useful. It was similar to that with which Jeroboam was
afflicted. (1 Kings 13: 4-6.)

    7 **And the scribes and the Pharisees watched him,**—The
"scribes" were those who copied the law and finally became

would heal on the sabbath; that they might find how to accuse him. 8 But
he knew their thoughts; and he said to the man that had his hand withered,
Rise up, and stand forth in the midst. And he arose and stood forth. 9 And
Jesus said unto them, I ask you, Is it lawful on the sabbath to do good, or to

teachers of it; the "Pharisees" were those of that sect or party
of the Jews who were particular about the traditions of the fathers. They had a bad motive in observing what Jesus would
do. (Luke 14: 1; Acts 9: 24.) They were watching Jesus
maliciously. The growth of opposition is seen in that they
now watch intently for an occasion to censure him. Possibly
they thought that he would heal this man on the Sabbath;
they thought that they had Jesus in a dilemma; either he
must heal the man on the Sabbath, or he must refuse to do
good when he has the power to do it; they thought that they
had the grounds for bringing charges against him whatever he
did.

8 **But he knew their thoughts;**—This was an evidence of
the divinity of Christ. Luke does not stop to prove his divinity, but takes it for granted. In the Old Testament God's existence is treated this way. John expresses it as follows: "Because he needed not that any one should bear witness concerning man; for he himself knew what was in man." (John
2: 25.) Jesus commanded the man that had the withered
hand to "rise up, and stand forth in the midst." He did this
so that all could see the man with the afflicted hand, and could
see when it was healed. The man obeyed him and "stood
forth." Jesus makes the misery and the healing of the man
conspicuous, yet he performs the cure with the word.

9, 10 **And Jesus said unto them,**—Jesus now put them in a
dilemma; he asked them: "Is it lawful on the sabbath to do
good, or to do harm?" They must admit that it was lawful to
do good; they must also admit that it is wrong to do harm or
fail to do good when one has an opportunity. Some understand this to mean that the question is used in a general sense
other than in a particular sense. However, Jesus first asks in
regard to doing good or evil in a general sense on the Sabbath, and then in a particular sense, to destroy life or to save
life.

do harm? to save a life, or to destroy it? 10 And he looked round about on them all, and said unto him, Stretch forth thy hand. And he did *so;* and his hand was restored. 11 But they were filled with ⁵madness; and communed one with another what they might do to Jesus.

⁵Or, *foolishness*

And he looked round about on them all,—Matthew (12: 11, 12) records the reference to a sheep that had fallen into a pit, but Mark and Luke omit this point. Jesus "looked" "on them all." That "look" of Jesus was very significant. Mark records (3: 5) that Jesus "looked round about on them with anger"; he had a righteous indignation because of the hardness of their hearts. He silenced his opposer and then proceeded to heal the afflicted hand. He performed the miracle without any bodily effort, or any word except the command, "stretch forth thy hand." The man obeyed and "his hand was restored." The enemies of Jesus could not charge him with laboring on the Sabbath; he did no work, but spoke to the man. The healing took place immediately; Jesus had only to speak and the man had to obey. The faith of the man is brought into its natural relation to his obedience and cure. Jesus gave the command; the man believed, and obeyed, and received the blessing.

11 But they were filled with madness;—The scribes and Pharisees were answered before they had expressed their thoughts; Jesus had looked into their hearts and had answered them; they were displeased with this. They were deprived of legal ground of objection since the miracle was performed without any action on the part of Jesus; there was nothing left for them to do except to receive the testimony of Jesus that he was the promised Messiah, or reject him and all the evidence that he had furnished. They could not deny the evidence. They seek to satisfy themselves with a senseless rage; this was a foolish thing for them to do.

9. THE CHOICE OF THE TWELVE
6: 12-19

12 And it came to pass in these days, that he went out into the mountain to pray; and he continued all night in prayer to God. 13 And when it was day, he called his disciples; and he chose from them twelve, whom also he

12 **And it came to pass in these days,**—Parallel accounts of this are found in Matt. 10: 1-4 and Mark 3: 13-19. "In these days" designates the period during which the miracles just related were wrought, and the Pharisees and others were seeking how they might destroy him. He went "into the mountain to pray." There are several mountains in Galilee on the west side of the Sea of Galilee, some think that it was the same mountain from which the "Sermon on the Mount" was preached. It is significant that he went there "to pray" and that he continued "all night in prayer to God." Luke makes special reference to Jesus at prayer. (Luke 3: 21; 5: 16; 9: 18; 11: 1.) Jesus resorted to special prayer before great and important events. (Mark 6: 46; Luke 22: 41-44; John 11: 41, 42; 17: 1.)

13 **And when it was day,**—We must distinguish between the call of these men to discipleship (John 1: 35-45), their call to be constant attendants, preachers, or evangelists (Matt. 4: 18-22; Mark 1: 16-20), and their selection as apostles which is here related. After their selection they were endowed with miraculous gifts and sent out on their "limited commission." (Matt. 10: 1-4.) The next morning after the night had been spent in prayer "he called his disciples," and from his disciples he "chose from them twelve, whom also he named apostles." The word "chose" means "he made or constituted" to be "apostles." From the many disciples which he had made up to this time, he selected twelve of them and appointed them as his "apostles." "Apostle" means one "sent forth." Jesus is named or called an "Apostle." (Heb. 3: 1.) Luke uses this term more than the other writers do. (Luke 9: 10; 11: 49; 17: 5; 22: 14; 24: 10.) They are sometimes called "the twelve" (Mark 4: 10; 6: 7), or "the twelve disciples" (Matt. 20: 17), or simply "disciples" (Luke 9: 12). Mark (3: 14) gives the reason for their appointment "that they might be with him, and that he might send them forth to preach."

named apostles: 14 Simon, whom he also named Peter, and Andrew his brother, and [6]James and John, and Philip and Bartholomew, 15 and Matthew and Thomas, and [6]James *the son* of Alphæus, and Simon who was called the Zealot, 16 and Judas *the* [7]*son* of [6]James, and Judas Iscariot, who became a

[6]Or, *Jacob*
[7]Or, brother. See Jude 1

14-16 **Simon, whom he also named Peter,**—There are four catalogues of the apostles, and Luke gives two of the four; Matthew and Mark give the other two. Each catalogue is divided into three classes, the names of which are never interchanged, and each class headed by a leading name. Peter heads the first class, Philip the second, James the third, and Judas Iscariot stands the last, except in the Acts, where his name is omitted because of his apostasy and death. Matthew enumerates the apostles two by two, in pairs; Mark and Luke one by one, individually; and Luke in the Acts, mixedly. This shows that the writers wrote independent of each other.

MATT. 10: 2-4	MARK 3: 16-19	LUKE 6: 14-16	ACTS 1: 13
Simon Peter	Simon Peter	Simon Peter	Peter
Andrew, his brother	James	Andrew	John
James, son of Zebedee	John	James	James
John, his brother	Andrew	John	Andrew
Philip	Philip	Philip	Philip
Bartholomew	Bartholomew	Bartholomew	Thomas
Thomas	Matthew	Matthew	Bartholomew
Matthew	Thomas	Thomas	Matthew
James, son of Alphaeus	James, son of Alphaeus	James, son of Alphaeus	James, son of Alphaeus
Lebbaeus or Thaddaeus	Thaddaeus	Simon Zelotes	Simon Zelotes
Simon, the Cananaean	Simon	Judas, son of James	Judas, son of James
Judas Iscariot	Judas Iscariot	Judas Iscariot	....

Peter stands at the head of the apostles; was given the keys of the kingdom; had a prominent part in the early church; wrote two books of the New Testament. Andrew was the brother of Peter; was born at Bethsaida and afterwards lived at Capernaum; nothing is known of his work.

James, the son of Zebedee, was called "James the Greater," and is never mentioned in the New Testament apart from John his brother; he was the first martyr among the apostles. (Acts 12: 2.) John, the brother of James, ranked next to Peter; he was the beloved apostle; he wrote five books of the New Testament—John, First John, Second John, Third John, and Revelation. Philip was a native of Bethsaida, a disciple

traitor; 17 and he came down with them, and stood on a level place, and a great multitude of his disciples, and a great number of the people from all Judæa and Jerusalem, and the sea coast of Tyre and Sidon, who came to

of John the Baptist; his labors and death are not recorded in the New Testament. Bartholomew was the son of "Bar-Tholmai," or son of Tholmai; nothing is said of his labors. Matthew was also called Levi; he was a publican; he wrote the first book of the New Testament; nothing further is known of his labors. Thomas was also called "Didymus" (John 11: 16), which means "a twin"; he has been called "doubting Thomas," but this should not be applied to him (John 20: 24-29). James was the son of Alpheus; he is called "James the less" (Mark 15: 40); some think that he was the cousin of our Lord (Luke 24: 10; John 19: 25) and that he had a brother Joses (Matt. 27: 56). Simon was called the "Zealot"; Mark calls him "the Cananaean"; nothing is known of his work. Judas "the son of James" was probably the same as "Lebbaeus" or "Thaddaeus"; some think he was the same as the author of Jude. Judas Iscariot is always designated as the traitor; he is thought to have been the only apostle who was not by birth a Galilean; the climax of his sins was the betrayal of Jesus and his suicide.

17-19 **and he came down with them,**—Jesus now descended from the mountain and further instructed his disciples and taught the multitudes. He is now to be accompanied with his apostles. He "stood on a level place"; we do not know where this was. Some think that it was near Capernaum. "A great multitude" of his disciples and many from Judea, Jerusalem, and the seacoast of Tyre and Sidon came to hear him. Luke here gives us a glimpse of the great crowds that attended his preaching; Jesus was at this time at the height of his popularity as a teacher; in fact, he was popular with all except those who decided against him with the Pharisees. Judea was south of Samaria and Jesus at this time was in Galilee. Palestine was divided into three divisions at this time—Galilee on the north, Samaria in the middle, and Judea on the south.

hear him, and to be healed of their diseases; 18 and they that were troubled with unclean spirits were healed. 19 And all the multitude sought to touch him; for power came forth from him, and healed *them* all.

---

and they that were troubled with unclean spirits—Those who were "troubled with unclean spirits were healed"; troubled" in the original first meant "a crowd or mob" with the idea of "want of arrangement and discipline," and therefore of "confusion" and "tumult." It is applied to the noise and tumult of a crowd, and so passes into the sense of the "trouble" and "annoyance" caused by these, and of trouble generally. It is a term frequently used in medical language; here again we see evidence of Luke's profession. Many were possessed with demons and were harassed with even crowds of evil spirits. It is significant that they were healed. These "unclean spirits" manifested their power through the bodies of men, and to a greater or less extent caused physical diseases.

And all the multitude sought to touch him;—All those who were diseased, and there was a multitude of them, sought to touch Jesus. Their eagerness was so great and their faith in his power to heal was so strong that their touching Jesus was sufficient to affect their cleaning. Theirs was a touch of faith; "for power came forth from him, and healed them all." The multitudes were all the while seeking to touch him, for his virtue was going out of him. (Matt. 14: 36; Mark 6: 56.) Luke is more technical, using the strictly medical term, "healed," which occurs twenty-eight times in the New Testament, and seventeen of these are mentioned by Luke. Luke also uses the two words employed by Matthew and Mark, but always with some addition showing the nature of the saving, or healing.

10. THE GREAT SERMON
6: 20-49

20 And he lifted up his eyes on his disciples, and said, Blessed *are* ye

---

20 And he lifted up his eyes on his disciples,—A parallel of this sermon is found in Matt. 5: 1 to 7: 28. This "sermon" is a synopsis of a continuous discourse, spoken at one time; it

poor: for yours is the kingdom of God. 21 Blessed *are* ye that hunger now:

may have been repeated a number of times and Luke gives a
record of the sermon which was repeated at some later time
than the record given by Matthew. Many think that Luke's
account is in chronological order, while Matthew's is not.
Both accounts in Matthew and Luke represent a great multitude present, but that Jesus spoke directly to his disciples;
both Matthew and Luke present the main topics in the same
order throughout; both begin with "the beatitudes" and end
with the illustration of the necessity of doing as well as hearing. Matthew records nine beatitudes, while Luke gives only
four; yet Luke adds four "woes" upon different classes of men
which Matthew does not record. Luke puts the discourse in
the second person, "blessed are ye," while Matthew has it in
the third person.

Blessed are ye poor:—The poor as used here means those
who are "poor in spirit," and not the penniless. The humble
in spirit and the contrite of heart are those who are poor in
the spirit. The word here means the same as that used in Isa.
66: 1-3. The poor in this sense may lay just claims to "the
kingdom of God." "The kingdom of God" is the same as
Matthew calls "the kingdom of heaven." Matthew uses
"kingdom of heaven" frequently, and Jesus used that phrase
to describe the kingdom. "Kingdom of heaven" and "kingdom of God" are equivalent terms, though the pre-eminent
title was "kingdom of God," since it was expected to be fully
realized in the Messianic era, when God should take upon
himself the kingdom by a visible representative. "Kingdom
of heaven" had a double meaning with the Jews—the historical kingdom and the spiritual kingdom.

21 **Blessed are ye that hunger now:**—Luke adds the word
"now," that is, in this life and at the present time. Those who
earnestly and even painfully desire righteousness "shall be
filled"; that is, they shall be satisfied. They shall find complete satisfaction in Christ, having his righteousness accounted to them and being satisfied and conformed to his
image. (Prov. 21: 21; Isa. 41: 17; 60: 21; 2 Pet. 3: 13.)

for ye shall be filled. Blessed *are* ye that weep now: for ye shall laugh. 22 Blessed are ye, when men shall hate you, and when they shall separate you *from their company,* and reproach you, and cast out your name as evil, for the Son of man's sake. 23 Rejoice in that day, and leap *for joy*: for behold, your reward is great in heaven; for in the same manner did their fathers

Blessed are ye that weep now:—Again Luke gives the word "now," its proper emphasis, and restricts the weeping. This is a stronger expression than Matthew uses—"they that mourn." It signifies that deep anguish of spirit which manifests itself in groans and tears; it does not include all kinds of weeping, for the sorrow "of the world worketh death." (2 Cor. 7: 10.) It includes those who weep over their sins. "Ye shall laugh"; not only shall they be comforted, as Matthew expresses it, but they shall rejoice with open joy. Their sins shall be forgiven; they shall be supported in trial and cheered with the blessings of God. Their joy shall be complete, both with respect to the present and the future state. (2 Cor. 1: 4; 4: 17; Rev. 21: 4.)

22 **Blessed are ye, when men shall hate you,**—This expresses in strong terms the enemies of the disciples of Christ; they shall be hated. The disciples of Christ represent the kingdom of God on earth, and the world hates the kingdom of God. The disciples of Christ are hated, reproached, persecuted, and separated from their synagogues, their society, and outcasts among men. They are hated because they are the children of God; they are cast out as evil persons. All this is done "for the Son of man's sake." "Son of man" is a phrase frequently used in the Old Testament. It was applied to man in general (Num. 23: 19; Job 25: 6; 35: 8; Psalm 8: 4), and is used eighty-nine times in Ezekiel. It had also a Messianic meaning in the Old Testament. (Dan. 7: 13.) Jesus most frequently used this phrase when speaking of himself; and there are but two instances in which it is applied to him by another, namely, by Stephen (Acts 7: 56) and by John (Rev. 1: 13; 14: 14). As "Son of man" Jesus asserts his authority over all flesh.

23 **Rejoice in that day,**—They are to rejoice in the day that they are persecuted, when they are reproached for the name of

unto the prophets. 24 But woe unto you that are rich! for ye have received
your consolation. 25 Woe unto you, ye that are full now! for ye shall hunger. Woe *unto you,* ye that laugh now! for ye shall mourn and weep. 26

Christ. They were even to "leap for joy"; they should be so
overjoyed that they were counted worthy to suffer for Christ
that they could not contain themselves without a physical
demonstration of their job. Christians have reason to rejoice
amid persecutions in view of a reward so great and glorious.
(2 Cor. 4: 17.)

24-26 **But woe unto you that are rich!**—Luke here records
four woes which Matthew does not record. These woes are
not the expression of anger, but of lamentation and warning.
"Woe unto you" or "alas for you!" Jesus is not uttering as a
judge condemnation, but as the great Teacher and Prophet he
declares the miserable condition of certain classes and warns
them against it. The first woe is pronounced over those that
are rich; this is the opposite of spiritual poverty; it includes
those that make this world their possession and wealth and
trust in riches. (Mark 10: 24; Luke 12: 21; 18: 24, 25; 1 John
2: 15.) Worldly riches are deceitful in their influence, chok-
ing the word and rendering it unfruitful.

Woe unto you, ye that are full now!—This is the opposite
of those who have spiritual hunger. This class has no cravings
after spiritual food, but are satisfied with the worldly pleasures which only the earth can give. There is coming a time
when they shall "hunger." When they are brought to their
senses and are bereft of all spiritual food, then they shall fam-
ish for need of that which only can make the soul happy in the
world to come. This will be an endless hunger.

Woe unto you, ye that laugh now!—This woe is the opposite of weeping in verse 21. Those who engage in worldly
pleasure, who indulge in frivolity, and dissipation, who live in
gaiety and mirth in this world, shall in the world to come
"mourn and weep." The frivolity will be turned into sorrow
when they discover their miserable end, and are cast out into
outer darkness where there is wailing and gnashing of teeth.
(Prov. 1: 25-28; James 4: 9.)

Woe *unto you,* when all men shall speak well of you! for in the same manner did their fathers to the false prophets.

27 But I say unto you that hear, Love your enemies, do good to them that hate you, 28 bless them that curse you, pray for them that despitefully

Woe unto you, when all men shall speak well of you!—This was spoken to his disciples; they should not court the favor of men; neither should they seek to please men. The reason given here is that "in the same manner did their fathers to the false prophets." This woe is opposite to the beatitudes in verses 22 and 23. "All men" is a term used to include the world. A Christian should strive to have "good testimony from them that are without" (1 Tim. 3: 7), but when his words and conduct are such as to please and delight the ungodly, affording no reproof for their wicked practices, he should be alarmed. "Know ye not that the friendship of the world is enmity with God? Whosoever therefore would be a friend of the world maketh himself an enemy of God." (James 4: 4.) The fathers sought to please "the false prophets" by encouraging them in their wicked ways, and the false prophets sought to please the people by crying "peace, peace"! when there was no peace. (1 Kings 22: 6-14; Jer. 23: 14; 28: 10, 11; Ezek. 13: 10, 11.)

27, 28 But I say unto you that hear,—Jesus here puts in contrast his teachings with that of the traditions of the scribes and Pharisees. He had told his disciples that they would have enemies and would suffer persecution; he now instructs them how they should treat their enemies. He enforces the duty of love, its extent, and its standard. Luke here arranges his account of this sermon very different from that given by Matthew. Jesus enforced this by saying: "I say unto you"; he speaks not like their scribes. "Love your enemies." This sublime moral precept takes rank at the head of all moral duties toward our fellow beings, for the obligation to love enemies carries with it the obligation to love all who are not enemies, but who are more or less friendly.

bless them that curse you,—They would be persecuted and spoken evil against, but they were not to retaliate, and speak evil of their enemies, but were to bless them; speak words of

use you. 29 To him that smiteth thee on the *one* cheek offer also the other;
and from him that taketh away thy cloak withhold not thy coat also. 30
Give to every one that asketh thee; and of him that taketh away thy goods

peace, kindness, and love to those who insulted and reviled
them. They were to pray for them; that is, pray that their
enemies might cease to be enemies and to become disciples of
Jesus. Praying for their enemies is the opposite of cursing
their enemies. Jesus set the example for them when he
prayed on the cross: "Father, forgive them." (Luke 23: 34.)
Stephen prayed the same prayer when he said: "Lord, lay not
this sin to their charge." (Acts 7: 60.)

29, 30 **To him that smiteth thee on the one cheek**—Jesus
gives two examples to illustrate the treatment of enemies in
addition to enjoining the principle of love. The first example
is that of turning the other cheek when smitten on one.
"Cheek" literally means "the jaw"; the blow intended is not a
mere slap, but a heavy blow, an act of violence rather than
contempt. It was regarded as an affront of the worst sort to
be struck in the face; it was severely punished both by Jewish
and Roman laws. It was a proverb to turn the other cheek
when receiving injury. (Lam. 3: 30.) This sets forth a principle, and is not to be taken too literally. The other example
is that if the cloak is taken from one then the coat should be
given. This illustrates the same principle. From personal violence Jesus descends to the demanding of property by legal
means. The "cloak" was the outer garment; it was worn
loose around the body; the "coat" was the undergarment.
We are here taught to suffer wrong rather than do wrong; we
are to do good for evil. We are not to retaliate; this course, if
followed by the disciples of Christ, would win a victory over
our enemies.

Give to every one that asketh thee;—This is to be interpreted by the principles of Christian love; Jesus is here opposing a retaliating and revengeful spirit; his disciples must not
out of revenge withhold help from any who may need it.
Christians should be ready and willing to help the needy at all
times, even if they are enemies. (2 Cor. 8: 12; Gal. 6: 10.) If
anyone should take "away thy goods ask them not again."

ask them not again. 31 And as ye would that men should do to you, do ye also to them likewise. 32 And if ye love them that love you, what thank have ye? for even sinners love those that love them. 33 And if ye do good to them that do good to you, what thank have ye? for even sinners do the same. 34 And if ye lend to them of whom ye hope to receive, what thank have ye? even sinners lend to sinners, to receive again as much. 35 But love

---

The disciples of Jesus are not to show a revengeful spirit, and should not do violence to anyone that despoils their goods; but they should be kind and liberal and strive to win back the offender to right conceptions of living. Christians should show a forbearing spirit at all times and never retaliate.

31 **And as ye would that men should do to you,**—This is called the "Golden Rule"; Jesus gives it as a test of love toward others. We should make the case of others our own, and as we would as honest and righteous people that others should do to us, we should do in like manner to them. This was a new requirement, but simply the application of the law to love our neighbor as ourselves. (Matt. 7 : 12.) Many have quoted similar statements from heathen authors, but those gave the negative part of this command, while Christ gave the positive. Not only are we to avoid doing to others what we in their situation would dislike, but we are to do to them whatever we would in righteousness wish them to do to us. This principle of determining what we shall do to others by first determining what we would have others do to us would keep down many of the difficulties that arise in society. This excludes all selfishness and enforces right thinking about others as well as righteous conduct toward them. It is the rule that Jesus gave, and hence is the one that regulates Christian conduct toward each other and all others.

32-36 **And if ye love them that love you,**—Sinners do good to others for policy's sake, not from principle; they do good to others, hoping to receive good from others, and not for the good that they love to do. Jesus here lays down a higher and nobler course of conduct; Christians are to do good to others with no thought of receiving again any good from others; they are to do it because they love to do good; do it because God does and will provide for those who follow Christ. If Christians only did good to those in the world who did them,

your enemies, and do *them* good, and lend, [1]never despairing; and your reward shall be great, and ye shall be sons of the Most High: for he is kind
toward the unthankful and evil. 36 Be ye merciful, even as your Father is
merciful. 37 And judge not, and ye shall not be judged; and condemn not,
and ye shall not be condemned: release, and ye shall be released: 38 give,
and it shall be given unto you; good measure, pressed down, shaken to-

[1]Some ancient authorities read *despairing of no man*

good, they would do very little good in this world; if they did
no more good than many church members do to each other,
again they would be doing very little good. Christ gives a
higher standard of conduct for his disciples. He sums up his
teachings by saying that his disciples should love their enemies, "and do them good, and lend, never despairing." There
is no moral credit in simply loving those who love us; the
wicked do that much; it is no mark of godliness simply to do
good to those who do good to us; many godless people do like
that.

Be ye merciful,—Prove yourself merciful by the conduct
above described that you may be like your Father. Matthew
says "be perfect." God is the "Father of mercies" (2 Cor. 1:
3), and as mercy is one of the chief attributes of God shown to
man, to be merciful like him is to reach completeness in our
sphere, as he is completely "perfect" in his sphere.
"Merciful" means "pitiful, compassionate"; it is the feeling
produced by the misery and want of others. In James 5: 11 it
is very properly translated "tender mercy."

37, 38 **And judge not,**—This forbids harsh, censorious judgments of the character of others; it also forbids unjust criticisms of the conduct of others. It does not forbid the forming
of opinions as to what is right or wrong. It does admonish us
that those opinions should be in love, never severe.
Christians should not form hasty judgments, nor unkind judgments; they should never form judgments based on jealousy,
suspicion, envy, or hate. The Golden Rule should govern one
here; one should judge another as he would wish to be
judged; one should not condemn with severity, but weigh in
Christian love every judgment formed. One should not seek
to judge, but if one must, let it be a "righteous judgment";
consider it as Christian.

gether, running over, shall they give into your bosom. For with what
measure ye mete it shall be measured to you again.
39 And he spake also a parable unto them, Can the blind guide the blind?

---

give, and it shall be given unto you;—There are two things
which are forbidden here, namely, "judge not" and "condemn
not"; one will be judged and condemned with the same degree
of severity, both by man and God, that he passes on others.
There are also two things commanded here, namely, "release"
and "give." One will receive what one gives; the Christians'
law of conduct here is to "give and forgive." This rule will
keep peace and happiness in the church, in the community,
and in the family. If one will follow this rule, one will receive
full measure for it; "good measure, pressed down, shaken together, running over, shall they give into your bosom."
"Pressed down" as dry articles, "shaken together" as soft
goods, "running over" as liquids. Full measure shall be given
to the one who so deports himself. This "good measure"
"shall they give into your bosom." The gathered folds of the
wide upper garment, bound together with the girdle, formed a
pouch. In the eastern country people who wore a loose, outer
garment used the bosom to pour the contents of grain or other
articles into as they would a sack. In Ruth 3: 15 Boaz said
to Ruth: "Bring the mantle that is upon thee, and hold it; and
she held it; and he measured six measures of barley, and laid
it on her: and he went into the city." (See also Isa. 65: 7;
Jer. 32: 18.)

39 **And he spake also a parable unto them,**—This "parable"
is more like a proverb; it is put in the interrogative form and
the original shows that a negative reply is expected. "Can
the blind guide the blind?" The blind were very numerous in
that country; Luke uses the word "parable" some fifteen
times instead of "proverb" and for the longer narrative comparisons. This is the only use of the term parable concerning
the metaphors in the "Sermon on the Mount." One blind
man is very unfit to guide another; so those who undertake to
teach others when they do not know the truth themselves are
unfit, for they are blind guides. The "pit" is an emblem of destruction; the Pharisees are described as "blind guides."

shall they not both fall into a pit? 40 The disciple is not above his teacher:
but every one when he is perfected shall be as his teacher. 41 And why
beholdest thou the mote that is in thy brother's eye, but considerest not the
beam that is in thine own eye? 42 Or how canst thou say to thy brother,
Brother, let me cast out the mote that is in thine eye, when thou thyself
beholdest not the beam that is in thine own eye? Thou hypocrite, cast out
first the beam out of thine own eye, and then shalt thou see clearly to cast

---

(Matt. 15: 14; Matt. 23: 16.) The reference here is to censorious and critical teachers who may have a "beam" in their
eye. If ignorant and unskillful leaders attempt to guide people,
they themselves will be the first to fall into the ditch or be de-
sroyed. No one who is blind to spiritual truth can guide others into it.

40 **The disciple is not above his teacher:**—Here Jesus uses
another proverbial statement that the disciple, so long as he is
a disciple, or learner, cannot be above his master or teacher.
The nature of the relationship of teacher and disciple is such
that the teacher is above the disciple, and the disciple cannot
become wiser and better than his teacher so long as this relationship exists. "But every one when he is perfected shall
be as his teacher." The disciple naturally makes his teacher
his model and imitates him. If they are blind and censorious
teachers, they would infuse the same spirit into their disciples; hence they would be unsafe and unfit instructors.
"Perfected" as used here signifies in the original to "readjust,
restore, to set right," whether in a physical or moral sense.
In Gal 6: 1 it is used as restoring a brother taken in a fault; in
medical language it means to set a bone or joint when it has
been broken or dislocated.

41, 42 **And why beholdest thou the mote**—Jesus here rebukes and instructs those who would be teachers; suggestions
to those who undertake to teach others are used here, and specific application made to the Pharisees and other religious
teachers. In their censorious spirit, they magnify and are
quick to see the smallest fault in their neigibor, but do not
perceive the enormous faults in their own character. Some
can always see the faults of others quicker than they can see
their own faults; again the faults in others always seem much
larger than their own faults; yet in reality their own faults

out the mote that is in thy brother's eye. 43 For there is no good tree that
bringeth forth corrupt fruit; nor again a corrupt tree that bringeth forth
good fruit. 44 For each tree is known by its own fruit. For of thorns men
do not gather figs, nor of a bramble bush gather they grapes. 45 The good
man out of the good treasure of his heart bringeth forth that which is good;
and the evil *man* out of the evil *treasure* bringeth forth that which is evil:
for out of the abundance of the heart his mouth speaketh.

---

may be much greater than those in the other person, whom
they are criticizing. Jesus uses here "the mote" and "the
beam" to enforce his teaching. The "mote" and the "beam"
are proverbial contrasts, the "mote" being the finest particle
of dust or chaff against the "beam" of timber for a house
frame—like the contrast between sawdust and the saw log itself.

43, 44 **For there is no good tree that bringeth forth corrupt
fruit;**—The general principle here announced by Jesus was
that which all believe. The good tree cannot bear corrupt
fruit, nor can a rotten tree bring forth good fruit. The character of the tree is determined by the kind of fruit it bears.
The tree and its fruit illustrate the heart and the life; the bad
heart yields a wicked life; the good heart, a worthy life.
Honest and pure intentions, the sincere purpose to do right,
yield naturally the fruit of right doing; so Jesus teaches us to
estimate what the inner man is by what the outer man does.
Men do not gather figs from thorn trees, nor grapes from a
"bramble bush." Matthew uses "thistle," while Luke uses
"bramble bush." Some think that Luke was acquainted with
the "bramble bush" and used it for medicinal purposes, as he
was a physician.

45 **The good man out of the good treasure**—The figure was
changed from the general tree to the particular horn tree; the
thorn tree was abundant in that country. So the figures are
now applied to man's character and conduct; out of the good
man come good words and deeds, because there is a treasury
of goodness in his heart. His thoughts and affections are
pure. Out of the evil man comes evil, because the store of
things in his heart is evil. Language is the overflowing of the
soul and indicates its state and condition. (Matt. 15: 18;
Rom. 10: 9, 10; 2 Cor. 4: 13.) Jesus has passed by degrees

46 And why call ye me, Lord, Lord, and do not the things which I say?
47 Every one that cometh unto me, and heareth my words, and doeth them, I
will show you to whom he is like: 48 he is like a man building a house, who
digged and went deep, and laid a foundation upon the rock: and when a
flood arose, the stream brake against that house, and could not shake it: [2]be-
cause it had been well builded. 49 But he that [3]heareth, and [4]doeth not, is

[2]Many ancient authorities read *for it had been founded upon the rock:* as in Mt.
7.25
[3]Gr. *heard*
[4]Gr. *did not*

from the conditions of the Christian life, the beatitudes, to the
life itself; he has presented first the principle, then the life
that is governed by the principle.

46 **And why call ye me, Lord, Lord,**—The force of this question is seen when we look at the meaning of "Lord"; "Lord"
means master, ruler; it is inconsistent to call one "Lord" and
yet not obey him. The question implies: "Why do ye admit
my right to rule and to lay down the law of your life, and yet
not do the things which I command?" It seems that many,
both real and professed friends, were thus addressing him; the
repetition emphasizes a habitual profession. If they truly accepted Jesus as Lord, they would do what he commanded
them; this was applicable to his apostles, also to his disciples
today. The interrogative form makes this a two-edged
sword; an emphatic warning, on one hand, against a mere
profession, and an emphatic command, on the other, to make
their profession and practice agree. Matthew (7: 21-23)
makes a different application of this.

47, 48 **Every one that cometh unto me,**—The one who comes
to Christ in the proper sense as used here becomes a disciple
or learner. Doing, obeying, comes by hearing and implies
faith. (Rom. 10: 14.) The "words" as here used include all
that Jesus had spoken during this sermon. Hearing is important, but there is something else needed; faith and obedience
must be added to hearing. "But be ye doers of the word, and
not hearers only, deluding your own selves." (James 1: 22.)
The one that both hears and does what Jesus says is like the
man building a house, who digged deep, and placed a foundation on the solid rock.

like a man that built a house upon the earth without a foundation; against which the stream brake, and straightway it fell in; and the ruin of that house was great.

---

49 **But he that heareth, and doeth not,**—The foolish hearer who fails to do what the Lord requires, yet because he has heard, thinks himself secure, finds his professed Christian character swept away in a sudden flood of evil, like the house stuck upon the earth, which the sudden floods undermine and sweep away into ruin. The hearer, who does not obey, has no solid foundation for his character or hope. His hearing is commendable, but his failing to do or obey is condemned. The same figure is used here of the wind, rain, and flood beating against the house of the one who had built his house upon the rock. The difference is great; the one withstood all the furiousness of the storm, but the other went down in hopeless ruin; so it will be with those who hear but do not obey.

11. THE CENTURION AT CAPERNAUM
7: 1-10

1 After he had ended all his sayings in the ears of the people, he entered into Capernaum.

---

1 **After he had ended all his sayings**—Having ended his sermon, Luke proceeds to narrate other events. A parallel of this account is found in Matt. 8: 5-13. Luke's account is fuller at the beginning, but Matthew's record is fuller at the close; Matthew records some things that Luke omits, and Luke records some that Matthew does not. The context here shows that this discourse which has just been narrated was delivered at one time, and not a mere collection of sayings or detached parts of different discourses. Jesus had ended all of these sayings "in the ears of the people"; the discourse recorded in chapter 6 was for the instruction of the people as well as his disciples. "He entered into Capernaum." The language implies that he was not far from Capernaum when he delivered this discourse; Capernaum was the center of his operations, and to it he frequently returned from his preaching tours.

2 And a certain centurion's ⁵servant, who was ⁶dear unto him, was sick
and at the point of death. 3 And when he heard concerning Jesus, he sent
unto him elders of the Jews, asking him that he would come and save his
¹servant. 4 And they, when they came to Jesus besought him earnestly, say-

⁵Gr. *bondservant*
⁶Or. *precious to him*   Or, *honorable with him*
¹Gr. *bondservant*

2, 3 **And a certain centurion's servant,**—A "centurion" was
a Roman officer commanding a hundred men. This one was
probably in the service of Herod Antipas, and stationed at
Capernaum as an important provincial town and a place of
considerable traffic on the Sea of Galilee, to preserve order
there and in the adjacent country. Matthew tells us that he
was a gentile (Matt. 8: 10), but he seems to have been very
strongly attached to the Jewish nation. He may have been a
proselyte to the Jewish faith; he would be called a "proselyte
of the gate," one who lived among the Jewish people and conformed to what were called the seven precepts of Noah, which
prohibited blasphemy, idolatry, murder, robbery, rebellion,
and eating of blood and things strangled. Those who submitted to circumcision and became naturalized Jews were termed
"proselytes of righteousness." The New Testament mentions
three other centurions, and all of them are favorably mentioned. (Luke 23: 47; Acts 10: 1; 27: 1, 3, 43.) His servant
was sick and "at the point of death." This servant was very
dear to the centurion. Matthew reports the servant as being
grievously tormented.

And when he heard concerning Jesus,—He heard of the miraculous power of Jesus and "sent unto him elders of the
Jews." They were persons who were elders or magistrates of
the city; they may have been officers of the synagogue which
this centurion had built. The term "elder" was first applied
to men of age (Gen. 24: 2; 50: 7); and as persons of right age
and experience would naturally be called to the management
of public affairs (Josh. 24: 31), it afterwards became an
official title (Ex. 3: 16; 4: 29; 19: 7; 24: 1, 9). The office grew
out of the patriarchal system. Matthew makes no mention of
the elders of the Jews coming to Jesus. It may be that the
centurion followed the elders, or what he did through his rep-
resentatives may be said of himself as doing.

ing, He is worthy that thou shouldest do this for him; 5 for he loveth our
nation, and himself built us our synagogue. 6 And Jesus went with them.
And when he was now not far from the house, the centurion sent friends to
him, saying unto him, Lord, trouble not thyself; for I am not ²worthy that
thou shouldest come under my roof: 7 wherefore neither thought I myself
worthy to come unto thee: but say ³the word, and my ⁴servant shall be
healed. 8 For I also am a man set under authority, having under myself
soldiers: and I say to this one, Go, and he goeth; and to another, Come, and
he cometh; and to my ¹servant, Do this, and he doeth it. 9 And when Jesus
heard these things, he marvelled at him, and turned and said unto the multitude that followed him, I say unto you, I have not found so great faith, no,

²Gr. *sufficient*
³Gr. *with a word*
⁴Or, *boy*

4, 5 **And they, when they came to Jesus,**—The elders were
very urgent in their request that Jesus go as quickly as possible to the centurion's house. They give as their reason that
he was "worthy" that Jesus should do this for him. The Jews
pleaded the worthiness of the centurion, but the centurion declared his own unworthiness; truly greatness and humility go
together. The elders of the Jews wanted to repay him for
what he had done in building a synagogue for them. This
centurion had built a synagogue at his own expense. Every
town where there were Jews had its synagogue.

6, 7 **And Jesus went with them.**—Messengers were sent in
succession to an important person of whom a favor was desired, making the request in varied form with many expressions of humility in the East. Even when it was known that
the request would be granted, it was customary to send again,
urging the great one not to put himself to trouble, and offering apologies and expression of unworthiness. So the centurion followed this custom; he sent his friends to Jesus, saying: "Lord, trouble not thyself; for I am not worthy that thou
shouldest come under my roof."

8-10 **For I also am a man set under authority,**—Being a centurion this man would be under the authority of higher
officials, as the centurion had command of only one hundred
soldiers; however, he could say to those under him: "Go, and
he goeth; and to another, Come, and he cometh." He could
command his servants to do anything that he wished done,
and they would do it. This centurion appears to have regarded the sickness of his servant either as due to some pecu-

not in Israel. 10 And they that were sent, returning to the house, found the
¹servant whole.

liar state of body or to demons, which were under the authority of Jesus, precisely as the centurion's soldiers were subject
to his order.   It is remarkable that while Matthew calls the
disease "palsy," Luke, a physician, does not name the disease.

I have not found so great faith,—When Jesus heard what
the centurion had said about commanding and having it done,
he turned to the multitude that was following him and said: "I
have not found so great faith, no, not in Israel."   These words
were spoken to the Jews who followed Jesus.   The centurion,
a Gentile and a military man, Jesus commended as having
greater faith than anyone he had found among God's chosen
people.   This is the first recorded instance of faith in Christ's
power to heal at a distance; this great faith was not found in
some favored Israelite, but in one far less privileged and favored, a Gentile.   When those who had been sent to Jesus returned, they "found the servant whole."   Jesus had healed or
restored to health the servant as the centurion had requested.

12. RAISING THE SON OF THE WIDOW OF NAIN
7: 11-17

11 And it came to pass ⁵soon afterwards, that he went to a city called
⁵Many ancient authorities read *on the next day*

11 And it came to pass soon afterwards,—Soon after the
restoration of the centurion's servant in Capernaum, Jesus
and his disciples and the great multitude went to the city
"called Nain."   "Nain" is not used anywhere else in the Bible;
its exact location has not been determined.   Many think that
it was on the northern slope of Mount Hermon, immediately
west of Endor, which lies in a further recess of the same range
of mountains.   It was probably about twelve or fifteen miles
from Capernaum.   Luke is the only writer of the gospel that
records this miracle, as John is the only one that records the
miracle of raising Lazarus from the dead.   We do not know
why others omitted the record of this miracle.   Jesus was on

Nain; and his disciples went with him, and a great multitude. 12 Now when he drew near to the gate of the city, behold, there was carried out one that was dead, the only son of his mother, and she was a widow and much people of the city was with her. 13 And when the Lord saw her, he had compassion on her, and said unto her, Weep not. 14 And he came nigh and touched the bier: and the bearers stood still. And he said, Young man, I

---

one of his preaching tours through Galilee when he went to Nain.

12 **Now when he drew near to the gate of the city,**—This small town was a walled city, hence the "gate" of entrance to it. Most of the towns and villages were walled for protection. As Jesus and his company came near to the gate, "there was carried out one that was dead." The burial of bodies within the town or city was forbidden, hence the sepulchers and tombs were located without the limits of the cities and villages. Luke describes very minutely the scene; it was a "funeral procession" of "the only son of his mother" and this mother "was a widow."

13 **And when the Lord saw her,**—It is significant that the "Lord saw her"; no bereaved heart or contrite spirit ever escaped his attention. It seems that Jesus and his disciples with a multitude following him were going into the city of Nain and met the funeral procession as it came out of the city. It is very probable that this mother had never seen Jesus before; he was a stranger to her so far as we know, and yet when he saw her he said in his compassion for her, "Weep not." The sympathies of Jesus are in full and lively exercise for this bereaved mother. The word translated "weep" is that which denotes the outward expression of grief. The people in the East gave vent to their sorrow in loud shrieks and lamentations over the bodies of the dead. Oftentimes they employed persons whose office it was to sing dirges and utter dolorous groans and lamentations; they were "professional mourners." The louder they would groan and shriek the greater was the grief supposed to be. It is not known whether there were such "professional mourners" in this funeral procession that Jesus met.

14 **And he came nigh and touched the bier:**—"The bier" was an open frame upon which the dead body, wrapped in

say unto thee, Arise. 15 And he that was dead sat up, and began to speak.

folds of linen, was placed and carried on the shoulders of four, and sometimes six persons, to the grave or tomb. Jesus touched the bier as a signal for the bearers to stand still. "The bearers stood still." There must have been a dignity and air of authority in our Lord to stop in this way the procession of such a solemn occasion by a simple gesture, or the mere laying his hand upon the bier. When the bearers stopped Jesus simply said: "Young man, I say unto thee, Arise." The authority and power with which Jesus spoke should be observed. There are three records of Jesus' raising the dead. The first is the raising of the daughter of Jairus (Matt. 9: 18, 19, 23-26; Mark 5: 22-24, 35-43; Luke 8: 41, 42, 49-56); the widow's son (Luke 7: 11-17); and the raising of Lazarus (John 11: 35-53). In all of these miracles Jesus' authority is expressed by "Damsel, I say unto thee, Arise"; "Young man, I say unto thee, Arise"; and "Lazarus, come forth." All of these forms are expressive of our Lord's power to perform the act.

There are seven instances of restoration to life recorded in the Bible: (1) the child of the widow of Zarephath (1 Kings 17: 22); (2) son of the Shunammite woman (2 Kings 4: 33-36); (3) the case of a man raised by touching Elisha's bones (2 Kings 13: 21); (4) Jairus' daughter (Matt. 9: 18, 19, 23-26; (5) the widow's son (Luke 7: 11-17); (6) the raising of Lazarus (John 11: 35-53); and (7) Tabitha or Dorcas by Peter (Acts 9: 36-42). Our Lord's resurrection differs from all these; these all died again, but Jesus arose never to die again.

15 **And he that was dead sat up,**—The young man that was dead obeyed the voice of Jesus and sat up and began to speak. His speaking proved the reality of the raising from the dead to the large company. It should be recalled that Jesus and his disciples were present and a great multitude had followed them; again there was a great multitude that waas following the funeral procession; putting these two large groups together, we have many witnesses to this resurrection. In no case where the dead were restored to life does the Bible tell us what they said; their experience and their knowledge of any-

And he gave him to his mother. 16 And fear took hold on all: and the glorified God, saying, A great prophet is arisen among us: and, God hath visited his people. 17 And this report went forth concerning him in the whole of Judæa, and all the region round about.

thing beyond death are withheld from us. The body was in full view and there was no possible chance for deception in this case. It is a beautiful touch of sympathy described by Luke when he reports that Jesus "gave him to his mother."

16, 17 **And fear took hold on all:**—The people were filled with awe, and praised God for what they had seen. In their praise they said: "A great prophet is arisen among us; and, God hath visited his people." They at once recalled Elijah and Elisha and declared that a great prophet like these had arisen "among us," and that God had visited his people again with a prophet. It had been about four hundred years since the prophets ceased to bring God's message to the people.

And this report went forth concerning him—Such a miracle would be reported quickly and would have a wide circulation; the whole country would ring with the many accounts and rumors of his work. All Galilee, Samaria, and Judea would be talking of this great prophet and of his wonderful power. With the rumor would go the probability that this prophet was the Messiah himself. The crowds that witnessed this would help to norate the report. One crowd followed Jesus and another was following the bier and friends of the widow and her son; both crowds help to broadcast the great miracle which they had witnessed.

13. JESUS COMMENDING JOHN THE BAPTIST
7: 18-35

18 And the disciples of John told him of all these things. 19 And John

18 **And the disciples of John told him**—A parallel of this is found in Matt. 11: 2-19. The whole country was in excitement over Jesus; the report of his wonderful works had reached the ears of both his enemies and his friends. The disciples of John the Baptist learned of the increased fame of

calling unto him ⁿtwo of his disciples sent them to the Lord, saying, Art thou he that cometh, or look we for another? 20 And when the men were come unto him, they said, John the Baptist hath sent us unto thee, saying, Art thou he that cometh, or look we for another? 21 In that hour he cured

ⁿGr. *certain two*

Jesus from the reports that went out. John had been cast in prison; we do not know just how long he had been in prison, but his disciples found a way of telling John while he was in prison at Machaerus about the works and fame of this new prophet who seemed to outstrip John himself.

19 **And John calling unto him two of his disciples**—John was at this time in prison, but his disciples seemed to have had free access to him; so far as Luke's account is concerned we would not know that John was in prison; we learn this from Matthew. John was probably seventy miles away from the place where Jesus was preaching and in prison. We do not know what his purpose was in sending two of his disciples to Jesus; some think that John was in doubt; others think that he sent his disciples to Jesus that they might be strengthened in their faith. John had designated Jesus to his disciples as the Lamb of God that taketh away the sin of the world (John 1: 29.) It matters not whether John sent these disciples to relieve his own doubts or those of his disciples; the fact remains that he sent two of them to ask Jesus: "Art thou he that cometh, or look we for another?"

20 **And when the men were come unto him,**—Since John was in prison at Machaerus, fifteen miles southeast from the northern extremity of the Dead Sea, and about seventy miles from the cities on the Sea of Galilee, it would take these two disciples of John several days to bring the message from John to Jesus. They were faithful to the trust imposed upon them, and came directly to Jesus and reported that they were messengers from John the Baptist and that John had propounded the question. The question was: "Art thou the coming one, the Messiah, or should we look for another?" The Greek implies by another, one of a different kind. The point in John's mind seems to have been—it is time for the Messiah.

21 **In that hour he cured many of diseases**—In the presence

many of diseases and [7]plagues and evil spirits; and on many that were blind he bestowed sight. 22 And he answered and said unto them, Go and tell John the things which ye have seen and heard; the blind receive their sight, the lame walk, the lepers are cleansed, and the deaf hear, the dead are raised up, the poor have [8]good tidings preached to them. 23 And blessed is he, whosoever shall find no occasion of stumbling in me.

[7]Gr. *scourges*
[8]Or, *the gospel*

of these two disciples that John had sent Jesus "cured many of diseases and plagues and evil spirits." The disciples of John witnessed all of these miracles. Jesus cured diseases of ordinary kind, such as plagues and scourges, which meant diseases that were believed to be sent as special punishments from God. He cast out evil spirits and restored sight to many that were blind. Luke, as a physician, carefully divides the diseased into three classes, and distinguishes each of these from the blind. The three classes are "diseases and plagues and evil spirits."

22, 23 **And he answered and said unto them,**—Jesus gave a very emphatic answer to the messengers of John; they were to report to John what they had seen and heard. There was no mustering of military forces; no gathering of armies; no training of men for carnal war; no preparation for breaking down the towers of the Herods of that day and releasing his prisoners at the point of his conquering sword; no amassing of wealth to finance any great movement. But there was every demonstration of tender sympathy with human woes and of miraculous power, stooping low to touch the blind, the lame, the leper, the deaf, and the dead. The only detailed account of raising the dead in the ministry of Jesus up to this time is that of the widow's son and, possibly, according to a few historians, of Jairus' daughter; but we do not know how many cases of raising the dead there were that are mentioned. We know that many miracles were performed by Jesus of which we have no detailed account. (John 21: 25.) As great as these things were, the greatest spiritual miracle, which is the climax of this list of marvelous works and of evidence, was the poor "have good tidings preached to them."

24, 25 **And when the messengers of John were departed,**— Jesus began his eulogy of John so soon as the messengers of

24 And when the messengers of John were departed, he began to say unto the multitudes concerning John, What went ye out into the wilderness to behold? a reed shaken with the wind? 25 But what went ye out to see? a man clothed in soft raiment? Behold, they that are gorgeously apparalled, and live delicately, are in kings' courts. 26 But what went ye out to see? a

John left. He began by asking some vivid questions about the interest of the people in John. Matthew records the same questions (11: 7, 8). Jesus' testimony concerning John is one of those tender, earnest, and exquisitely beautiful utterances of our Lord that sparkles like diamonds in the twilight. This testimony is reserved until after John's messengers have gone that it may not seem to be words of compliment so common in speeches of flattery. John's work was done chiefly in the wilderness of Judea; hence the people went out there to hear him. Jesus asked them if they went out to see "a reed shaken with the wind?" The "reed" was a tall, slender plant, easily shaken about by the wind; it grew in abundance along the Jordan where John baptized. John was no slender, trifling character blown about by every new doctrine; he was no delicate, spiritual character, merely amusing himself by turning himself into a preacher; he was more like the sturdy oak which cannot be moved so easily.

But what went ye out to see?—This is another one of those questions which Jesus asked about John; it helped to drive home the answer that Jesus gave to it. John was no man clothed in soft raiment; he was clothed in a garment of rough "camel's hair, and a leathern girdle about his loins." (Matt. 3: 4.) He was not clothed in fine raiment, neither did he seek any "soft, easy" places, but his work was done in the wilderness. He did not live in luxury and was not dressed in gorgeous apparel. Luke adds "in kings' courts"; John did not live in idle ease in the palace of kings. His work and manner of dress belonged to the sturdy yeomanry of the wilderness, and those who came out of the cities to hear him.

26, 27 But what went ye out to see? a prophet?—If the people did not go out to see a person living in luxury and dressed in fine apparel, that is, an effeminate person, then what did they expect to find? Anticipating their reply he asks: "A

prophet? Yea, I say unto you, and much more than a prophet. 27 This is
he of whom it is written,

> [9]Behold, I send my messenger before thy face,
> Who shall prepare thy way before thee.

28 I say unto you, Among them that are born of women there is none
greater than John: yet he that is [10]but little in the kingdom of God is greater
than he. 29 And all the people when they heard, and the [11]publicans, justified God, [1]being baptized with the baptism of John. 30 But the Pharisees and

---

[9]Mal. 3.1
[10]Gr. *lesser*
[11]See marginal note on ch. 3.12
[1]Or, *having been*

---

prophet?" A "prophet" was not only one who foretold future
events, but also one who was divinely commissioned as a religious teacher, or who would instruct men as to the will of
God. John was more than an ordinary prophet; he had a
message far different from that of any prophet; he had a work
far different from the work that any prophet had done. All
the people accepted John as a prophet (Luke 20: 6), but Jesus
ranked John far higher than a prophet. John was the special
messenger (Mal. 3: 1) to get the people ready for the coming
of Christ; therefore he was much more than a prophet; he
was the great forerunner of the Messiah. Jesus here points
John out as the one who fulfilled the prophecy uttered by Malachi. The word "prophet" in the original means to "speak
before, in front of, in behalf of, or for another."

28 **I say unto you, Among them that are born**—Jesus here
means to say that there is none greater than John the Baptist;
none enjoyed the distinction that he enjoyed; his relative position to the Messiah placed him far above everyone else who
had lived on the earth. This does not mean that John ex-
celled all others in piety and purity of character; it only
means that the position John held and his relation to Jesus as
the Messiah placed him out of the class of all others. Jesus
adds, "Yet he that is but little in the kingdom of God is
greater than he."

29 **And all the people when they heard,**—Matthew does not
record this verse; Luke throws in a brief allusion to the effect
of these teachings on his hearers. Many think that verses 29
and 20 belong to the language of Jesus; others think that
Luke adds these verses to the speech of Jesus. They do not

the lawyers rejected for themselves the counsel of God, [2]being not baptized of him. 31 Whereunto then shall I liken the men of this generation, and to what are they like? 32 They are like unto children that sit in the market-place, and call one to another; who say, We piped unto you, and ye did not

[2]Or, *not having been*

seem to belong to the discourse of Jesus; their whole diction and form are historical. However, they show the success of John's ministry. The people who heard and the publicans "justified God" by being baptized with the baptism of John. In the strictest sense no one can make God more just than he is, since he is infinitely just; it means that the people perceived, confessed, and declared God's justice in all of his acts among men. These had been prepared to make this confession as they had been baptized of John, and must have openly confessed their sins.

30 **But the Pharisees and the lawyers**—There were two classes, Pharisees and lawyers, not included among the first two classes mentioned above, the people and the publicans, who did not join in praising God, but "rejected for themselves the counsel of God, being not baptized of him." These Pharisees and lawyers thwarted the good purpose of God toward them by refusing to submit to John's baptism. They did not confess their sins, and hence were not baptized by John. They annulled God's purposes of grace so far as they applied to them. Had they submitted to John's baptism they would have received God's blessings, because they would have been carrying out God's purpose with them. "Pharisees" were a sect of religionists who were strict conformists to the traditions of the fathers; "lawyers" were those who were well informed in the traditions of the fathers and the law of Moses; both classes were teachers of the people. They set the example of disobedience to God.

31-35 **Whereunto then shall I liken the men**—Here again Jesus asks some pointed questions to stimulate an interest in what he is about to say; he does this to make his answers the more emphatic. He answered his own questions by saying that they were "like unto children that sit in the marketplace,

dance; we wailed, and ye did not weep. 33 For John the Baptist is come eating no bread nor drinking wine; and ye say, He hath a demon. 34 The Son of man is come eating and drinking; and ye say, Behold, a gluttonous man, and a winebibber, a friend of ³publicans and sinners! 35 And wisdom ⁴is justified of all her children.

³See marginal note on ch. 3.12
⁴Or, *was*

and call one to another." His illustration here was familiar to the people. The market place was open like our modern city squares, where people trade, hear the news, and the children have their games and sports. The Jews at this time were as foolish and perverse and hard to please as a lot of children at play, calling one to another in the market place, "We piped unto you, and ye did not dance"; that is, they played on the pipe as at a wedding, but they would not respond. The children were imitating a marriage procession or feast in their play, but some of them refused to respond. Jesus changed the figure; the children first imitated the glad wedding march, but some of them would not play; then they went to the extreme and imiated a funeral procession, and some would not play that either; they were contrary and would not respond to either play. Jesus says that these Jews were like these children playing in the market place.

For John the Baptist is come—Jesus made his own application; the point of his illustrations was the unreasonableness common to children and to childish men. John the Baptist came among them with very abstemious habits—his food not bread, but locusts and wild honey; his drink not wine, but probably cold water. They could not bear that, for they said, "He hath a demon"; that is, no man would live as he lived if he were not possessed with a demon. "The Son of man" came "eating and drinking" like the most of men, but this did not suit them any better; they railed at him and said: "Behold, a gluttonous man, and a winebibber, a friend of publicans and sinners!" Neither mode of life would satisfy them; they were sulky, sour, and as unreasonable as a group of disagreeable children.

14. JESUS ANOINTED BY A SINFUL WOMAN
7: 36-50

36 And one of the Pharisees desired him that he would eat with him. And he entered into the Pharisee's house, and *sat down to meat. 37 And behold, a woman who was in the city, a sinner; and when she knew that he was *sitting at meat in the Pharisee's house, she brought *an alabaster cruse

⁵Or, *reclined at table*
⁶Or, *reclining at table*
⁷Or, *a flask*

36 **And one of the Pharisees desired him**—Luke gives the only record we have of this incident. He records two other incidences of Pharisees who invited Jesus to meals and he alone gives them. (Luke 11: 37; 14: 1.) Jesus would dine with a Pharisee or with a publican (Matt. 9: 10; Mark 2: 15; Luke 5: 29), and he even invited himself to be the guest of Zaccheus who was a publican (Luke 19: 5). In this account two characters are brought together; they are not only diverse, but strongly contrasted. Valuable lessons may be learned from these two opposite characters. Jesus accepted the invitation to eat with this Pharisee. This Pharisee seems not to have been as hostile toward Jesus as many other Pharisees were; there is no evidence that he invited Jesus to his table to do him harm.

37, 38 **And behold, a woman who was in the city,**—It is probable that this woman was from Capernaum. There has been much speculation as to who this woman was. Some have thought that she was Mary Magdalene, others that she was Mary of Bethany, the sister of Lazarus. In some respects this account is similar to the anointing of Jesus by Mary as narrated in Matt. 26: 7; Mark 14: 3; and John 12: 3, but this does not seem to be an account of the same event. The name of the Pharisee who entertained Jesus happens to be the same in both instances; however, the Simon of Bethany was a very different man from the one here mentioned. Nor can this woman, who seems to have been of a notoriously bad reputation, be identical with the Mary of Bethany who had sat at Jesus' feet, and by her gentle confiding love and won so strong a hold upon his affections. (Luke 10: 38-42.) These incidents must have been two distinct events.

of ointment, 38 and standing behind at his feet, weeping, she began to wet his feet with her tears, and wiped them with the hair of her head, and °kissed his feet, and anointed them with the ointment. 39 Now when the Pharisee that had bidden him saw it, he spake within himself, saying, This man, if he were °a prophet, would have perceived who and what manner of woman this is

°Gr. *kissed much*
°Some ancient authorities read *the prophet.* See Jn. 1.21, 25

and when she knew that he was sitting at meat—It was the custom at that time for the guests to remove the sandals before the meal and recline on the left elbow or side with the feet outward from the table. They did not have the custom of sitting in chairs as we have today. It was also customary for anyone to come into the house during a feast and sit and converse with those who were invited to the feast; the invited guests reclined at the table, while the uninvited guests sat around the wall. This woman brought an "alabaster cruse of ointment," and anointed the feet of Jesus. It seems that she was standing behind his feet weeping, and was drawn irresistibly by gratitude to Jesus and "wet his feet with her tears, and wiped them with the hair of her head." It was regarded among the Jews as a shameful thing for a woman to let down her hair in public but she made this sacrifice because of her affection for Jesus.

39 **Now when the Pharisee that had bidden him**—The emphasis is put here on "the Pharisee"; he had invited Jesus to come into his house and dine with him; Jesus had accepted the invitation and the penitent woman had approached Jesus and paid great honor and respect to him. The Pharisee had witnessed the whole affair and was "saying" "within himself" that Jesus was not a prophet as he claimed to be. Thoughts passed through his mind, or he reasoned with himself that Jesus could not be a prophet. He had already reached the conclusion that Jesus was not a prophet; if he had been one, as he claimed to be, he would have known "who and what manner of woman this is that toucheth him." This woman was regarded as a great sinner; she was notorious in person and character. Surely if Jesus had known who she was, the Pharisee reasoned, he would not have permitted her to have touched him. For a woman of such abandoned character to

that toucheth him, that she is a sinner. **40 And Jesus answering said unto him, Simon, I have somewhat to say unto thee. And he saith, Teacher, say on. 41 A certain lender had two debtors: the one owed five hundred** [10]**shillings, and the other fifty. 42 When they had not** *wherewith* **to pay, he forgave them both. Which of them therefore will love him most? 43 Simon**

---

[10]The word in the Greed denotes a coin worth about eight pence half-penny, or nearly seventeen cents

---

touch one was regarded as the highest species of defilement. The Pharisee thought that Jesus did not know her character, or he would never have permitted her to touch him, much less to remain at his feet kissing them and continuing to express her love for him by such demonstrations. His reasoning was fallacious.

40 And Jesus answering said unto him,—The Pharisee had concluded that Jesus was not a prophet, because he did not know the life and character of this woman; he had not spoken aloud on this point; he had only reasoned with himself. But Jesus now does the very thing which the Pharisee considered as a mark or characteristic of a prophet—he reads the mind of the Pharisee. Jesus spoke directly to him; he addressed him as "Simon," and then stated emphatically that he had something to say to him. The Pharisee is very brief and emphatic in his reply; he said: "Teacher, say on." Jesus answers the thoughts and doubts of Simon and shows that he knows about Simon's thoughts and therefore knows all about this woman; there is a kind of Socratic irony in the speech of Jesus.

41, 42 A certain lender had two debtors:—A lender of money for interest is here meant as the original shows. The parable which Jesus now proposed for the instruction of this self-righteous Pharisee is based on well-known facts. This lender of money for interest "had two debtors"; the first one owed him "five hundred shillings," while the second one only owed him "fifty." The term used here is "denarius," which was the chief silver coin of the Romans at this time, and of the value of about seventeen cents. It was the rate of wages for a day's work. Five hundred would amount to about eighty-five dollars, while fifty would amount to eight dollars and fifty cents; hence expressed in our values one of these debtors

answered and said, He, I suppose, to whom he forgave the most. And he
said unto him, Thou hast rightly judged. 44 And turning to the woman, he
said unto Simon, Seest thou this woman? I entered into thy house, thou
gavest me no water for my feet: but she hath wetted my feet with her tears,
and wiped them with her hair. 45 Thou gavest me no kiss: but she, since

owed eighty-five dollars and the other owed eight dollars and
fifty cents.

When they had not wherewith to pay,—Neither one of
these debtors could pay the lender the amount owed him; the
lender, out of the kindness and generosity of his heart, released them of their indebtedness. Favor, kindness, benevolence, compassion, and sympathy are the sole basis of the act,
all merit on the part of the recipient being excluded. After
presenting this parable in its simplicity to the Pharisee, Jesus
asked him: "Which of them therefore will love him most?"
Jesus by this question forces the Pharisee to draw the only
conclusion that was possible to draw from the parable, and
then Jesus makes the application. The point of the parable
then is the attitude of the two debtors toward the lender who
forgave both of them.

43 **Simon answered and said,**—It seems that Simon began to
see the point that Jesus was making; hence he said, "He, I
suppose, to whom he forgave the most." The Pharisee's reply
indicates a descent from his lofty and arrogant tone to one of
more humility. Simon saw how his answer would convict
himself as he had perceived in part the drift of the illustration.
Jesus did not leave him in doubt as to what he had said; he
replied to Simon: "Thou hast rightly judged." This was the
end of the argument; there was nothing further to say.
Leaving the matter thus as did Jesus made the point more
emphatic.

44-46 **And turning to the woman,**—Jesus now directed Simon's attention to the woman who had bestowed such gracious favors upon him. It seems that this was the first time
that Jesus looked at the woman, and he asks the Pharisee to
look at her; she was behind Jesus, hence he would have to turn
to look at her. Jesus was an invited guest; the Pharisee had
neglected some points of common and customary hospitality;
the contrasts here made, scholars tell us, have the rhythm of

the time I came in, hath not ceased to [11]kiss my feet. 46 My head with oil thou didst not anoint: but she hath anointed my feet with ointment. 47 Wherefore I say unto thee, Her sins, which are many, are forgiven; for she loved much: but to whom little is forgiven, *the same* loveth little. 48 And he said unto her, Thy sins are forgiven. 49 And they that [12]sat at meat with

[11]Gr. *kiss much*
[12]Gr. *reclined*

Hebrew poetry; in each contrast the first word is the point of defect in Simon's conduct toward Jesus. "Water," "kiss," and "oil" are the points of emphasis. The water which Simon had failed to give was supplied by the tears of the woman; the failure of Simon to show affection for his guest was supplied by the kisses of the woman; and the failure of Simon to honor his guest was supplied by the precious oil with which she anointed the feet of Jesus. Simon had failed as a host to anoint the head of Jesus, the nobler part, with ordinary oil, but the woman had anointed his feet with costly oil. This penitent, sinful woman had done far more for Jesus than had the Pharisee; it was expected of the Pharisee to show such acts of customary honor to Jesus as his guest, but it was not expected of this woman to bestow any acts of honor upon him.

47, 48 **Wherefore I say unto thee,**—Jesus now turns from Simon and speaks to the woman; this seems to be the first time that he has spoken to her. "Wherefore" introduces the conclusion which is drawn from what has been said. Jesus says, "Her sins, which are many, are forgiven." Here Jesus shows that he knew her condition, and that the Pharisee had misjudged him and his ability to know the hearts of people. Jesus not only refers to her public and scandalous sins, but to all which she had ever committed. His forgiveness is most ample, covering the sins of a whole life. Jesus gave the reason for his forgiving her. "For she loved much" is the assuring statement that Jesus made. All that she had done for Jesus showed her love for him; her coming to Jesus showed her consciousness of a need of a Savior; Jesus' words to her showed that he was willing to save. Jesus then stated the conclusion from his parable by saying: "But to whom little is forgiven, the same loveth little."

him began to say [13]within themselves, Who is this that even forgiveth sins?
50 And he said unto the woman, Thy faith hath saved thee; go in peace.

[13]Or, *among*

49, 50 And they that sat at meat with him—The friends of
the Pharisee who sat at meat with Jesus began to reason with
themselves and made inquiry of their own hearts as to who
this man was. They thought that he was presumptuous to
claim to forgive sins; they did not speak aloud or speak to
each other, but they were unanimous in their conclusion that
he was a presumptuous sinner. Perhaps their surprise was
expressed in their faces. Jesus without answering them or
their thoughts changed the form of his address to the woman,
perhaps that she might not be misled into thinking that her
acts of devotion were misjudged. Jesus said to her: "Thy
faith hath saved thee; go in peace." This shows that Jesus
knew the full condition of her heart; he knew her life; he
knew her faith in him. Jesus ignored the old question which
the Pharisaic mind raised about his claim to forgive sins; he
had fully answered them, and had taught them an important
lesson. They were not disposed to receive the lesson. There
was a wide contrast in the faith of this woman and the lack of
faith on the part of the Pharisee; the width between these two
is emphasized in the contrast between what the woman did
for him and what the Pharisee had failed to do.

15. THE MINISTERING WOMEN
8: 1-3

1 And it came to pass soon afterwards, that he went about through cities
and villages, preaching and bringing the [14]good tidings of the kingdom of

[14]Or, *gospel*

And it came to pass soon afterwards,—Luke is the only writer that gives an account of these events. From the account
of the forgiven woman (7: 45-50), Luke naturally goes on to
narrate the ministering of other women to Jesus during the
preaching tour that was made about this time. Soon after the
events recorded in chapter 7 Jesus "went about through cities

God, and with him twelve, 2 and certain women who had been healed of
evil spirits and infirmities: Mary that was called Magdalene, from whom

---

and villages, preaching and bringing the good tidings of the
kingdom of God." "Soon afterwards" means "in the order" or
"succession"; the same word is used in Luke 1: 3, and is rendered "in order," and means "in close succession." This is
probably the second tour that Jesus made through Galilee.
He went "about through cities and villages" on this circuit.
He took city by city and village by village on this tour. Luke
in this brief paragraph covers the entire circuit. The first circuit may be referred to in Luke 4: 42-44, and more definitely
in Matt. 4: 23-25 and Mark 1: 35-39, before the formal selection of the twelve. This second circuit is mentioned only by
Luke and was made after the twelve apostles were chosen. A
third circuit in Galilee seems to be referred to in Matt. 11: 1
and Mark 6: 6, though it is not certain that there were three
distinct circuits in Galilee. The purpose of Jesus in traveling
through the cities and villages was to preach and bring the
good tidings of the kingdom of God to the attention of the
people.

2 and certain women who had been healed—These women
are referred to again in Luke 23: 55; 24: 10; and the names of
some are given in Matt. 27: 56 and Mark 15: 40. They seem
to have been attached to the company of Jesus and his disciples; they were very grateful for the remarkable cures that
they had received. The first mentioned is "Mary that was
called Magdalene"; she is the one out of whom Jesus had cast
seven demons. This fact is stated also in Mark 16: 9. The
presence of seven demons in one person indicates special ma-
lignity. (Mark 5: 9.) See Matthew (12: 45) for the parable
of the demon who came back with seven other demons worse
than the first. It is not known where Magdala was, from
whence Mary gets part of her name. There is no valid reason
for identifying her with the sinful woman in chapter 7. She
was terribly afflicted with demons and Jesus cured her. She
was truly grateful to him and showed her gratitude by ministering to him.

seven demons had gone out, 3 and Joanna the wife of Chuzas Herod's steward, and Susanna, and many others, who ministered unto [15]them of their substance.

[15]Many ancient authorities read *him*

3 **and Joanna the wife of Chuzas Herod's steward,**—Joanna
is mentioned here as the wife of Chuzas who was steward of
Herod; some think that he was a nobleman (John 4: 46-53)
who believed on Jesus and all of his house. It is notable that
Jesus had a disciple from the household of Herod Antipas
who had such curiosity to see and hear him; again there was
later Manaen, "the foster-brother of Herod the tetrarch," who
was a disciple . (Acts 13: 1.) Joanna is mentioned again with
Mary Magdalene in Luke 24: 10. These women with "many
others" ministered unto Jesus and his company. The very
fact that Jesus now had twelve men going with him called for
help from others, and these women of means responded to the
demand. They ministered with "their substance." They ministered with the things which belonged to them; their gratitude and zeal were such that they were willing to do everything that they could to help Jesus and his company. They
were benevolent, full of good deeds, and gentle ministrations.
Through the gratitude for blessings received these women
contributed freely to the necessities of Jesus. They appear
again in the scenes at and after his crucifixion; they provided
costly spices for his body after his death; they may be classed
with the godly women who "adorn themselves in modest apparel, with shamefastness and sobriety; not with braided hair,
and gold or pearls or costly raiment; but (which becometh
women professing godliness) through good works." (1 Tim.
2: 9, 10.)

16. THE PARABLE OF THE SOWER
8: 4-18

4 And when a great multitude came together, and they of every city re-

4 **And when a great multitude came together,**—Parallel accounts of the "parable of the sower" are found in Matt. 13:
3-23 and Mark 4: 3-25. A study of all these records will show
that Mark has the fullest account in detail, and that Luke has

sorted unto him, he spake by a parable: 5 The sower went forth to sow his
seed: and as he sowed, some fell by the way side; and it was trodden under

the least number of details. The great points of the parable
are found in all, and yet the three accounts should be studied
in order to obtain a clear and connected view of this important scripture. A fuller comment on this parable may be had in
the author's "Commentary on the Gospel According to Matthew," pages 285-295. Mark and Luke place this parable before the stilling of the tempest, the cure of the demoniacs of
Gadara, and the raising of Jairus' daughter; this seems to be
the correct chronological order for it. When a great multitude came together, and especially "they of every city resorted unto him," Jesus taught "by a parable." This multitude may have come together as a result of his "preaching"
circuit mentioned in verses 1-3. The parable was a very easy
and simple style of teaching. Mark uses "parables" as does
Matthew (13: 3; Mark 4: 2), while Luke uses "a parable."
There are ten of these parables in Matthew and Mark, but
only two recorded in Luke; Luke uses the expression "in parables" in verse 10.

5 **The sower went forth to sow his seed:**—The scene described here was very familiar to the hearers of Jesus. The
sower went out from his house, from the village or city into
his field or country to sow his seed. The time is indefinite,
but the fact was of common occurrence. It may be that a
sower was present or near at hand in a field, making the preparation for the sowing of his seed; this would make the parable more striking and impressive. Some of the seed fell "by
the way side." Fields were very commonly unenclosed, or
separated only by a narrow footpath. The ordinary roads also
were not fenced; hence the seed of the sower was liable to fall
beyond the plowed ground upon the hard ground, path or
road which formed the "way side." The seed was thus exposed to a double danger. "It was trodden under foot" by
those who passed along and "the birds of the heaven devoured
it." The birds, such as the lark, sparrow, and raven "devoured it."

6 **And other fell on the rock;**—"The rocky ground" (Matt.

foot, and the birds of the heaven devoured it. 6 And other fell on the rock; and as soon as it grew, it withered away, because it had no moisture. 7 And other fell amidst the thorns; and the thorns grew with it, and choked it. 8 And other fell into the good ground, and grew, and brought forth fruit a hundredfold. As he said these things, he cried, He that hath ears to hear, let him hear.

9 And his disciples asked him what this parable might be. And he said,

---

13: 5) was "the rocky places," or the places where the soil was very thin over the rock. The grain sprang up quickly above the surface, and then quickly died; the hot sun soon scorched it and "it withered away, because it had no moisture." There was no chance for the plant to grow, as the soil was not deep enough above the rock, hence it withered away.

7 And other fell amidst the thorns;—This seed fell in the midst of or among the thorns, where the roots of the thorns remained, not having been carefully taken away. When the seed germinated it could not grow because it was choked by the thorns. These thorns stifled the grain by pressing upon it, overtopping it, shading it, and exhausting the soil. Thorny shrubs and plants abounded in Palestine.

8 And other fell into the good ground,—The "good ground" was the rich, deep soil, which was free from rocks, thorns, and hard surface of the wayside. The seed therefore sprang up and brought forth "fruit a hundredfold." Matthew and Mark give the different increase, thirty, sixty, and a hundredfold; Matthew begins with the greatest and descends to the lowest, thirty; while Mark begins with the lowest and ascends to the highest; Luke records only the greatest increase. "Hundredfold" is used with respect to the increase which Isaac received when he sowed in the land of the Philistines. (Gen. 26: 12.) Of the four kinds of soil only one was fruitful. When Jesus presented this parable "he cried" and said: "He that hath ears to hear, let him hear." "He cried," that is, with a loud voice he spoke this last warning to the people; both Matthew and Mark record this statement of Jesus.

9, 10 And his disciples asked him—His disciples asked him the meaning of this parable; they did not ask him what the parable was, for they knew what it was, but did not know its *meaning.* This is one of the parables of Jesus that we need

Unto you it is given to know the mysteries of the kingdom of God: but to the rest in parables; that seeing they may not see, and hearing they may not understand. 11 Now the parable is this: The seed is the word of God. 12

not misunderstand its meaning, for Jesus here gives the meaning of it. His disciples were perplexed over this parable; it was a new mode of teaching for Jesus to use; so when the twelve and a few others were alone (Mark 4: 10) they asked him several questions as to what the meaning of the parable was and why he had spoken in parables. Jesus replied that it was given to them "to know the mysteries of the kingdom of God: but to the rest in parables." He meant to say that his disciples had a desire to know the truth, and that these truths could be understood by them. A similar thought was expressed at another time when Jesus said: "If any man willeth to do his will, he shall know of the teaching." (John 7: 17.) The "mysteries" or secrets, the hidden power of spiritual truth, are revealed to those who sincerely desire to know them. "Mysteries" is from "musterion" and means to close or shut. The disciples had been initiated into the secrets of the kingdom of heaven; so Jesus here explains that this parable is open to the disciples, but shut to the Pharisees with their hostile minds. In the gospels "musterion" is used only here and in the parallel passages. (Matt. 13: 22; Mark 4: 11.) If the truths were explained to those having no heart to receive them, the truths would not be appreciated nor understood; they would tend to harden the heart, and would be as pearls cast before swine.

11 **The seed is the word of God.**—Jesus now proceeds to interpret his own parable. The word of God is the seed of the kingdom; the phrase "the word of God" does not appear in Matthew and only once in Mark (7: 13) and John (10: 35), but four times in Luke (5: 1; 8: 11, 21; 11: 28) and twelve times in Acts. In Mark 4: 14 we have only "the word." In Mark 3: 35 we have "the will of God," and in Matt. 12: 50 "the will of my Father" where Luke 8: 21 has "the word of God." Luke means the word that comes from God. The truths of the gospel mean the same thing as the word of God; hence the same thing as the seed is "the word of God." (1

And those by the way side are they that have heard; then cometh the devil, and taketh away the word from their heart, that they may not believe and be saved. 13 And those on the rock *are* they who, when they have heard, receive the word with joy; and these have no root, who for a while believe, and in time of temptation fall away. 14 And that which fell among the

---

Pet. 1: 23.) The word of God or gospel is preached, people hear it, believe it, and obey it, and are brought into the kingdom of God; hence it is the seed of the kingdom. "Of his own will he brought us forth by the word of truth." (James 1: 18.) "So belief cometh of hearing, and hearing by the word of Christ." (Rom. 10: 17.) "Whosoever believeth that Jesus is the Christ is begotten of God." (1 John 5: 1.) These explain how the word of God is the seed, because it is essential to one's becoming a Christian.

12 **And those by the way side**—This parable has long been known as the "Parable of the Sower," but some in recent years have suggested that a more appropriate name would be the "Parable of Different Soils," and others have called it the "Parable of Different Hearers." The first kind of hearers Jesus represents by those who hear but when they have heard the devil cometh and "taketh away the word from their heart, that they may not believe and be saved." The word of God finds no entrance and Satan taketh it away as a bird picks up the grain which falls by the wayside. These hearers do not care to believe; the word of God is good, the teacher is faithful in preaching it, but the heart is not prepared for it.

13 **And those on the rock**—Other hearers are compared to the thin layer of earth which covers a ledge of stone; seed which fall into such soil spring up quickly because warmed by the underlying rock; but as the roots cannot go to any depth, the blade soon withers beneath the hot sun. Some hearers "receive the word with joy"; they give the impression at first that they will make faithful children of God; "who for a while believe, and in time of temptation fall away." They are impulsive, demonstrative, and ardent for a little while, but when trials and testings come through putting their profession into practice, they give up and go back into the world. They cannot stand persecution and trials; they quickly desert the Christ in the hour of temptation.

thorns, these are they that have heard, and as they go on their way they are choked with cares and riches and pleasures of *this* life, and bring no fruit to perfection. 15 And that in the good ground, these are such as in an honest and good heart, having heard the word, hold it fast, and bring forth fruit with [1]patience.

16 And no man, when he hath lighted a lamp, covereth it with a vessel, or putteth it under a bed; but putteth it on a stand, that they that enter in

[1]Or, *stedfastness*

14 **And that which fell among the thorns,**—Other hearers are compared to seed which fall where thorns are growing; the seed springs into life, but it has no room for development; it is robbed by the thorns of its needed nourishment. So some Christians are so preoccupied by "cares and riches and pleasures of this life" that they "bring no fruit to perfection." They may have some evidence of bearing fruit for a time, but the spiritual fruit is blasted and never comes to rightness or completeness. They have conviction of sin, show signs of sorrow and repentance, but the heart is divided, and the full powers of body and soul are not given to Christ. They are not thoughtless hearers, like those of the first class, neither like those of the second; they hear, hear seriously, enter upon a conflict with the world, but fail to conquer. They are not fully consecrated and hence they let the riches and pleasures of this life draw away their heart from God. Many are in the church today like this class of hearers.

15 **And that in the good ground,**—This class of hearers are like seed which fell on "good ground" and "brought forth fruit a hundredfold." They receive the truth "in an honest and good heart," and patiently and perseveringly they produce in their lives a golden harvest of grain. Of the four kinds of hearts or hearers, only one kind really is profited by the hearing of the word of God. This class with constancy of purpose, with a consistent perseverance, through a life of discouragements and trials "bring forth fruit with patience."

16 **And no man, when he hath lighted a lamp,**—Jesus here uses a very vivid figure; it was contrary to custom, and even to reason, to light a lamp and cover it with a vessel or put it under a bed. Mark 4: 21 has a more definite figure; he uses "under the bushel" as does Matt. 5: 15. The purpose of a

may see the light. 17 For nothing is hid, that shall not be made manifest; nor *anything* secret, that shall not be known and come to light. 18 Take heed therefore how ye hear : for whosoever hath, to him shall be given ; and whosoever hath not, from him shall be taken away even that which he ²thinketh he hath.

²Or, *seemeth to have*

---

light is to enable one to see something else, not the light. Jesus had told his disciples that it was given to them to know "the mysteries of the kingdom of God," but the unbelieving multitude could not know ; hence one reason for his speaking in parables. The apostles might infer that these "mysteries" of the great truths of his kingdom were to be kept secret, and that instruction in parables is, in its very nature, adapted to darken and becloud truth rather than enlighten people. Jesus at this time dispels any such ideas by this figure which he used. It is the nature of truth to enlighten ; if truth darkens, it is the fault of the hearer and not the truth. The truths of the gospel are like the lamp ; they are designed, not to cover up, but to be made known, so as to give light to the world.

17 **For nothing is hid,**—Here Jesus gives the use of his figurative language ; it is to enlighten and instruct. It is not the teaching of Jesus to say that secret sins will be revealed, though that is a truth elsewhere taught ; he teaches here that everything pertaining to the kingdom of God shall be revealed ; nothing shall be kept back that may enlighten and instruct those who are anxious to know. All the truth pertaining to the kingdom of God which was spoken in parables should be revealed and broadcast to the world.

18 **Take heed therefore how ye hear:**—The manner of hearing is important ; Mark 4 : 24 gives the warning to take heed "what ye hear." Putting these two records together, the disciples were to give heed to *how* they heard *what* they heard. They were to take heed how they heard, for now they are hearing for themselves, and for others, since they must teach what they heard to others. The manner of hearing and the matter heard are both supremely important ; some things possibly should not be heard at all ; others that are heard should be forgotten ; still others heard should be treasured and prac-

ticed. Those who had the truth and taught it to others would receive a clearer conception of the truth themselves; "for whatsoever hath, to him shall be given."

17. THE KINDRED OF JESUS
8: 19-21

19 And there came to him his mother and brethren, and they could not come at him for the crowd. 20 And it was told him, Thy mother and thy brethren stand without, desiring to see thee. 21 But he answered and said

---

19 And there came to him his mother and brethren,—Parallel records of this incident are found in Matt. 12: 46-50 and Mark 3: 31-35. The place of this visit is not mentioned, but it is generally supposed that it was in or near Capernaum. "His mother and brethren" came to see him. Both Matthew and Mark place the time of this visit before the speaking of the parable of the sower; usually Luke follows Mark's order, but he does not do so here. At first the brothers of Jesus, who were younger sons of Joseph and Mary, were not unfriendly to the work of Jesus, as seen in John 2: 12, when they with the mother of Jesus are with him and the small group of disciples in Capernaum after the wedding in Cana. But as Jesus went on with his work and was rejected at Nazareth (Luke 4: 16-31), there developed an evident disbelief in his claims on the part of the brothers who ridiculed him six months before the end (John 7: 5). It seems that at this time they had come with Mary to take Jesus home out of the excitement of the crowds, perhaps sharing in the sentiment of others, that he was beside himself. (Mark 3: 21.)

20 And it was told him,—Jesus was in the crowd; he was busy teaching and healing; someone brought him word that his mother and brethren were desiring to speak to him. Who the "brethren" were has caused much discussion. Many think that they were only "cousins" or near relatives, but not "brothers," that is, sons of Mary. Others think that they were sons of Joseph by a former marriage, hence only half brothers in a legal sense. The natural meaning would be that they were his own "brothers." There is no evidence that Mary had no other children, and the easy, natural construc-

unto them, My mother and my brethren are these that hear the word of God, and do it.

---

tion of this and the parallel accounts is that they were his brothers in the flesh. This view must be accepted until some valid objection is established against it.

21 But he answered and said unto them,—Here Jesus makes spiritual ties take precedence above fleshly ties; family ties are at best temporal, but spiritual ties are eternal. Luke gives a very brief statement of Jesus and makes it clear that those who "hear the word of God, and do it," are mother and brothers to him. No one is a child of God because of human parentage. (John 1: 13.) Luke emphasizes that they must "hear" the word of God and "do" it in order to be called his brethren. Jesus makes "doing" a test of friendship for him. (John 15: 14.) Hence those who hear the word of God and do it are the nearest relatives of Jesus; this spiritual relationship outranks in tenderness the natural or fleshly relationship. The spiritual kinship is more vital than any relationship of blood or of nature; it results in a fellowship at once blessed which is possible for all. The reply of Jesus could not have offended his brethren even though it did contain a delicate rebuke.

18. JESUS STILLING THE STORM
8: 22-25

22 Now it came to pass on one of those days, that he entered into a boat, himself and his disciples; and he said unto them, Let us go over unto the other side of the lake: and they launched forth. 23 But as they sailed he

---

22 Now it came to pass on one of those days,—Parallel accounts of this are found in Matt. 8: 18-27 and Mark 4: 35-41. Luke is not definite with respect to the time; "on one of those days" is a very indefinite time. Jesus was preaching in Galilee and Luke places the time during his Galilean ministry. Jesus and his disciples entered into a boat in the Sea of Galilee; he desired to go to the other side; hence he said: "Let us go over unto the other side of the lake." He had entered a ship in order to discourse to the people. (Matt. 13: 2; Mark

fell asleep: and there came down a storm of wind on the lake; and they were filling *with water,* and were in jeopardy. 24 And they came to him, and awoke him, saying, Master, master, we perish. And he awoke, and re-buked the wind and the raging of the water: and they ceased, and there was

4: 1.) It seems from Matthew that after preaching from the boat, he retired for a short time to the house, probably where he resided at Capernaum (Matt. 13: 36); then he returned to the boat and possibly discoursed again for some time; but seeing the multitude continuing (Matt. 8: 18), he commands to depart to the opposite side, which was the east side of the lake.

23 **But as they sailed he fell asleep:**—Luke describes the de-tails very accurately; his graphic and accurate language makes him a good historian. Jesus had been busy all day, and this was probably about sunset when they left the coast near Capernaum. He needed sleep, like other men, especially after a day of hard work. However, the storm which came upon them simultaneously with his sleep was not an accident. His disciples needed to feel their extremity and be the more deeply impressed with his power over the elements. Like Jonah, he slept in the midst of the storm; but how different from Jonah was the Christ! Luke describes the storm as coming "down" "on the lake." The rain from the heavens and the surrounding mountains upon the lake fits Luke's descrip-tion. It was one of those sudden, violent whirlwinds, at-tended with some rain, which Luke here describes. The boat was "filling with water" and all were in jeopardy. Matthew says "that the boat was covered with the waves." (Matt. 8: 24.)

24 **And they came to him,**—It seemed strange to his disci-ples that Jesus would be sleeping amidst such danger. His disciples aroused him by saying: "Master, master, we perish." Matthew records their saying: "Save, Lord; we perish." (Matt. 8: 25.) Mark (4: 38) says: "Teacher, carest thou not that we perish?" Jesus in this incident is spoken of as "Mas-ter," "Teacher," and "Lord." The disciples recognized in Jesus one who filled all three of these offices to them. They appealed to him for help. Jesus arose, rebuked the wind and

a calm. 25 And he said unto them, Where is your faith? And being afraid
they marvelled, saying one to another, Who then is this, that he commandeth
even the winds and the water, and they obey him?

---

the surging of waves, and they ceased and there was a calm.
Luke narrates all of these events with simple dignity; there is
no effort on his part to amplify, give needless details, or excite
wonder; there is a sublimity of truth.

25 **Where is your faith?**—After all the miracles they had
witnessed, after all the wisdom and power Jesus had shown,
and after all his teaching for months past, why should they
not have had faith? They should have had faith enough to
feel secure in the presence of Jesus; they should have known
that if they perished Jesus would also perish with them.
They should have understood that the work of Jesus had not
been completed, and that nothing could prevent his completing the Father's will. They marveled and said one to another: "Who then is this, that he commandeth even the winds
and the water, and they obey him?"

19. THE GERASENE DEMONIAC HEALED
8: 26-39

26 And they arrived at the country of the [3]Gerasenes, which is over

---

[3]Many ancient authorities read *Gergesenes;* others, *Gadarenes:* and so in ver 37.

---

26 **And they arrived at the country of the Gerasenes,**—Parallel accounts are found in Matt. 8: 28-34 and Mark 5: 1-21.
Of the three accounts of this miracle Matthew speaks of two
demoniacs, while Mark and Luke speak of only one. This
slight discrepancy is of no importance since Mark and Luke
give attention to the one which was the most fierce. The old
maxim: "He who tells of two includes the one, and he who
tells of the one does not deny the two" holds good as an explanation in this case. There are two difficulties presented
here. One is with respect to the exact name of the place, and
the other is with respect to its location. The name is "Gadarenes," "Gerasenes," "Gergesenes." Matthew uses "Gadarenes," while Mark uses "Gerasenes" as does Luke. Its loca-

against Galilee. 27 And when he was come forth upon the land, there met
him a certain man out of the city, who had demons; and for a long time he
had worn no clothes, and abode not in *any* house, but in the tombs. 28 And
when he saw Jesus, he cried out, and fell down before him, and with a loud
voice said, What have I to do with thee, Jesus, thou Son of the Most High
God? I beseech thee, torment me not. 29 For he was commanding the unclean spirit to come out from the man. For ⁴oftentimes it had seized him:

---

⁴Or, *of a long time*

---

tion is on the east side of the Sea of Galilee; however the
exact location cannot be determined. Students of Bible geog-
raphy are not agreed as to its exact location. Many think
that it was not far from "Gadara." It was a political district
extending to the southeast shore of the Sea of Galilee with
Gadara as its capital.

27 **And when he was come forth upon the land,**—It seems
that Jesus and his disciples had sailed down the coast and
came "forth upon the land." Luke, like Mark, fixes attention
upon one of the demoniacs and says that "there met him a
certain man out of the city." The man belonged to, or had
lived in one of the towns which was called "Gergesa" until
this affliction of demons came upon him; after his affliction he
dwelt in the caves also used as burial places for the dead.
Luke is very minute in describing the man, and says, "for a
long time he had worn no clothes, and abode not in any house,
but in the tombs."

28 **And when he saw Jesus,**—When the demoniac saw Jesus
"he cried out, and fell down before him." There seems to
have been a dual or double will in this poor man; he had consciousness of his own, and there seems to have been a consciousness of the demons manifesting themselves in his speech
and in his acts. When the two wills came into collision, the
man fell down before Jesus; he recognized the superior authority and power and divinity of Jesus. He said: "What
have I to do with thee, Jesus, thou Son of the Most High
God?" He then added a request in the words "torment me
not." The demons knew Jesus; they knew who he was and
the power that he possessed. They made confession of their
knowledge and feared his mighty power.

29 **For he was commanding the unclean spirit**—The man

and he was kept under guard, and bound with chains and fetters; and breaking the bands asunder, he was driven of the demon into the deserts. 30 And
Jesus asked him, What is thy name? And he said, Legion; for many demons are entered into him. 31 And they entreated him that he would not
command them to depart into the abyss. 32 Now there was there a herd of

---

possessed with the evil spirit is described as having an "unclean spirit," or possessing a demon. While in this verse
Luke speaks of the "evil spirit" in the singular; in the next
verse he speaks of demons in the plural. This possession
gave the man extraordinary strength at times, and caused him
to break the "chains and fetters" and bands with which the
guard had attempted to keep him bound. After breaking the
bands he would rush away from the guards into the wilderness or "into the deserts." Matthew describes the man as
being so dangerous "that no man could pass by that way."
(Matt. 8: 28.) Mark describes him as being so that "no man
had strength to tame him." (Mark 5: 4.)

30 **And Jesus asked him, What is thy name?**—We do not
know why Jesus asked his name; it may have been asked to
bring the man himself to a consciousness of his state; the answer of the demon was "Legion"; for many demons were entered into him. "Legion" means many; it was a military term
used by the Romans; a full Roman legion had 6,000 men.
This may not have been a full legion, for Mark 5: 13 notes
that the number of hogs was "about two thousand." The
demon answered rather than the man; it is best to consider
the general meaning of "legion" to mean "many." Some
think that there was one chief demon which was superior and
a number of inferior ones under him. This shows the overwhelming power over the entire nature of the man.

31 **And they entreated him**—The demons earnestly besought him; they feared the power of Jesus; they recognized
him as being the Son of God, and hence they knew that he
was opposed to them. Their entreaty was that "he would not
command them to depart into the abyss." There is no evidence that the demons meant by "the abyss" the deep sea or
"abyss" of the Sea of Galilee; they meant the place or prison
of evil spirits. The same Greek word occurs in Rom. 10: 7,

many swine feeding on the mountain: and they entreated him that he would give them leave to enter into them. And he gave them leave. 33 And the demons came out from the man, and entered into the swine: and the herd rushed down the steep into the lake, and were drowned. 34 And when they that fed them saw what had come to pass, they fled, and told it in the city and in the country. 35 And they went out to see what had come to pass; and they came to Jesus, and found the man, from whom the demons were gone out, sitting, clothed and in his right mind, at the feet of Jesus: and they

---

and in Rev. 20: 3. They did not wish to be sent into the abyss of torment or special punishment. They were willing to go any place to get out of the fearful presence of the Son of God.

32, 33 **Now there was there a herd of many swine**—The demons made the further request that they be permitted to enter the swine; Jesus granted their request. The herd of about two thousand were "feeding on the mountain." Jesus did not forbid or restrain them from going into the swine; the Greek word for "suffered' or "gave leave" means primarily "to turn over," hence to suffer, allow, or permit. We do not know why Jesus did not restrain the demons from entering the swine, which led to the drowning of the herd. When granted the permission, the "demons came out from the man, and entered into the swine." When they entered the swine, they caused the herd to rush "down the steep into the lake," and they were "drowned." They were feeding on the mountainside and rushed down into the sea and were strangled which resulted in their death. This miracle and that of the withered fig tree which Jesus cursed (Luke 11: 12-14, 20) are the only ones which resulted in any destruction of property.

34, 35 **And when they that fed them**—The feeders of the swine were astonished and frightened; nothing had occurred in all of their experience like this; the frenzied destruction of the whole herd in the sea was enough to frighten those who kept them; so they fled and reported in the city what had taken place. Their report reached far into the country and all who heard it were astonished. They came out to verify the report, and when they did so they "found the man, from whom the demons were gone out" acting in a normal way. He was no longer a demoniac. Matthew records (8: 34) that "all the city came out to meet Jesus"; they were anxious to see one who had such authority. The man who had been af-

were afraid. 36 And they that saw it told them how he that was possessed with demons was ¹made whole. 37 And all the people of the country of the Gerasenes round about asked him to depart from them; for they were holden with great fear: and he entered into a boat, and returned. 38 But the man from whom the demons were gone out prayed him that he might be with him: but he sent him away, saying, 39 Return to thy house, and de-

¹Or, *saved*

flicted was "sitting, clothed and in his right mind, at the feet of Jesus." He was clothed like others; his mind was sound and sane; he was sitting at the feet of Jesus and learning of the great Teacher.

36, 37 **And they that saw it told them**—Those who had been eyewitnesses, and others who may have gathered through curiosity, reported how the man who had been afflicted with the demons was "made whole." The keepers of the swine who had fled and told the owners may have returned with others and related what had taken place. "And all the people of the country of the Gerasenes round about asked him to depart from them." The effect of this miracle brought together a great multitude of people from the surrounding country. When they saw and heard what was done they made a unanimous request or entreaty that Jesus "depart from them." They were afraid of him; they were not only filled with a superstitious awe at such exhibition of power, but with fear that similar results might attend other miracles. Other owners of swine may have thought their traffic in danger. (Acts 19: 24-31.) It may be that the loss of the swine concerned the people more than did the curing of this unfortunate man.

38, 39 **But the man from whom the demons were gone—** There is a wide contrast between the request of the people of the community and that of the man who had been made whole. This man "prayed him that he might be with him." Jesus was entering the boat (Mark 5: 18) when this man came to him and asked to accompany him. There may have been several reasons for the man making this request; he had a warm desire of gratitude and love for what Jesus had done for him; the mean and selfish request and treatment of the Gerasenes strengthened his feelings for Jesus. It may be that this man feared a repossession by the demons after Jesus

clare how great things God hath done for thee. And he went his way, pub-
lishing throughout the whole city how great things Jesus had done for him.

departed. (Matt. 12: 43-45.) The demons prayed, and their
prayers were granted to their own discomforture (verses 10,
12); the Gerasenes prayed, and their prayer also was granted
by Jesus leaving them to their own destruction; the man
made whole prayed and his petition is not granted for it was
not best and he had a work to do.

Return to thy house,—Jesus instructed the man to return to
his house and declare all that "God hath done for thee." The
man returned and published "throughout the whole city how
great things Jesus had done for him." This man had a great
message to tell and he could tell it with power. The young
ruler was required to sell his possessions and follow Jesus
(Matt. 19: 21); this young man did not obey. The leper was
charged to say nothing to any man, but to go show himself to
the priest (Mark 1: 44); but he went out and published
abroad what was done for him. The disciple was not allowed
to go home and bury his father. (Matt. 8: 21.) But this man
was sent home to his friends to publish abroad what had been
done for him. The whole country had stoutly urged Jesus to
leave their country so that he could not spread the news of his
kingdom there; but the healed man was sent to the same people to tell the story of his miraculous cure. He obeyed; he
published in the whole city how great things Jesus had done
for him. Mark 5: 20 says that he spread the news in Decapolis, the region of the ten cities.

20. JAIRUS' DAUGHTER RAISED; THE WOMAN WITH
AN ISSUE OF BLOOD
8: 40-56

40 And as Jesus returned, the multitude welcomed him; for they were all

40 **And as Jesus returned,**—Parallel accounts of this miracle
are recorded in Matt. 9: 18-26 and Mark 5: 21-34. Mark gives
the fullest account; Luke comes next in detail. According to
Matthew, this miracle was performed immediately after Jesus'

waiting for him. 41 And behold, there came a man named Jairus, and he was a ruler of the synagogue: and he fell down at Jesus' feet, and besought him to come into his house; 42 for he had an only daughter, about twelve years of age, and she was dying. But as he went the multitudes thronged him.

---

discourse on fasting at Matthew's feast. For some reason unknown to us Mark and Luke deferred giving an account till after the healing of the demoniac. There is a wide contrast between the multitude that "welcomed him" and the one that he had just left who had earnestly besought him to leave their country; one multitude almost drives him away, but the other was waiting to welcome him; driven from Decapolis, he is welcomed in Capernaum.

41 **And behold, there came a man named Jairus,**—Mark says that he was "one of the rulers" (Mark 5: 22); the synagogue was under the direction of an officer who sometimes exercised judicial power. According to Matthew (9: 10, 14, 18) Jesus seems to have been in the house of Matthew. It is not certain, however, as to the exact house. The ruler of the synagogue was sometimes an elder; it was his duty to convene the assembly, preserve order, invite readers and speakers. (Acts 13: 15.) Jairus was probably a Jew, as his name seems to be the same as the Hebrew name "Jair" (Num. 32: 41), meaning "whom Jehovah enlightens." He came to Jesus and prostrated himself at his feet in a very reverent and earnest manner. He entreated him to come into his house.

42 **for he had an only daughter,**—Luke gives the reason that Jairus besought Jesus to come to his house. He had an only daughter and she lay dying. She was "about twelve years of age." Mark says (5: 23) that she was "at the point of death." However, Matthew records (9: 18) that she was "even now dead." Jairus on reaching Jesus may have first given vent to his fears by the strong statement that she "is even now dead," or rather has just now died, and then have explained himself by saying that she was at the point of death. His strong faith is shown by his leaving his dying daughter to seek the aid of Jesus, and by his earnest entreaty for him to come at once. It is to be noted that he made this request for his "daughter"; in

43 And a woman having an issue of blood twelve years, who ²had spent
all her living upon physicians, and could not be healed of any, 44 came behind him, and touched the border of his garment: and immediately the issue
of her blood stanched. 45 And Jesus said, Who is it that touched me? And
when all denied, Peter said, ³and they that were with him, Master, the mul-

²Some ancient scholars omit *had spent all her living upon physicians, and*
³Some ancient authorities omit *and they that were with him*

the East daughters were and still are regarded as of small importance in the family; but the birth of a son is cause for
great congratulation. This incident shows how Jewish life
differed from ordinary Eastern ideas in esteem for girls in the
family. Luke brings out the touching fact that this was an
"only daughter." So he mentions an "only son" of the widow
of Nain (7: 12), and the "only child," the lunatic boy (9: 38).

43, 44 **And a woman having an issue of blood**—As Jesus had
responded to the entreaties of Jairus, he started to his house,
but as he crowded through the multitude, a woman having a
chronic disease which, according to the law, rendered her unclean (Lev. 3: 25), came near enough to touch the border of
his garment. Her hopeless case and the incurableness of her
disease are shown in the fact that she had been afflicted for
twelve years, that she had spent "all her living upon physicians," and they had failed to cure her. As a physician, Luke
strongly puts her case as incurable. The woman had heard of
Jesus and had faith in his power to heal her; she approached
him in the crowd from behind. Perhaps she felt her unworthiness and was timid. Some think that "the border of his
garment" was that which the law required to be worn.
(Num. 15: 38-40.) It may have been a fringe or tassel which
was worn at each of the four corners of the outer garment.

45 **And Jesus said, Who is it that touched me?**—The question implies neither ignorance nor deceit in Jesus; he asked it
in order to call forth the confession of the woman for her own
good and the good of others. Jesus asked questions of the
two on their way to Emmaus. (Luke 24: 17-19.) These questions were asked, not for his own information, but to draw out
a statement of their views. All near Jesus denied touching
him, and "Peter said, and they that were with him, Master,
the multitudes press thee and crush thee." There was no un-

titudes press thee and crush *thee*. 46 But Jesus said, Some one did touch me; for I perceived that power had gone forth from me. 47 And when the woman saw that she was not hid, she came trembling, and falling down before him declared in the presence of all the people for what cause she touched him, and how she was healed immediately. 48 And he said unto her, Daughter, thy faith hath 'made thee whole; go in peace.

---

conscious healing virtue in Jesus; he was conscious of all things about him. When healing went forth from him he willed it to go. When all the disciples denied any knowledge of a special touch, Peter in his naturally impulsive way, speaking for the others, reminded Jesus of the crowd that were pressing and crushing upon him. The question to Peter seemed unreasonable since there was such a multitude pressing upon him from every side. Luke alone mentions the name of Peter in this connection.

46 **But Jesus said, Some one did touch me;**—Jesus knew that someone had touched him; he even knew who had touched him; nothing was hidden from him. He gave as his reason that he perceived "that power had gone forth from me." Jesus felt the senation of power already gone; he was conscious of the afflicted woman and her touch; he knew her faith. Her cure was the result of an answer of her touch of faith, which reached beyond the fringe of his garment to his divine nature.

47 **And when the woman saw that she was not hid,**—Mark 5: 32 says that "he looked round about to see her that had done this thing." This shows that Jesus knew, and now by his look he brings out her confession. The woman came "trembling, and falling down before him," and declared in the presence of all the people that she had touched Jesus and that "she was healed immediately." In humility and reverence she came to him and prostrated herself before him, giving herself up to his power and mercy. The woman publicly acknowledged what she had done, why she did it, and the blessings that she received.

48 **And he said unto her,**—After the woman had made her confession public, Jesus now spoke words of comfort to her. He said: "Daughter, thy faith hath made thee whole." It was

49 While he yet spake, there cometh one from the ruler of the synagogue's *house,* saying, Thy daughter is dead; trouble not the Teacher.   50
But Jesus hearing it, answered him, Fear not: only believe, and she shall be
¹made whole.   51 And when he came to the house, he suffered not any man

¹Or, *saved thee*

not the touch of Jesus that healed her, neither was it the
touch of the woman that brought the cure; her faith was the
ground of her blessing.   Having made this open confession
Jesus bids her depart with his blessings completely healed.
Jesus spoke tenderly to her.   He said: "Go in peace."
Matthew records him as saying "be of good cheer." (Matt. 9:
22.)   "Go in peace" was a usual form of parting salutation,
especially to inferiors; it expressed the friendship and good
wishes.   (Ex. 4: 18; 1 Sam. 1: 17; Luke 7: 50; James 2: 16.)

49 **While he yet spake,**—Jesus had started to the house of
Jairus, but was delayed by the curing of the woman with the
issue of blood.   This took some time; we know not how
much.   A messenger arrived from "the ruler of the synagogue's house," which said: "Thy daughter is dead; trouble
not the Teacher."   It appears that Jairus had come with the
knowledge and consent of his family; they seem to have
known why he had gone to Jesus.   Since the child died Jairus
received word from his house that he need not trouble Jesus
as his daughter was dead.

50 **But Jesus hearing it,**—While the messenger brought the
word to Jairus, and reported it to him, yet Jesus heard that
the daughter was dead.   He then said to Jairus: "Fear not:
only believe, and she shall be made whole."   While Jesus was
talking with the woman this messenger came to Jairus, and
Jesus, in deep sympathy for him, as he was for the afflicted
woman, gave him assurance that his daughter should be made
whole.   This must have astonished those who thought that he
might cure her, but could not raise her from the dead.

51 **And when he came to the house,**—Jesus proceeded on his
way to the house, and when he came to the house "he suffered
not any man to enter in with him, save Peter, and John, and

to enter in with him, save Peter, and John, and James, and the father of the maiden and her mother. 52 And all were weeping, and bewailing her: but he said, Weep not; for she is not dead, but sleepeth. 53 And they laughed him to scorn, knowing that she was dead. 54 But he, taking her by the

James, and the father of the maiden and her mother." Peter, James, and John are now privileged to go with him and Jairus into the house, and into the apartment where the body of the daughter was lying. (Mark 5: 37, 40.) The multitude and other disciples remained on the outside; possibly some, after learning that the daughter was dead, had not followed him to the house.

52 **And all were weeping,**—All were expressing loud lamentations. According to Matthew, Jesus saw in the house "the flute-players, and the crowd making a tumult." (Matt. 9: 23.) They were making doleful music according to their custom of mourning for the dead. When Jesus saw this he said: "Weep not; for she is not dead, but sleepeth." Jesus said that they should not regard her as dead, but as though she was sleeping. Matthew records them as laughing him to scorn. Jesus used a similar expression when he said "Lazarus sleepeth," which he explained to mean death. (John 11: 11, 14.) Jesus allowed the parents and others to regard the damsel as really dead and raised to life again.

53, 54 **And they laughed him to scorn,**—The company of mourners was certain that the child was dead. The people did not understand the language nor the power of Jesus, hence they "laughed him to scorn." They thought that he ought to know that she was dead. They reasoned that he claimed to be a prophet, the Messiah, the Son of God, yet he did not know the difference between one who was asleep and one who was dead. They thought that he either knew the difference or did not know the difference; if he knew the difference, he was falsifying when he said that she was asleep. In either case he was not what he claimed to be.

But he, taking her by the hand,—Some authorities say that he put all out of the house, but this clause is omitted in the

hand, called, saying Maiden, arise. 55 And her spirit returned, and she rose up immediately: and he commanded that *something* be given her to eat. 56 And her parents were amazed: but he charged them to tell no man what had been done.

best translations. Jesus took the maiden by the hand and then said: "Maiden, arise." Mark gives the exact Aramaic words which Jesus used: "Talitha cumi." (Mark 5: 41.)

55, 56 And her spirit returned,—At the command of Jesus her life came back to her at once; this was the actual return of her spirit. She had been really dead, but now has full life and in normal condition. Jesus commanded that they give her something to eat. This would be proof positive that she was healed as well as restored to life. If one is able to eat, one is in normal condition. It is probable that she had not eaten for some time as she had been sick. Her parents "were amazed," but Jesus charged them that they should "tell no man what had been done." The parents did not obey Jesus, for Matthew tells us (9: 26) that "the fame hereof went forth into all that land."

21. THE MISSION OF THE TWELVE
9: 1-9

1 And he called the twelve together, and gave them power and authority over all demons, and to cure diseases. 2 And he sent them forth to preach

1 And he called the twelve together,—Parallel accounts of this incident are found in Matt. 10: 1-42 and Mark 6: 6-13. Luke hastily passes over several months, touching only upon the leading points. It is thought that this took place while Jesus and his disciples were making their third general preaching tour throughout Galilee. It is not known at what place these events occurred. There is but little variation in the different accounts. The apostles had been called and appointed for their work; they had been with Jesus for some time and are now to be endowed with miraculous power. Jesus called "the twelve together," and gave them power to perform miracles to confirm that which they preached. The

the kingdom of God, and to heal ⁵the sick. 3 And he said unto them, Take
nothing for your journey, neither staff, nor wallet, nor bread, nor money;
neither have two coats. 4 And into whatsoever house ye enter, there abide,

⁵Some ancient authorities omit *the sick*

number twelve is significant in the scriptures. Jacob had
twelve sons; there were twelve tribes of Israel; twelve stones
in the breastplate of the high priest (Ex. 28: 17-21); twelve
loaves of showbread (Lev. 24: 5-8); the altar and the twelve
pillars which Moses erected at Mount Sinai (Ex. 24: 4); the
altar of twelve stones of Elijah (1 Kings 18: 31); the twelve
spies who went to search the promised land (Num. 13: 1;
Deut. 1: 23); twelve stones taken from the bed of the Jordan
(Josh. 4: 3). The woman with a crown of twelve stars (Rev.
12: 1) and the new Jerusalem with twelve foundation stones
(Rev. 21: 14) are mentioned.

2 **And he sent them forth to preach**—The purpose of their
being endowed with "power and authority" was that they
might preach "the kingdom of God" with the greatest effect.
In doing this they would heal the sick and cast out demons.
They had a double office of proclaiming the gospel of the
kingdom and healing the sick. Their first business was "to
preach," in the sense of proclaiming the kingdom of God; that
is, proclaim that the kingdom was near. The healing was to
attest the preaching.

3 **And he said unto them,**—Luke agrees with Matthew in
telling what they were to take; there is a slight variation in
the record given by Mark (6: 8). Mark records that they
could take a "staff," but Matthew and Luke omit that. This
discrepancy has given trouble to commentators; however, it
may mean the second staff. The record as given by Matthew
and Luke would forbid an extra staff, while the record given
by Mark mentions only the common staff that everyone carried on his journey. They were to take nothing extra; no
extra staff, no wallet, no bread, no money, no extra coat.
They were to make no preparation for the journey, but go just
as they were. The "wallet" was generally made of leather for
carrying provisions. This has been called the "limited com-

and thence depart. 5 And as many as receive you not, when ye depart from that city, shake off the dust from your feet for a testimony against them. 6 And they departed, and went throughout the villages, preaching the gospel, and healing everywhere.

1Or, *good tidings*

mission" of the twelve. The entire "outfit" of these twelve shows that they were plain fishermen, farmers, or shepherds.

4, 5 And into whatsoever house ye enter,—When they arrived at any town or village they were to go into the house as invited and welcome proclaimers of the coming kingdom; they were to make that house their temporary abode until they should depart; they were not to go from house to house, shifting their place of abode. They were to seek first a suitable place to lodge and there abide till the work in that city was accomplished. Mark tells us that they were sent "forth by two and two" (Mark 6: 7) ; hence when they went into a house they were to remain there and preach the tidings of the kingdom in that town.

And as many as receive you not,—This tells how they should act toward the rejector of their message as well as themselves. If any person or persons, family or city, rejected them they should "shake off the dust" from their feet as a testimony of the condemnation. The Jews were accustomed to shake off the dust of the heathen when they returned from a foreign country to their own land. This meant that they renounced all fellowship with those who rejected them. Paul shook off the dust from his feet against his persecutors at Antioch in Pisidia (Acts 13: 51), and shook out his garments against the Jews at Corinth (Acts 18: 6).

6 And they departed,—After receiving their commission, they followed the instruction of Jesus and "went throughout the villages." The names of the villages are not given. It seems that they went through the southern and southeastern portion of Galilee. Jesus cautioned them against entering a city of the Samaritans (Matt. 10: 5), which implies that they would at least come near the borders of Samaria. It also seems that Herod had his attention directed to Jesus by this mission of the twelve. (See verse 7.) It is probable that they

7 Now Herod the tetrarch heard of all that was done: and he was much
perplexed, because that it was said by some, that John was risen from the
dead; 8 and by some, that Elijah had appeared; and by others, that one of

visited Tiberias or its vicinity, the capital of Galilee, where
Herod resided most of the time. As they went they preached
"the gospel." They announced the glad tidings to the people,
individually and collectively, as they had opportunity. Mark
records that they preached that men should repent. (Mark 6:
12.) They healed the sick in all of the villages. Luke is brief,
but comprehensive. Mark 6: 13 says "they cast out many demons, and anointed with oil many that were sick, and healed
them."

7-9 **Now Herod the tetrarch**—Herod's opinion of Jesus may
be found also in Matt. 14: 1-12 and Mark 6: 14-29. Mark's record is the fullest; Luke comes next in detail; but Matthew as
well as Mark relates the recent beheading of John the Baptist,
which Luke omits. "Tetrarch" is a Greek word meaning "a
ruler of the fourth part," which became a common title for
those who governed any part of a province, subject only to
the Roman emperor. In popular language, and from courtesy,
he is styled "king." (Matt. 14: 9; Mark 6: 14.) This was
Herod Antipas, son of Herod the Great. He ruled over Galilee, Samaria, and Perea. He first married a daughter of Aretas, king of Arabia, but afterwards took Herodias, his brother
Philip's wife. Aretas, indignant at the insult offered his
daughter, waged war against Herod and defeated him. When
Herod heard of Jesus he was at a loss to know what to think
of it; he was in a state of painful uncertainty.

by some, that Elijah had appeared;—They were willing to
assign Jesus any place but his rightful place. Some thought
that Elijah had been brought back to earth according to a mis-
interpretation of Mal. 4: 5. Still others thought that he was
"one of the old prophets" who had been raised from the dead.
There were those who were not ready to regard him as John
the Baptist, neither would they regard him as Elijah, but they
thought that he was some prophet who had come from among
the old prophets. The people, however, accorded to Jesus a
higher mission; some higher than others, but none so high as

the old prophets was risen again. 9 And Herod said, John I beheaded: but who is this, about whom I hear such things? And he sought to see him.

that of the Messiah. His Messiahship was perceived by faith. (Matt. 16: 16, 17.)

And Herod said, John I beheaded:—Herod reluctantly beheaded John the Baptist. This is the only reference by Luke to the death of John, which at first seems remarkable, since he gives so particular account of his birth. However, Luke gives John's history only as he was connected with Jesus as his forerunner. John's death occurred about seventeen months after his imprisonment. Herod in his perplexity now inquires: "Who is this, about whom I hear such things?" Matthew (14: 2) and Mark (6: 14) do not record the doubt in Herod's mind as the feelings and convictions of a guilty conscience.

22. THE FIVE THOUSAND FED
9: 10-17

10 And the apostles, when they were returned, declared unto him what things they had done. And he took them, and withdrew apart to a city

10 **And the apostles, when they were returned,**—The twelve returned in twos, as they went out, and told Jesus what they had done. They gave a faithful report of what was done, but neither of the writers of the gospels tells us what their report was or what they did. Some think that their success was small compared with that of the seventy. If it had been great, and had excited their wonder, it would have been natural for some of the writers to have recorded that fact. Jesus took them away from the multitude and went to "a city called Bethsaida." Here Luke speaks of the twelve as "apostles"; the word means "persons sent forth." Jesus gave this title (Luke 6: 13) to the twelve when he selected them from among his disciples. Mark appropriately applies this title now to the twelve just returning from their mission. "Bethsaida" means "house of fish"; it was the native place of Andrew, Peter, and Philip. (John 1: 44; 12: 21.) It was on the east side of the Sea of Galilee. Jesus and his disciples had

called Bethsaida. 11 But the multitudes perceiving it followed him: and he welcomed them, and spake to them of the kingdom of God, and them that had need of healing he cured. 12 And the day began to wear away; and the twelve came, and said unto him, Send the multitude away, that they may go into the villages and country round about, and lodge, and get provisions: for we are here in a desert place. 13 But he said unto them, Give ye them to

gone there for rest, but the multitude would not let them have time to rest.

11 **But the multitudes perceiving it followed him:**—This miracle of feeding the five thousand is recorded by all four of the writers of the gospels. Compare Matt. 14: 13-21; Mark 6: 30-44; John 6: 1-14 with Luke's record. Jesus had withdrawn with his disciples from the people without making known the place where he would go. Matthew and Mark state that the people followed him on foot, which was easy enough to do if Jesus went by boat across the lake. The popularity of Jesus among the common people and their eagerness to hear his teaching and witness his miraculous power are here very briefly presented. Jesus welcomed them instead of being displeased that they should encroach upon his retirement. Matthew and Mark state that he was moved with compassion at the sight of the multitude; instead of dismissing them that he and his disciples might enjoy quiet, he spoke unto them concerning the kingdom of God. The idea of the original is that he continued the work of "teaching" and "healing" till the day was far spent.

12 **And the day began to wear away;**—The fact that it was near the close of the day suggested to the twelve that Jesus should dismiss the multitude that they might go and find food and lodging in some of the villages not very far away. This implies that there were villages and places not far away sufficient to provide for a crowd of five thousand men with their women and children. The disciples reminded Jesus that they were "in a desert place." This means that they were away from villages and thoroughfares where lodging and food could be obtained.

13-15 **But he said unto them,**—Jesus commanded his disciples to give the multitude something to eat, declaring that

eat. And they said, We have no more than five loaves and two fishes: except we should go and buy food for all this people. 14 For they were about five thousand men. And he said unto his disciples, Make them ²sit down in companies, about fifty each. 15 And they did so, and made them all ²sit down. 16 And he took the five loaves and the two fishes, and looking up to heaven, he blessed them, and brake; and gave to the disciples to set before

²Gr. recline

there was no necessity for sending them away. (Matt. 14: 16.) This was done to excite their expectation and to strengthen their faith. Philip was addressed in order to try his faith; he was asked where food could be obtained; he answered that two hundred pennyworth, or about thirty dollars, would not be sufficient. (John 6: 5-7.) The twelve apostles then asked if they should go and buy that amount. (Mark 6: 37.) They had discovered that there were five loaves and two fishes, but they observed that this was a very small amount to feed such a multitude. However, Jesus commanded that the five thousand men be seated in companies of about fifty in each company. The disciples followed his instruction and the multitude was seated. Luke gives only the number of men present; Matt. 14: 21 records that there were five thousand men "besides women and children." Some have estimated that there were probably seven or eight thousand in all. It will be observed that Jesus commands order even in feeding the multitude. The plain where they were seated was covered with grass.

16 **And he took the five loaves and the two fishes,**—Jesus took the loaves and fishes and implored the blessings of God on them. John 6: 11 says that he gave thanks. The giving of thanks is included in blessing. The word translated "bless" is used in praising God for favors (Luke 1: 64); also in invoking God's blessing (Luke 2: 34); also in God's conferring favors (Heb. 6: 14; Acts 3: 26). These three senses really met in Jesus. He praised God and implored his blessing. The same diversity is seen in the account of the Lord's Supper. Matthew (26: 26) and Mark (14: 22) have "blessed"; Luke (22: 19) and Paul (1 Cor. 11: 24) have "gave thanks." The usual way of preparing bread for eating was by breaking it; the scriptures speak of "breaking bread," but never of "cutting it."

the multitude. 17 And they ate, and were all filled: and there was taken up that which remained over to them of broken pieces, twelve baskets.

---

17 And they ate, and were all filled:—Jesus "blessed" the food, gave it to his disciples, and they distributed it to the multitude. There are three facts stated here that should be noted, namely: (1) "they ate"; (2) "were all filled"; (3) twelve basketfuls were taken up of the broken pieces. John 6: 12 records the fact that Jesus told them to gather up the fragments so that nothing should be lost. We know the number of baskets was twelve, and that each basket was filled, but we do not know the size of the baskets. There remained of the loaves and fishes much more than was had at the beginning. Probably the baskets were the small provision baskets in which a Jew commonly carried his food to avoid pollution when going abroad, or among other people. In the miracle of the four thousand soon after, the basket was the larger rope basket. In the larger basket Paul was let down from the wall at Damascus and escaped from the fury of his enemies. (Acts 9: 25.)

23. JESUS FORETELLS HIS DEATH
9: 18-27

18 And it came to pass, as he was praying apart, the disciples were with him: and he asked them, saying, Who do the multitudes say that I am? 19

---

18 And it came to pass,—Compare Matt. 16: 13-28 and Mark 8: 27-31 with the record given here by Luke. Both Matthew and Mark give more details of this scene than Luke does, both locating it on the "coasts" or "towns" of Caesarea Philippi. There was a Caesarea on the eastern shore of the Mediterranean Sea, but Caesarea Philippi was on the extreme northern boundary of the ancient land of Israel, near the latitude of Tyre, and at the head of one of the principal tributaries of the Jordan. Jesus and his disciples had retired to this remote district of Galilee to evade and forestall the uprising of the people to "take him by force, to make him king." (John 6: 15.) He had just performed the miracle of feeding the five thousand and was very popular with the people at this time.

And they answering said, John the Baptist; but others *say* Elijah; and others, that one of the old prophets is risen again. 20 And he said unto them, But who say ye that I am? And Peter answering said, The Christ of God.

19 **And they answering said,**—Jesus had asked his disciples: "Who do the multitudes say that I am?" Jesus did not ask this question to gain information; he knew the minds of all; he did not ask his disciples to learn what they thought of him. He knew their mind. He asked the question that he might correct the views of his disciples and to strengthen their faith. The disciples answered that some of the people thought that he was John the Baptist, others that he was Elijah, and still others that he was "one of the old prophets." Herod was one who believed that he was John the Baptist; in fact, Herod seems to have started this report. (Matt. 14: 2.) Some thought that he was Elijah, while others placed him among the old prophets. It is not clear whether they thought that an old prophet had arisen from the dead, or that Jesus as a prophet had the spirit of one of the old prophets. It seems strange that they did not in their various answers think that he was the Messiah. Probably they did not class him as the Messiah because he did not fulfill their preconceived notions of the earthly dignity and glory of their coming king.

20 **And he said unto them,**—Jesus was not so much concerned about what the multitudes thought of him as he was about what his disciples thought of him. Hence he put the question directly to them and said: "But who say ye that I am?" So soon as they answered his first question, he asked a second personal and pointed question. This is an emphatic question; it means "but ye, who do ye say?" It should not have mattered much to the disciples as to what the multitudes thought of Jesus, but it was a matter of great moment as to what they thought about Jesus. Peter answered for the group and declared, "The Christ of God." Each writer records Peter's confession differently. Matthew records him as confessing: "Thou art the Christ, the Son of the living God." (Matt. 16: 16.) Mark records the confession: "Thou art the

21 But he charged them, and commanded *them* to tell this to no man; 22 saying, The Son of man must suffer many things, and be rejected of the elders and chief priests and scribes, and be killed, and the third day be raised up. 23 And he said unto all, If any man would come after me, let him deny

Christ." (Mark 8: 29.) "Christ" is the Greek word for "anointed"; "Messiah" is the Hebrew word which means the same. "The Christ of God" would mean the anointed of God.

21, 22 But he charged them,—The disciples were to be silent now about his Messianic nature; the time had not arrived for them to proclaim it. Perhaps they did not clearly understand it, and hence could not successfully proclaim it to others. There were some things which must befall him before they were to proclaim him as the Son of God. The things which he now enumerates, when they behold, will deepen their faith in him as "the Christ of God." Jesus does not say here, but it is implied, that after he shall have suffered these things, they may then proclaim him as the Christ. Among the things which he mentions that he must suffer, are that he should "be rejected of the elders and chief priests and scribes," "be killed," and "be raised up" on the third day. The "elders" were the rulers of the people; "chief priests" were the heads of the twenty-four courses or classes of the priests. David had divided the priests into the twenty-four classes. "The scribes" were those who transcribed the law and were also teachers of the people; since they transcribed the law, they were supposed to know it and teach it. All of these would reject Jesus; the verb for "rejected" in the original means to reject on scrutiny or trial, and therefore implies *deliberate* rejection. "The third day" means "after three days," as Mark expresses it. (Mark 8: 31.) "After three days" is just another way of saying "on the third day" and does not mean "on the fourth day."

23, 24 And he said unto all,—Jesus wanted all to understand the lesson of self-sacrifice; they could not yet understand the full meaning of the words of Jesus as applied to his approaching death of which he had been speaking. The shadow of the cross is already across the path of Jesus, but his disciples do

himself, and take up his cross daily, and follow me. 24 For whosoever
would save his life shall lose it; but whosoever shall lose his life for my
sake, the same shall save it. 25 For what is a man profited, if he gain the
whole world, and lose or forfeit his own self? 26 For whosoever shall be
ashamed of me and of my words, of him shall the Son of man be ashamed,

not see it. Jesus said to his disciples if ye would continue to
be followers of the Messiah that ye call me, you will need further denial of self. There are no high positions, no places of
ease and honor, no wealth or power to gratify the earthly ambitions of men as you might expect in the company of an
earthly king; but there are daily crosses, a life of hardship, obscurity, persecution, and dishonor in the world if you follow
Jesus. (Rom. 8: 36; 1 Cor. 15: 31.) If his apostles shared in
the delusions of the scribes in respect to the glorious temporal
reign of the Messiah, this language of Jesus must have dazed
and bewildered them.

For whosoever would save his life—Here Jesus presents a
remarkable paradox to impress and to fasten the truth upon
all his disciples. In an attempt to save the present life, the
body, one risks and often loses the true life, the soul. We
gain the pleasure of time and lose the bliss of eternity. The
natural life is doomed to death; we strive to save it, we lose it,
and do not gain spiritual life in Christ. But losing this life in
Christ we save it by having it transformed into a new life in
him who is the life and light of the world.

25 **For what is a man profited,**—Here Jesus puts the case in
a very common-sense question of profit and loss. If a man
gains the world, yet forfeits his own self, his true self, becoming a castaway in God's great kingdom, what a sorrowful bargain! The loss is eternal. There can be no means of profit to
the one who loses heaven, it matters not what he may gain on
earth. Loss as a consequence of seeking the world and not
following Jesus cannot recompense for gain of all of this
world.

26 **For whosoever shall be ashamed of me**—Jesus identifies
himself with his word; he said that those who were ashamed
of him and his word that he would be ashamed of them. The
cross, the trials, the persecutions, the loss of life itself are

when he cometh in his own glory, and *the glory* of the Father, and of the holy angels. 27 But I tell you of a truth, There are some of them that stand here, who shall in no wise taste of death, till they see the kingdom of God.

awful tests of Christian faith and fidelity. No wonder some stop and stagger in the face of such a thorny pathway to heaven. To turn aside, to waver is to be "ashamed" of Christ, and of such he will be ashamed in the day of his glorious appearance. Jesus endured the shame of the cross. (Heb. 12: 2.) The man at the feast who had to take a lower seat did it with shame. (Luke 14: 9.) Paul declared that he was not ashamed of the gospel. (Rom. 1: 16.) Onesiphorus was not ashamed of Paul. (2 Tim. 1: 16.) Jesus speaks of himself here as he often does "as the Son of man." He is going to come again; at his next advent he will come "in his own glory." His first advent was attended with humiliation and suffering, but the next time he will come in all of his glory with his angels. He will be accompanied with "the glory of the Father" and the glory of "the holy angels" when he comes the second time. This makes a threefold glory that shall attend Christ when he comes again.

27 **But I tell you of a truth,**—Jesus speaks with the greatest emphasis when he says that he tells of a truth. He gives assurance that some who were standing in his presence at that time should not "taste of death" until they should see the kingdom of God; that is, the kingdom of God would come before some who were present would die. The word "taste" is used in the sense of "experience." It is often used in this sense in classical Greek. It is used in the New Testament only with respect to Christ here and in the parallels, Matt. 16: 28; Mark 9: 1; Heb. 2: 9. This shows that the kingdom of God had not at this time been established.

24. THE TRANSFIGURATION
9: 28-36

28 And it came to pass about eight days after these sayings, that he took

28 **And it came to pass**—This remarkable scene of the transfiguration of Jesus is recorded with only the slightest diversities by Matt. 17: 1-8 and by Mark 9: 2-8; it is alluded to also

with him Peter and John and James, and went up into the mountain to pray. 29 And as he was praying, the fashion of his countenance was altered, and his raiment *became* white *and* dazzling. 30 And behold, there talked with him two men, who were Moses and Elijah; 31 who appeared in glory, and

by Peter in 2 Pet. 1: 17, 18.   The time was one week after the conversation just previously recorded.   The place is a point of quiet subordinate importance.   Commentators are not agreed as to the mountain on which the transfiguration took place. Tradition has located it on Mount Tabor, but the probabilities are that it was on some of the peaks of Mount Hermon immediately adjacent to Caesarea Philippi, where, as we learn from Matt. 16: 13 and Mark 8: 27, this conversation commencing with Luke 9: 18 was held.   However, a full week had intervened before the transfiguration, and no record remains to show whether they had or had not been traveling during this time.   Jesus took Peter and John and James with him "up into the mountain to pray."   Luke is the only one who records the purpose of their going into the mountain; they went up there "to pray."   Jesus had taken these three apostles with him on other occasions; they were with him when he raised the daughter of Jairus (Luke 5: 37) and they alone were the witnesses of his agony in the garden of Gethsemane (Luke 14: 33).

29 **And as he was praying,**—He had gone into the mountain to pray, and now as he was engaged in prayer the transfiguration took place.   The transfiguration of Christ is closely associated with his predictions both of his death and his return in his threefold glory.   His countenance was altered; that is, the appearance of his face became different; Matt. 17: 2 says that "his face did shine as the sun."   Luke does not use the word "transfigured," but Matthew and Mark do.   His raiment became white and dazzling; Mark 9: 3 says that it was "exceeding white," and Matt. 17: 2 says it was as "white as the light." His face did shine as the sun, and his garment was white as the light.   The texture of his garment was not changed, but it was bright with a radiant light of his glorified body.

30 **And behold, there talked with him two men,**—Glory was not only manifested in and around the person of Jesus, but

spake of his [3]decease which he was about to accomplish at Jerusalem. 32 Now Peter and they that were with him were heavy with sleep: but [1]when they were fully awake, they saw his glory, and the two men that stood with

[3]Or, *departure*
[1]Or, *having remained awake*

---

heavenly visitors attended him. "Moses and Elijah" were there and "talked with him." Matthew and Luke say "Moses and Elijah," while Mark says "Elijah with Moses." Moses was the representative of the law and Elijah was the representative of the prophets; Luke presents them as both talking with him. We need not ask *how* Peter, James, and John knew Moses and Elijah; the records do not inform us. There were many ways by which they could have had this knowledge. Jesus could have saluted them by their names, or conversation may have indicated it, or they may have known them through the Holy Spirit. Moses had died more than fourteen hundred years before this on Mount Nebo and Jehovah "buried him in the valley in the land of Moab over against Bethpeor; but no man knoweth of his sepulchre unto this day." (Deut. 34: 6.) Elijah had been translated nine hundred years before this event. (2 Kings 2: 11.)

31 **who appeared in glory,**—As Jesus was praying he was suddenly transfigured, and as suddenly there appeared Moses and Elijah who were similarly robed in glory and began talking with Jesus; these three, Jesus, Moses, and Elijah, were holding a conversation. What was their subject? Luke is the only one who tells us the subject of their conversation. They were talking about "his decease which he was about to accomplish at Jerusalem." Jesus had announced his death to his disciples six days before this; now these messengers from heaven are speaking upon the same subject. Their thoughts and conversation were of heaven, but they spoke in the language of earth. They spoke of the work which Jesus was to complete at Jerusalem for the redemption of man. We do not know just what words were spoken.

32 **Now Peter and they that were with him**—The three apostles were weighted down with sleep. This is almost the same condition that we find recorded of them in Matt. 26: 43

him. 33 And it came to pass, as they were parting from him, Peter said
unto Jesus, Master, it is good for us to be here; and let us make three [12]tab-
ernacles; one for thee, and one for Moses, and one for Elijah: not knowing
what he said. 34 And while he said these things, there came a cloud, and
overshadowed them: and they feared as they entered into the cloud. 35 And

---

[2]Or, *booths*

---

and Mark 14: 40. The same expression is used in Acts 20:
9, where actual sleep is meant. This is the most natural
meaning here. Peter is made prominent, being the only one
mentioned in this connection. When they were fully awake
from the sleep they passed through the state of drowsiness
into that of full wakefulness. Luke makes it clear that it was
not a dream, but an actual sight that they had seen. They
saw the glory of Jesus and the "two men that stood with
him." The glory of the scene may have had something to do
with their awakening. But now when they were aroused and
awake they saw what was before them, and hence they are
competent witnesses. It seems that they had not seen the beginning of the transfiguration.

33 **And it came to pass,**—While Moses and Elijah were leaving Jesus, Peter made the suggestion that it was good to be
there. The departing of Moses and Elijah apparently accompanied Peter's remark as given by all three of the records.
Peter addressed him here as "Master," while Matthew records
him as saying "Lord" (Matt. 17: 4), and Mark records him as
saying "Rabbi" (Mark 9: 5). It was near the feast of the tabernacles, which came the middle of the seventh month of the
Jewish year. So Peter proposed that they celebrate the feast
upon the mountain instead of going to Jerusalem. However,
Peter did not understand the full import of his remark. "For
he knew not what to answer; for they became sore afraid."
(Mark 9: 6.) Peter acted according to his impulsive nature
and spoke up even though he did not know what to say or
even what he was saying when he spoke.

34 **And while he said these things,**—Two more wondrous
events occurred—the cloud and the voice. The cloud came
and overshadowed them; it seems that all six were overshadowed by the cloud. The three apostles feared as they entered into the cloud. Matt. 17: 5 says that it was a bright

a voice came out of the cloud, saying, This is ³my Son, my chosen: hear ye him. 36 And when the voice ⁴came, Jesus was found alone. And they held their peace, and told no man in those days any of the things which they had seen.

³Many ancient authorities read *my beloved Son* See Mt. 17.5; Mk. 9.7
⁴Or, *was past*

cloud; it was the symbol of the divine presence, as was the cloud over the tabernacle in the wilderness. (Ex. 40: 38.) The cloud also overshadowed Mount Sinai (Ex. 24: 16, 17), and the cloud overshadowed Solomon's temple (1 Kings 8: 10, 11.) It was similar to the cloud that was present at the ascension of Jesus. (Acts 1: 9.) Some claim that only Jesus, Moses, and Elijah were overshadowed by the cloud; others claim that only the disciples were overshadowed by it; still others claim that all six were overshadowed. It seems that all six were in the cloud.

35 **And a voice came out of the cloud,**—This voice was the voice of the Father, like that at the baptism of Jesus. (Matt. 3: 17; Mark 1: 11; Luke 3: 22.) It was also like the voice when the people thought it was a clap of thunder or an angel. (John 12: 28-30.) The voice said: "This is my Son, my chosen: hear ye him." Matt. 17: 5 records the voice as saying: "This is my beloved Son, in whom I am well pleased; hear ye him." Mark 9: 7 records the voice as saying: "This is my beloved Son: hear ye him." Both Matthew and Mark use the words "my beloved." The words, "hear ye him," are added to what the voice said at his baptism. These disciples were commanded to hear Jesus as the Son of God, even when he predicts his death. Moses as a representative of the law was present and passed away; the time was when they could hear the law, but now they are to hear Jesus. Elijah was present as a representative of the prophets; the time was when they could hear the prophets, but now they are to hear Jesus. This is an important lesson impressed in a most emphatic way.

36 **And when the voice came,**—As the voice spoke no one was present but Jesus and his disciples. After hearing the voice, the prostrate disciples were gently touched by Jesus, and they saw that he was again alone; the heavenly visitors

had disappeared and left Jesus alone to occupy the prominent place in the great scheme of the redemption of man. God had pointed him out as his Son and heaven had commanded that he, and he alone, be heard. In Matt. 17: 9 and Mark 9: 9 Jesus commanded Peter and James and John not to tell the vision until after his resurrection from the dead. Luke notes that they in awe obeyed that command, and they finally forgot the lesson of this night's great experience.

25. THE DEMONIAC BOY
9: 37-45

37 And it came to pass, on the next day, when they were come down from the mountain, a great multitude met him. 38 And behold, a man from the multitude cried, saying, Teacher, I beseech thee to look upon my son; for he is mine only child: 39 and behold, a spirit taketh him away, and he sud-

37 **And it came to pass, on the next day,**—Parallel records of this miracle are found in Matt. 17: 14-20 and Mark 9: 14-29. Jesus and the three disciples spent the night on the mount of transfiguration; in the morning they came down to the foot of the mountain where the nine disciples and a great multitude were assembled. The miracle which followed is peculiar, as a case of failure on the part of the disciples; it gave the occasion for our Lord to rebuke their unbelief, and to manifest at the same time his own power. Mark, whose account is fuller, adds that the scribes were around the nine disciples troubling them with perplexing questions and taunting them about their failure to cure the demoniac child.

38 **And behold, a man from the multitude cried,**—This man addressed Jesus as "Teacher"; Mark 9: 17 records the same address; while Matthew 17: 15 records the address as "Lord." He besought Jesus "to look upon" his son; he wanted Jesus to heal his son. Luke adds that he was an "only child." This is peculiar to Luke as we have seen on other occasions. (See Luke 7: 12; 8: 42.) This father cried unto Jesus as soon as he appeared. The agony and the earnestness of the father were very intense.

39 **and behold, a spirit taketh him**—The father describes the terrible handling of the child by the demon. He said that "a spirit taketh him"; Mark records that it was a "dumb and

denly crieth out; and it ⁵teareth him that he foameth, and it hardly departeth
from him, bruising him sorely. 40 And I besought thy disciples to cast it
out; and they could not. 41 And Jesus answered and said, O faithless and
perverse generation, how long shall I be with you, and bear with you? bring

⁵Or, *convulseth*

deaf spirit." (Mark 9: 25.) In Matt. 17: 15 the boy is described as an "epileptic, and suffereth grievously." He was
"possessed" with a demon which caused deafness, dumbness,
and fits of epilepsy; it was a severe and complicated case.
His dumbness consisted in his inability to utter articulate
sounds. This evil spirit seized him as if to destroy him; at
any time the demon might exert his frenzied power upon the
child, producing sudden and violent paroxysms. The child
would suddenly cry out, which showed that dumbness was an
inability to articulate correct words. The demon, having possession of the child, would tear him, causing him to foam at
the mouth, and cause bruising the body of the child. Matt.
17: 15 says that "oft-times he falleth into the fire, and oft-
times into the water." Mark records that the dumb spirit
would "dash him down" and cause him to foam at the mouth
and grind his teeth. The three descriptions taken together
form a fearful picture of the frenzied paroxysms which were
added to his afflictions.

40 **And I besought thy disciples**—Apparently while the
scene of the transfiguration was transpiring this very severe
case of demonical possession was brought before the nine
apostles; they attempted to cast out the demon, but were unable. There is no other record of any case of sickness which
the disciples, apart from the Master, could not cure by the
power which he had given them. Here is a case of signal failure; it is a case of complex afflictions; demoniac, and a "lunatic," or, judging from the symptoms more accurately, it was
epilepsy. The cure baffled the nine disciples; the severity of
the disease may have filled them with distrust.

41 **And Jesus answered and said,**—This was in the presence
of the scribes and the multitude and his disciples. It showed
his nine disciples up in a bad light. However, Jesus rebuked
the faithless and perverse generation. The rebuke must be

hither thy son. 42 And as he was yet a coming, the demon ⁹dashed him down, and ⁷tare *him* grievously. But Jesus rebuked the unclean spirit, and healed the boy, and gave him back to his father. 43 And they were all astonished at the majesty of God.

But while all were marvelling at all the things which he did, he said unto his disciples, 44 Let these words sink into your ears: for the Son of man

⁹Or, *rent him*
⁷Or, *convulsed*

applied to the multitude as well as to the scribes; it applies also to his disciples, though perhaps with not the same force as to the scribes. Jesus asked how long he should be with them and bear with them. Here the two questions of Mark 9: 19 (only one in Matt. 17: 17) are combined in one sentence. After asking the question Jesus commanded the father and his friends to bring his son to him.

42, 43 **And as he was yet a coming,**—As the child was brought to Jesus "the demon dashed him down" and convulsed him grievously. Luke's description as a physician is very vivid; the description seems to be an attack by the demon and by a fit of epilepsy. Mark adds the piteous plea of the father: "If thou canst do anything [after thy disciples have failed], have compassion on us." Mark also gives the response of Jesus and his answer to the "if." Jesus showed that the "if" was not his to remove, but belonged to the father. "If thou canst! All things are possible to him that believeth." (Mark 9: 23.) Jesus rebuked the unclean spirit and "healed the boy, and gave him back to his father." All were astonished at the "majesty of God." Calmness, dignity, sympathy, and power were blended in this act of Jesus. People were compelled to ascribe all these to the majesty of God; though nine disciples had failed, the Master had with a word prevailed.

43, 44 **But while all were marvelling at all the things**—This verse shows a poor division in verse division; the division should have been at the end of the sentence with the words "majesty of God." The latter part of verse 43 has nothing to do with the first part of the verse. Mark 9: 30 relates that they now departed from the vicinity of Caesarea Philippi and passed through Galilee; Matt. 17: 22 speaks of Jesus abiding in Galilee; and from John 7: 1-9 we may infer that Jesus, dur-

shall be ⁸delivered up into the hands of men. 45 But they understood not
this saying, and it was concealed from them, that they should not perceive it;
and they were afraid to ask him about this saying.

ᵏOr, *betrayed*

ing this whole period, rather sought retirement. While the
multitude was wondering Jesus spoke to his disciples and
said: "Let these words sink into your ears." It is probable
that his disciples were nearest to him and that he could give
them special instruction. The words which he was about to
speak he wanted to lodge permanently in the minds and
hearts of the twelve apostles. Again he announced that he
should be "delivered up into the hands of men." He should
be betrayed by Judas and given up by the Father to men in
order that he may suffer and die. (Acts 2: 23.) The divine
plan of his sufferings and death had formed the topic of discourse on the mount of transfiguration, and now it is the topic
of his nearest circle of disciples.

45 **But they understood not this saying,**—They did not understand what Jesus meant. The original Greek may be
translated "it was concealed from them"; this may relieve in
part the disciples to some extent of the full responsibility for
their ignorance about the death of Jesus. They were afraid to
ask Jesus about what he meant. It may be that they were not
allowed to understand, but that they would more fully understand later. After the resurrection and ascension they saw
the truth very clearly; the Holy Spirit guided and enlightened
their minds, and wrought a great change in their perception of
Christ's teaching. There is a natural diffidence in speaking to
a person regarding near approaching death. And this diffidence was increased to fear by the all-inspiring presence and
power of Jesus. It may be that the personal dignity precluded questions.

26. JESUS TEACHING TRUE GREATNESS
9: 46-50

46 And there arouse a ⁹reasoning among them, which of them was the

⁹Or, *questioning*

46 **And there arose a reasoning among them,**—The parallel
passage of this is Mark 9: 33-37, and Matt. 18: 1-15 is analo-

[10]greatest. 47 But when Jesus saw the reasoning of their heart, he took a little child, and set him by his side, 48 and said unto them, Whosoever shall

[10]Gr. *greater*

gous to it. As they went along the way a dispute arose, or "a reasoning among them," as to who would be the greatest in this earthly kingdom that they supposed Jesus would establish. It seems that this argument followed immediately after the words of Jesus about his death. They were afraid to ask Jesus about that subject, but Matt. 18: 1 states that they came to Jesus to settle it. Luke makes it plain that it was not an abstract problem about greatness in the kingdom of heaven as they put it to Jesus, but a personal problem as to who would be the greatest in their own group; rivalries and jealousies had arisen and now sharp words had been spoken. A little later James and John became bold enough to ask for the first places for themselves in this political kingdom which they expected to be established. (Matt. 20: 20; Mark 10: 35.)

47 **But when Jesus saw the reasoning of their heart,**—Jesus looked into their hearts and saw their ambitions and motives; he did not need that they should tell him what they were discussing along the way. The disciples seem to have gained some vague and indefinite idea from the predictions of Jesus that he would soon be declared the Messiah and would assume his royal power and set up his kingdom as an earthly ruler would do. Hence, the occasion of the "reasoning" among the disciples; they desired to know who would have the highest and most honorable place in this kingdom and who would have the greatest authority. If Jesus had intended that Peter should become the "pope," this would have been the time and the place for his declaring it. Jesus rebuked their worldly ambitions and their jealousies by taking a little child and placing "him by his side." Literally he took a child to himself, as Mark 9: 36 has it, "in his arms," and as Matt. 18: 2 says "in the midst of them." All three attitudes follow one another as the disciples were probably in a circle around Jesus. Some have conjectured that this child belonged to Peter, since it is supposed that they were in the home of

receive this little child in my name receiveth me: and whosoever shall receive me receiveth him that sent me: for he that is [11]least among you all, the
same is great.

49 And John answered and said, Master, we saw one casting out demons
in thy name; and we forbade him, because he followeth not with us. 50 But

[11]Gr. *lesser*

Peter. There is no evidence as to the truthfulness of this tradition.

48 Whosoever shall receive this little child—The links of
the chain are stated here; those that receive the child "in my
name," said Jesus, and those who received Jesus, received
God, as God had sent him. The honored disciple is the one
who welcomes little children "in my name" upon the basis of
the name and authority of Jesus. This was a rebuke of the
selfish ambition of the twelve. Ministry to Jesus is a mark of
true greatness; ministry to children in the name of Jesus is a
mark of greatness; ministry in the name of Jesus to anyone is
a mark of greatness. True greatness is in service; those who
serve most unselfishly are the greatest in the kingdom of God.
The disciples of Jesus had not learned this, and many of his
disciples have not yet learned this lesson.

49 And John answered and said,—There is some difficulty
in locating the order of events here. Some place these events
later in the ministry of Jesus as occurring on the way to the
feast of tabernacles. (John 7: 2-10.) There were persons
among the Jews who attempted to exorcise demons by various
methods, and some, like this person and the sons of Sceva in
Acts 19: 13, 14, did it by using the name of Jesus. It is probable that John introduced this at this time because he wanted
to change the subject after the embarrassment of the rebuke
for their dispute concerning greatness. John addressed Jesus
as "Master"; Luke has already recorded this address four
times. (Luke 5: 5; 8: 24, 45; 9: 33.) The disciples of Jesus
were intolerant; they had a zeal for Jesus which was narrow
and biased. Joshua forbade Eldad and Medad to prophesy because he was jealous for Moses. (Num. 11: 27-29.) Moses
and Jesus were more tolerant than their followers. They forbade this man because he would not follow this special group
of disciples of Jesus.

Jesus said unto him, Forbid *him* not: for he that is not against you is for you.

50 **But Jesus said unto him, Forbid him not:**—Luke is the only writer that expresses so briefly this incident. Mark 9: 38-40 develops the words of Jesus somewhat more fully. The incident is related here by Luke because it is connected with the suggested link "in my name." This man did not belong to the group of apostles, so John relates to the Master that they forbade his doing that work in the name of Jesus because he would not follow them. We are not told as to what result the apostles had in forbidding this man to do the work in the name of Jesus; we only have Jesus rebuking his disciples for forbidding him. Jesus said: "For he that is not against you is for you."

SECTION FOUR

THE MINISTRY OF JESUS IN PEREA; JOURNEYS
TOWARD JERUSALEM
9 : 51 to 19 : 28

1. THE INHOSPITABLE SAMARITANS
9 : 51-56

51 And it came to pass, when the days, [12]were well-nigh come that he

[12]Gr. *were being fulfilled*

At this point Luke begins to narrate a new portion of the ministry of Christ, which is not found in the other writers of the gospel. Only a few notes of time and place as recorded by Matthew and Mark are parallel to Luke's history. This portion of Luke's record has been regarded as one of the most difficult parts to harmonize and bring into chronological order; some have regarded the task as impossible, while others have supposed that Luke from this point to Luke 18: 15 has thrown together a mass of discourses and incidents without reference to chronology or order. However such a supposition in regard to about one-third of Luke's record is hardly consistent with the accuracy, research, and order proposed by Luke in chapter 1, verses 1-4. It seems easy to find order and connection, but little apparent chronology. Luke's record has been found regular and orderly thus far when compared with the records of Matthew and Mark. Why should we not expect the same characteristic in this portion of Luke's writings?

During the last six months of Christ's ministry John records our Lord's journey to the feast of tabernacles (John 7: 10), his presence at the feast of dedication (John 10: 22), his going down from Perea to Bethany to raise Lazarus (John 10: 40-42; 11: 1-17), and his final journey to Jerusalem from a city called Ephraim (John 11: 54; 12: 1).

51 **And it came to pass, when the days**—The language of Jesus makes it clear that he was fully conscious of the time of his death; it was rapidly drawing near to the close of his ministry. The time when "he should be received up" means the

should be received up, he stedfastly set his face to go to Jerusalem, 52 and
sent messengers before his face: and they went, and entered into a village of
the Samaritans, to make ready for him. 53 And they did not receive him,
because his face was *as though he were* going to Jerusalem. 54 And when

time of the ascension of Jesus after his resurrection. Luke as
well as John 17: 5 reveals a yearning on the part of Jesus to
return to the Father; this was in the mind of Christ at the
transfiguration. He now "stedfastly set his face to go to Jerusalem." This is emphatic; Jesus himself with fixedness of
purpose set his face against the difficulties and dangers that
would befall him. This look on the face of Jesus as he went
to his doom is noted later in Mark 10: 32. Luke three times
mentions Jesus making his way to Jerusalem; here and in
Luke 13: 22 and 17: 11. John mentions three journeys to Jerusalem during the later ministry. (John 7: 10; 11: 17; 12:
1.) It is natural to take these journeys to be the same in each
record. However, Luke does not make definite location of
each incident, and John merely supplements here.

52 **and sent messengers before his face:**—Jesus was going
from Galilee; it seems that he would pass through Samaria
and he sent messengers before him to make ready. These
messengers went into Samaria to fulfill the orders which they
had received. The Samaritans did not object when people
went north from Jerusalem through their country, but they
objected seriously to the Jews going through their country up
to Jerusalem. Jesus repudiated Mount Gerizim as the place
of worship by going to Jerusalem. This was an unusual pre-
caution by Jesus, and we do not know why he sent messengers before him at this time.

53 **And they did not receive him,**—Jesus was going to Jerusalem, and the Samaritans refused to receive him "because his
face was as though he were going to Jerusalem." This was
the reason that they refused to receive him. When the Samaritans found that it was a Jewish party going to one of the
Jewish feasts, they refused to entertain Jesus and his company. The Jews had no dealings with the Samaritans, and
the Samaritans naturally retaliated in the same spirit upon all

his disciples James and John saw *this,* they said, Lord, wilt thou that we bid fire to come down from heaven, and consume them?[13] 55 But he turned, and rebuked them.[14] 56 And they went to another village.

[13]Many ancient authorities add *even as Elijah did.* Comp. 2 K. 1.10-12
[14]Some ancient authorities add *and said, Ye know not what manner of spirit ye are of.* Some, but fewer, add also *For the Son of man came not to destroy men's lives but to save* them: Comp. ch. 19.10; Jn. 3.17; 12.47.

who accepted the Jewish place of worship to the neglect of the Samaritan place on their sacred mountain.

54 And when his disciples James and John—Perhaps the recent appearance of Elijah on the mount of transfiguration reminded James and John of the incident in 2 Kings 1: 10-12. These two disciples, who afterwards showed great moderation and love, here exhibited the fiery zeal of their misguided loyalty to Jesus by asking should they call "fire to come down from heaven, and consume them?" This may be why they were called "Sons of thunder," or "Boanerges." (Mark 3: 17.) They were indignant at the failure of the Samaritans to receive their Lord. There was no love between the Jews and the Samaritans at any time, and now for them to treat their Lord in such a way was more than James and John could stand. The allusion seems to be to the attempt of Ahaziah to capture Elijah.

55, 56 But he turned, and rebuked them.—Certain it is that here Jesus rebuked the bitterness of James and John toward the Samaritans, as he had already done to John for his intolerance in forbidding the man to cast out demons in the name of Christ, because he had refused to follow them. Jesus taught them a spirit of tolerance. The disciples of Jesus were to learn that his spirit was not that of Elijah, not that which would burn and destroy to make converts.

2. THE COST OF DISCIPLESHIP
9: 57-62

57 And as they went on the way, a certain man said unto him, I will

57 And as they went on the way,—Matt. 8: 19 calls this man "a scribe"; he said that he would follow Jesus wherever he.would go. There is a certain kind of zeal in the proposition of this man which is to be commended; but it does not

follow thee withersoever thou goest. 58 And Jesus said unto him, The foxes have holes, and the birds of the heaven *have* [15]nests; but the Son of man hath not where to lay his head. 59 And he said unto another, Follow me. But he said, Lord, suffer me first to go and bury my father. 60 But he said unto him, Leave the dead to bury their own dead; but go thou and pub-

[15]Gr. *lodging-places*

---

sound like one who had carefully counted the cost. It may be that the scribe was looking for a life of ease and comfort in following a teacher of such power and popularity; however we know that Jesus impressed upon him the fact that it was not an easy life to follow him. It seems that this man regarded Jesus as the Messiah, but, like his disciples in general, had wrong conceptions of the nature of the kingdom of God.

58 **And Jesus said unto him,**—Jesus knew the measure of the scribe's enthusiasm; he knew that the scribe did not appreciate the full meaning of his own words. Jesus pictured to him the extreme condition that might be imposed upon one who would be his disciple. "The foxes have holes" means that they had a lurking hole or place to which they could go for safety and for rest. "The birds of the heaven have nests," which means that they had a place to roost and rest at night. But in contrast to the foxes and the birds, "the Son of man" did not have any place "to lay his head." Jesus often speaks of himself as the "Son of man." Others do not speak of him as such; they do not refer to him as "the Son of Man," but Jesus frequently uses that term with respect to himself. It may be that Jesus had reference to the fact that the Jews were seeking to destroy him; that there was no place where he could go for rest or safety from the scheming and plotting Jews.

59, 60 **And he said unto another, Follow me.**—The scribe volunteered an offer to follow Jesus, but in this instance Jesus commands this one to follow him. Matt. 8: 21 does not give the command of Jesus to follow him, and seems to make this man also volunteer instead of responding to a command. There is no contradiction between the two records. The man excused himself by requesting that he be allowed sufficient time to bury his father. One of the problems of life is the re-

lish abroad the kingdom of God. 61 And another also said, I will follow
thee, Lord; but first suffer me to bid farewell to them that are at my house.
62 But Jesus said unto him, No man, having put his hand to the plow, and
looking back, is fit for the kingdom of God.

---

lation of duties to each other, which comes first. The burial
of one's father was a sacred duty (Gen. 25: 9), but this man is
to learn that the first duty that man owes is his duty to God.
It is not known that this man's father was dead at this time;
many think that he wanted to wait and take care of his father,
and after his father died then he would give all of his time to
following Jesus. This is probably the meaning; Jesus means
to teach that there is nothing that should come between one
and his obedience to God; that the first and highest and most
important duties of all are those which we owe to God.

61, 62 **And another also said, I will follow thee,**—This case
is like the first; this man volunteers to follow Jesus. Luke is
the only one that records this case. This man had something
that he wanted to come "first"; he wanted to bid farewell to
those who were at his house. Within itself that was a good
thing to do, but he needed to know that he must put the
things of God "first." Perhaps he meant that he would like to
have a formal parting with his friends by setting a feast; however it does not matter what his motive was; he is to learn the
lesson that nothing can come first but God and his work.
This is a lesson that many need to learn today. Jesus answered this one by quoting an old proverb taken from agricultural life: "No man, having put his hand to the plow, and
looking back, is fit for the kingdom of God." It has always
been the ambition of the plowman to run a straight furrow; in
order to do this one must look straight forward; he must look
to the things which are in front. Looking back would be fatal
to a plowman in running a straight furrow. This is a very
vivid picture; while engaged in labor, the plowman must keep
his eye clear and straightforward. The application that Jesus
makes is clear and simple.

3. MISSION OF THE SEVENTY
10: 1-24

1 Now after these things the Lord appointed seventy[1] others, and sent them two and two before his face into every city and place, whither he himself was about to come. 2 And he said unto them, The harvest indeed is plenteous, but the laborers are few: pray ye therefore the Lord of the harvest, that he send forth laborers into his harvest. 3 Go your ways; behold, I send you forth as lambs in the midst of wolves. 4 Carry no purse, no wallet,

[1]Many ancient authorities add *and two:* and so in ver. 17

1 **Now after these things**—The mission of the "seventy" is given by Luke only. Jesus was probably near Capernaum when this was given. Many think that the seventy were sent out before the incidents recorded in Luke 9: 51-56, and therefore before Jesus left Galilee for the feast of tabernacles at Jerusalem. (John 7: 2-10.) The places to which the seventy were sent are not known; they were probably in lower Galilee and along the Jordan valley in Perea and Judea. "After these things" simply means after the general series of events narrated in the previous chapter. They were to go in twos. The number seventy reminds us of the seventy elders appointed by Moses (Num. 11: 16) and the Jewish Sanhedrin, which was composed of seventy or seventy-two. These seventy were appointed in addition to the other disciples or apostles which had been selected. Their mission was to go before him and announce his coming.

2 **And he said unto them,**—As they were to go by twos, they had a specific mission. He said to them, "the harvest indeed is plenteous," but there were very few laborers. The language used by Luke here is the same that was used in sending the twelve. (Matt. 9: 37, 38.) They were to pray that "the Lord of the harvest" should send forth sufficient laborers to take care of the harvest. Christ was the Lord of the harvest; it is he who sent them out. "The harvest" refers to the great multitude of people who were eager to learn of his teaching. This is another passage which very vividly represents the need of laborers to work for Jesus.

3 **Go your ways; behold, I send you forth**—These seventy likewise were sent as lambs among wolves; notice that here the word is "lambs," while in Matt. 10: 16 it is "sheep," but

no shoes; and salute no man on the way. 5 And into whatsoever house ye shall ²enter, first say, Peace *be* to this house. 6 And if a son of peace be there, your peace shall rest upon ³him: but if not, it shall turn to you again. 7 And in that same house remain, eating and drinking such things as they give: for the laborer is worthy of his hire. Go not from house to house. 8

²Or, *enter first. say*
³Or, *it*

the thought is the same, only intensified by lambs. These seventy were to go in gentleness and simplicity as lambs, and as defenseless as they, among the rough people who would act like wolves toward them. Lambs and wolves are natural enemies; the lambs are innocent and defenseless, the wolves are malicious and cruel. It is a pathetic picture of the risk and dangers that they had to endure. It is like taking one's life into one's own hands. It was necessary that these dangers be made emphatic to them so that they would know what they would have to meet.

4, 5 **Carry no purse, no wallet,**—The provision for their journey was very much like that of the twelve when sent out on their limited commission. "Purse" means moneybag; "wallet" was a bag for carrying provisions; they were to take no extra shoes or sandals. These sandals were fastened to the bottom of the feet with straps passing over the foot and ankle. They were to go just as they were, without making preparation, and depend on the hospitality of the people. They were to salute no man on the way; the King's business required haste. The greeting or salutation to the house was the common Jewish greeting. To salute one by the way after the Eastern custom would consume much time, but this greeting to a house when they entered it was brief, and required no waste of time. The brief salutation was "peace be to this house." Whatever house they should happen to enter, they were to greet it with this usual salutation. (1 Sam. 25: 6.) This salutation was both a prayer and a blessing, and which indicated the gracious mission which they had in coming to that house.

6, 7 **And if a son of peace be there,**—"Son of peace" means one who is inclined to peace and properly belongs to the household. The figure here is that the peace and blessing

And into whatsoever city ye enter, and they receive you, eat such things as
are set before you: 9 and heal the sick that are therein, and say unto them,
The kingdom of God is come nigh unto you. 10 But into whatsoever city ye
shall enter, and they receive you not, go out into the streets thereof and say,
11 Even the dust from your city, that cleaveth to our feet, we wipe off
against you; nevertheless know this, that the kingdom of God is come nigh.

which they pronounced upon this household would return to
them; they would receive blessings for blessing the household. However if the head of the house did not receive them,
their blessings should not abide with that house; it should return "to you again." If they had a favorable reception, they
were to remain in that house until they had finished their
work in that village. They were not to go "from house to
house" in their abiding; it does not mean that they should not
go from house to house in their teaching. The laborer is worthy of his hire. It would be easier for them to do their work
by remaining in the same house, and avoid waste of time with
such elaborate entertainments as might be offered them.

8, 9 **And into whatsoever city ye enter,**—The same rules
were to apply to them on entering a city that applied to them
on entering a house if they had a welcome; they were to remain there and to eat such things as would be set before
them; they were not to expect a great feast, but were to live a
simple life so that they could render the most efficient service.
To eat to gluttony and to drink to drunkenness would unfit
them for the work that they were to do; they were not to be
gormandizers. They were to heal the sick that were there
and to preach that "the kingdom of God is come nigh unto
you." Healing is here placed before preaching; this was an
emphatic way of demanding attention to their message.

10, 11 **But into whatsoever city ye shall enter,**—Jesus knew
that his cause would have enemies; he knew that some would
not accept his disciples; he knew that some would not believe,
as he knew that some would believe and receive his message.
Hence, he tells them how to deport themselves in the presence
of those who refused to believe their message. Dust was a
plague in the East; they should shake off the dust as a witness
against those who rejected them. There was to go with this a

12 I say unto you, It shall be more tolerable in that day for Sodom, than for that city. 13 Woe unto thee, Chorazin! woe unto thee, Bethsaida! for if the 'mighty works had been done in Tyre and Sidon, which were done in you, they would have repented long ago, sitting in sackcloth and ashes. 14 But it shall be more tolerable for Tyre and Sidon in the judgment, than for you.

'Gr. *powers*

condemnation because they had refused to accept the message. The kingdom of God had come nigh to them, and they had spurned it, and invited the condemnation of the kingdom upon themselves. As those who received them invited the blessings of the kingdom, so those who rejected the message invited the condemnation of the kingdom upon them.

12 I say unto you,—Jesus had just given instruction to the seventy, and had told them that if a city refused to receive them that they should wipe off the dust from their feet as a testimony against that city. He now says that it will be "more tolerable" in the day of judgment "for Sodom" than for the city that rejects the messengers of Christ. Lot witnessed against the evil of the Sodomites, but he was a less perfect and clear witness than were the seventy in their mission to the towns of Palestine; hence the greater light rejected, the greater condemnation. This rule holds good now since it expresses a general truth: the more light and truth rejected, the greater the condemnation. (See Luke 12: 47.) The many and the few stripes suggest this principle. Sodom was situated where the southern portion of the Dead Sea now is. Its wickedness was great. (Gen. 13: 13; 18: 20; Jude 7.) Its retribution was also great. (Deut. 29: 23; Isa. 13: 19; Jer. 49: 18; Amos 4: 11; 2 Pet. 2: 6.)

13, 14 Woe unto thee, Chorazin!—Chorazin is not mentioned save here and in Matt. 11: 21. Its exact location is not known. The cities mentioned here were probably located west of the Jordan. Bethsaida was at the north end of the Sea of Galilee and probably on the west of the Jordan. It was evidently not far from where the Jordan flowed into the Sea of Galilee. Jesus evidently did many notable miracles in Chorazin and Bethsaida. Jesus did many mighty works of which we have no special record. (Matt. 4: 24; 8: 16; 9: 35.)

15 And thou, Capernaum, shalt thou be exalted unto heaven? thou shalt be
brought down unto Hades. 16 He that heareth you heareth me; and he that

Bethsaida is supposed to be the name of two towns, one on
the east and the other on the west of the Sea of Galilee. The
name means "a house of fishing or fishery." The Bethsaida
on the northeastern border of the lake may be referred to in
Mark 6: 32; 8: 22; Luke 9: 10. The one mentioned here was
on the west side near Capernaum, the birthplace of Andrew,
Peter, and Philip. (John 1: 44; 12: 21.) Tyre and Sidon
were located on the Mediterranean coast. They were the two
principal cities on the eastern coast of the Mediterranean.
"Sidon" means "fishery" and was one of the oldest cities of
the world; it is thought to have been founded by Sidon, the
oldest son of Cain. (Gen. 10: 15; 49: 13.) Tyre means "a
rock" and was about twenty miles south of Sidon; it was not
so old as Sidon, but grew in importance and became a greater
city. They were the subjects of much prophecy and of divine
judgments. (Isa. 23; Ezek. 26: 27, 28; 29: 18.) These old
heathen cities of Tyre and Sidon would have repented long ago
had such works been done in them as have been done in
Chorazin and Bethsaida. "Sackcloth and ashes" were symbols of penitence. "Sackcloth" was a coarsely woven cloth; it
was made of goats' or camels' hair, and was a material similar
to that which Paul used in making tents. It was used for
rough garments of mourners (1 Kings 21: 27; Esth. 4: 1) in
which the sackcloth was put next to the flesh in token of extreme sorrow. "Ashes" was a sign of mourning, and the defil-
ing of oneself with dead things; sometimes this was done by
using dirt.

15, 16 **And thou, Capernaum,**—Capernaum was situated on
the northwestern coast of the Sea of Galilee. It had exalted
privileges; Jesus had resided there for some time; its privileges and honors were great. (Matt. 9: 1.) It was situated
on the hill that rises from the plain of the sea; it could boast
of being a great city. The prophecy of Christ is that it should
be brought down "unto Hades." Hades is not the same as
Gehenna; "Hades" was originally the name of the god who

rejecteth you rejecteth me; and he that rejecteth me rejecteth him that sent me.

17 And the seventy returned with joy, saying, Lord, even the demons are subject unto us in thy name. 18 And he said unto them, I beheld Satan

presided over the realm of the dead; hence the phrase, "house of Hades." "Sheol" has a similar meaning. The classical "Hades" embraced both good and bad men, though divided into "Elysium," the abode of the righteous, and "Tartarus," the abode of the wicked. In the New Testament, "Hades" is the realm of the dead; it is not merely the place for the wicked. Capernaum would be reduced from its high and exalted state to the lowest state.

He that heareth you heareth me;—These solemn words close the instruction that Jesus gave the seventy. The fate of Chorazin, Bethsaida, and Capernaum will befall those who set aside the mission and message of those sent out by Christ. To receive these seventy would be to receive Christ; to reject the seventy and their message would be to reject Christ. Those who rejected Christ rejected God. Today when people reject the word of God they reject Jesus, and those who reject Jesus reject God. To reject the New Testament today is to reject God.

17 **And the seventy returned with joy,**—They had followed the directions of Jesus, and had gone into all of the cities where he had directed them to go. They now returned with joy and rejoicing. They had been given power over demons; the demons were merely one sign of the conflict between Christ and Satan. The twelve had been endowed with this power when they were sent out (Luke 9: 1), but the seventy were only told to heal the sick as stated by Luke in 10: 9. Not only did they heal the sick which Jesus commanded them to do, but their faith was so active and strong that they cast out demons. This was the more remarkable, as even nine apostles had sometime before this failed to cast out a demon. (Luke 9: 40.) There is great simplicity and honesty in their report.

18-20 **And he said unto them,**—With a prophetic eye Jesus saw the downfall of Satan. The demons being subject to the

fallen as lightning from heaven. 19 Behold, I have given you authority to tread upon serpents and scorpions, and over all the power of the enemy: and nothing shall in any wise hurt you. Nevertheless in this rejoice not, that the spirits are subject unto you; but rejoice that your names are written in heaven.
21 In that same hour he rejoiced [5]in the Holy Spirit, and said, I [6]thank thee, O Father, Lord of heaven and earth, that thou didst hide these things from the wise and understanding, and didst reveal them unto babes: yea,

[5]Or, *by*
[6]Or, *praise*

seventy gave the occasion for Jesus to utter this prophecy. The fact that demons were subject to the disciples of Jesus indicated that Satan himself should be defeated by Christ. As a flash of lightning out of heaven, so quick and startling, so the victory of the seventy over the demons, the agent of Satan, forecast his downfall and Jesus in vision pictured it as a flash of lightning. Jesus now enlarged their authority over evil. They were to have authority "to tread upon serpents and scorpions," and all phases of their enemies' efforts to harm them. Jesus gives them power to do the work that he had for them to do; they were qualified to do his work, and Satan should not have power to prevent their successful work. The power to tread upon serpents is repeated in Mark 16: 18, and exemplified in Paul's case in Melita. (Acts 28: 3-5.) Protection from physical harm is not the main point in this struggle with Satan. (Matt. 13: 25; Rom. 16: 20; 1 Pet. 5: 8.) Nothing can really "hurt" God's people; they may be persecuted, but their spiritual life cannot be touched by any of the agents or weapons of Satan. (Rom. 8: 27-39.) "Serpents" were poisonous reptiles; "scorpions" were large insects, several inches long, with a poisonous sting at the extremity of the tail; they live in warm climates and are found in dry and dark places.

21 In that same hour he rejoiced—Jesus had just told his disciples to rejoice and he now sets the example as "he rejoiced in the Holy Spirit" and prayed to his Father. Similar sublime words were spoken on another occasion. (Matt. 11: 25-27.) The thanksgiving as expressed here by Jesus acknowledges God as "Lord of heaven and earth." The thanksgiving arises from the wisdom of God in hiding these things from the

Father; [7]for so it was well-pleasing in thy sight. 22 All things have been delivered unto me of my Father: and no one knoweth who the Son is, save the Father; and who the Father is, save the Son, and he to whomsoever the Son willeth to reveal *him.* 23 And turning to the disciples, he said privately, Blessed *are* the eyes which see the things that ye see: 24 for I say unto you, that many prophets and kings desired to see the things which ye

[7]Or, *that*

wise and understanding, those who fancied themselves to be so, and having revealed them to babes in wisdom and understanding. The Holy Spirit expressed through Paul a similar thought. (Rom. 9: 11-17. See also Matt. 16: 17; 18: 3, 4; Luke 9: 47, 48; 1 Cor. 1: 21, 26; 2 Cor. 4: 3, 4.) This result was not a mere arbitrary act of God; it follows a law of mind and of truth. People who refuse to see and accept spiritual truth gradually render themselves unable to understand it; those of little spiritual apprehension, mere babes in experience, yet willing to get and use what they can, gain more and more capacity to apprehend that kind of truth; thus it is hidden from the first and revealed unto the latter class.

22 **All things have been delivered unto me**—Jesus was given all power and authority on earth and in heaven; he is Revealer, Creator, Redeemer, and will be final Judge of all mankind. (Matt. 28: 18; John 1: 1-5, 41; 17: 2.) No one knew the Father except as revealed through Christ; Christ knew the Father and revealed him. The Father knew Christ and revealed him to man; each revealed the other to man. We read of no patriarch or prophet, or priest, or apostle or saint of any age, who ever used words like these; they reveal to us the mighty majesty of our Lord's nature and person. They reveal the very intimate relation between the Father and Son; both are incomprehensible, and are understood only so far as they are revealed.

23, 24 **And turning to the disciples,**—The prayer that Jesus uttered was a soliloquy, spoken in the presence of the seventy on their return. Jesus now turned and spoke "privately," or to his twelve disciples. It may have been on this same occasion or a little later. "Blessed" here introduces a beatitude, a beatitude of privilege. Their eyes were blessed because they

see, and saw them not; and to hear the things which ye hear, and heard them not.

---

saw; they understood in some degree what Jesus was saying. They were indeed blessed in contrast to the blinded scribes and Pharisees around them, who both hated and rejected the truth; these humble followers of Jesus, having teachable spirits, had beheld him as the Messiah, and had received from him lessons of heavenly wisdom.

many prophets and kings desired to see—The Old Testament prophets like Isaiah, and kings like David, Hezekiah, Jehoshaphat, and Josiah longed to see the fulfillment of the promise in the coming Messiah, and to hear the wonderful truths he would reveal, but did not see the one nor hear the other. They lived and died in the hope and faith that these things would be accomplished. We live in the full light of that kingdom already set up, and yet how little do we realize the force of these remarkable words of Jesus! (2 Sam. 23: 5; Job 19: 23, 24; Isa. 52: 7; 1 Pet. 1: 10.)

4. THE GOOD SAMARITAN
10: 25-37

25 And behold, a certain lawyer stood up and made trial of him, saying, Teacher, what shall I do to inherit eternal life? 26 And he said unto him, What is written in the law? how readest thou? 27 And he answering said,

---

25 And behold, a certain lawyer stood up—This parable is peculiar to Luke. "A certain lawyer," that is, one who was skilled in the law of Moses, one who could interpret the law and who could teach it. The lawyer "stood up," which showed this was some formal meeting or gathering. His purpose was to make trial of Jesus. He was not wanting to know the truth; the question of the ensnaring lawyer and the answer with their explanatory parable were fitted to give truer views of God's law, further break down Jewish exclusiveness, and to prepare the way for the acceptance of the universal brotherhood of man. The question asked was "What shall I do to inherit eternal life?"

26, 27 And he said unto him,—The lawyer's question implied that he knew what the rabbis taught, but you are a new

¹Thou shalt love the Lord thy God ²with all thy heart, and with all thy soul, and with all thy strength, and with all thy mind; ³and thy neighbor as thyself. 28 And he said unto him, Thou hast answered right: this do, and thou shalt live. 29 But he, desiring to justify himself said unto Jesus, And who is

¹Dt. 6.5
²Gr. *from*
³Lev. 19.18

teacher; what do you say? Jesus did not ask what the law taught, but he asked, "What is written in the law? how readest thou?" Jesus asked how do you understand the law to teach regarding this? How would you sum up the law respecting this particular matter? The lawyer answered by quoting Deut. 6: 3; 11: 13, which were written on the phylacteries. The second part of his answer was from Lev. 19: 18 and shows that the lawyer knew the law. At a later time Jesus himself in the temple gave a like summary of the law to a lawyer who wanted to catch him by his question. (Matt. 22: 34-40; Mark 12: 28-34.)

28, 29 **And he said unto him,**—The rich young ruler had asked the same question and this lawyer was not as sincere as the ruler. Jesus gave an unexpected turn and said: "This do, and thou shalt live." The lawyer was not prepared for this answer of Jesus; he expected Jesus to give a different answer. He did not see that following the law in its deep significance would lead him to accept the Messiah; he did not see that every sacrifice offered unto the law pointed to Jesus as the great sacrifice for the sins of the world; he did not see that the law was tutor to bring one to Christ. The lawyer seeking to justify himself, asked: "Who is my neighbor?" The lawyer admitted that it was hard to keep this law fully, and that Jesus had answered him correctly. He was seeking a loophole by which he could escape. He had come to ensnare Jesus, but had been caught in his own trap; hence he sought to justify himself by asking a question which diverted the mind from the main question. The lawyer asked whom he was to love as himself. He was hoping, perhaps, that Jesus would limit the word neighbor to the Jews. (Matt. 5: 43.) The Pharisees restricted the term so as to exclude not only Gentiles and Samaritans, but also publicans and those who

my neighbor? 30 Jesus made answer and said, A certain man was going
down from Jerusalem to Jericho; and he fell among robbers, who both
stripped him and beat him, and departed, leaving him half dead. 31 And by
chance a certain priest was going down that way: and when he saw him, he
passed by on the other side. 32 And in like manner a Levite also, when he

---

shared not their own peculiar views. If Jesus should make a
different application, the lawyer would have hope to refute
Jesus. The word "neighbor" signified one living near, and
was used in a limited sense to mean a friend; in its broader
sense, Jesus shows that it meant a fellow man in need.

30 **Jesus made answer and said,**—This is a very good point
with respect to the teachings of Jesus. The lawyer had given
this turn to his question and asked whom he is to love as himself. How near must he live to him; how near in the gradations of social life; how exactly on the same plane of social
rank? This shows that the astuteness of the lawyer was
brought to his aid in this conversation; he presents the many
difficulties of interpreting the second table of the law so as to
make it thoroughly practical. Jesus presents the case of a
Jew who was journeying from Jerusalem to Jericho. This
road was indeed a going "down," for Jericho was about eight
hundred feet below the Mediterranean Sea, while Jerusalem
was about two thousand five hundred feet above it, making a
descent of three thousand three hundred feet in about sixteen
to eighteen miles. This road to Jericho was through a narrow, deep ravine with holes, caves, and hiding places for robbers.

31 **And by chance a certain priest**—It seems accidental, yet
there are no accidents in God's arrangements. Jericho was a
city of priests, where twelve thousand lived. As they served
at Jerusalem, it would be no uncommon thing for a priest to
be traveling that road, even though they more commonly took
the longer route by Bethlehem. When the priest saw this
man wounded and dying, he passed by "on the other side."
This presents a vivid and powerful picture of the vice of Jewish ceremonial cleanliness at the cost of moral principle and
duty. This priest was under obligation to help this man, but
he did not do so.

came to the place, and saw him, passed by on the other side. 33 But a certain Samaritan, as he journeyed, came where he was: and when he saw him, he was moved with compassion, 34 and came to him, and bound up his wounds, pouring on *them* oil and wine; and he set him on his own beast, and brought him to an inn, and took care of him. 35 And on the morrow he took out two ⁴shillings and gave them to the host, and said, Take care of him; and whatsoever thou spendest more, I, when I come back again, will

⁴See marginal note on ch. 7.41

32 **And in like manner a Levite also,**—"A Levite" was one who belonged to a class, the descendants of Gershon, Kohath, and Merari; these were the sons of Levi who assisted the priest in sacrificing and other services; they also guarded the temple. (Num. 3: 17; 8: 5-22.) The Levite was probably returning to Jericho from the temple service at Jerusalem. When he drew near to the wounded man, he just looked at the miserable object and got an idea of the critical condition of the poor, wounded sufferer. He immediately crossed the road, passing on without doing anything to relieve the man. The priest had showed great and even selfish indifference, but the Levite showed a cool and calculating selfishness; both acted in a manner unbecoming humanity and utterly unworthy of their sacred professions and office. Their conduct was a striking violation of the law. (Ex. 23: 4, 5; Deut. 22: 1-4; Isa. 58: 7; Mal. 2: 6, 7.)

33-35 **But a certain Samaritan,**—The wounded man was apparently a Jew, and the Jews had no dealings with the Samaritans. (John 4: 9.) This Samaritan traveling the same road found the man who had been robbed and wounded; he had mercy on him; he took him up and gave him treatment, "pouring on them oil and wine," and put him on his own beast and took him to an inn. Of all men in the world to do a neighborly act, a Jew would not expect this of a Samaritan. The Samaritan did not side-step or dodge the wounded man, but had compassion on him. Oil and wine were used for medicinal purposes in the East. (Isa. 1: 6.) They were very commonly carried by travelers. (Gen. 28: 18; Josh. 9: 13.) The wine may have been used for bathing and cleansing the wounds, and the olive oil for relieving the pain and for its healing qualities. Jews also used a mingling of oil and wine

repay thee. 36 Which of these three, thinkest thou, proved neighbor unto him that fell among the robbers? 37 And he said, He that showed mercy on him. And Jesus said unto him, Go, and do thou likewise.

together for healing wounds. The Samaritan was not contented with merely taking him to the inn and seeing that he had a place of safety, but he took care of him during the remainder of the day and night, attending to his wants, nursing him, and thus denying himself of needed rest and sleep.

36, 37 **Which of these three,**—Jesus is now ready to have the lawyer answer his own question. The lawyer had asked who was his neighbor and the great Teacher has led him up to the point that he can answer his own question. So Jesus asks the lawyer which of the three "proved neighbor unto him that fell among the robbers?" The lawyer answered promptly and said: "He that showed mercy on him." The Master Teacher had changed the lawyer's standpoint and put it up to him to decide, and the lawyer could not answer the question incorrectly; the lawyer could not say that the priest or the Levite acted neighborly toward the wounded man; such an answer would have stultified his own intelligence; he had to answer the question correctly; there was no way to evade. He had come to ensnare Jesus, but is now entangled in his own net. Jesus then said to him: "Go, and do thou likewise." He had asked what he should do to inherit eternal life, and he now has his answer. He avoided in answering Jesus' question, saying "the Samaritan" proved neighbor, and used the clause, "he that showed mercy on him."

5. MARY AND MARTHA
10: 38-43

38 Now as they went on their way, he entered into a certain village: and a certain woman named Martha received him into her house. 39 And she

38 **Now as they went on their way,**—Jesus was traveling toward Jerusalem; they came to "a certain village." We learn from John 11: 1 that this was Bethany. The time is not definite; there is nothing in the language to indicate just when this event took place. As Jesus and the twelve were on their journey whither the seventy had already gone, they came to

had a sister called Mary, who also sat at the Lord's feet, and heard his word. 40 But Martha was ⁵cumbered about much serving; and she came up to him, and said, Lord, dost thou not care that my sister did leave me to serve alone? bid her therefore that she help me. 41 But the Lord answered and

⁵Gr. *distracted*

Bethany—Bethany, the village of Mary and her sister Martha. The characters of the two sisters as here presented agree with those described in John. Lazarus is not named here by Luke; it seems that Luke's design was merely to present these two sisters with their different traits and their relations to Jesus. Bethany was situated less than two miles from Jerusalem on the eastern slope of the Mount of Olives. Jesus went into the house of these sisters Many think that this was before the sickness and death of Lazarus.

39 **And she had a sister called Mary,**—Martha was probably the older of these sisters, and had charge of the domestic duties of the house; she received Jesus to her hospitalities. Very little is said about Mary; in fact, these sisters are mentioned only three times in gospel history. Mary "sat at the Lord's feet, and heard his word." Pupils were accustomed to sit at the feet of their teacher; Paul sat and learned at the feet of Gamaliel. (Acts 22: 3.) Mary is described as sitting in John 11: 20, in contrast to the active Martha. In Mary we see a quiet, childlike, teachable, and contemplative spirit eagerly seeking after the truth. The good Samaritan presents us an example of active love; Mary of devoted and receptive love.

40 **But Martha was cumbered about much serving;**—In contrast to Mary at her Master's feet is Martha bustling amid anxious cares and overburdened with much labor. She is "cumbered," which means "perplexed, overoccupied"; with her domestic duties weighing heavily upon her in preparing the table for the entertainment of Jesus, she complains to Jesus about her sister Mary. Jesus frequently visited this home; hence he was not a stranger. Martha came with some haste to Jesus into the room where he was sitting and asked that he bid her sister to help her. There seems to be a reproach to Jesus in her speech as she asked if he did not care that Mary had left her alone to serve. It was an explosive act

said unto her, ⁶"Martha, Martha, thou art anxious and troubled about many
things: 42 ⁷but one thing is needful: for Mary hath chosen the good part,
which shall not be taken away from her.

⁶A few ancient authorities read *Martha, Martha, thou art troubled; Mary hath
chosen &c.*
⁷Many ancient authorities read *but few things are needful, or one*

of Martha to so speak to Jesus. Jesus overlooked the apparent rebuke that Martha gave him, and looked into her heart
and answered according to her good and his own wisdom.

41, 42 But the Lord answered and said unto her,—Jesus
said: "Martha, Martha." This was an impressive and emphatic
repetition, calling her attention to the important truth he was
about to utter. Martha was fretted with work, and Jesus
kindly and calmly answered her outburst of feeling and said
that she was "anxious and troubled about many things." The
manifold cares in providing for his entertainment were not
necessary. Jesus reproved her, not so much to the entertaining him as to her state of mind; not to the mere providing for
the company, but to her needless solicitude and restless agita-
tion of spirit which could well have been spared on that occasion. Martha was anxious about "many things," but Jesus informed her that only "one thing is needful." Here Jesus puts
in contrast the "many things" with the "one thing"; that contrast is not only in regard to number, but also in regard to
kind. Martha was absorbed with the physical and earthly.
Jesus points her to the spiritual and heavenly. The one thing
needful was a proper state of heart for receiving Jesus, and
also the receiving of his truth. With proper attention to the
one thing needful, Martha as well as Mary could have done
well in attending to her household duties. Jesus commended
Mary because she had "chosen the good part," and he adds
that it should "not be taken away from her."

6. JESUS' TEACHING ABOUT PRAYER
11: 1-13

1 And it came to pass, as he was praying in a certain place, that when he

1 And it came to pass, as he was praying—Jesus had taught
his disciples to pray by precept (Matt. 6: 7-15) and example

ceased, one of his disciples said unto him, Lord, teach us to pray, even as John also taught his disciples. 2 And he said unto them, When ye pray, say, ⁸Father, Hallowed by thy name. Thy kingdom come.⁹ 3 Give us day by day

⁸Many ancient authorities read *Our Father, who art in heaven.* See Mt. 6.9
⁹Many ancient authorities add *Thy will be done, as in heaven, so on earth.* See Mt. 6.10

(Luke 9: 29). The example of Jesus on this occasion stirred them to fresh interest in prayer and reminded them of the teachings of John the Baptist. (Luke 5: 33.) Jesus gave them the substance of a model prayer as recorded in Matt. 6: 7-15. Jesus was praying "in a certain place"; this indefinite statement shows that Luke did not make a definite time or place, but that his "order" is one of thought. This occasion may have followed close upon the visit at Bethany, the "one of his disciples" in that case perhaps being a later one, and Jesus here repeating what had been taught the twelve disciples in Matt. 6: 9. The "certain place" would then be near Jerusalem. This disciple said: "Lord, teach us to pray, even as John also taught his disciples."

2-4 **And he said unto them, When ye pray,**—Two causes may be listed for this request—the example of Jesus and the fact that John had taught his disciples to pray. Many think that his form is different in time and place from that given in Matt. 6: 9-13; however this is of little consequence. The importance of prayer justifies a repetition of teaching concerning it. In Matthew the suggestive occasion is the habit of "vain repetitions"; in Luke the occasion is a direct request. In Matthew the prayer is followed with a fuller statement of the condition of forgiveness, while in Luke Jesus gives encouragement to persevering in prayer. The simplicity, brevity, beauty, directness, generality, and spiritual fitness make this prayer a model one.

Father, Hallowed be thy name.—God is to be addressed, not as Creator, or Ruler, or Almighty, or as the Omniscient One —but as "Father." This form of address is comprehensive enough to include all the rest. It puts in the foreground his love and care, and is chosen to suggest our relation to him and his relation to us. His name is to be hallowed; this

[10]our daily bread. 4 And forgive us our sins; for we ourselves also forgive every one that is indebted to us. And bring us not into temptation.[11]

[10]Gr. *our bread for the coming day.* Or, *our needful bread:* as in Mt. 6.11
[11]Many ancient authorities add *but deliver us from the evil* one (or, *from evil*). See Mt. 6.13

means that we are to give reverence, honor and homage to it; it forbids our using his name in an irreverent way; we are to hold it with majesty, purity, and glory. "Thy kingdom come." The first petition is not for ourselves, but for the interest of his kingdom; his kingdom must be put first. Our interests are to be identified with the interests of his kingdom. At the time that this prayer was taught, the kingdom had not been established; it was still in the future, and they were to look forward with prayer to its coming.

Give us day by day our daily bread.—This phrase or petition may have been suggested from the daily gift of the manna in the wilderness. After we have sought first the things pertaining to the kingdom of God, we may make request for bread, daily needs for the body, and daily bread for the soul may be fairly understood as included in this prayer. We are dependent on God, and the petition of this prayer for daily bread keeps before us our dependence on him. The asking each day for the bread of the day carries with it efforts on our part to earn our daily bread. We are to work for it. When we pray for the kingdom to spread, we obligate ourselves to work for the spreading of the kingdom; so when we pray for our daily bread, we are pledging ourselves to cooperate with God through all of the laws that he has given for the production of bread.

And forgive us our sins;—Jesus teaches us here to ask God for forgiveness, as we ourselves have already forgiven those who have sinned against us. One ground, and apparently the only ground, except the mercy of God, on which we can ask to be forgiven, is that we have forgiven all—every one from our heart. It is useless to ask God to forgive us when we have neglected or refused to forgive others. Jesus teaches emphatically and clearly the conditions of God's forgiving us, and one of these conditions is that we already have a forgiving heart

5 And he said umto them, Which of you shall have a friend, and shall go unto him at midnight, and way to him, Friend, lend me three loaves; 6 for a friend of mine is come to me from a journey, and I have nothing to set before him; 7 and he from within shall answer and say, Trouble me not: the door is now shut, and my children are with me in bed; I cannot rise and give thee? 8 I say unto you, Though he will not rise and give him because he is his friend, yet because of his importunity he will arise and give him

---

toward others. We pray that we may not be led into temptation. Jesus and God may permit us to be tempted but we ask not to be led into temptation, and not to be tempted above that we are able to bear. (1 Cor. 10: 13; 2 Pet. 2: 9.)

5, 6 **And he said unto them,**—This has a close connection with the prayer which just precedes it. The request made of Jesus was "Lord, teach us to pray"; Jesus not only gives instruction, but gives an illustration which puts the greatest stress upon persistent importunity. One had a friend who came to his house "at midnight," and requested the loan of "three loaves" to set before his guest who was on a journey, and had stopped to remain overnight with him. This request came at an unusual hour; his friend must arise from slumber, tear himself from his little ones, unbolt his well-fastened door, and hand out three loaves of bread. The man had come for the bread and would not return without it. Some have suggested that "three loaves" were asked for, because of a custom —one loaf for the guest, one for the host, and one to show abundance.

7, 8 **and he from within shall answer and say,**—The man awakened at midnight is severely tested; he responded to the call of his friend in a vexed tone. He did not wish to be bothered; his door was shut; his children were in bed with him or in the same sleeping place. The Greek word for bed applied to any room or place used for sleeping, as well as to a bed or couch. There were so many obstacles in the way, and it would be so much trouble to unbar the door, find the loaves, and disturb the children that the friend answered that he could not be bothered with him. His friendship would not move him to grant the request, but the importunity, literally "the shamelessness" of the caller would cause him to "arise and give him as many as he needeth."

¹²as many as he needeth. 9 And I say unto you, Ask, and it shall be given you; seek, and ye shall find; knock, and it shall be opened unto you. 10 For every one that asketh receiveth; and he that seeketh findeth; and to him that knocketh it shall be opened. 11 And of which of you that is a father shall his son ask ¹a loaf, and he give him a stone? or a fish, and he for a fish give him a serpent? 12 Or if he shall ask an egg, will he give him a scor-

¹²Or, whatsoever things
¹Some ancient authorities omit a loaf, and he give him a stone? or

9, 10 **And I say unto you, Ask,**—"Ask," "seek," and "knock" represent the three ways of striving to have our wants supplied. Not content with asking, we are to follow it by seeking and searching (Deut. 4: 29), and to add to that knocking. When asking does not bring all that is needed, we continue seeking, as well as asking (John 15: 7; 16: 23); and when there are obstacles as locked doors, barred gates, knock for help , that the difficulties may be removed and a door opened for spiritual blessings and spiritual opportunities. The three-fold repetition—"ask," "seek," and 'knock"—comes naturally from the illustration that has just been given. Ask and seek as the man who went to his sleeping friend at midnight; "knock" at the door earnestly as he did; for to such asking, seeking, knocking, God's door of mercy will be opened. These three repetitions of command are more than mere repetitions; since to seek is more than to ask, and to knock more than to seek. These emphasize the deep earnestness and persistency that must be exercised in prayer.

11, 12 **And of which of you that is a father**—This is another illustration emphasizing prayer. A loaf of bread in the East bore resemblance to a flat stone, suggestive of this compari-son; some fish also resembled a serpent in form, as an eel. These two illustrations are given by Matthew. (Matt. 7: 9, 10.) Luke only gives the third illustration of the comparison between the egg and scorpion. The scorpion was a crab-shaped animal, and some species were exceedingly poisonous. If a child should ask for any form of food, an earthly parent would not give him a hurtful thing in answer to the child's request; hence God would not give harmful things to his chil-dren who ask him in earnest prayer. Some think that "a scor-

pion? 13 If ye then, being evil, know how to give good gifts unto your children, how much more shall *your* heavenly Father give the Holy Spirit to them that ask him?

---

pion for an egg" was a proverbial expression. Jesus now makes his own application of these illustrations.

13 **If ye then, being evil, know how to give good gifts**— There is no longer a comparison, but a contrast; the contrast is between man and Jehovah as our Father. It may also signify the contrast between Jehovah God and the gods of the heathen. If earthly parents know how to give "good things" to their children, how much more shall God our Father "give the Holy Spirit to them that ask him?" It is worthy of notice that the argument for persevering prayer increases. First from a friend, then from a father, who is more than a friend, and now from the relation of heavenly Father, who is infinitely more than an earthly father.

7. BLASPHEMY AND UNBELIEF REBUKED
11: 14-36

14 And he was casting out a demon *that was* dumb. And it came to pass, when the demon was gone out, the dumb man spake; and the multitudes marvelled. 15 But some of them said, [2]By [3]Beelzebub the prince of the demons casteth he out demons. 16 And others, trying *him*, sought of him a

[2]Or, *in*
[3]Gr. *Beelzebul*

---

14 **And he was casting out a demon**—The demoniac spirit in the man seems to have made the man dumb. If this is the same case as that noticed in Matt. 12: 22 he was blind also. When the demon was cast out by the power of Jesus, the man's powers of speech were restored to him, and the people marveled at this power in Jesus to drive out evil spirits. Others think that this was a different case to that mentioned by Matt. 12: 22 and Mark 3: 19-30. The greatness of the miracle excites the astonishment of many; this leads to the charge and the demand in the next two verses.

15, 16 **But some of them said,**—As presented here by Luke, there are two classes of objectors: (1) those who charged him with working through Beelzebub, the prince of demons, and (2) those who, discrediting all the testimonies he had given in

sign from heaven. 17 But he, knowing their thoughts, said unto them, Every kingdom divided against itself is brought to desolation; ⁴and a house *divided* against a house falleth. 18 And if Satan also is divided against himself, how shall his kingdom stand? because ye say that I cast out demons ²by ³Beelzebub. 19 And if I ²by ³Beelzebub cast out demons, by whom do your sons cast them out? therefore shall they be your judges. 20 But if I by the finger of God cast out demons, then is the kingdom of God come upon you.

⁴Or, *and house falleth upon house*

support of his claims, demanded yet other signs from heaven. When this demon was cast out of the man he had instantaneous relief. "Beelzebub" comes from the Aramaic, and was the name for the chief of demons; Beelzebub was a Philistine god of the flies, and this title may not unnaturally have been transferred to Satan. The issue between Jesus had his enemies was too vital to be omitted, hence all three of them give a record of this accusation against Jesus. We have it in Matt. 9: 32-34 and much more fully in 12: 22-32.

17-20 **But he, knowing their thoughts,**—Jesus first answered the charge that his power came from Satan. The kingdom or a house divided, filled with discord, strife, dissension, and anarchy cannot stand; a kingdom is destroyed by internal civil war. If Jesus cast out demons because he was in league with Satan, then his kingdom was divided against itself; Satan is casting out Satan; how can his kingdom stand? (Mark 3: 23.) To ask the question was the most forceful way of saying it cannot stand. But if Satan cast out demons, by whom did their sons cast them out? The pretended power of the Pharisees to cast out evil spirits belonged to their sons. This was a keen and justifiable term of the charge upon them, popularly known as "argumentum ad hominem." Even your sons will become your judges to condemn you on the charge; demons to do cast out demons.

But if I by the finger of God—If he, by "the finger of God," or power of God, or Holy Spirit, cast out demons, then the kingdom of God had come unawares upon them. On the phrase, "finger of God," compare the expression of the magicians to Pharaoh—"this is the finger of God." (Ex. 8: 19.) The "kingdom of God," not kingdom of heaven, is the uniform phrase used by Luke. It will be noticed here that Satan is

21 When the strong *man* fully armed guardeth his own court, his goods are in peace; 22 but when a stronger than he shall come upon him, and overcome him, he taketh from him his whole armor wherein he trusted, and divideth his spoils. 23 He that is not with me is against me; and he that gathereth not with me scattereth. 24 The unclean spirit when [5]he is gone out of the man, passeth through waterless places, seeking rest, and finding none, [5]he saith, I will turn back unto my house whence I came out. 25 And when [5]he is come, [5]he findeth it swept and garnished. 26 Then goeth [5]he, and taketh *to him* seven other spirits more evil than [6]himself; and they enter in and dwell there: and the last state of that man becometh worse than the first.

[5]Or, *it*
[6]Or, *itself*

represented as a real personal being, not a mere principle of evil.

21-23 When the strong man fully armed—The reasoning here is clear and forceable. So long as Satan, the strong man armed kept his palace and no mightier foe assailed him, he had things his own way and his household goods were undisturbed; but when the Son of God came down upon him with far mightier forces, he wrests from him his old weapons and quickly divides his spoils. Jesus, if he had been in league with Satan, would have left him to keep his power over men in peace; but by his casting out demons, he showed that he is an enemy to Satan and superior to him—that he had himself overpowered Satan and conquered him.

He that is not with me is against me;—This is a proverbial saying and was probably repeated often by Jesus; it was suited to the various classes of his hearers, many of whom were secret enemies or undecided and wavering or timid friends. Jesus emphatically declares that there can be no middle ground. He that does not take part with God and Christ must take part with Satan.

24-26 The unclean spirit when he is gone—Here Jesus teaches the law of Satanic operations; this especially relates to demonical possessions. When a spirit of Satan is cast out of one person or place, it seeks another favorable place. The meaning here is that the evil spirit wanders about and finds no rest; then it decides to return, and taking to itself seven other evil spirits does return. The evil spirit returns to its house, the human soul, and finds it swept and garnished as a reformed, yet unconverted, person might be.

27 And it came to pass, as he said these things, a certain woman out of the multitude lifted up her voice, and said unto him, Blessed is the womb that bare thee, and the breasts which thou didst suck. 28 But he said, Yea rather, blessed are they that hear the word of God, and keep it.

29 And when the multitudes were gathering together unto him, he began to say, This generation is an evil generation: it seeketh after a sign; and there shall no sign be given to it but the sign of Jonah. 30 For even as

27-28 **And it came to pass,**—"A certain woman" was impressed with the wisdom and moral grandeur of Jesus as a great Teacher, and in true womanly ways cried out aloud in the multitude and gave expression to her praise. Tradition says this woman was a maidservant to Martha and Mary; there is no evidence of the truthfulness of this tradition. The woman's expressions indicate that she was a mother, as she voices motherly instincts and feelings. Her beatitude is similar to that of Elisabeth, the mother of John the Baptist. (Luke 1: 42.) This good woman is fulfilling Mary's own prophecy. (Luke 1: 48.) One way of praising Jesus was to praise his mother.

But he said, Yea rather, blessed are they—The instant response of Jesus turns the thought to the far higher blessedness of those who "hear the word of God, and keep it." The woman's sentiment was a true expression of her heart, but Jesus showed who should receive the richest blessings. She was blessing Jesus through his mother, but Jesus in contrast turns attention to others and gives them a beatitude. Jesus gives praise to his mother, but he never intended that she be worshiped; he does not deny the woman's words, but points out who, rather than his natural mother, are to be counted as blessed, even those who hear and keep the word, the whole counsel, commands, and will of God. Hearing is not enough; one must hear and do or "keep" the commandments of God.

29 **And when the multitudes were gathering**—When the multitudes were thronging together, or assembling, Jesus announced certain truths. Matt. 12: 38-45 may be compared with Luke's record here. Luke does not state a definite time; he does not tell us when the multitudes were assembling. It is very probable that frequent gatherings during Christ's ministry were had. Jesus now answers those noticed in verse 16,

Jonah became a sign unto the Ninevites, so shall also the Son of man to be this generation. 31 The queen of the south shall rise up in the judgment with the men of this generation, and shall condemn them: for she came from the ends of the earth to hear the wisdom of Solomon; and behold, [7]a greater

[7]Gr. *more than*

---

who were seeking a sign from heaven. The generation was an evil one, for it was unbelieving, and demanded unreasonable evidences of the divinity of Jesus; they wanted a heavenly sign, but the only sign granted was that of Jonah. The preaching of Jesus ought to have been sign enough as in the case of Jonah.

30 **For even as Jonah became a sign**—As Jonah became a sign to the Ninevites, so Jesus and his preaching should have been sufficient sign to his generation. Jonah had been commanded to go to Nineveh and warn them against impending destruction; but instead of going to Nineveh he went in the opposite direction, and went aboard a vessel. A storm arose and Jonah was thrown overboard by the crew; Jehovah had prepared a great fish and Jonah was swallowed and remained in the fish for three days and nights; he was then thrown out of the fish on the dry land, and was then instructed to go to Nineveh. He went to Nineveh and preached to the Ninevites. Jonah came forth from the sea monster to preach to the Ninevites; so Jesus came forth from the heart of the earth to send forth the gospel to every creature. Jonah's remaining in the belly of the fish became a type of Jesus remaining in the grave. This is the sign that Jesus gave as his proof of his Messiahship.

31 **The queen of the south shall rise up**—"The queen of the south" was the queen of Sheba (1 Kings 10: 1); Sheba is supposed to be the southern part of the Arabian peninsula. It is called here "the ends of the earth"; this is an expression to denote a great distance. (Jer. 6: 20.) She came to hear the wisdom of Solomon, and was filled with admiration. She had faith; she was not unbelieving; for she made the long journey to hear the wisdom of Solomon. There was in the very presence of the people something or a sign greater, or superior to that of Jonah or to Solomon. The miracles and preaching of

than Solomon is here. *32* The men of Nineveh shall stand up in the judgment with this generation, and shall condemn it: for they repented at the
preaching of Jonah; and behold, [7]a greater than Jonah is here.
   33 No man, when he hath lighted a lamp, putteth it in a cellar, neither
under the bushel, but on the stand, that they which enter in may see the
light. *34* The lamp of thy body is thine eye: when thine eye is single, thy
whole body also is full of light; but when it is evil, thy body also is full of

Jesus were more significant and superior in kind and degree
than those in the day of Jonah or of Solomon when the people
believed.

   32 The men of Nineveh shall stand up in the judgment—Jesus passes on in his discourse and contrasts that generation
with the Ninevites, whom they despised as heathens and Gentile sinners. They would be witnesses against that generation
for rejecting Jesus; the unreasonableness of the impenitent of
this generation would be condemned by the example of the
Ninevites and the queen of Sheba. The Ninevites repented at
the preaching of Jonah, who only made them a temporary
visit and performed no miracles. Jesus was living among
them and preaching the gospel of the Messiah, yet they did
not believe him. Jonah preached to the Ninevites about 840
B.C. Jesus as recorded by Luke here contrasted the Ninevites and the queen of the south; the climax is greater; it was
more terrible to be condemned by the Ninevites than by the
queen of Sheba.

   33 No man, when he hath lighted a lamp,—In the discourses
of Jesus this illustration occurs repeatedly, being used for various purposes, yet always appropriate. (See Matt. 5: 15; 6:
22; Mark 4: 21; Luke 8: 16.) Jesus uses a very apt illustration; a lamp was used for light, and no one would put it in a
secret place, or "in a cellar," or "under the bushel"; when
lighted, it was placed on the stand that it might give light to
those who were in the room. The Greek word for "secret
place" or "cellar" means any concealed place, like a vault,
crypt, or covered way, or place like a cellar, a mere hole where
persons would not enter. The "bushel" was a common household measure holding about a peck.

   34 The lamp of thy body is thine eye:—As the lamp is made
for light and its useful purposes, so the eye was made for vi-

darkness. 35 Look therefore whether the light that is in thee be not darkness,
36 If therefore thy whole body be full of light, having no part dark, it shall
be wholly full of light, as when the lamp with its bright shining doth give
thee light.

sion, needing therefore to be in perfect condition so as to fulfill its functions well. In like manner the moral light of God
comes into this world through Christ to be accepted by men
honestly and with unprejudiced mind. For as a blurred eye
dooms the whole body to darkness, so does a prejudiced,
worldly heart shut off the light of God and doom the miserable man to the darkness of delusion and death. The "eye is
single" when it is undimmed and has its natural and proper
powers for straight and clear seeing; when the eye is evil, that
is, it lacks its powers of clear and correct sight, the body is
full of darkness.

35, 36 **Look therefore whether the light**—If the only source
of light be darkness, great indeed is the darkness. The eye
gives expression and radiance to the face and person; when
the eye is dark the whole person is gloomy and sad. The eye
has been called "the window of the soul"; hence through the
eyes the different moods of the soul are expressed. Disputing
and questioning the work and authority of Jesus as these
Pharisees and others were doing, and demanding unreasonable signs, and disbelieving the signs which he had already
given them, was like having an eye that is dark; the whole
spiritual man is soon filled with evil, with deep spiritual darkness. (John 3: 19; 2 Cor. 4: 4.)

8. CONDEMNATION OF PHARISAISM
11: 37-54

37 Now as he spake, a Pharisee asketh him to ⁸dine with him: and he
went in, and sat down to meat. 38 And when the Pharisee saw it, he mar-

⁸Gr. breakfast

37, 38 **Now as he spake, a Pharisee asketh him**—A Pharisee
invited Jesus to dine with him. This Pharisee was more
friendly than many of the Pharisees. The Pharisees were a
religious sect among the Jews who were very particular
about the ceremonies of the law; in fact, they had added many

velled that he had not first bathed himself before [1]dinner. 39 And the Lord
said unto him, Now ye the Pharisees cleanse the outside of the cup and of

[1]Gr. *breakfast*

of their traditions to the law; they were as careful to observe
their traditions as they were to observe the law. This Pharisee was not a disciple of Jesus. Jesus accepted the invitation.
The original shows that it was an early meal, perhaps "breakfast." It was less formal than a dinner. Who the Pharisee
was, or why he asked Jesus, we are not informed; some think
that he invited him to criticize his teachings and his life.

And when the Pharisee saw it,—Jesus accepted the invitation and went into the house and dined with the Pharisee. It
was the Jewish custom to dip the hands in water before eating
and often between courses for ceremonial purification. In
Galilee the Pharisees and scribes had criticized Jesus severely
and often because he ate with unwashed hands. (Matt. 15:
1-20; Mark 7: 1-23.) On this occasion Jesus had reclined at
the breakfast without this ceremonial dipping in water his
hands. This neglect of Jesus to follow the custom of the
Pharisees caused them to wonder. It became an occasion for
Jesus to teach them a lesson. Perhaps this Pharisee was hor-
rified, not that the hands of his guest were unclean, but that
he had not conformed to the Pharisaic ceremony of washing
before the meal.

39 **And the Lord said unto him,**—Though Jesus was a guest
in the house and at the table of this Pharisee, yet he did not
hesitate to condemn the tradition which had been added to the
law, and which stood in the way of this Pharisee accepting
the truth. Jesus charged the Pharisees with making the outside clean, but neglecting the inside. He did not object to
cleansing the outside, but his objection was the cleansing of
the outside and leaving the inside unclean; the Pharisees
would substitute the outside cleansing for the inward cleansing; this Jesus severely condemned. Jesus used the common
illustration of "the cup and of the platter" because these were
on the table while they were eating. It was a severe charge
to say that they were "full of extortion and wickedness." The

the platter; but your inward part is full of extortion and wickedness. 40 Ye foolish ones, did not he that made the outside make the inside also? 41 But give for alms those things which ²are within; and behold, all things are clean unto you.

42 But woe unto you Pharisees! for ye tithe mint and rue and every herb, and pass over justice and the love of God: but these ought ye to have done,

²Or. ye can

Pharisees kept the external regulations, but their hearts were full of plunder and wickedness. The psalmist had said: "Thou desirest truth in the inward parts." (Psalm 51: 6.) A cleansed body does not make a pure heart any more than fine clothes make a noble character.

40, 41 Ye foolish ones, did not he that made—God had made the outside and the inward part also; he required cleanliness of both parts. They are called "foolish ones" because they put the emphasis on the wrong thing; at other times Jesus called them hypocrites. The Pharisees gave alms and thought that they were acceptable to God because of their mere giving of alms. They gave alms of what they had and then claimed that all things that they had were clean because they had given alms of it. It mattered not how they had obtained their possession, they acted as though their fraudulent gains were sanctified because they gave a part of them to Jehovah. They thought that they could use lawfully and enjoy all things of which they gave alms. (Luke 19: 8, 9; Rom. 14: 14; 1 Tim. 4: 4, 5; Tit. 1: 15.)

42 But woe unto you Pharisees!—A curse is pronounced upon the Pharisees; Jesus was not talking "about" the Pharisees, but he was talking "to" them. The reason assigned is that they carefully "tithe mint and rue and every herb," and fail to appreciate the full significance of this. To "tithe" meant to take a tenth of anything and give it to Jehovah. "Mint" was a garden plant like our spearmint"; "rue" was a shrubbery plant about two feet high and was grown in their gardens; "herb" was a general term to include similar plants. Matt. 23: 23 has "anise" and "cummin." These were garden plants used principally for flavoring purposes. They were careful to tithe these things, but neglected the important things of "justice and the love of God." Mathew adds

and not to leave the other undone. 43 Woe unto you Pharisees! for ye love
the chief seats in the synagogues, and the salutations in the marketplaces. 44
Woe unto you! for ye are as the tombs which appear not, and the men that
walk over *them* know it not.

45 And one of the lawyers answering saith unto him, Teacher, in saying

---

"faith." It was right for them to tithe these things, but
wrong for them to neglect the important things. These
things ye ought to do, said Jesus, but you ought not to have
left undone "the weightier matters of the law, justice, and
mercy, and faith." (Matt. 23: 23.)

43 **Woe unto you Pharisees!**—This "woe" is pronounced
upon these Pharisees because they loved to occupy the "chief"
or "first" seats in the synagogue. The chief seats were elevated in a semicircle at one end of the synagogue and facing
the congregation. Sometimes these seats were sold to those
who were able to pay the best price for them. Matt. 23: 6 has
also the chief place at feasts, given by Luke (14: 7: 20: 46) as
a mark characteristic of the Pharisees. The Pharisees loved
these positions of honor; they also loved reverential salutations, titles of honor, and praise of men. They liked to receive the plaudits of men in the market places. In all these
places they appeared to be very pious and wanted praises for
their pretended loyalty to the law.

44 **Woe unto you!**—This condemnation is pronounced upon
them by Jesus for their hypocrisy. Matthew includes the
scribes and other hypocrites with the Pharisees.
"Hypocrites" were like stage actors who put on masks and assumed characters that did not belong to them; they were base
pretenders. They were like graves or tombs that are hidden
from view by age or the growth of grass or weeds and men
passing over them are defiled. So people were spiritually defiled by these hypocrites, whose pretended righteousness hid
from view their depraved character. These hidden graves
would give ceremonial defilement for seven days. (Num. 19:
16.)

45 **And one of the lawyers answering saith**—The "lawyers"
were generally Pharisees; they were oftentimes the same as
the "scribes." This lawyer felt the reproach that Jesus had

this thou reproachest us also. 46 And he said, Woe unto you lawyers also!
for ye load men with burdens grievous to be borne, and ye yourselves touch
not the burdens with one of your fingers. 47 Woe unto you! for ye build the
tombs of the prophets, and your fathers killed them. 48 So ye are witnesses

---

given to the Pharisees and so informed him. He felt that
what Jesus had said was an insult to the lawyers or to his
class. They were interpreters of the law, and were not lawyers in our modern use of that word. He was shrewd enough
to see the force of what Jesus had said and felt that the denunciations applied to the lawyers as well as to the Pharisees;
he felt that his dignity had been insulted as well as that of the
Pharisees.

46 **And he said, Woe unto you lawyers also!**—The "lawyers," one of whom now rebuked Jesus, justly merited the
condemnation, and Jesus pronounced three woes upon this
class. Jesus showed them to be hypocrites, for they by their
interpretations and traditions placed heavy burdens upon the
people, but they did not get under the load and help bear
them; they would not even touch the burden with their fingers. While they made the law fearfully burdensome to the
people they touched not those burdens themselves with one of
their fingers; but, on the contrary, they exempted themselves
by their interpretations entirely from those burdensome con-
structions which they imposed upon the people. To make law
bear heavily on the people, but light as air upon the lawyers
and Pharisees, was the uttermost moral abomination.

47 **Woe unto you! for ye build the tombs of the prophets,**—
Sepulchres among the Jews were often caves, or were hewn
out in rocks on the sides of hills and the entrance decorated
with ornaments. (Gen. 23: 9; Isa. 22: 16.) Some interpret
this speech of Jesus as being severe irony. They now pretend
greatly to honor the prophets, but their fathers had killed the
prophets, and they were walking in the footsteps of their fathers; they did not condemn their fathers for killing the prophets, but went to great trouble and expense to adorn heir
graves. This sounds very much like much of our modern hypocrisy, both as individuals and as nations.

and consent unto the works of your fathers: for they killed them, and ye build *their tombs.* 49 Therefore also said the wisdom of God, I will send unto them prophets and apostles; and *some* of them they shall kill and persecute; 50 that the blood of all the prophets, which was shed from the foundation of the world, may be required of this generation; 51 from the blood of Abel unto the blood of Zachariah, who perished between the altar and the

48 **So ye are witnesses and consent**—The generation to which Jesus was talking became guilty of the sins of their fathers by consenting or endorsing the crimes which they did in killing the prophets. Jesus knew that these Pharisees and lawyers were getting ready to destroy him. Their fathers killed the prophets, and now they were building tombs of costly stones, and were adding endless burdens by their traditions. Their fathers had disobeyed the prophets and had destroyed them; the present generation was concealing them under their whitewash of tradition, so that men could not recognize them nor their teaching. In this way they were witnesses and consenting unto the works of their fathers. It is a high crime against God to persecute and destroy God's prophets of the present generation, but destroy those of a former generation.

49-51 **Therefore also said the wisdom of God,**—"The wisdom of God" as used here does not refer to any book of the Old Testament; it has reference to Jesus as Paul says in 1 Cor. 1: 30. Possibly it may mean that God in his wisdom said what Jesus now states; hence there is no reference to a previous revealed "saying." This wisdom of God now announced that God would send his prophets and apostles to them and that they would persecute and kill them. The generation to which Jesus was speaking was no better than the generation that killed the prophets of God; the present generation was seeking to do even a greater crime than their fathers had done; hence, the condemnation that fell upon their fathers would come with greater force upon them. The sins of the fathers should be visited upon the children (Ex. 20: 5), especially of that generation which sanctioned the sins of the past, and even went beyond them.

from the blood of Abel unto the blood of Zachariah,—Abel, the second son of Adam, was the righteous martyr, and the

³sanctuary: yea, I say unto you, it shall be required of this generation. 52
Woe unto you lawyers! for ye took away the key of knowledge: ye entered
not in yourselves, and them that were entering in ye hindered.

53 And when he was come out from thence, the scribes and the Pharisees

³Gr. *house*

first recorded in the Bible, and Zachariah, the son of Jehoiada,
is the last one recorded, according to the Jewish arrangement
of the Old Testament. (2 Chron. 24: 20-22.) His last words
were: "Jehovah look upon it, and require it." However there
is some difficulty in determining definitely who this Zachariah
was. Many of God's prophets between Abel and Zachariah
had been slain. Some think that this Zachariah was the son
of Barachiah; however the usual explanation is that it has reference to Zachariah, the son of Jehoiada, the priest who was
slain in the court of the temple. Matt. 23: 35 gives Zachariah
as the son of Barachiah. Some think that in some way "Barachiah" as used by Matthew should be "Jehoiada"; they think
these names have been interchanged. Chronologically the
murder of Uriah by Jehoiakim was later (Jer. 26: 23), but this
climax is from Genesis to Second Chronicles. Zachariah was
slain between the altar and the sanctuary; that is, between the
brazen altar in the court and the temple. The condemnation
should be cumulative, bringing the blood or the guilt for shed-
ding the blood of all of the prophets upon this generation.

52 **Woe unto you lawyers!**—This is the third woe pronounced upon the lawyers. This woe is pronounced upon them
because they had taken away "the key of knowledge."
Spiritual wisdom is represented as a treasure in a room or
house, on which were lock and key; the lawyers had locked
the door, and either carried, that is, "kept" the key, or it may
mean, they had taken it away. In either case they were responsible as teachers of the law for the ignorance of the people.
They had not entered in, neither had they permitted others to
enter in. Jesus was revealing the will of God unto the people;
these lawyers had refused to accept this teaching and were
hindering the people from accepting it.

53, 54 **And when he was come out from thence,**—The mali-
ciousness of the scribes and Pharisees is clearly and strongly

began to ⁴press upon *him* vehemently, and to provoke him to speak of ⁵many things; 54 laying wait for him, to catch something out of his mouth.

⁴Or. *set themselves vehemently against* him
⁵Or, *more*

described here. The original Greek may mean that they terribly pressed him, enraged, and plied him with questions concerning more things, setting a trap for him, to catch (or "hunt artfully") something from his mouth. So soon as Jesus went out from the Pharisee's house (verse 37) these scribes and Pharisees were ready to spend all of their fury upon him. Jesus had in no uncertain terms very severely rebuked their hypocrisy; they were enraged against him and now sought to take some word and pervert it into some accusation against Jesus. What became of the breakfast that Jesus went in to eat, we know not, but the rage of both Pharisees and lawyers, together with the scribes, knew no bounds. Jesus had pronounced three woes upon the Pharisees and three upon the lawyers. They were "laying wait for him"; this vivid picture of the anger of these Pharisees and lawyers which Luke draws presents them as treating Jesus as if he were a beast of prey.

9. A CHARGE TO HIS DISCIPLES
12: 1-12

1 In the mean time, when ⁶the many thousands of the multitude were gathered together, insomuch that they trod one upon another, he began to

⁶Gr. *the myriads of*

1 In the mean time, when the many thousands—"In the mean time" is a classic idiom to start a sentence, or even a paragraph; Luke has no expressed antecedent other than the incidents of Luke 11: 53, 54, and is frequently found in Luke's writings. Some think that what Luke here presents is compiled from several discourses of our Lord spoken at different times and places. However, this seems to introduce the events which follow; Luke gives an accurate account of events without giving the chronological order of them. The report of the public attack upon Jesus by the scribes and Pharisees brought together "many thousands of the multi-

[7]say unto his disciples first of all, Beware ye of the leaven of the Pharisees, which is hypocrisy. 2 But there is nothing covered up, that shall not be revealed; and hid, that shall not be known. 3 Wherefore whatsoever ye have said in the darkness shall be heard in the light; and what ye have spoken in the ear in the inner chambers shall be proclaimed upon the housetops. 4 And I say unto you my friends, Be not afraid of them that kill the body,

[7]Or, *say unto his disciples, First of all beware ye*

tude," and there were so many that, in their excitement and wonder, "they trod one upon another." Jesus addressed himself to his disciples. What he relates now may be found in Matt. 16: 6 with respect to the Sadducees, and in Mark 8: 15 what is said about the Pharisees. The occasion was opportune for what Jesus warned his disciples against the hypocrisy of the leading Pharisees; their hypocrisy was hidden by a professed sanctity of heart. The "leaven of the Pharisees" was their hypocrisy.

2 **But there is nothing covered up,**—We have a parallel of this in Matt. 10: 26-33. Jesus had warned them against the "leaven" or the hypocritical influence of these Pharisees; he now tells them that there is nothing covered up, whether false or true, that shall not be revealed. Jesus used here a proverbial saying which meant that hypocrisy would be unmasted, truth would be displayed and vindicated. The secret designs of his enemies would be made known, exposed to the light of truth, and condemned at the judgment. (1 Cor. 4: 5; Eph. 5: 13.)

3 **Wherefore whatsoever ye have said**—The thought in the preceding words is expanded here and applied to the words of the apostles. Whatever may be spoken privately, secretly, as in the darkness of night, or whispered as it were in the retired chambers, shall be made public. The roofs of their houses were flat and the people were accustomed to sitting on them in the evening and talking to each other in neighborly conversation. Hence whatever might be spoken in secret should be proclaimed from the housetop; this means that whatever may be told to them in secret or in the secret room should be proclaimed in public conversation on the top of their houses.

4, 5 **And I say unto you my friends,**—Jesus is here still addressing his disciples; he calls them "friends" in opposition to

and after that have no more that they can do. 5 But I will warn you whom ye shall fear: Fear him, who after he hath killed hath [8]power to cast into [9]hell; yea, I say unto you, Fear him. 6 Are not five sparrows sold for two pence? and not one of them is forgotten in the sight of God. 7 But the very hairs of your head are all numbered. Fear not: ye are of more value than many sparrows. 8 And I say unto you, Every one who shall confess

[8]Or, *authority*
[9]Gr. *Gehenna*

the scribes and Pharisees. "No longer do I call you servants," but friends. (John 15: 14, 15.) The furiously angry attack of the Pharisees which had just been made seems to suggest the coming persecutions of his disciples. Jesus spoke comforting words to them; they were not to fear those who could only destroy the body; they were to fear only him who was able to destroy both body and soul. Socrates is reported as saying when they were about to kill him: "Slay me, they may; hurt, me, they cannot. The body is not the 'me,' not the 'real being.'" The soul and body are together not said to be killed, but "cast into hell." "Gehenna" is the place of future torment, which punishment is distinctly stated to be everlasting. (Matt. 25: 46.)

6, 7 **Are not five sparrows sold for two pence?**—Sparrows were very abundant in Palestine; there were many species of them. These birds were caught, strung together, and sold in the market at the exceedingly small price of five for two farthings, or about three cents in our money. Matthew says: "Are not two sparrows sold for a penny?" (Matt. 10: 29.) Luke says: "Are not five sparrows sold for two pence?" The variation in price depends upon the number purchased. They are not forgotten in the sight of God, though they are small and bring an insignificant price. In like manner the "very hairs of your head are all numbered." Nothing is too small for God to take note of it; God made the small and insignificant things as well as the planets and satellites; hence one need not think that God overlooks the minutest details that affect his children. His care is so minute as to number every hair of our heads.

8, 9 **And I say unto you, Every one who shall confess**—This is similar to Matt. 10: 32; the time is at hand when disciples

[10]me before men, [11]him shall the Son of man also confess before the angels of God: 9 but he that denieth me in the presence of men shall be denied in the presence of the angels of God. 10 And every one who shall speak a word against the Son of man, it shall be forgiven him: but unto him that blasphe-

[10]Gr. *in me*
[11]Gr. *in him*

must take a stand; they must confess Christ or deny him. The time would come when confessing Christ would cost the confessor persecution and even death. To give courage to his disciples to make the confession in the presence of men, Jesus first reminds them of God's minute care of his creatures, even of the almost worthless sparrows, and now adds the reward of such confession. If his disciples would confess him before men, he would confess them "before the angels of God." On the other hand, if they should deny him "in the presence of men," he would deny them "in the presence of the angels of God." "In the presence of men" and before "the angels of God" are put in contrast. To confess Jesus was to own him as Lord and Master; it meant to place oneself as a servant under Christ as a Master.

10 And every one who shall speak a word against the Son —From the denial of Jesus, he passes to blasphemy; he brings the two classes of blasphemy into prominence—the blasphemy against the "Son of man" and the blasphemy "against the Holy Spirit." There are gradations of blasphemy: to blaspheme primarily means "to speak evil of, to rail, or to slander." Hence the word in scripture, when applied to God, took upon itself the strongest meaning; to blaspheme means to speak irreverently and impiously to God, or of God, or of sacred things. One can speak evil of or to a fellow man; this implies a malicious purpose, so blasphemy presupposes an impious intention to detract from the glory of man or God; it means to alienate the minds of others from the love and reverence of God. An idea of this sin may be seen in Lev. 24: 10-16; other instances are recorded in 2 Kings 18: 28-35; 19: 1-6, where Jehovah and his perfections are maliciously reviled.

What is it to blaspheme "against the Holy Spirit"? Some call it "unpardonable sin"; some call it the "sin unto death."

meth against the Holy Spirit it shall not be forgiven. 11 And when they bring you before the synagogues, and the rulers, and the authorities, be not anxious how or what ye shall answer, or what ye shall say: 12 for the Holy Spirit shall teach you in that very hour what ye ought to say.

God spoke to man through the law of Moses; the time came when he next spoke to man through his Son. (Heb. 1: 1.) Some who heard Christ could and did blaspheme him; they spoke evil to him and of him; they even attributed the power that he used in casting out demons to Beelzebub; this was speaking evil against the "Son of man." Jesus was crucified, buried, raised from the dead, and ascended back to the Father; he then sent the Holy Spirit. Jesus stated that his testimony was incomplete, and that he would send the Holy Spirit to complete or further perfect the testimony that God furnished. (John 16: 7, 8, 13, 14.) The Holy Spirit came and perfected the testimony by guiding the apostles into all truth, and inspiring those who wrote the New Testament. If one finally rejects the Holy Spirit and the teaching that he gave in the New Testament, there is no hope for that one. The Holy Spirit with his teachings is the last that God has to offer man. If one blasphemes the Holy Spirit by rejecting the words of the New Testament, there is no chance for forgiveness because no other agency from heaven will be given.

11, 12 **And when they bring you before the synagogues,—** The apostles, after Jesus ascended to heaven, would be brought before the rulers of the synagogue and before the Sanhedrin; in the hour of peril the Holy Spirit would be present with them to assist them in their confession of Jesus and defense of what they preached in his name. They should be brought before all kinds of tribunals, but they should not fear, as the Holy Spirit would be with them. (See Acts 4: 8-12.) They should be so completely under the influence of the Holy Spirit that they needed not to be anxious how or what they should say; the Holy Spirit would speak through them. Here is a promise that the Holy Spirit should be given to the apostles and should inspire them on occasions to speak for Jesus. (Matt. 6: 34; 1 Cor. 7: 34; Phil. 4: 6.) The Holy Spirit is here promised to be the divine teacher and guide to the apostles. Paul was brought before Agrippa, but he spoke more of Jesus than he did of his own defense.

10. WARNING AGAINST COVETOUSNESS
12: 13-21

13 And one out of the multitude said unto him, Teacher, bid my brother divide the inheritance with me. 14 But he said unto him, Man, who made me a judge or a divider over you? 15 And he said unto them, Take heed, and keep yourselves from all covetousness: ¹for a man's life consisteth not in

¹Or, *for even in a man's abundance his life is not from the things which he possesseth*

13 **And one out of the multitude said unto him,**—This volunteer from the crowd drew attention to the multitude; he does not ask for arbitration, and there is no evidence that his brother was willing to settle the matter that way. This man wanted a decision from Jesus against his brother. The law of Moses (Deut. 21: 17) divided the estate, giving the elder brother two-thirds and the younger one-third. Some think that this was the younger brother who was complaining; others think that it was the older brother who had not received his two-thirds according to the law. The man probably had a just claim, or he would not have appealed to one so well known to oppose injustice as Jesus. The man appealed to Jesus as "Teacher," but there was nothing unusual in his appeal.

14, 15 **But he said unto him, Man, who made me a judge**— Jesus emphatically refused to become an arbitrator or umpire in secular matters. He repudiated the position of judge in family fusses and lawsuits. Jesus here is rendering unto Caesar the things of Caesar (Luke 20: 25), and showed that he had nothing to do with worldly affairs, that his kingdom was not of this world (John 18: 36). Jesus frequently corrected mistaken views of his mission, and while he gave rules to guide disciples in worldly matters, he declined to decide disputes, or to assume authority concerning temporal things. This gave Jesus an occasion to give a warning against the sin of covetousness; the eager request of the man is made the occasion for this warning. "Covetousness" means greedy and unlawful desire for anything; Jesus warns against "all cove-

the abundance of the things which he possesseth. 16 And he spake a parable unto them, saying, The ground of a certain rich man brought forth plentifully: 17 and he reasoned within himself, saying, What shall I do, because I have not where to bestow my fruits? 18 And he said, This will I do: I will pull down my barns, and build greater; and there will I bestow all my grain and my goods. 19 And I will say to my ²soul, ²Soul, thou hast much goods laid up for many years; take thine ease, eat, drink, be merry. 20 But God said unto him, Thou foolish one, this night ³is thy ²soul required of thee; and

²Or, *life*
³Gr. *they require thy soul*

tousness," against all kinds and degrees of greediness or grasping for gain; covetousness is greedily keeping one's own as well as desiring and grasping for the things of others. It takes the affections and the heart which belong to God (Col. 3: 5), and unites with it trust in uncertain riches (1 Tim. 6: 17.)

16-19 **And he spake a parable unto them,**—This parable shows that abundance of earthly possessions did not save the rich man, but his earthly possession became the means of his condemnation. This rich man gained his wealth honestly from the fruitfulness of his grounds. He had such an abundance of things that he did not know what to do with his increase; finally he decided what he would do. He decided to pull down his barns, and build greater; he would store away all of his goods in his new barn, and then he would take things easy and "eat, drink, be merry." In pulling down his barns and building greater ones he was not directly injuring anyone, neither was he doing anything mean; he may have been helping some by giving them employment. Neither did he purpose a life of drunkenness, dissipation, nor crime. He withheld giving to the poor, as the rich young ruler was required to do. (Matt. 19: 21; Luke 18: 22.) He proposed to hoard selfishly everything for himself; he was planning to enjoy ease, not considering the ease of anyone else; he planned to eat, drink, and make merry, whether anyone else had the necessities of life or not; he planned a life of respectable comfort and pleasure.

20, 21 **But God said unto him, Thou foolish one,**—This man was foolish because he lacked sense, or good judgment. (Luke 11: 40; 2 Cor. 11: 19.) This man was foolish because

the things which thou hast prepared, whose shall they be? 21 So is he that layeth up treasure for himself, and is not rich toward God.

---

he was not living with the right aim or motive; he was a miserably misguided man; his mistake was fatal. While the rich man was telling his soul of the abundance stored up for years, the swift messenger of God came and said to him: "This night is thy soul required of thee." This was a striking rebuke of this man's soliloquy. How awful do these words of God peal forth, as thunder from the bosom of a dark cloud, darkening the heavens, which but a few moments previous were glowing with the splendor of the noonday sun. How disappointed this man was! Jesus then asks who shall possess the wealth that the rich man left. The implication is that his wealth will no longer be his. It is true that we brought nothing into this world, and that we can take nothing out of it. Furthermore it is true that shrouds have no pockets. Earthly possessions can give no comfort in the hour of death, but may be the means of condemnation. (Job 27: 16-19; Psalm 39: 6; Eccles. 2: 18, 19, 26.)

11. EARTHLY ANXIETY DISCOURAGED
12: 22-34

22 And he said unto his disciples, Therefore I say unto you, Be not anxious for *your* ⁴life, what ye shall eat; nor yet for your body, what ye shall put on. 23 For the ⁴life is more than the food, and the body than the rai-

⁴Or, *soul*

22, 23 And he said unto his disciples,—Jesus now turns from the crowd to his disciples; the material presented here appears in Matthew, but not in the connection that it appears there. Jesus has rebuked the hoarding of possessions, as the rich man did, and now turns to his disciples and instructs them with regard to the interest that they should take in food and clothing. They should trust God for food and clothing; their first thoughts belong to the kingdom of God. They should use wisely the powers and opportunities granted them, and believe that God would bless their plans and labors by adding such temporal things as they needed. Luke 12: 22-31 corresponds to Matt. 6: 25-33. It seems that the parable of

ment. 24 Consider the ravens, that they sow not, neither reap; which have
no store-chamber nor barn; and God feedeth them: of how much more value
are ye than the birds! 25 And which of you by being anxious can add a
cubit unto ⁵the measure of his life? 26 If then ye are not able to do even
that which is least, why are ye anxious concerning the rest? 27 Consider

⁵Or, *his stature*

the rich fool was spoken to the crowd, but this instruction
was given to his disciples. It is to be noted that this is given
in the negative form, teaching what *not* to do; how *not* to
feel. The life is more, that is, of greater importance, than
food, and the body than raiment. We should place the
greater importance on things of the greatest value; we should
give to the higher and better things the greater care and
labor.

24 **Consider the ravens, that they sow not,**—"Ravens" include the whole crow group of birds. Matt. 6: 26 has only
"the birds"; Matthew puts the statement in an interrogative
form. The raven abounds in that country and is frequently
referred to in scripture. Noah sent one from the ark (Gen. 8:
7), and the ravens fed Elijah (1 Kings 17: 4-6). (See also Job
38: 41; Psalm 147: 9; Prov. 30: 17.) The ravens neither sow
nor reap; they have no "store-chamber nor barn," yet they
live; they have no anxiety about their food for God feeds
them. God's people are of far greater value, and he will take
care of them. Though the birds neither sow nor reap, yet
they build their nests and seek their food; Jesus is not dis-
couraging work and industry, but does discourage undue anxiety in regard to our temporal needs.

25, 26 **And which of you by being anxious**—The birds or
ravens illustrate God's universal care and wisdom as to the
lower animals; his intelligent children should remember his
care and refrain from anxiety. They cannot by worry add to
their stature or measure of life. If they cannot change what
is comparatively of least importance, that is, how tall or how
old they shall be, then why should they worry about these
other things? Luke only adds the conclusion found in verse
26. The argument is from the less to the greater; to add a
little to life is a small thing with God, but to give life and to

the lilies, how they grow: they toil not, neither do they spin; yet I say unto you, Even Solomon in all his glory was not arrayed like one of these. 28 But if God doth so clothe the grass in the field, which to-day is, and to-morrow is cast into the oven; how much more *shall he clothe* you, O ye of little

sustain it year after year, to give the fruits of the field and the animal creation for food, belong to the greater exercise of infinite power. Why should one be distressed about the greater things when anxiety about the less can accomplish nothing? These are unanswerable questions and put a strong argument in the interrogative form.

27, 28 Consider the lilies,—The lily group of plants is very numerous in Palestine. Some of them are very brilliant in color, and very beautiful; more than a dozen varieties are peculiar to that country. Jesus now passed from food to raiment; he might have drawn his illustration here also from the animal creation, but he descended to the vegetable kingdom, and presented his instruction in a more impressive way. Some have speculated as to the kind of variety that Jesus had in mind here; no one knows, as liles grew wild in the fields and were noted for their beauty and fragrance. (Song of Solomon 2: 1, 16; 5: 13; 6: 2, 3.) The lilies did not toil nor spin, yet "even Solomon in all his glory" was not to be compared in beautiful array to the lily. The external splendor of Solomon's reign, and especially his royal state and dress as he sat upon his throne of ivory, was proverbial. (1 Kings 10: 18; 2 Chron. 9: 15-28.) Solomon and his servants were continually striving to keep up the beauty and splendor of his attire; yet even any one of the lilies of the field was regarded as being more beautiful and fragrant.

But if God doth so clothe the grass—Matthew uses "the grass of the field" instead of "the grass in the field." (Matt. 6: 30.) The wild flowers were cut down with the grass; their existence at best was very brief. Dried grass and stalks of flowers were used for fuel. The Jews had a kind of earthen or iron oven, shaped like a large pitcher, open at the top, in which they made a fire. When it was well heated they made a paste of mingled flour and water and applied it to the outside where it was quickly baked and taken off in thin layers.

faith? 29 And seek not ye what ye shall eat, and what ye shall drink, neither be ye of doubtful mind. 30 For all these things do the nations of the
world seek after : but your Father knoweth that ye have need of these things.
31 Yet seek ye °his kingdom, and these things shall be added unto you. 32

°Many ancient authorities read *the kingdom of God*

The flowers and the grass had a brief existence, yet God made
them and they served a useful purpose ; the disciples of Christ
have a much longer existence and a more important work so
they may expect God to take care of them. Those who do not
see this have but little faith in God.

29, 30 **And seek not ye what ye shall eat,**—It is foolish to
spend the most of one's strength and time on what one shall
eat or drink or wear. The application of the argument from
the two illustrations just given of God's care over the birds of
the air and the lilies of the field is very evident. Jesus warns
against seeking with anxiety after things which perish with
the using. Neither should they be of "doubtful mind"; that
is, they should not be held in suspense, wavering, fluctuating
with unsettled mind between hope and fear ; they should have
firm faith in God and not be disturbed with the material
things of life. The Gentiles who have no God to trust are
seeking after all these things with restless anxiety ; but the
disciples of Jesus should not be unstable, fickle, or changeful ;
they should let the nations of the world have their care and
anxiety, but should not share in them. People of the world
live only for the present ; they ignore God, and have no trust
in him ; but they are continually seeking to get pleasure and
satisfaction out of the possession of worldly affairs. God
knows what one needs, and he has promised to take care of
his children.

31 **Yet seek ye his kingdom,**—The disciples of Jesus are to
put the emphasis of their life on the spiritual side of things ;
they are to seek the interest of God's kingdom ; they are to
put these things first, and God has promised to provide the
lesser things or material things for them. The world seeks
first the lower, less important things ; his disciples should not.
God knows what they need, and if they will put his kingdom
first and all the righteousness of his kingdom, he will give

Fear not, little flock; for it is your Father's good pleasure to give you the
kingdom. 33 Sell that which ye have, and give alms; make for yourselves
purses which wax not old, a treasure in the heavens that faileth not, where

those things which are needed in the physical realm. No one
can in extravagance and idleness seek the kingdom of God
first; putting the interests of the kingdom of God first implies
giving necessary attention to the lower things of life. God
will support the earthly life and will give eternal life to those
who seek his kingdom first and the righteousness of that kingdom.

32 **Fear not, little flock;**—Jesus here uses a term of endear-
ment; and speaks words of love and tenderness to them.
They are called "little flock"; that is, my sheep and my
lambs; they are encouraged not to fear. Jesus is a Good
Shepherd, and will take care of his flock. It is his delight to
"give you the kingdom." Disciples are not to worry about
their spiritual food and support; they are a little flock, helpless in a great world; yet how assuring when Jesus says to
them "fear not"! The kingdom had not at this time been established; hence, he could speak of it in the future; that it
would be given to them. He means his church with its privileges and blessings; they are encouraged to seek his kingdom,
and now he promises that it shall be given to them. The
apostles became the charter members of that kingdom.

33, 34 **Sell that which ye have,**—The disciples of Christ
should not hoard their riches but should distribute to those
who have need. Christians of the early church sold their possessions and gave to such as had need; earthly provision bags
or purses, like the possessions, become old and worthless; the
bags would decay with the wealth that it contained.
Christians should regard that which they hold as God's, not
their own; they are only stewards for God. This does not
mean that a Christian should give up everything that he has
to those who are not trying to serve God; neither does it
mean that a Christian should give up what he has to those
who are living a life of idleness and wickedness. Lazy, useless, trifling beggars are not to be supported by Christians
giving up what they have to them; Christians must use what

no thief draweth near, neither moth destroyeth. 34 For where your treasure is, there will be your heart be also.

they have to the glory of God, which means that it must be used to accomplish the greatest good. Instead of laying up treasures on earth, Christians are to lay them up in heaven. Treasures on earth contained all kinds of material possessions; thieves then as now would break through and steal; moths would consume and destroy some of the wealth.

For where your treasure is,—The treasure and the heart go together; hence, the Christian's chief good should be in God; the heart will be fixed supremely on the highest good in laying up treasures in heaven. If one's treasure is in this world, one's affections are fixed upon it; Jesus gives the reason for laying up treasure in heaven that it may draw the heart thither, and so make heaven more precious to the soul. This is another way of saying "set your mind on the things that are above, not on the things that are upon the earth." (Col. 3: 2.)

12. EXHORTATION TO WATCHFULNESS
12: 35-48

35 Let your loins be girded about, and your lamps burning; 36 and be ye yourselves like unto men looking for their lord, when he shall return from the marriage feast; that, when he cometh and knocketh, they may straight-

35, 36 Let your loins be girded about,—In verses 22-30, Jesus gives the negative side of things, but from verse 31 onward he has the positive duties of his disciples. To gird the loins about was to fasten the garments with a girdle; the long garments of the people then made speed difficult; it was important to use the girdle before starting on a journey. They could travel better with the long garment girded up so that it would not interfere with rapid motion. Another exhortation is that they should keep their "lamps burning." The lamps were to be kept burning, like those of a company of servants waiting for the coming of their lord from a wedding feast at night. They should be watching that they might be ready to open the door for him at the first knock. This is the same point in the parable of the ten virgins. (Matt. 25: 1-13.) They were not only to be girded, ready for active service, but

way open unto him. 37 Blessed are those ⁷servants, whom the lord when he cometh shall find watching: verily I say unto you, that he shall gird himself, and make them sit down to meat, and shall come and serve them. 38 And if he shall come in the second watch, and if in the third, and find *them* so, blessed are those *servants*. 39 ⁸But know this, that if the master of the house had known in what hour the thief was coming, he would have

⁷Gr. *bondservants*
⁸Or, *But this ye know*

their lamps were to be burning, prepared for immediate use. They were not to be anxious about food and raiment, but they were to be alert and ready to do their duty to their Master in faithful watching and service. Constant readiness is enjoined as well as constant watchfulness. They should be ready to receive Christ at the first signal.

37, 38 **Blessed are those servants,**—Jesus encourages watchfulness by describing the happy condition of those servants who shall be thus found at his coming. Jesus uses very emphatic language in expressing these important truths. By their fidelity the servants become guests, waited upon by the lord himself. The condescension is great here; first the lord girds himself; next he causes them to recline at the table; then he comes forth to minister to their wants and wait upon them. In this he treats them not as servants, but as honored guests. Jesus gave an example of this when he washed the feet of his disciples. (John 13 : 4-8.)

And if he shall come in the second watch,—The Romans divided the night into four watches; the first watch is not named here, as it would be too early to expect one from a wedding feast in that watch; the fourth is omitted, perhaps because it was unusual for one to return so late as that watch; the teaching of Jesus here is that all should be ready when the Lord comes. The time of his coming is uncertain. The master of the house does not know what hour the robber will come, or he would watch, and not allow him to dig through the earthen cover of his roof. At an earlier period the night had been divided into three equal parts or watches. Those servants are blessed who are awake, faithful to duty, and watching for the master.

39, 40 **But know this, that if the master of the house**—Jesus here illustrates the necessity of constant readiness and watch-

watched, and not have left his house to be ⁰broken through. 40 Be ye also
ready: for in an hour that ye think not the Son of man cometh.

41 And Peter said, Lord, speakest thou this parable unto us, or even unto
all? 42 And the Lord said, Who then is ¹⁰the faithful and wise steward,
whom his lord shall set over his household, to give them their portion of
food in due season? 43 Blessed is that ¹servant, whom his lord when he
cometh shall find so doing. 44 Of a truth I say unto you, that he will set

⁰Gr. *digged through*
¹⁰Or, *the faithful steward, the wise* man *whom &c.*
¹Gr. *Bondservant*

fulness by the case of theft. We find a parallel of this in
Matt. 24: 43-51. Eastern houses were built of stone or clay;
sometimes the roofs were made of clay or thatch. Thieves
could easily break through and plunder. This shows how
thieves planned to come and dig through and plunder the
house while the master of it was away. Had the master
known when the thief would come, he would have been ready
to prevent his plundering his house. Jesus makes his own application when he exhorts his disciples to be ready, "for in an
hour that ye think not the Son of man cometh." The application of this warning is to the coming of the Son of man; it
applies to every individual in principle, for no one knows
when death will come.

41 **And Peter said, Lord,**—This entire paragraph from verse
22 to verse 40 had been addressed directly to his disciples;
hence Peter asked this question. He wanted to know if Jesus
meant the parable to belong to the disciples exclusively, or if
it was general, belonging "even unto all." It seems that he
knew that the disciples were included in the teaching, but he
did not know whether it belonged to others. Peter's question
gave occasion for the reply that Jesus now gave.

42-44 **And the Lord said, Who then is the faithful**—Peter
was impulsive, frank, and inquisitive; Jesus did not directly
answer Peter's question, but added another parable of a steward, whom his lord put in charge of his house during a temporary absence. This was a common occurrence in the East.
Jesus still enforces his teaching on watchfulness and a constant readiness for his coming by the parable of a servant left
in charge of his master's house. The question was asked as to

him over all that he hath. 45 But if that ¹servant shall say in his heart, My lord delayeth his coming; and shall begin to beat the menservants and the maidservants, and to eat and drink, and to be drunken; 46 the lord of that ¹servant shall come in a day when he expecteth not, and in an hour when he knoweth not, and shall ²cut him asunder, and appoint his portion with the

²Or, *severely scourge him*

who was the faithful and wise steward. The interrogative form makes the sentence the stronger, and leads every hearer and reader to reflect more and to make a personal application. The duties and responsibilties of the apostles and others are involved in this. Jesus answered in an indirect way the question that Peter asked, but he never attempted to satisfy the curiosity of people. His teachings were given for the spiritual profit, not only of his apostles, but all of his disciples in all ages. The steward was a slave or a bond servant; the servant that had charge of his master's things would be blessed when the master returned and found him faithful in his duties.

45, 46 **But if that servant shall say in his heart,**—After blessing the faithful servant, Jesus then gives the other side; the unfaithful servant is described as one who said "in his heart" that his master would not return for some time, and began to treat the servants under him in a shameful and brutal way. He used the time which belonged to his master and the money which the master had left in his care eating and drinking; he even drank to drunkenness; he spent his time in revelry. He took advantage of the absence of his master, betrayed the trust imposed in him, and proved himself unworthy of the position that he held. While the servant was in charge and beating his fellow servants and living an idle, drunken life, the master returned and saw his servant in the height of his folly. The master will punish with terrible affliction this unfaithful servant. This is a vivid picture of the sudden and terrible punishment that shall be brought upon the unfaithful servant. There is a wide contrast in the treatment of the unfaithful servant and the faithful one. "Cut him asunder" is an expression of fearful punishment. (1 Sam. 15: 33; Dan. 2: 5; 3: 29; Heb. 11: 37.)

unfaithful.   47 And that ¹servant, who knew his lord's will, and made not
ready, nor did according to his will, shall be beaten with many *stripes;* 48
but he that knew not, and did things worthy of stripes, shall be beaten with
few *stripes.* And to whomsoever much is given, of him shall much be required: and to whom they commit much, of him will they ask the more.

47, 48 And that servant, who knew his lord's will,—Here
Jesus makes his own application and expresses the general
principle by which punishment will be inflicted on different
persons.   It seems that people will be treated according to
their   opportunities   and   the   light   which   they   have.
Opportunity and ability measure one's responsibility; some
have greater opportunities than others; some have greater
ability than others; therefore the responsibilities vary; so it
seems that the reward and punishment will vary according to
the responsibilities.   (Matt. 25: 14-30.)   The one who knows
the will of God and does it not "shall be beaten with many
stripes"; this implies severe punishment and degrees of punishment.   The law of Moses recognized different degrees of
punishment for different offenses; the number of stripes could
not exceed forty.   (Deut. 25: 2, 3; Amos 3: 2; James 4: 17.)

but he that knew not,—The one who was ignorant of what
should be done was punished, but with fewer stripes than the
one who knew but did not do.   One may be responsible for
not knowing the will of God.   The law of Moses recognized
the sin of ignorance, yet it was a sin.   (Lev. 5: 17.)   Those
who are without the law should be judged without the law.
"Few stripes" implies punishment, but a lighter degree than is
indicated by "many stripes."   The punishment will be propor-
tioned to the powers, gifts, opportunities, and knowledge of
the offender.

And to whomsoever much is given,—The principle here
seems to be that the possession of great gifts involves a corresponding responsibility; the accumulation of gifts, graces, and
influence is the measure of responsibility to God; whoever
violates that principle must suffer; if one lets his talents lie
dormant or squanders them, he will bring upon himself the
condemnation of God.   Of those to whom much is given,
much is required; the one who has ability to use five talents is

required to use that many; the one who has ability to use only one talent is held responsible if he does not use that one talent.

13. DIVISIVE INFLUENCE OF JESUS
12: 49-59

49 I came to cast fire upon the earth; and ³what do I desire, if it is already kindled? 50 But I have a baptism to be baptized with; and how am

³Or, *how would I that it were already kindled!*

49 **I came to cast fire upon the earth;**—There has been much discussion as to the difficulties involved in this verse; it has received a variety of interpretations and many conflicting comments. No speculation need 'be advanced as to the meaning of this verse. Jesus had just stressed the necessity of watchfulness and readiness; this led him to refer to one object of his coming, to the sufferings he should endure, and the effect of the gospel in producing divisions among people. He simply declared that he came to "cast fire upon the earth." Fire was a powerful purifier. (Mal. 3: 2.) There have been many different meanings given to "fire" as used here. Some think that it may mean the fire of destruction; others the fire spoken of by John the Baptist (Matt. 3: 11); still others think that it refers to the fires of persecution. "Fire" cannot here be a symbol of blessings; Jesus had just emphasized the fact that punishment would be meted out to those who were unfaithful; the fire would represent the process of purification, and also the judgment.

50 **But I have a baptism**—Jesus here calls his suffering a baptism; it is an overwhelming in suffering. He had challenged James and John, when they asked for the chief seats in his kingdom, if they could be baptized with his baptism. (Matt. 20: 22; Mark 10: 32.) The cross was before Jesus at the time that he spoke these words and he said: "How am I straitened till it be accomplished!" The Greek word "baptizo" means overwhelm, plunge, dip, immerse; hence, Jesus on the cross was to be overwhelmed with sorrow, suffering and death. There is implied in this figure not only the painful submersion, a dying, but also a joyful rising. Jesus was

I straitened till it be accomplished! 51 Think ye that I am come to give
peace in the earth? I tell you, Nay; but rather division: 52 for there shall
be from henceforth five in one house divided, three against two, and two
against three. 53 They shall be divided, father against son, and son against
father; mother against daughter, and daughter against her mother; mother
in law against her daughter in law, and daughter in law against her mother
in law.

"straitened" until this should be accomplished. "Straitened"
means pressed, as it were on every side with anxiety; Paul expresses the same idea in Phil. 1: 23. Jesus lived daily with
the cross in view.

51, 52 **Think ye that I am come to give peace**—Here Jesus
teaches that strife and persecution are to be expected as a consequence of his proclaiming the will of God to the people; one
should not shrink from the fear of disturbing people by
preaching the truth. Christ is the Prince of Peace; but in a
sinful world, a righteous king can have and give peace only by
destroying error and evil; to do this will bring war; not because Christ and his people have the spirit of strife and war,
but because the truth they urge is resisted, and made the occasion for strife, division, and contention by others. The conflict that may be waged among the different advocates of error
will often unite in their opposition to the truth. The truth
taught by Jesus is opposed to error; there can be no compromise between truth and error. When one member of the
household accepts the truth and others reject it, there is opposition and antagonism.

53 **They shall be divided, father against son,**—The purifying
process of the truth of God would occasion division among
those bound by the closest and most sacred ties. Some in the
house would accept the truth and some reject; then the division would fall between even father and son, the tender affection of mother and daughter would be broken, and so stoutly
would the gospel be resisted that angry persecutions would
follow, as is sadly pictured here by the words of Jesus. This
teaching of Jesus has caused divisions in many homes; almost
in every community there may be found sad illustrations of
the divisive teachings of Jesus. Terrible commotions must
arise; old social affinities be broken up; the ties of household

54 And he said to the multitudes also, When ye see a cloud rising in the
west, straightway ye say, There cometh a shower; and so it cometh to pass.
55 And when *ye see* a south wind blowing, ye say, There will be a [4]scorch-
ing heat; and it cometh to pass. 56 Ye hypocrites, ye know how to
[5]interpret the face of the earth and the heaven; but how is it that ye know
not how to [5]interpret this time? 57 And why even of yourselves judge ye

[4]Or, *hot wind*
[5]Gr. *prove*

---

be rent asunder; some will love more strongly than ever before; but the many will hate with bitterness. Jesus wanted
his disciples to know that such would be the result when the
truth of God was preached. We need not be surprised to see
the same resulting today.

54 **And he said to the multitudes**—Jesus now turns to the
multitudes again as in verse 14. There are similar teachings
in Matt. 5: 25f.; 16: 1f. There is some difference in the phra-
seology, but the teaching is similar. In Matthew the Pharisees and Sadducees were asking for a sign from heaven as
they often did. These signs of the weather are given; they
have a more or less general application. Jesus does not verify
the signs and make them invariable; he recites the signs
which they were accustomed to giving in conversation with
each other. They claimed to be able to discern the weather
conditions, but were unable to understand the signs of the
time with respect to the Messiah; hence, Jesus rebukes them.

55 **And when ye see a south wind blowing,**—The south
wind came from the Arabian desert and reached Palestine
from the south; it was extremely hot. (Job 37: 17.) Jesus
here continues his rebuke to the multitudes. They could read
the signs of rain in the rising of the cloud from the Mediterranean Sea on the west (1 Kings 18: 44); they also knew that a
south wind soon brought heat; but they did not know the
signs of the time with respect to the Messiah; they should
have known both from the prophets and from the work that
Jesus did among them.

56, 57 **Ye hypocrites, ye know how to interpret**—A "hypocrite" is a pretender, a dissembler; one who assumes to be
what he is not. This statement of Jesus refers to verse 1
of this chapter. These people could read the signs of rain
in the clouds and foretell the heat waves by the wind from

not what is right? 58 For as thou art going with thine adversary before the magistrate, on the way give diligence to be quit of him; lest haply he drag thee unto the judge, and the judge shall deliver thee to the "officer, and "officer shall cast thee into prison. 59 I say unto thee, Thou shalt by no means come out thence, till thou have paid the very last mite.

"Gr. *exactor*

---

the south, but they could not see the clear and sure signs of the presence of the Son of God among them. He had taught them as never man taught; he had worked signs and wonders in their presence; the miracles of healing which he had wrought among them all bore witness to his claim as the Messiah; the spotless purity of his life and the wisdom and perfection of his teaching emphasized his claim. They were rebuked and condemned for their pretended wisdom.

58, 59 **For as thou art going with thine adversary**—A man under indictment for crime against his adversary and on his way for trial is admonished to settle the case before the trial comes on; it can be settled easier out of court than to be followed by a long-drawn-out lawsuit, in which animosity is stirred up. The process of trial may move on with such intricacies that the outcome, though the claim be just, may result in condemnation; hence, it is wise to settle it, if it can be done, before the judge or jury pronounces sentence. If one is on the way to the magistrate with his adversary in law, whom he has wronged, it is right to become reconciled with him before he drags him to the judge and the judge pass the sentence and inflict the punishment. The application is that they should be reconciled to God and be discharged from the punishment due for their sins. The multitude to whom Jesus was speaking understood the physical facts concerning the wind and rain, but they were ignorant of the signs of the times about the Messiah.

Thou shalt by no means come out—This is the conclusion of the application that Jesus made of his parable. The Jewish nation was under indictment for great national sin against God; it was at that time being brought to issue on the momentous question of receiving their long-promised Messiah, and through him, making peace with their offended God.

They were at that time moving on to the courtroom of the
Great Judge; the hour of trial for the nation as well as for individuals was at hand. They should make peace with their
adversary while they had opportunity to do so. Some think
that Jesus makes the application only to the nation, while others think that the principle is the same whether applied to a
nation or an individual.

14. THE NEED OF REPENTANCE
13 : 1-9

1 Now there were some present at that very season who told him of the
Galilæans, whose blood Pilate had mingled with their sacrifices. 2 And he
answered and said unto them, Think ye that these Galilæans were sinners

1 **Now there were some present at that very season**—This is
connected with the discourse that has just been recorded.
"At that very season" means on that same occasion. A pause
or interruption in the discourse was made by some who were
present. They evidently made no application of the truth that
had been spoken by Jesus to themselves, but like the covetous
man (12: 13), were thinking of other things which had recently taken place. They may have related to Jesus the occasion of Judas of Galilee referred to in Acts 5: 37. However,
we do not know who these Galileans were, neither do we
know on what occasion the soldiers of Pilate had killed these
and "mingled with their sacrifices" the blood of them that
were slain. Uprisings and rebellions were common at that
time and especially on feast days. It was considered a great
curse to have the blood of the worshiper mingled with the
sacrifices of the worshiper.

2 **Think ye that these Galilaeans were sinners**—Evidently
those who told Jesus of this incident were breaking the force
of his teachings as applied to themselves; they attempted to
divert attention to something else. Many are prone to talk
about the death of others rather than about their own death;
they rather speak about the sins of others than their own sins.
But Jesus does not let them escape the force of his discourse.
These Galileans had suffered and the idea was prevalent then

above all the Galilæans, because they have suffered these things? 3 I tell you, Nay: but, except ye repent, ye shall all in like manner perish. 4 Or those eighteen, upon whom the tower in Siloam fell, and killed them, think ye that they were [7]offenders above all the men that dwell in Jerusalem? 5 I tell you, Nay: but, except ye repent, ye shall all likewise perish.

[7]Gr. *debtors*

---

as now that sufferings were brought on because of sin. Job's friends had this idea. Jesus does not deny that these Galileans were sinners; neither does he deny that the calamity that befell them was because of their great sin; he does not deny that divine judgment is visited because of sin. He raises the question as to whether they were greater sinners than those who were present.

3 I tell you, Nay: but, except ye repent,—In answer to the question that Jesus raised, he said of them that no such preeminence in sin is to be attributed to them. It is wrong to conclude that their fate was due to any great wickedness that they had committed. "Except ye repent, ye shall all in like manner perish." This declaration brings their attention to their own sin; it is emphatic and solemn. It is a warning that a similar or greater punishment would be brought upon them if they did not repent. This is a severe rebuke to these men who reported this to Jesus and to all others who may be in sin; no one can ward off the force of the truth here spoken by Jesus. "Repent" is used many times in the New Testament. It means a change of mind, disposition, governing purpose; unless one changes from an impenitent heart doom certainly awaits one. The suffering of these becomes a warning to all others to repent or to perish. There is no alternative; it is either repent or perish.

4, 5 Or those eighteen, upon whom the tower in Siloam fell, —Jesus further forcibly impresses this truth upon his hearers by citing another example. There were eighteen persons who were killed by the fall of the tower in Siloam. It is not known the exact location of this tower; probably it was near the pool of Siloam which was near the foot of Mount Zion. There were large porches around the pools where many sick lay. On some occasion some building had fallen upon certain

6 And he spake this parable; A certain man had a fig tree planted in his vineyard; and he came seeking fruit thereon, and found none. 7 And he said unto the vinedresser, Behold, these three years I come seeking fruit on this fig tree, and find none; cut it down; why doth it also cumber the ground? 8 And he answering saith unto him, Lord, let it alone this year also till I shall

persons and the hearers of Jesus were familiar with the incident. This building is referred to by Jesus as "the tower in Siloam" and was probably the one mentioned in John 9: 7, and which may have included the dwellers in Jerusalem. Some have conjectured that these eighteen were confined in the tower as prisoners, but does not matter why they were in or near the tower; the point that Jesus makes is that they had perished and that they had not perished simply because of their great wickedness. Their death came, not from the discriminating judgments of God, nor the bloody hands of men, but by the falling tower in Siloam; it was not necessary for them to trace the fall of the tower and its consequences to any judicial act of God.

6 **And he spake this parable;**—Luke seems to be the only writer that records this parable; it is called "the parable of the barren fig tree." Figs were native to that country; this tree was planted in a "vineyard," or a place of vines. Isaiah and David used a parable like this to describe the Jewish people. (Isa. 5; Psalm 70: 5.) Jesus applies the same truths by the idea of a fig tree growing in a sheltered field and protected and carefully cultivated, but fruitless. The doom pronounced upon the Jewish nation, unless it was averted by timely repentance, is still more forcibly illustrated by this parable. The long-suffering of God, as well as the threatened destruction of the wicked, is clearly set forth.

7-9 **And he said unto the vinedresser,**—A "vinedresser" was one whose duty it was to take care of the vines. "These three years" has been used by many to represent the three years of the personal ministry of Jesus on earth; however, there is no reference to this in the text. For three years after this fig tree should have borne fruit, its owner came each year and sought fruit in vain. Why should he waste both time and labor upon a worthless fig tree? The land was cumbered with it and

dig about it, and dung it: 9 and if it bear fruit thenceforth, *well;* but if not, thou shalt cut it down.

something else could be produced upon the plot that this tree occupied. The gardener begged for one more year of trial; he would nurture it and fertilize it and wait and see the results before destroying it. Increased culture might help it, but left to itself, it had failed to bear fruit. God had waited patiently on the Jewish nation for the fruits of righteousness; so far it had failed. One more period was now set for the Jews to avoid the punishment of their sins. While the fig tree refers primarily to the Jewish nation, in a secondary sense it refers to every impenitent sinner who enjoys the opportunities of salvation, but fails to avail himself of them. Evidently, there is a limitation to divine forbearance; unless averted by timely repentance, the threatened destruction will come, and there will be no power to escape the dreadful doom. It is clear that the Jewish people brought on their own destruction by their obstinate neglect of all the messages which God sent to them; John the Baptist had warned them and predicted that the kingdom of God was at hand; Jesus was in their midst and giving them the opportunities to repent. If ever there was a people that had been spared for a long time and patiently instructed and warned, and had such opportunities to be fruitful, that was the Jewish people.

15. HEALING ON THE SABBATH
13: 10-21

10 And he was teaching in one of the synagogues on the sabbath day. 11

10 **And he was teaching in one of the synagogues**—It seems that Luke passes over some incidents and takes up that which Jesus had done after his final leave of Galilee and had retired to the region beyond the Jordan or in Perea. Some place this incident after John 11: 47-54, where we are told that in consequence of the counsel of Caiaphas against Jesus, he retired from Jerusalem to a city called Ephraim, near the wilderness. (John 11: 54.) Jesus frequently taught in the synagogue; it was while he was teaching in the synagogue that the follow-

And behold, a woman that had a spirit of infirmity eighteen years; and she was bowed together, and could in no wise lift herself up. 12 And when Jesus saw her, he called her, and said to her, Woman, thou art loosed from thine infirmity. 13 And he laid his hands upon her: and immediately she was made straight and glorified God. 14 And the ruler of the synagogue,

---

ing miracle took place. It appears that this woman was a regular attendant at the synagogue worship.

11 **And behold, a woman that had a spirit of infirmity**—This woman was a Jewess; she had access to the synagogue worship, being "a daughter of Abraham." She was afflicted with "an infirmity eighteen years"; we are not told the nature of her affliction. Luke was a physician and would naturally refer to this miracle of healing. Her disease caused physical debility and deformity; it may have been caused by the wicked spirits, as she had "a spirit of infirmity." She was "bowed together, and could in no wise lift herself up." Her disease was spinal and extending down to the loin; she was so bent down as to be totally unable to raise herself up, or even to look up.

12, 13 **And when Jesus saw her,**—Jesus was in the synagogue teaching and evidently this woman came in; many were worshiping in the synagogue and this woman seems to have been one among the many. Jesus called her to him; others observed him, and the ruler of the synagogue saw it. It seems that Jesus abruptly said to her, after she responded to his call, that she was "loosed from thine infirmity." In a moment when the woman least expected it, her prayers had been answered and she was released beyond her expectation. Jesus struck at the root of the evil; the miracle was evident to all and it was most merciful.

And he laid his hands upon her:—She showed her faith by her gratitude; she glorified God. It should be noted that this miracle was one of those which our Lord worked unsolicited and unasked; the widow at Nain is another instance (Luke 7: 11ff.); in both cases the person to whom kindness was shown was a woman. The miracle was wrought instantaneously; there was no gradual inprovement in her condition, but she was made whole immediately.

being moved with indignation because Jesus had healed on the sabbath, answered and said to the multitude, There are six days in which men ought to work: in them therefore come and be healed, and not on the day of the sabbath. 15 But the Lord answered him, and said, Ye hypocrites, doth not each one of you on the sabbath loose his ox or his ass from the ¹stall, and lead

¹Gr. *manger*

14 **And the ruler of the synagogue,**—Each synagogue had its ruler; it was his duty to take care that all things were done decently and in order in the services of the synagogue; however, there was no occasion for this rebuke. The woman had not come there to be cured; she had not solicited Jesus to cure her, but Jesus had done so on his own initiative. If any rebuke was due, it should have been administered to Jesus, as he was entirely responsible for it. The ruler was "moved with indignation" because she had been "healed on the sabbath." The ruler seems to have vented his indignation upon the worshipers, as he said to them: "There are six days in which men ought to work: in them therefore come and be healed, and not on the day of the sabbath." There was no labor, no toil, no violation of the Sabbath law in any respect; but the ruler administered a severe rebuke to the multitude; it seems that he was afraid to rebuke Jesus.

15 **But the Lord answered him,**—Jesus was ever ready to answer his critics; he was always in the right, and those who opposed him were in the wrong. He used a very strong word in his condemnation of the ruler and those who sympathized with him: "Ye hypocrites, doth not each one of you on the sabbath loose his ox or his ass from the stall, and lead him away to watering?" The ruler had said one thing and had meant another. He had rebuked the woman and her sympathizers, when in reality he meant to rebuke Jesus; hence, he was a hypocrite. He envied Jesus and desired to injure him and his influence, but not daring to show it, he pretended a most pious interest in the observance of the Sabbath. Many of those who were present had, doubtless, that very morning led an ox or an ass to water, and did not think of violating the Sabbath, but they were growling at Jesus for healing this unfortunate woman on the Sabbath.

him away to watering? 16 And ought not this woman, being a daughter of Abraham, whom Satan had bound, lo *these* eighteen years, to have been loosed from this bond on the day of the sabbath? 17 And as he said these things, all his adversaries were put to shame : and all the multitude rejoiced for all the glorious things that were done by him.

18 He said therefore, Unto what is the kingdom of God like? and whereunto shall I liken it? 19 It is like unto a grain of mustard seed, which a man took, and cast into his own garden ; and it grew, and became a tree ; and the birds of the heaven lodged in the branches thereof.

16, 17 **And ought not this woman,**—If they could lead an animal to water without breaking the Sabbath law, why could not Jesus heal this woman without breaking the Sabbath law? Why should they criticize Jesus for doing such a merciful deed to this unfortunate woman, when they had done a less merciful act to one of the lower animals? Jesus represents this woman as being bound by Satan for eighteen years ; she had been in need of help for these many years ; her needs were far greater than the needs of the animals that day for water. They had done a merciful deed to an animal in giving it water on the Sabbath, but he had done a far greater deed by healing this woman who was far more valuable than an animal ; why then should they criticize him? His adversaries were "put to shame," and in contrast the "multitude rejoiced for all the glorious things that were done by him."

18, 19 **Unto what is the kingdom of God like?**—A parallel of this is found in Matt. 13 : 31-33 and Mark 4 : 31, 32. Matthew records the parable of the leaven in connection with the parable of the mustard seed, but Mark records only the parable of the mustard seed. Matthew states particularly that this seed is the least of its class, and that the plant becomes the greatest of herbs, so that the sense of the parable becomes obvious. From the smallest beginning its rapid growth carries it to the greatest size ; such is the kingdom of God. In its nature it *must* grow ; the law of growth and progress is its most vital element ; in its nature love moves to activity ; begets labor ; and such labor as cannot fail of success. This kingdom belongs to God ; it is owned of God ; it is recognized by him, and his power is an element of glorious vitality.

20 And again he said, Whereunto shall I liken the kingdom of God? 21
It is like unto leaven, which a woman took and hid in three ²measures of
meal, till it was all leavened.

²See marginal note on Mt. 13.33

**20, 21 And again he said, Whereunto shall I liken the king-
dom of God?**—This parable is also recorded by Matthew (13:
33); its meaning is evident. "Leaven" was very common in
the houses of that day; it is yeast and an element used in
making bread. The kingdom of heaven is like "leaven," for it
will permeate and influence all with which it comes in contact; leaven hid in meal will diffuse itself by its very nature
and will permeate the entire mass. The term "three measures" was the amount usually used for one meal; it has no
further significance. The parable simply means that the truth
of God when planted in the heart will influence the life, and
that life will continue to influence others until society is affected by it. Some have seen an allegorical meaning in the
"woman," the number "three measures," and the "meal."
However, there seems to be no significance attached to these
words other than it was customary for the women to bake the
bread.

16. THE NARROW DOOR
13 : 22-30

22 And he went on his way through cities and villages, teaching, and
journeying on unto Jerusalem. 23 And one said unto him, Lord, are they

22 And he went on his way through cities and villages,—Jesus now has his face set toward Jerusalem; Jesus now makes
a fourth circuit through the villages and towns of Galilee previous to his going up to Jerusalem to attend the feast. Many
think that this was the summer and fall before he was crucified, and that the "cities and villages" mentioned here are the
cities and villages in Perea. If they mean the cities in Galilee,
it was the fourth time that he had visited the cities in that
country; but if it is meant that he visited the cities and villages in Perea he did not make the long circuit to Galilee.
Authorities differ with respect to the meaning of these "cities
and villages." He could have gone through Galilee on a cir-

few that are saved? And he said unto them, 24 Strive to enter in by the
narrow door: for many, I say unto you, shall seek to enter in, and shall not
be [3]able. 25 When once the master of the house is risen up, and hath shut

[3]Or, *able, when once*

cuit and then crossed the Jordan south of the Sea of Galilee
and visited Perea and then proceeded to Jerusalem; it is possible for him to have visited the cities on both sides of the Jordan, and thus visited Galilee and Perea. However, the point
is clear that he was headed toward Jerusalem and that he visited cities and villages on the way to Jerusalem. It is to be
noted that he taught in all of these villages.

23, 24 **And one said unto him,**—Jesus is here asked a question. We are not told what city Jesus was in at this time.
Someone asked Jesus: "Lord, are they few that are saved?"
He seems to inquire if there are few that be saved or many.
The Jews are said to have had many curious theories on this
subject. Some supposed all Israelites would be saved; others,
that very few would escape, as of all who came out of Egypt,
but two entered Canaan. The question clearly means whether
the saved would be few or many, and it is supposed that he
had reference to the Jews. Jesus did not answer the curiosity
of this inquirer, but gave answer to an infinitely more vital
question: "How could they themselves be saved? Jesus directed his answer not to the one who made the inquiry only,
but to "them," or to the masses who were about him. He exhorts all to strive "to enter in by the narrow door." This is
similar to the teaching in Matthew (7: 13, 14), where Jesus
contrasts the two ways. "Strive" is the word used in con-
tending for a prize in the games, and denotes the utmost effort put forth. It takes all that one can do to enter heaven;
no one need think that he can work only part of the time and
enter heaven. Many will "seek to enter in," but "shall not be
able." Many seek halfheartedly, while others will put forth
their utmost.

25-27 **When once the master of the house is risen up,**—It is
difficult to determine the connection of this verse. "The master of the house" is the one who controls the house; when he
has arisen from his seat in order to shut the door, all comers

to the door, and ye begin to stand without, and to knock at the door, saying, Lord, open to us; and he shall answer and say to you, I know you not whence ye are; 26 then shall ye begin to say, We did eat and drink in thy presence, and thou didst teach in our streets; 27 and he shall say, I tell you, I know not whence ye are; depart from me, all ye workers of iniquity. 28 There shall be the weeping and the gnashing of teeth, when ye shall see Abraham, and Isaac, and Jacob, and all the prophets, in the kingdom of God, and yourselves cast forth without. 29 And they shall come from the east and

---

are shut out. The figure of a wedding feast is still preserved, and the guests are called; the doors are left open for their entrance; the servants are sent out to call them, and when the feast begins the doors are shut upon those who refused to come or those who came too late. The late-comers knock and ask admission, but the master answers them and turns them away. This teaches that the gospel call has its limitations of time; the door of mercy is open for a time, but not indefinitely; if men would enter they must pass in while the door stands open. The master will rise in his dignity and authority and close the door and will say: "I know not whence ye are; depart from me, all ye workers of iniquity." These Jews had heard Jesus; he had taught in their streets; they had witnessed his wonderful miracles, but had rejected him, and had judged themselves unworthy of his blessings. "Workers of iniquity" mean those who do evil; they are the ones who have followed unrighteous practices as a trade; their occupation was sin.

28 **There shall be the weeping**—The "workers of iniquity," those who were hired for the wages of sin to do evil, shall reap their reward in due season. The weeping, the gnashing mentioned here, expresses intense and unexampled anguish. In this life pain is not pain as compared to the anguish of soul in perdition. They shall weep because they have lost their favor with God, and shall gnash their teeth in anguish because others enter in and they are rejected. Those who by procrastination and inaction suffer the time of admission to the gospel feast to pass by, will mourn and lament when they see from afar the banquet of bliss where Abraham, Isaac, Jacob, and the prophets are permitted to feast, while they are excluded from the presence of God.

29 **And they shall come from the east and west,**—Salvation

west, and from the north and south, and shall ⁴sit down in the kingdom of
God. 30 And behold, there are last who shall be first, and there are first
who shall be last.

⁴Gr. *recline*

will be extended to the Gentiles; not only those who were
near, but all those most distant, from all parts of the earth
shall be called. (Isa. 45: 6; 49: 6.) They shall come from all
quarters and recline at the table according to the prediction of
the prophets and the commission given by Jesus. To recline
at the table with Abraham, Isaac, and Jacob was to the Jewish
mind a representation of the highest honors and the greatest
happiness. Many Gentiles shall become spiritual descendants
of the fathers in faith (Heb. 11: 8-10), participators of the
kingdom of God below (Col. 1: 13) and above (2 Pet. 1: 11).
Some think that this has reference to the second coming of
Christ, while others that it has reference to the privileges and
blessings of the gospel.

30 **And behold, there are last who shall be first,**—Jesus used
this expression at the close of the parable of the "laborers in
the vineyard." (Matt. 20: 16.) It seems that there will be
such a reversal of present relations; that many of those who
seemed most likely to have been the favored guests will be excluded; while others, whose prospects for such an honor were
far less favorable, will be selected as the recipients. The last
are first in being permitted to enjoy a banquet from which the
others were excluded.

17. MESSAGE TO HEROD AND LAMENTATIONS
OVER JERUSALEM
13: 31-35

31 In that very hour there came certain Pharisees, saying to him, Get
thee out, and go hence: for Herod would fain kill thee. 32 And he said unto

31 **In that very hour there came certain Pharisees,**—The
Pharisees were enemies of Jesus; they came to him at this
time with an appearance of friendship, but in reality upon the
wicked suggestion of Herod. Luke is the only one that records this incident. This was Herod Antipas; he had slain
John the Baptist and was jealous of the influence which Jesus

them, Go and say to that fox, Behold, I cast out demons and perform cures to-day and to-morrow, and the third *day* I [5]am perfected. 33 Nevertheless I must go on my way to-day and to-morrow and the *day* following: for it

[5]Or, *end my course*

had gained over the people. Great multitudes followed Jesus and many supposed that he would at some favorable juncture proclaim himself king and set up his kingdom on earth; this would make him a rival of Herod, and Herod thought that he would destroy Jesus. He adopted this plan of sending the Pharisees to him, to induce Jesus to leave Galilee and hasten to Jerusalem, and there to be in greater danger from the Sanhedrin. Herod Antipas was the son of Herod the Great; he had now ruled over Galilee and Perea for thirty years. Herod did not want to kill Jesus as he had John the Baptist, for he feared the people; but he thought that he would drive Jesus out of his territory and that the Jews would kill him at Jerusalem.

32, 33 **And he said unto them, Go and say to that fox,**—Jesus was not afraid of any earthly power; he had a work to perform, and he did that without fear. Some think that the Pharisees were as anxious to get Jesus to Jerusalem as was Herod. It was a cunning warning from Herod and from the Pharisees; it was more cunning than friendly; hence, Jesus tells them: "Go and say to that fox." This shows the steadfastness and fearlessness of Jesus in carrying out his purpose to remain in that region until he had finished his work there. Herod was cunning and crafty; some think that the people had already given him the name "fox." While Jesus applied this term to Herod, in reality it also applied to the crafty efforts of the Pharisees to effect his ruin or at least his disgrace.

I cast out demons and perform cures to-day and to-morrow, —Again Jesus uses proverbial phrases and designates the time as being short for his work. It is parallel to John 11: 9, 10. Jesus meant to say that he had an appointed time in which he would continue his work with fearlessness and without interruption. "The third day I am perfected." This seems to refer to his death. In the plan of God Jesus must die at Jerusalem; he must finish his work before that time. The time was defi-

cannot be that a prophet perish out of Jerusalem. 34 O Jerusalem, Jerusalem, that killeth the prophets, and stoneth them that are sent unto her! how
often would I have gathered thy children together, even as a hen *gathereth*
her own brood under her wings, and ye would not! 35 Behold, your house
is left unto you *desolate*: and I say unto you, Ye shall not see me, until ye

---

nitely marked and Jesus had set his face toward Jerusalem,
where he would finish his work. The time was to be very
short, during which he must accomplish the remainder of his
work on earth. "The third day" does not mean within three
days, but a very short time. It is thought that Jesus went up
to Jerusalem to the feast of the tabernacle, and was seen no
more in Galilee.; but from Jerusalem he went through Samaria
and Galilee to the regions beyond the Jordan.

it cannot be that a prophet perish out of Jerusalem.—So
cruel and bloody had been the conduct of the Jews toward
their prophets that it was beyond probability that a prophet
could perish out of Jerusalem; hence, Jesus did not feel any
fear of malice from Herod in his territory. He knew exactly
how his hands were tied by a fear of offending the people of
Galilee; he could have easily excited sedition; he gave assurance to Herod that he had no such design, but looked rather
to a brief ministry, and a bloody end. A prophet was tried
only by the Sanhedrin, which met in Jerusalem. Jesus foretold that he would be tried by that court.

34 O Jerusalem, Jerusalem,—This exclamation seems to
have the same meaning as Matt. 23: 37-39. The repetition of
Jerusalem is emphatic, and was repeated by Jesus at a later
time in Jerusalem itself, as his closing sentence before his retirement to the sacrifice of himself for the sins of the world.
Some think that Jesus made this lamentation only one time,
and that Luke has the lamentation out of its chronological
order; there is no reason why Jesus could not have spoken the
lamentation more than once. Jerusalem had killed the prophets and the leaders were then plotting to kill him. Jesus at
a single glance reviews the whole history of Jerusalem in
which the persecution of prophets was common and often repeated.

35 Behold, your house is left unto you desolate:—Jesus had
earnestly longed to gather the sons and daughters of Jerusa-

shall say, Blessed *is* he that cometh in the name of the Lord.

lem unto himself as a hen gathers her brood for comfort and protection; but they would not accept him. Their house is now left desolate; the temple that has long been desecrated is doomed to destruction. To be left "desolate" is like land thrown up as no longer worth cultivating.

18. HEALING ON THE SABBATH; A GUEST ON
THE SABBATH
14: 1-24

1 And it came to pass, when he went into the house of one of the rulers of the Pharisees on a sabbath to eat bread, that they were watching him. 2 And behold, there was before him a certain man that had the dropsy. 3 And

1 **And it came to pass, when he went into the house**—Jesus was probably still in Perea at this time. He had been invited into the house of "one of the rulers of the Pharisees." Some think that this was a chief man among the Pharisees and some have even said that he was a member of the Sanhedrin; we cannot determine whether he was a man of such prominence; his house seems to have been in Perea, and Jesus was his invited guest. He was a man of distinction and probably wanted to satisfy himself concerning Jesus and what he taught. It was on the Sabbath. The Jews were accustomed to meet as families in social converse on the Sabbath and other holy days; they thought it proper and lawful to spend part of the Sabbath in quiet conversation. (See Neh. 8: 10.) Jesus did not hesitate to accept the invitation. Others were watching Jesus to see what he would so; they were seeking an occasion to accuse him of violating the Sabbath. They observed him closely as spies, bent on finding fault, if he violated any of the customs or rules governing conduct on the Sabbath.

2, 3 **And behold, there was before him a certain man**—These words seem to inply that this man was there by design of those who watched Jesus; he was put there to meet Jesus; perhaps the man himself knew of their evil designs and lent himself to the occasion. He was afflicted with "dropsy." Luke, being a physician, singles out this case and records the

Jesus answering spake unto the lawyers and Pharisees, saying, Is it lawful to heal on the sabbath, or not? 4 But they held their peace. And he took him, and healed him, and let him go. 5 And he said unto them, Which of you shall have [1]an ass or an ox fallen into a well, will not straightway draw him

[1]Many ancient authorities read *a son.* See ch. 13.15

healing of this man. This seems to be the only case on record where Jesus healed one with the "dropsy." This disease seems to have been produced by an accumulation of water under the skin, in various parts of the body, often the result of a previous disease, and generally incurable.

And Jesus answering spake—Jesus spoke to the "lawyers and Pharisees." It seems that these were the ones who had arranged this affair. If Jesus healed the man at once, they were ready to accuse him of laboring on the Sabbath; if he did not heal him, they were ready to report abroad a failure to extend mercy, or a sign of fear. It is interesting to note how Jesus spoiled their dilemma. He asked: "Is it lawful to heal on the sabbath, or not?" This question of Jesus put the lawyers and Pharisees to flight. If they answered that it was lawful to heal the man, it would spoil their chance of accusation against him; but if they answered in the negative, they would be considered unmerciful, unsympathetic, and unhelpful to one in distress. They knew that certain things *must* be done on the day of rest; sickness and natural exigencies constantly compel men to do some work; they must do some work other than that of healing.

4 **But they held their peace.**—On the one hand they could not deny the benevolent act of healing the man on the Sabbath; and on the other, they were fearful of compromising themselves with him in some way, if they replied in the affirmative. Hence, they prudently kept silent; this was the cowardly way out of the dilemma that they were in. Jesus thus exposed them to all who observed. He then took the man "and healed him, and let him go." Jesus took hold of the man and healed him; he put himself in physical contact with the man according to his usual custom. There is a striking antithesis between this heartless silence in regard to the cure of the man and the readiness with which Jesus healed him.

up on a sabbath day? 6 And they could not answer again unto these things.
    7 And he spake a parable unto those that were bidden, when he marked
how they chose out the chief seats; saying unto them, 8 When thou art bid-

---

5, 6 And he said unto them,—Jesus had already completely
routed his enemies, but he further presses them to greater embarrassment. He now forces them to break their silence by
asking them a direct question. "Which of you shall have an
ass or an ox fallen into a well, and will not straightway draw
him up on a sabbath day?" This is similar to the argument
that Jesus made in Matt. 12: 11, where the argument is fully
expressed, but is left here to be mentally supplied. What
Matthew uses as a sheep, Luke uses an ass or an ox; but the
term Matthew uses is comprehensive enough for all kinds of
domestic animals. (Ex. 20: 17; Isa. 1: 3.) They would immediately draw out an ass or an ox if it had fallen into a well;
this would require great labor and the services of several men
to pull an ox or an ass out of a well. They would not let the
animal remain in the well until after the Sabbath passed. The
argument put in the interrogative form here is made complete
by substituting Matt. 12: 12: "How much then is a man of
more value than a sheep?"

7 **And he spake a parable unto those that were bidden,**—Jesus now gives three parable as he dined at the table of the
chief Pharisee who had invited him. The first (verses 7-11)
refers to the conduct of those who are invited to a feast; the
second (verses 12-14) is directed against the selfishness of inviting those only who are able to give entertainments in return; the third (verses 16-24) is designed to correct false
views with respect to the blessings of the Messianic kingdom.
While Jesus sat or reclined at the feast "he marked" how
those who were bidden selected the chief seats. The Greek
word for "marked" means "gave attention," or "observed"; it
is sometimes translated "gave heed." (Acts 3: 5.) They had
spied on Jesus when he went into the feast with the purpose
of criticizing him; he now observes their conduct that he may
help them and teach others. "The chief seats" were the best
seats; they did not have seats as we have at the table, but reclined on couches. The most honorable station at an enter-

den of any man to a marriage feast, [2]sit not down in the chief seat; lest haply a more honorable man than thou be bidden of him, 9 and he that bade thee and him shalt come and say to thee, Give this man place; and then thou shalt begin with shame to take the lowest place. 10 But when thou art bidden, go and sit down in the lowest place; that when he that hath bidden thee cometh, he may say to thee, Friend, go up higher: then shalt thou have glory in the presence of all that [3]sit at meat with thee. 11 For every one that

[2]Gr. *recline not*
[3]Gr. *recline.* Comp. ch. 7.36, 37, marg.

tainment among them as well as among the Romans was the middle part of the middle couch, each couch holding three.

8, 9 When thou art bidden of any man to a marriage feast, —Jesus now proceeds to point out how different dispositions and traits of character are manifested by the conduct at this feasts. One when invited should come and "sit not down in the chief seat," but should occupy a humble place and let the one who has invited arrange according to his own judgment and inclination. It shows egotism, self-conceit, and haughtiness to go into a feast and occupy the chief place without an invitation. Humility would suggest a different course.

and he that bade thee and him shall come and say—Humility and modesty should be practiced. If one enters and occupies the chief seat, another more honorable might come in and the host would have to humiliate the one who has occupied the chief place by inviting him to take a lower, or less honorable seat. It is better to be invited to a higher place than to be requested to take a lower place. "Begin with shame to take the lowest place" means that one reluctantly does so with shame. The one who is ousted from the self-selected honorable seat must be requested to take the lowest place with shame. All the higher and more inviting seats were already occupied; no seat was vacant for his use except the one furthest removed from the chief place. He was not told to take the lowest seat, but he must do this from necessity.

10 But when thou art bidden, go and sit down in the lowest place;—Jesus has given negative teaching; he has told them what not to do, and now he tells what they should do. "Sit down" literally means "lay yourself back" in a convenient

exalteth himself shall be humbled; and he that humbleth himself shall be exalted.

12 And he said to him also that had bidden him, When thou makest a dinner or a supper, call not thy friends, nor thy brethren, nor thy kinsmen, nor rich neighbors; lest haply they also bid thee again, and a recompense be made thee. 13 But when thou makest a feast, bid the poor, the maimed, the

place or couch and wait until invitation is given to come up higher. Jesus does not teach hypocrisy here, neither a mock humility, which takes the lowest seat in order that the eyes of the whole company may be directed to the efforts of the master of the feast, to prevail upon the person who does this to go up higher; there is no greater evidence of pride than such an overdoing of humility.

11 **For every one that exalteth himself**—This is Jesus' conclusion which he draws from the parable; its application is easily made. Jesus frequently repeated this. (Matt. 23: 12.) Pride and a haughty spirit come before a fall. This principle is applicable alike in the affairs of men and in the kingdom of God; Jesus probably intended to direct their mind, not merely to abasement and exaltation among men, but also in a higher, spiritual sense in his kingdom and before God. This principle is taught throughout the Bible. (Prov. 16: 18; Ezek. 21: 26.)

12 **And he said to him also that had bidden him,**—This second parable of chapter 14 is intended as a rebuke to those who in a selfish way invite others to a feast. Usually people invite those who will later invite them. This parable seems to be addressed to his host as the former one was addressed to his guests. It gave Jesus the occasion to give correct teaching on inviting people to a feast. It is customary to invite friends and kinspeople; but Jesus says not to invite "thy friends, nor thy brethren, nor thy kinsmen, nor rich neighbors." These four classes will very likely invite you because you have invited them. Jesus tells why they should not invite them—"lest haply they also bid thee again, and a recompense be made thee."

13 **But when thou makest a feast,**—Again, Jesus presents the negative teaching and then follows that with the positive teaching; he tells who should not be invited, and then tells who should be. Jesus does not mean that we should make a

lame, the blind: 14 and thou shalt be blessed; because they have not *where-with* to recompense thee: for thou shalt be recompensed in the resurrection of the just.

15 And when one of them that ⁴sat at meat with him heard these things, he said unto him, Blessed is he that shall eat bread in the kingdom of God.

⁴Gr. *reclined.* Comp. ch. 7.36, 37, marg.

feast for the "poor, the maimed, the lame, the blind" to mock their misery, but to extend to them the charity which they need. We need to give attention to the distressed and relieve them as far as we may be able. It is far better to give to relieve the distressed than to set a feast for those who do not need it and expect to be entertained in return. One should exert himself to feed the poor, help the maimed, heal the lame, and guide the blind rather than merely satisfy a selfish pride in entertaining those who do not need it.

14 **and thou shalt be blessed;**—One will not receive a reward merely for an exchange of entertainments, but will for helping the distressed in the name of Christ. The exchange of entertainments shows a selfishness that is to be condemned, but to help others, when no earthly reward may be had, is to lay up treasures in heaven. One should plan to do all the good possible to the suffering and helpless; Jesus counts all that is done to the distressed in his name as deeds done to him. (Matt. 25: 31-46.) One who helps those who need help shall be blessed here and hereafter. "Recompensed in the resurrection of the just" means that one shall be rewarded at the day of judgment when the righteous shall be raised from the dead. The unselfish and charitable believer in Christ shall then receive his reward in that resurrection where will be found multitudes of the poor and distressed of earth.

15 **And when one of them that sat at meat**—It should be remembered that Jesus was still in the house "of one of the rulers of the Pharisees on a sabbath" (14: 1), and that he was an invited guest. He had spoken the two parables above mentioned and one of the fellow guests heard and said: "Blessed is he that shall eat bread in the kingdom of God." Much discussion has been had by commentators as to why this one should have so spoken; there is also a diversity of opinion as to what his words man. Some think that he

16 But he said unto him, A certain man made a great supper; and he bade
many: 17 and he sent forth his [5]servant at supper time to say to them that
were bidden, Come; for *all* things are now ready. 18 And they all with one

[5]Gr. *bondservant*

meant literal bread eaten in Jerusalem at the great feast, while
others think that he had reference to eating bread in the Messianic kingdom, which, he thought, was an earthly kingdom.
The Jews believed that the kingdom of the Messiah would be
ushered in with a magnificent festival, at which all the members of the Jewish families should be guests. Some think that
this one understood Jesus' reference to the resurrection as
being the resurrection of the old kingdom of Israel. It is
thought that Jesus gave the following parable to correct that
false view. Some think that this man gave utterance to a religious thought because he was in company where religious
things were being discussed; however, we need not speculate
as to what he meant or what prompted him to so express himself. It remains as a fact that he did say what is recorded here.

16 **But he said unto him,**—Jesus here gave the third parable
at this time. It is called the parable of the "great supper."
This parable seems to be designed to correct the idea that it
was the prerogative of the whole Jewish nation to be partakers of the blessings of the Messianic kingdom, irrespective of
a change in life or character. Jesus was still at the feast and
the figure of a supper is continued in order to teach a funda-
mental truth. Jesus did not contradict others by opposing assertions, yet his teachings were obviously opposed to false
teaching. One of the guests had just spoken about eating
bread "in the kingdom of God," as if all Jews were to do this
by right of their Jewish birth; Jesus takes the words from him
to lift his mind to a better kingdom, into which he was invited.

17 **and he sent forth his servant at supper time**—This servant was to announce to the invited guests that all things
were ready. This parable implies that the man who made the
supper belonged to the wealthy and to the nobility of the
Jews. This was the second and final summons, the invita-
tions having been previously given. (Compare Esth. 5: 8; 6:

consent began to make excuse. The first said unto him, I have bought a field, and I must needs go out and see it; I pray thee have me excused. 19 And another said, I have bought five yoke of oxen, and I go to prove them; I pray thee have me excused. 20 And another said, I have married a wife,

---

14.) This servant was to announce to those invited that the supper was now in a state of readiness, and that they should at once come to enjoy it.

18 And they all with one consent began to make excuse.—"Consent" is not in the original; some think that it would be better to supply "mind," "spirit," or "accord." There was the same temper of mind manifested in the various excuses which these persons, made; they all exhibited an utter contempt for the honor done them, and showed their preference to things of comparatively trivial importance. They had not come together and formulated unanimous excuses, but their excuses were all of the same nature, and revealed the same disposition of heart and attitude of mind.

The first said unto him,—This represents the man of landed estate who pleads necessity. He said: "I have bought a field" and that he must needs go out and see it. Land was very valuable; this man must go from home and look after the real estate that he had purchased; this would be regarded as one of the most valid and reasonable excuses for not attending the feast. It was the best excuse that he could give; and if any excuse would be accepted this would come in that class. He would have to go out from the city in order to complete the trade, and would be away from home at the time of the feast. He courteously asked to be excused, thinking that he had a good reason for rejecting the invitation.

19 And another said, I have bought five yoke of oxen,—This was a man of business and he pleaded a bargain which he had made. "Yoke" means two or more animals yoked together; he has purchased "five yoke of oxen" and had to go and "prove them." The spirit of this excuse is the same as the former; the language seems to be less polished, as it is that of a rustic. "To prove" them is to try them by putting them to the plow; he wished to test their strength, endurance, and ability. It is evident that he could have deferred this until

and therefore I cannot come. 21 And the ⁵servant came, and told his lord
these things. Then the master of the house being angry said to his ⁵servant,
Go out quickly into the streets and lanes of the city, and bring in hither the

---

after the supper; his excuse seems to represent men in the excitement of business, and he did not have the time to attend
the supper. He politely asked to be excused.

20 **And another said, I have married a wife,**—This man did
not plead any business engagements, but offered domestic en-
joyment and pleasure. "I have married" puts this in the past
tense; it refers to an act gone by in contrast to a present action. Here we have the force of temptations which lie in the
field of difficulty of reconciling conflicting duties. Attendance
on the feast did not entail the violation of any duty arising out
of his new relation, but simply the holding it of inferior importance on a given occasion. A newly married man has special favors granted him. (Deut. 24: 5; 1 Cor. 7: 33.) He
bluntly stated that he could not attend the feast.

21 **And the servant came, and told his lord these things.**—
The three classes of excuses are drawn from the different
phases of life; they are not "flimsy" excuses, ridiculous excuses, as some have sought to make them; they were the most
important excuses that could be given. They are taken from
the honorable stations of life in business and social intercourse. Yet, it was considered an insult to refuse to accept
the invitation. These reasons assigned could be put aside;
they could have been attended to at another time; those making them could have attended the supper, and later attended
to the business and social affairs.

Go out quickly into the streets—No time was to be lost; the
supper was ready, provisions abundant and should not be
wasted; every place at the table must be filled without delay.
He was to go into "the streets and lanes of the city." The
servant would go first into the city. The better class of people will be passing to and fro in the streets or broad ways, and
the poor would naturally be found in the "lanes of the city" or
narrow streets and alleys. It is evident that both rich and
poor are included in the terms and conditions of this invita-

poor and maimed and blind and lame. 22 And the ⁵servant said, Lord, what thou didst command is done, and yet there is room. 23 And the lord said unto the ⁵servant, Go out into the highways and hedges and constrain *them* to come in, that my house may be filled. 24 For I say unto you, that none of those men that were bidden shall taste of my supper.

tion. The rich will be passing to and fro in the broad streets and the poor would be in the lanes and alleys. Instead of a select company of invited guests, a promiscuous company was now to be invited; however, the prominence is given to the poorer class in the words "the poor and maimed and blind and lame." This is the same class as mentioned in verse 13. "Bring in hither" does not mean that he was to compel, but rather the invitation was urgent.

22-24 **And the servant said,**—The servant obeyed. He was commanded to "go out" quickly, and he did this. It seems that after his urgent invitation not enough guests were found to occupy all of the places at the table; there was yet room for others. This shows that there was provided sufficient food for a great many; hence it is called the "parable of the great supper"; a very large hall was made ready for this banquet. The servant was then commanded to "go out into the highways and hedges" and "constrain" others to come in. "Highways" meant public roads which led into the city, and "hedges" meant the narrow hedge paths, the vineyards and gardens. "Hedges" may mean either a "hedge" or a "place inclosed with a hedge." The vagrants usually rested along the hedge.

For I say unto you,—None who had despised his offer and had rejected the invitation should enjoy this feast. They had showed themselves unworthy of the honor and blessings which had been offered them; hence they were not to receive or enjoy that which had been prepared for them. Various interpretations and applications have been made of this parable. It is obvious and undeniable that not a man of all those first invited should partake of this supper; the master of the house had fully determined that somebody should enjoy it, but not one of those who had spurned his invitation should have access to it. Jesus had offered the blessings of the gospel to the

Jews; they had refused his invitation; they had offered various excuses, and had rejected him. The Gentiles and others more worthy of the blessings of God should receive the blessings first extended to the Jews.

19. COUNTING THE COST
14: 25-35

25 Now there went with him great multitudes: and he turned, and said unto them, 26 If any man cometh unto me, and hateth not his own father, and mother, and wife, and children, and brethren, and sisters, yea, and his

25 Now there went with him great multitudes:—Be it remembered that Jesus was on his way to Jerusalem; he had paused in the house of the Pharisee and had remained there at the feast and had spoken the three parables discussed above. It seems that he is now proceeding toward Jerusalem and a great multitude is following him. The Jews traveled in companies to Jerusalem to attend the feast. (Luke 2: 44.) This discourse is recorded only by Luke; there are similar declarations in Matt. 10: 37, 38; Mark 9: 50. This is another proof that Jesus repeated many of his sayings and interwove them into different connections and discourses. As Jesus proceeded on the way the multitude that followed him increased; however, it is not necessary to infer that the crowds followed him all the way to Jericho and thence to Jerusalem.

26 If any man cometh unto me,—Jesus here shows the cost of being his disciple; the great multitude that enthusiastically followed him at this time thought that the would establish an earthly kingdom, and that they would receive all of its blessings without an change of life. They are to know that they cannot follow Jesus without taking up their own cross, without bearing burdens and suffering persecution. One must hate "his own father, and mother, and wife, and children, and brethren, and sisters, yea, and his own life" in order to be a disciple of Jesus. "Hateth" does not mean that one must do them evil or hold malice against them; Jesus taught otherwise. (John 19: 25-27.) "Hate not" frequently means to love less. (Gen. 29: 31; Deut. 13: 6; 33: 9.) Matthew records Jesus as saying: "He that loveth father or mother more than

own life also, he cannot be my disciples. 27 Whosoever doth not bear his
own cross, and come after me, cannot be my disciple. 28 For which of you,
desiring to build a tower, doth not first sit down and count the cost, whether
he have *wherewith* to complete it? 29 Lest haply, when he hath laid a foundation, and is not able to finish, all that behold begin to mock him, 30 saying,

me is not worthy of me; and he that loveth son or daughter
more than me is not worthy of me." (Matt. 10: 37.) This
shows that "hate"is to be taken in a comparative sense. "To
hate" stands for "to love less"; when a choice between relatives or one's own life and Christ is before us, we must choose
to follow Christ; in doing this, we are hating our relatives and
loving Christ more.

27 **Whosoever doth not bear his own cross,**—We are to see
here that everything is to be given up for Christ; we must not
let anything come between us and Christ. To choose between
relatives and Christ is a cross that many must bear; to choose
between one's own life and Christ is a burden placed upon us.
Jesus tells whose cross one must bear; it is "his own cross";
all must bear a cross, but not all the *same* cross; each one
must "bear his own cross." One cannot be a disciples of
Christ without taking this cross and following Jesus.

28 **For which of you, desiring to build a tower,**—Jesus had
just taught the conditions of discipleship—one must take up
his cross and follow Jesus; he now teaches the cost of discipleship. This is illustrated by a man building, or proposing to
build a tower. Before doing this a wise, prudent man will
"first sit down and count the cost." The word "tower" may
designate a military tower, or one to command a view of the
surrounding country, or a watchtower of a mansion, combin-
ing adornment with utility. We are not able to determine the
kind of tower, for it does not matter; the point is just the
same. "First sit down" shows deliberate calculation; it excludes haste and requires ample time and trouble to learn the
approximate cost before proceeding. A prudent man will
count the cost of building the tower and evaluate all resources
and determine whether he has sufficient funds to complete the
work.

29, 30 **Lest haply, when he hath laid a foundation,**—If one
does not take sufficient time to estimate his resources as well

This man began to build, and was not able to finish. 31 Or what king, as he goeth to encounter another king in war, will not sit down first and take counsel whether he is able with ten thousand to meet him that cometh against him with twenty thousand? 32 Or else, while the other is yet a

as the cost of building, one may start the building and be unable to complete it. If he can build only the foundation or any part of it, but unable to complete the building, the unfinished building will stand as a monument to his folly and lack of good judgment and deliberation in the affair. Those who look upon the unfinished building will "begin to mock him." They will deride and scoff because he had so little judgment to begin that which he could not complete. They will say, "This man began to build, and was not able to finish." The imprudent tower builder will be put to shame before his fellows because of his foolish attempt at that which he was unable to do. The enemies of Jesus scoffed at him while he was on the cross. (Matt. 27: 40-42.) The folly of this man is also seen in the waste of money in laying a foundation upon which he could not complete the building.

31 **Or what king, as he goeth to encounter another king**— The same thought is illustrated more vividly in two kings planning to engage in battle. No king will plan a military campaign without estimating the forces on both sides. He will estimate the number of soldiers that he can command; then he will seek to estimate as far as possible the number of men that he will have to meet; he will seek to find out the strength and weakness of the opposing king. Any other course would be foolish and rash. Like the man planning to build a tower, the king will "sit down first and take counsel" as to whether he will be able to meet his opponent. Again, the term "sit down" means to take deliberate counsel as to the wisdom of taking ten thousand men and arraying them against an opposing king with twenty thousand. It would be very unwise for any king with only ten thousand soldiers to go against one who has twenty thousand; it would be rash folly to do so. Wisdom and prudence would suggest that he not rush blindly against such odds.

great way off, he sendeth an ambassage, and asketh conditions of peace. 33
So therefore whosoever he be of you that renounceth not all that he hath, he
cannot be my disciple. 34 Salt therefore is good: but if even the salt have
lost its savor, wherewith shall it be seasoned? 35 It is fit neither for the

---

32 **Or else, while the other is yet a great way off,**—Good
judgment and keen foresight would suggest that he seek some
compromise before the enemy engages in battle; it would be
too late then. He would not wait until the opposing forces
were at his gate, but would make overtures before his enemy
discovered his weakness; he would get better terms if he
would act before the battle is really joined. While the enemy
is afar off, he may meet with his ambassadors on an equal
footing with the one who has double his strength.

33 **So therefore whosoever he be of you**—Here Jesus draws
his own conclusion and makes his own application. The one
who does not renounce all cannot be a disciple of Jesus. One
must "renounce" all; here the principle in the two parables of
the rash builder and of the rash king is applied; the minor details do not matter; the spirit of self-sacrifice is the point.
One should neither make a false start nor a hopeless stand,
but give up all at once for Christ, and give his life to him.
The cost is great; one must give his influence, his money, his
energy, his life, his all, if he would be a disciple of Jesus.

34, 35 **Salt therefore is good**:—These two verses seem to
have been thrown in without any close connection with what
precedes them. Some think that they are intended to emphasize that the disciple of Jesus must keep active in his service.
He had already compared them to salt. (Matt. 5: 13; Mark 9:
50.) Jesus shows the uselessness of a false profession and intimates the end of false professors; in this light these two
verses further emphasize what he has just taught. Salt is
good in its place and for that which it was intended. Salt
may lose its savor; it may lose its saltness; it may become in-
sipid and tasteless. There is a true similitude existing between the faithful disciples of Jesus and the properties of salt;
hence, Jesus frequently used this likeness to enforce and illustrate the great and important truths that he had just announced.

land nor for the dunghill: *men* cast it out. He that hath ears to hear, let him hear.

It is fit neither for the land—When salt has lost its saltness, it has lost its true nature; when it has lost its nature, it cannot function as salt and is unfit for that which people use salt. It is good for nothing and is cast away. Salt that has lost its savor does not make good fertilizer; rather it destroys the fertility of the soil and kills vegetation. There is no place about the house, yard, or garden where it can be used; no one will allow it to be thrown into his field, and the only place for it is in the street, and there it is cast to be trodden under foot of men. "Dunghill" is used here for "manure"; this is its only use in the New Testament; it is used a few times in the Old Testament. Jesus used strong terms to emphasize the worthlessness of a *mere* professor in his discipleship. He concluded with an oft-repeated saying: "He that hath ears to hear, let him hear." (Matt. 11: 15; 13: 43; Luke 8: 8.)

20. SOME PARABLES: LOST SHEEP, LOST COIN, PRODIGAL SON
15: 1-32

1 Now all the ¹publicans and sinners were drawing near unto him to hear

¹See marginal note on ch. 3.12

1 **Now all the publicans and sinners**—It is thought that these parables were spoken the next day after the dinner with the "ruler of the Pharisees." (14: 1.) This was probably in Perea near one of the fords of the Jordan and not far from Jericho, where publicans were numerous on account of trade centers. "Publicans" were tax gatherers; there were two classes of "publicans"—the first were Roman knights, who usually lived in Rome; the second class were subordinate collectors, each of whom was required to pay a certain sum to his superior with the privilege of raising as much more as he pleased for his own profit. Publicans were very odious in the sight of many Jews. They are usually classed with "sinners," who were depraved characters or open transgressors of the law of Moses. The publicans were infamous among the Jews

him. 2 And both the Pharisees and the scribes murmured, saving, This man
receiveth sinners, and eateth with them.
3 And he spake unto them this parable, saying, 4 What man of you, hav-

---

by their occupation and sinners were notorious offenders
against the tradition of the law. They had a noble purpose in
coming to Jesus; they came "to hear him." They did not
come through curiosity, but keenly felt a need of his blessings
and had a strong desire to be instructed by him. There is a
wide contrast between the purpose of their coming to Jesus
and that of the Pharisees and scribes.

2 And both the Pharisees and the scribes murmured,—The
Pharisees were a religious party or sect which originated
about a hundred and fifty years before Christ; their name
means "separatists"; they separated themselves from traditional impurity. To become a Pharisee one had to agree to
set apart all the sacred tithes and refrain from eating anything
that had not been tithed; they believed in the resurrection of
the dead. "Scribes" were learned men who preserved, copied,
and expounded the law and the traditions. (Ezra 7: 12; Neh.
8: 1; Matt. 15: 1-6.) They were called lawyers and doctors,
or teachers of the law. (Matt. 22: 35; Luke 5: 17-21.) Both
classes "murmured"; the original means that they were murmuring among themselves against him; the form of the verb
in the original is intensive, implying frequency, or in groups
among themselves, with mingled indignation. Their murmuring was because Jesus received and ate with sinners. He received them into his presence, instruction, and favor; he went
into their houses and ate with them. The Pharisees separated
themselves from such classes and would not even eat with
them.

3-7 And he spake unto them this parable,—This parable is
also recorded by Matthew (18: 12, 13); there are some points
of difference in the two records. The parable is addressed to
these murmuring scribes and Pharisees and in the presence of
publicans and sinners. This parable and the one following it
are introduced by questions. "What man of you, having a
hundred sheep, and having lost one of them, doth not leave
the ninety and nine in the wilderness, and go after that which

ing a hundred sheep, and having lost one of them, doth not leave the ninety
and nine in the wilderness, and go after that which is lost, until he find it?
5 And when he hath found it, he layeth it on his shoulders, rejoicing. 6 And
when he cometh home, he calleth together his friends and his neighbors, saying unto them, Rejoice with me, for I have found my sheep which was lost.
7 I say unto you, that even so there shall be joy in heaven over one sinner
that repenteth, *more* than over ninety and nine righteous persons, who need
no repentance.

---

is lost, until he find it?" The interrogative form served to fix
attention at once; Jesus appealed directly to that human feeling which leads a man to seek that which is lost, and rejoice
when he has found it. This flock consisted of one hundred
sheep in round numbers; a flock of this number would show
that the man was in very good circumstances. If one of them
is lost, the others are left while search is made for the lost
one. Very likely there were present some who had had such
experience as Jesus here related. The people were familiar
with such incidents in the life of shepherds. (Ezek. 34: 12.)
The seeking after the lost sheep shows the eager desire to find
it; it does not show that he thinks more of the one sheep than
he did of the ninety-nine. The ninety-nine were left and the
concern about them was suspended until the lost one was
found. The ninety-nine are left "in the wilderness," or the
rural section of pasture land. The search continues until the
lost is found, and then he "layeth it on his shoulders, rejoicing." The shepherds of the east often carried on their backs
the lost sheep of the flock; this could be done with less trouble than driving the sheep. When the shepherd returned
home with the lost sheep, he and his friends and neighbors
gathered in and rejoiced together.

I say unto you, that even so there shall be joy in heaven—
Here Jesus draws his own conclusion and makes the application of the parable. There is rejoicing "in heaven over one
sinner that repenteth"; the word "sinner" here points to verse
1; these sinners were repenting; the lost sheep were being
brought to the fold; the joy in heaven is in contrast with the
grumbling Pharisees and scribes. There is more rejoicing
over that which has been found than over "ninety and nine
righteous persons, who need no repentance." Jesus does not

8 Or what woman having ten ²pieces of silver, if she lose one piece, doth not light a lamp, and sweep the house, and seek diligently until she find it? 9 And when she hath found it, she calleth together her friends and neighbors, saying, Rejoice with me, for I have found the piece which I had lost. 10 Even so, I say unto you, there is joy in the presence of the angels of God over one sinner that repenteth.

---

²Gr. *drachma*. a coin worth about eight pence, or sixteen cents

---

mean to say that the Pharisees and scribes did not need to repent; he, for the sake of argument, accepts their claims about themselves and by their own words condemns them for their criticisms of his efforts to save the lost sheep. This is the same point that he made against them when they criticized him and his disciples for being at the feast of Levi. (Luke 5: 31ff.) They posed as "righteous"; they were not, but on their own claim, Jesus condemns them for murmuring against him in receiving and eating with sinners.

8-10 **Or what woman having ten pieces of silver,**—This parable is recorded only by Luke; it is introduced by a question, and has the same general meaning as the parable of the lost sheep. This parable advances the thought; the coin was lost and the place where it lay was concealed from the eye. The original word for "pieces of silver" was "drachma" and had a value of about sixteen or eighteen cents in our money. The name "drachma" is a term used in weighing medicines, but here it is applied to the value of the coin. The former parable represented a scene in the country and had to do with sheep; this was especially interesting to men. This parable is a scene in a house; the woman in the house usually kept the small treasury; hence this parable would be interesting to the women who were present. A woman had lost one of her ten pieces of silver. She lighted her candle, used her broom, and searched diligently until she found the coin. She then rejoiced and called her friends and neighbors to rejoice with her.

Even so, I say unto you, there is joy in the presence of the angels—In the former parable there was rejoicing "in heaven," but in this there is "joy in the presence of the angels"; however, the context shows that the two parables have the same meaning. The first parable is founded upon the affection, manifested by a shepherd toward a lost sheep; the

11 And he said, A certain man had two sons: 12 and the younger of them
said to his father, Father, give me the portion of [a]*thy* substance that falleth

[a]Gr. *the*

---

second parable relates to a poor woman who had lost a piece
of money, which she could not afford to spare from her scanty
treasury. The joy in the presence of the angels is the same as
the joy that shall be in heaven. Emphasis is put again upon
the "sinner that repenteth." This does not mean that God
finds more satisfaction in a repentant sinner than in a sinless
saint; Jesus was here referring definitely to the penitent publicans and to the self-righteous Pharisees. God did not take delight in the sins of the publicans, nor did he regard the state
of the Pharisees and scribes as perfect, even taking the Pharisees at their best.

11, 12 **And he said, A certain man had two sons:**—This parable is recorded only by Luke. It is said to be the most beautiful of all the parables; it is full of human sympathy and love.
Some have objected to calling this a parable; however, it
seems that no violence is done in classing it as a parable. By
common consent it has been called the "Parable of the Prodigal Son," yet the word "prodigal" is not used in the narrative.
The parables of the lost sheep and the lost coin help to introduce this parable. The three parables were spoken in the presence of "publicans and sinners" and the "Pharisees and the
scribes"; the first class had come to Jesus "to hear him" teach,
but the last class had come to spy, criticize, and accuse him.
It is well to keep these two classes in mind as we study the
parable. This may be called the "parable of the lost son" as
the other two and called the "lost sheep" and "lost coin."

and the younger of them said to his father,—The father had
two sons. In the first parable the lost sheep strayed of itself,
but a piece of money could not be lost of itself; in the one the
attention is fastened upon the condition of the thing lost,
while in the second case attention is fastened upon her sorrow of the one who lost it; but in the parable of the prodigal
son there is blame to be attached to the one that is lost.

to me. And he divided unto them his living. 13 And not many days after, the younger son gathered all together and took his journey into a far coun- try; and there he wasted his substance with riotous living. 14 And when he

There were two sons, and, according to Jewish law of inheri- tance, the older son would receive two portions; the younger son would receive only one-third of the inheritance. According to the custom, the father might, during his lifetime, dispose of all his property by a gift as he may wish.

13 **And not many days after, the younger son**—The father graciously gave the son his share, and soon this son, after gathering all his possions together, "took his journey into a far country." The father may have divided the estate in such a manner that the younger son could take his property away with him if he desired; or the son may have made such dispo- sition of it as to convert it into money and other valuables. He "took his journey," which shows that he resolved and acted deliberately; he not only went from home, but he went "into a far country." He not only wanted to be out of sight, but beyond the influence and control of his father; he was as far away in character as he was in geographical situation. He had taken all of his possessions out of his father's hands, and now he is placing himself beyond the reach of his father. We are not told into what country he went.

and there he wasted his substance with riotous living.—He "wasted." That is, dissipated, squandered; this was the very opposite of "gathered together." It means more exactly that he scattered his property like winnowing grain. (Matt. 25: 24.) We know how he "wasted his substance"; it was done "with riotous living." This means that he lived dissolutely or profligately; he was a spendthrift, a profligate, a prodigal. He plunged recklessly into extravagance, dissipation, and disso- lute living. (Prov. 28: 19; Gal. 5: 19-21; Eph. 4: 17-19.) This is a very dark picture and shows the depravity to which he had fallen; he was not so much a disturber of the peace, but had wasted his substance in "riotous living," and probably as the elder brother accused him later, he had "devoured" his substance by "living with harlots."

had spent all, there arose a mighty famine in that country; and he began to
be in want. 15 And he went and joined himself to one of the citizens of that
country; and he sent him into his fields to feed swine. 16 And he would fain
⁴have filled his belly with ⁵the husks that the swine did eat: and no man
gave unto him. 17 But when he came to himself he said, How many hired

⁴Many ancient authorities read *have been filled*
⁵Gr. *the pods of the carob tree*

14 **And when he had spent all,**—He soon spent all that he
had; one spends recklessly when one lives a dissipated life; he
had no income, and all that he spent diminished his capital; he
did not use good judgment even in spending what he had.
There is an end to be reached and this son soon reached that
end. After spending all in his riotous living, "a mighty famine" arose in that country. Famines were terrible scourges in
the east; they were caused by lack of rain in season, wars, and
pestilences. In ancient times there were no means of relieving the wants of a country by the products of another. They
did not have railroads, trucks, or other means of transporting
products from one country to another, as we now have; the
ships could go only along the water courses and caravans
would convey the products to the interior; but this was done
only on special occasions. People had to suffer. This son
"began to be in want."

15, 16 **And he went and joined himself to one of the citizens**
—He moved now from his haunts of vice and dissipation and
put himself in the service of some man of that country. He
"joined himself" to "one of the citizens of that country." The
verb here means to "glue or cement"; this implies that he
forced himself upon the citizen, who was unwilling to engage
him and who took him into service only upon persistent entreaty. This unhappy and miserable young man is now a useless appendage to a stranger who did not care for him. He
was sent "into his fields to feed swine." Presumably this
young man was a Jew; swine were unclean animals with the
Jews; this once proud and wealthy Jewish son is now the
feeder of unclean animals; it is worse than that, for he associates with the swine and "would fain have filled his belly
with the husks that the swine did eat." He had wanted the
wrong thing all along, and it was no better now; all he
wanted before was to fill his belly, and he now must fill it

servants of my father's have bread enough and to spare, and I perish here
with hunger! 18 I will arise and go to my father, and will say unto him,
Father, I have sinned against heaven, and in thy sight; 19 I am no more

---

with that which gives him no satisfaction. "Husks" generally
signifies a covering of grain, a dry and useless substance,
which is hardly fit for food for any animal. This means that
his food was so scanty that even the pods which the swine
were eating were the object of his craving appetite; but these
were denied him probably by the overseer.

17 **But when he came to himself**—He had been deaf to all
reason; his state was a form of reckless living, devoid of all
good reason; he had lost sight of all that was good, reasonable, and just; he had lost sight of his better nature and the
virtues of righteous living. His eyes were blind to all that
was good, his ears were deaf to wise counsel, and his appreciation of the better things of life was lost. Some describe his
state as being a state of insanity. The time came when he
"came to himself"; he comes back to his better self; he re-
gains his good judgment and opens his eyes and unstops his
ears and heightens his appreciation of the better things of life;
the spell of his youthful infatuation is broken and he begins to
take a sensible view of his own situation. When he thus
came to himself he remembered that even the servants in his
father's house had sufficient bread to eat and to spare, while
he was perishing with hunger. For the first time in his life he
now sees the folly of calling for his portion of the estate,
going into a far country, and spending his estate in riotous
living. While the servants in his father's house had plenty,
he, a born son, was starving; he had no one to blame but himself. His mind was soon made up.

18, 19 **I will arise and go to my father,**—When he came to
himself and made up his mind, he resolved to play the fool no
longer. There was no delay in making up his mind as to what
he would do; if he stayed longer, he would be too weak to
make the journey, as he was perishing at that time. He had
deserted his father, but now he is resolved to return to him.
He framed what he would say to his father: "I have sinned

worthy to be called thy son: make me as one of thy hired servants. 20 And
he arose, and came to his father. But while he was yet afar off, his father
saw him, and was moved with compassion, and ran, and fell on his neck, and

---

against heaven, and in thy sight." He will make no apology
for his sin, but frankly and fully confess his sins; he would
blame no one for his sin. No apology, no attempt to deceive,
nothing but a frank confession of sins repented of would he
say to his father. Sincere and humble confession is connected
with repentance. (2 Sam. 12: 13; Prov. 28: 13; Hos. 14: 2; 1
John 1: 9, 10.)

I am no more worthy to be called thy son:—This expressed
a true state of mind; he had not shown the love and respect of
a child to his father; he had reasonably forfeited all claim to
support as a son; he had been an ungrateful sinner, who had
remained among strangers until poverty and hunger had
forced him to change his course. He was willing to be taken
and treated as one of the hired servants. This shows how
deeply penitent he was. Though a son, he would not claim
that relationship; he would gladly act and be treated as any
one of the hired servants. He will gladly take whatever may
be offered him.

20 And he arose, and came to his father.—"He arose"; that
is, immediately put his resolution into action. He "came";
that is, he went directly to his father. We know not how
long it took him to go from this "far country" to his father's
home. "His father" in the original means 'his own father."
The picture is emphatic; he left the herd of swine and his association with it and came to his father—what a change in en-
vironment! Though forced by circumstances, yet it was an
exercise of his own will power in putting into execution his
good resolution; his decision and his execution of it were vol-
untary acts of this son.

But while he was yet afar off,—The father seems to have
been waiting and expecting his son; though he was at a distance in space, yet his son and the father were together in
thought and spirit. We do not know whether the worn and
dimmed eyes of his venerable father had been watching for
the return, but we do know that at some eminent place his

[6]kissed him. 21 And the son said unto him, Father, I have sinned against heaven, and in thy sight: I am no more worthy to be called thy son.[7] 22 But the father said to his [8]servants, Bring forth quickly the best robe, and put it

[6]Gr. *kissed him much.* See ch. 7.38, 45
[7]Some ancient authorities add *make me as one of thy hired servants.* See ver. 19
[8]Gr. *bondservants*

father caught sight of his prodigal son and "was moved with compassion" to receive his wayward son back into his home. His eagerness is shown in the fact that he "ran" to greet him. There is an eastern proverb which says: "Whoever draws near to me (God) an *inch,* I will draw near to him an *ell;* and whoso *walks* to meet me, I will *leap* to meet him." This expresses the eagerness with which the father ran to meet his son and the glow of affection with which he greeted him. The father "fell on his neck, and kissed him." Old man as his father was, yet he ran and fell on the neck of his son and kissed him. "Fell on his neck" refers to the act of embrace with which he greeted his son. (Gen. 45: 14.)

21 **And the son said unto him, Father,**—The son as quickly as he could free himself from the affectionate embrace of the father began to recite his oft-repeated confession that he had framed in his resolution to return to the father and had repeated over and over as he wearily wended his way back home. His confession was full and open as was the outburst of paternal love at the greeting. The son began his confession, and with trembling tones and many sad sobs had repeated the first part of his confession. He had sinned in the sight of God against his father and against heaven. Every sin is in some sense against God; it may be also against self or others, but always against God. It may be that this was the first awakening of filial love on the part of this prodigal son. Some ancient authorities add here: "Make me as one of thy hired servants." However, it is omitted from the manuscript from which the Revised Version was made. This phrase was in the resolution that he formed (verse 19), but it seems that he did not get to recite it to his father.

22-24 **But the father said to his servants,**—"Bondservants" is used here in the original, and there is a fine touch in bringing in the "bondservants" immediately after "my son." He

on him; and put a ring on his hand, and shoes on his feet: 23 and bring the fatted calf, *and* kill it, and let us eat, and make merry: 24 for this my son was dead, and is alive again; he was lost, and is found. And they began to be merry. 25 Now his elder son was in the field: and as he came and drew nigh to the house, he heard music and dancing. 26 And he called to him one

---

commanded the servants to "bring forth quickly the best robe" and put it upon his son. There was to be no delay; the "best robe," the first and most honorable one, was to be placed upon his son. This was a long flowing robe, a festive garment. (Mark 16: 5; Luke 20: 46.) The father commanded that "a ring" be put upon his hand, "and shoes on his feet." The "ring" was a symbol of restored sonship. Pharaoh placed a ring upon Joseph's hand to honor him. (Gen. 41: 42.) A "gold ring" on the hand was a distinguished honor. (James 2: 2.) Sandals were placed upon his feet. These were to take the place of the ragged garments with which his son was now clad. The son was a changed son and deeply penitent and affectionate, and the honorable dress in which he is now to be clad signifies the changed and forgiven son. The fatted calf was to be killed. This was the custom; an animal was kept for guests, and a refusal to kill the animal was an insult to the guest. The law of hospitality required the killing of the fatted calf.

for this my son was dead,—To the father he was dead, but now is very much alive. Here is an open and explicit acknowledgement of "this my son"; he was dead to the father, dead to all that was good and righteous, but now is alive in warm affection to the father, and alive to all that is good. He "was lost" in all that pertains to virtue and happiness; he is now found at home and restored to an honorable station. No wonder the joy of the father was expressed in a feast. "They began to be merry." This merrymaking took place at the close of the feast; in this joyful celebration the son himself doubtless took a prominent part, and in this there was a great advance on the preceding parables, the lost sheep and piece of money being insensible of joy which their recovery had inspired.

25 Now his elder son was in the field:—We now come to another scene in this most interesting and fruitful study of the

of the servants, and inquired what these things might be. 27 And he said
unto him, Thy brother is come; and thy father hath killed the fatted calf,
because he hath received him safe and sound. 28 But he was angry, and

---

parable of the prodigal son. There are several well-arranged
scenes that complete the picture—the first scene is in the
home with the younger son asking for his portion of the inheritance; the second scene is the prodigal son in a far country living riotously; the third, the prodigal son reduced to
poverty, feeding swine, and friendless, and homeless, coming
to himself and resolving to return home; the fourth, the meeting and greeting of the father and son, the making merry and
rejoicing together; the last scene, the elder brother coming to
the house, discovering what was doing on, rebuking the
father, and his cool treatment of his brother. Many conflicting interpretations have been given about the elder brother's
part in the scene. Some have regarded him as a type of the
angels in heaven; others have said that he represents the Jewish nation; still others make him represent the proud Pharisees. The music which the elder son heard was of that kind
which he knew to be accompanied with a dance; hence both
music and dancing are joined to the verb "heard." At wed-
dings, birthdays, and all other festal gatherings music was
their chief entertainment.

26, 27 **And he called to him one of the servants,**—Instead of
entering the house, as his position in the family would have
justified, upon learning what was going on, he called a servant
and inquired as to the particulars. His cool and calculating
selfishness betrays itself in this little incident. There are
three words in the Greek for servants in the parable; there are
"hired servants," "servants," and "footboys" or "lackeys"; the
elder brother called one of the "lackeys." These three classes
of servants may indicate the wealth and high standing of this
family. The servant reported: "Thy brother is come; and thy
father hath killed the fatted calf, because he hath received him
safe and sound." This should have been good news to the
elder brother. This servant seems to have thought that the
elder brother would receive the announcement with like emotions of the father; hence he says: "Thy brother" and "thy

would not go in: and his father came out, and entreated him. 29 But he
answered and said to his father, Lo, these many years do I serve thee, and I

---

father" are rejoicing together, and that the father had "killed
the fatted calf." No mention is made of the robe, ring, and
shoes with which the younger son had been clothed; only "the
fatted calf" was mentioned, which was enough to indicate that
great honor was bestowed upon the returned son. He was
"safe and sound," which was an added reason for the merrymaking; the returned son was in a healthful condition.

28 **But he was angry,**—The original means that he was not
angry with a mere temporary fit of passion, but with a deep-
seated wrath. "But" puts the elder brother's attitude and disposition in direct contrast with what the environments of the
occasion would seem to indicate. He "would not go in"; that
is, he was unwilling to go in the house and celebrate with his
father and brother; he refused in his anger to lend himself to
the joy of the occasion. While the house was resounding
with music and merrymaking, the elder brother stood sullenly
out and nursed his anger. He showed not only a lack of
brotherly love, but also of sympathy with the joy of his father
at the return of the son. When he refused to go in, his father
'came out, and entreated him." The father went forth to meet
the prodigal son; now he goes out to entreat the elder son to
lay aside his anger and enter the house; his happiness was not
complete even on the return of the prodigal, while his other
son stood without angry, displeased, and unhappy. The
father leaves the company within, in the presence of his long-
lost son, and condescends to go forth to plead with the elder
brother and to urge him to enter the house.

29, 30 **But he answered and said to his father,**—The elder
son was "in the field" and missed the affection at the scene of
the meeting of the aged father and the now penitent son; in
his deep anger he does not respect his venerable father when
he came out and entreated him to enter the house, but in his
reply he reflected upon his father. He said: "Lo, these many
years do I serve thee, and I never transgressed a commandment of thine." This seems a boastful statement, for such an

never transgressed a commandment of thine; and *yet* thou never gavest me a kid, that I might make merry with my friends: 30 but when this thy son came, who hath devoured thy living with harlots, thou killedst for him the fatted calf. 31 And he said unto him, [1]Son, thou art ever with me, and all that is mine is thine. 32 But it was meet to make merry and be glad: for

[1]Gr. *Child*

ugly disposition that he now showed would lead one to think that he was not so good and obedient as he claimed. He puts the "many years" which he had served his father in contrast with "when this thy son came" that moment the father began to make merry. The elder brother represents his own life in as favorable way as he can, and puts his younger brother's conduct in as unfavorable light as is possible; to him the contrast is very wide, and he has some ground to justify him in the contrast. According to his statement, he had not only served many years as a "slave," but he had "never transgressed a commandment" of his father, while his younger brother had "devoured thy living with harlots." Again, according to the elder brother, the father had never given him a kid that he, also a son, who had served him so long, might "make merry with" his friends. But, so soon as the prodigal son returned, the father killed the fatted calf and now was making merry; to the elder brother this seemed to be unfair; it showed that the father did not appreciate the elder brother's service, and seemed to put a premium on the dissipation and prodigality of the younger son. The elder brother thinks that he has made out a clear case of ungratefulness on the part of the father toward himself and convicted him of sanctioning the life that the younger son had lived. The elder brother speaks to his father of his brother as "thy son," not "my brother"; he puts the emphasis upon the dissolute life that the younger son had lived. In his own heart he thinks that he had been grossly neglected and abused. Again, the elder brother had accused the younger son of devouring "thy living with harlots."

31 **And he said unto him, Son, thou art ever with me,—**Note the calm and conciliatory address of the father; he speaks ten-

this thy brother was dead, and is alive *again;* and *was* lost, and is found.

---

derly, which is a contrast between his manner and that of his elder son. The elder son did not begin his address by saying "Father"; but this did not prevent his father from addressing him affectionately as "Son." True, "a soft answer turneth away wrath; but a grievous word stirreth up anger." (Prov. 15: 1.) The father not only addressed his son in this affectionate way, but he reminded him of the fact that "all that is mine is thine." This was another conciliatory statement; the father is the mediator between the two. He had given the younger son the portion that belonged to him, and as he had only two sons, all that he now possessed belonged to the elder brother; the father did not propose to take the portion that belonged to the elder brother and give it to his younger son. The father was just and fair, tender and affectionate, merciful and forgiving. This was a beautiful example for this elder brother.

32 **But it was meet to make merry and be glad:**—The last words of the father are at once truthful, temperate, and tender; they were calculated to destroy the force of the contemptuous and sneering words uttered apparently by the elder son with the express purpose of wounding the feelings of the father. It was fitting to "make merry and be glad," said the father. This was a very tactful way of rebuking the elder son's attitude. The father gives the reason for the rejoicing. "For this thy brother was dead, and is alive again; and was lost, and is found." The father tactfully refers to the younger son as "thy brother"; this was a gentle rebuke and reminder of the close relation of his two sons. It seems that the father has quoted from his son's language; the elder son had said: "This thy son." But the father says: "This thy brother." He was "dead"; he was as one dead to the father and to the elder brother; vicious persons are represented as dead. (1 Tim. 5: 6.) He was not only dead, but now "is alive again"; he is represented as being raised to a new life. He was lost to his

father and to all that was good, lost to his elder brother, but now he is "found." The father said the one long dead to us now lives again; the one long lost to us is now found and restored to us. The parable seems to end abruptly.

21. THE UNRIGHTEOUS STEWARD
16: 1-13

1 And he said also unto the disciples, There was a certain rich man, who had a steward; and the same was accused unto him that he was wasting his

1 **And he said also unto the disciples,**—This parable has been called the "Parable of the Unjust Steward"; it is here called the "Parable of the Unrighteous Steward." This parable is peculiar to Luke. Jesus had put to silence the murmuring Pharisees by the three foregoing parables; he now continues his discourse to his disciples, in the presence of the publicans and sinners, Pharisees and scribes. He introduces the parable with "a certain rich man" who had an unfaithful steward. "Steward," in the original, means one who distributes or dispenses affairs of a house; he is one who is a house manager or overseer of an estate (Luke 12: 42); the steward kept the household stores under lock and seal, giving out what was required; he was usually given a signet ring from his master to show his authority; he could execute bonds and notes in the name of his master by using the signet ring.

and the same was accused unto him—This servant was "accused," which, in the original, meant "to throw across," or "to carry across"; hence to carry reports from one to another; to carry false reports, and to culminate or slander. The word implies "malice," but not necessarily falsehood. The accusation against him was that he "was wasting his goods." He was wasting that which belonged to his master. "Wasting" is from the same root word as "wasted" in 15: 13, as used of the prodigal son, in wasting his substance in riotous living. The accusation against him may have come from jealous tenants and other servants in the house. The steward is not represented as denying the accusation or attempting to prove it to be false.

goods. 2 And he called him, and said unto him, What is this that I hear of thee? render the account of thy stewardship; for thou canst be no longer steward. 3 And the steward said within himself, What shall I do, seeing that my lord taketh away the stewardship from me? I have not strength to dig; to beg I am ashamed. 4 I am resolved what to do, that, when I am put

---

2 And he called him, and said unto him,—The day of reckoning had come; the steward was to be discharged. He was asked: "What is this that I hear of thee? render the account of thy stewardship." These words in the original imply anger. "Render the account of thy stewardship" literally means "give back" that which you have fraudulently taken; there is also implied "and now give back my signet; for thou shalt no longer be my steward." The proprietor must dismiss him from his service because he has proved himself to be unfaithful. Some think that there is implied that if the steward should successfully prove his innocence he might be retained in his position.

3, 4 And the steward said within himself,—It seems that the steward was conscious of his guilt and began to reflect as to "what" he should do; as a shrewd and prudent man he will strive either to hold his place or he will seek to provide for himself a comfortable living. It seems that he chose the latter alternative. He began to make preparation for a comfortable living. He was not yet dismissed and he had opportunity to further his unrighteous practices. In reasoning with himself he said: "I have not strength to dig; to beg I am ashamed." He either had to go to work or beg; he felt that he did not have strength to work; that is, he was not able to engage in manual labor which in agricultural pursuits consisted largely in upturning the earth by digging. He may have been strong enough to do that kind of work, but he was not inclined to do so, and thus persuaded himself that he was not able "to dig." The other alternative was that of begging, but he was "ashamed" or had a sense of pride, and did not wish to put himself in the class of mendicants. It was better to beg than to practice dishonesty, but he had nursed his pride and did not wish to beg. He was not "ashamed" to cheat or lie, but he was "ashamed" to beg.

out of the stewardship, they may receive me into their houses. 5 And calling to him each one of his lord's debtors, he said to the first, How much owest thou unto my lord? 6 And he said, A hundred ²measures of oil. And he said unto him, Take thy ³bond, and sit down quickly and write fifty. 7 Then said he to another, And how much owest thou? And he said, A hundred ⁴measures of wheat. He said unto him, Take thy ³bond, and write fourscore.

²Gr. *baths,* the bath being a Hebrew measure. See Ezek. 45.10, 11, 14
³Gr. *writings*
⁴Gr. *cors* the cor being a Hebrew measure. See Ezek. 45.14

I am resolved what to do,—He had fully made up his mind, and continues to soliloquize and expresses himself in a positive way as to what he will do, he had just thought of a plan that he could execute, and he is determined to do it. His plan was that when he was dismissed from his stewardship he would be received into the houses of those whom he had befriended. He planned to make friends so that they would receive him into their hospitality, out of gratitude for what he had done for them; he still hoped to enjoy life in the homes of those whom he had laid under obligation to him by an unrighteous use of his master's affairs. His plans as they are now revealed confirm the report that he was dealing falsely with his master's goods.

5-7 And calling to him each one of his lord's debtors,—He began speedily to execute his plan; he did not know just when he would be dismissed, so he must act in haste while he had the authority as a steward. He called each one of his "lord's debtors"; that is, he called them one by one. It is not known whether one debtor knew what he had done for the other debtor; his plans are to deal with each one separately. The first debtor was asked how much he owed his lord. He answered: "A hundred measures of oil." Literally, a "measure" means a "bath." The "bath" was a Hebrew measure, but the amount is uncertain, as there were three kinds of measurements in use in Palestine. The original Mosaic measure corresponded with the Roman; that of Jerusalem was a fifth larger, and the common Galilean measurement was about a fifth larger than the Jerusalem. The first standard made the bath consist of about fifty-six pints, or about seven gallons. Some make the bath to contain between eight and nine gallons. This is supposed to be olive oil, as it was used for vari-

8 And his lord commended [5]the unrighteous steward because he had done wisely: for the sons of this [6]world are for their own generation wiser than the sons of the light. 9 And I say unto you, Make to yourselves friends [7]by

[5]Gr. *the steward of unrighteousness*
[6]Or, *age*
[7]Gr. *out of*

---

ous purposes—food, cosmetics, embalming, light, surgery, etc. It was a great article of trade. (Rev. 18: 13.) The steward said to the debtor to sit down and write quickly "fifty." He reduced the debt one-half. He called another and asked the same question. This one said that his debt was "a hundred measures of wheat." He was told to "write fourscore" instead of the one hundred. The original for "measure" here is different from that in verse 6; a measure here means a "cor" or "homer," and was the largest Hebrew dry measure, equal to ten "baths" or about eleven bushels. (Ezek. 45: 14.)

8 **And his lord commended the unrighteous steward**—The lord admired the shrewdness of his steward, though he himself was defrauded; he commended, or praised, not the injustice or dishonesty of the steward, but his prudence and practical shrewdness. (Psalm 49: 18.) He had shown worldly foresight and had acted upon it. The unrighteous steward had been cunning in dishonesty; he had been prudent, though selfishly, and wrongly so. It should be kept clear that Jesus does not commend the dishonesty and trickery of this unrighteous steward; he does not commend the steward for his injustice or wrongdoing. "For the sons of this world are for their own generation wiser than the sons of the light." The lord of the steward does not excuse him from guilt, and he was apparently dismissed from his service; his shrewdness consisted in finding a place to go after he was dismissed; he was still an unrighteous steward even though his shrewdness was commended. "The sons of this world" are those who are studious and plan for the greatest possessions and pleasures of this world; they are opposed to "the sons of the light," who are those who are walking in the light. Men of the world act with better judgment oftentimes with respect to worldly affairs than do the disciples of Jesus with respect to spiritual af-

means of the mammon of unrighteousness; that, when it shall fail, they may receive you into the eternal tabernacles. 10 He that is faithful in a very little is faithful also in much: and he that is unrighteous in a very little is

fairs. This parable is spoken "unto the disciples." (Verse 1.)

9 And I say unto you, Make to yourselves friends—Jesus makes his own application of the parable. We should be satisfied with his explanation; sometimes the thought is lost amidst the drapery of the parable. The master of the unrighteous steward commended him for his prudent foresight, and Jesus, speaking to his disciples, said to them that they should use a like forethought in regard to their spiritual and eternal interests. Surely Christians should show better judgment in their relations with one another than "crooks" do in their dealings with one another; the devotees of material goods often use more sense in handling them than do Christians as custodians of eternal things.

by means of the mammon of unrighteousness;—"Mammon" is a word applied to wealth or riches; its probable derivation means trust; so the description of wealth, not merely as a possession, but also as something which is so generally made a ground of confidence. "Riches" is here personified as the "mammon of unrighteousness," which is about equivalent to unrighteous mammon. There is a contrast between the "mammon of unrighteousness" and "true riches." "The love of money is a root of all kinds of evil" (1 Tim. 6: 10) because it leads into every form of sin. Achan was tempted to his destruction by the "wedge of gold" and the goodly Babylonish garment. (Josh. 7: 21.) Judas betrayed the Savior for thirty pieces of silver. (Matt. 26: 15.) Ananias and Sapphira "lied to the Holy Spirit" and perished for the love of money. (Acts 5: 3.) Demas, the companion of apostles, forsook them, "having loved this present world." (2 Tim. 4: 10.) There is a right use of money and a wrong use; Jesus teaches the right use of money. He here teaches that his disciples should make such a use of their possessions as to secure heavenly treasures and gain friends, who, having gone before, would welcome them in the world to come to everlasting habitations.

unrighteous also in much. 11 If therefore ye have not been faithful in the
unrighteous mammon, who will commit to your trust the true *riches*?   12
And if ye have not been faithful in that which is another's, who will give
you that which is ⁿyour own? 13 No ⁰servant can serve two masters: for

ⁿSome ancient authorities read *our own*
⁰Gr. *household-servant*

---

10 **He that is faithful in a very little**—Jesus further instructs his disciples in lessons of faithfulness as stewards.
The right use of money, which is seeking the welfare of others
with it, applies not only to the rich, but also to the poor; the
one who is faithful in a very little may be faithful in much;
but if one is not faithful with little things, one will not be
with larger things. The one who is unfaithful in the use of
money here will not be faithful in dealing with spiritual and
eternal things. One's conduct in little things is a sure test of
what he is likely to do with greater things; we do not expect
one to be faithful in important things, if he has not been faithful in little things.

11 **If therefore ye have not been faithful**—If the disciples of
Jesus have not been faithful "in the unrighteous mammon"
then who will want to trust them with "true riches"? Here
"unrighteous mammon" is put in contrast with "true riches."
Riches are deceitful, fleeting, and uncertain; while "true
riches" are real, substantial, spiritual, and eternal. If the disciples of Jesus are not faithful in a righteous use of money,
the Lord could not trust them with the eternal verities of his
gospel. The one who is dishonest and unfaithful in the discharge of duties with respect to earthly possessions must not
expect to have heavenly treasures entrusted to him. One
must prove oneself to be faithful with the proper use of material things before one can be trusted with spiritual things.
Anyone who will not handle material things honestly will not
handle the truth honestly.

12, 13 **And if ye have not been faithful in that which is another's,**—This argument is further expanded and enforced by
Jesus. Here reference is again had to the mammon of unrighteousness; our faithfulness in that which God will make our
own may be judged by our care of the things of others. Jesus

either he will hate the one, and love the other; or else he will hold to one, and despise the other. Ye cannot serve God and mammon.

repeats a self-evident truth when he says, "No servant can serve two masters." These masters have different wills and purposes; they contradict each other in their demands; hence, it is impossible for one servant to serve two such masters. It is like attempting to travel in two directions at the same time, or attempting to love two entirely contradictory characters. A servant is supposed to obey his master; this obedience is called love. If one attempts to serve two masters, he will hate one and love the other; or he will honor one and dishonor the other.

22. PHARISEES ANSWERED; RICH MAN AND LAZARUS
16: 14-31

14 And the Pharisees, who were lovers of money, heard all these things; and they scoffed at him. 15 And he said unto them, Ye are they that justify yourselves in the sight of men; but God knoweth your hearts: for that which

14 And the Pharisees, who were lovers of money,—Jesus had dined with a Pharisee (14: 1), and had received publicans and sinners. He had been criticized by the Pharisees (15: 2) and had answered them with three parables, and had instructed his disciples on the righteous use of money. The Pharisees had heard what he had taught his disciples. They "were lovers of money." "Lovers of money" is from the Greek word which is used only twice in the New Testament —here and 2 Tim. 3: 2—it is closly connected in meaning with "covetousness." (1 Cor. 5: 10, 11; 6: 10.) When the Pharisees heard what Jesus had said about the use of money "they scoffed at him." "Scoffed," in the original, is used only here and in Luke 23: 35. Literally it means "to turn up the nose at one"; the Romans had a similar phrase, "to hang on the hooked nose," that is, to turn up the nose and make a hook of it on which (figuratively) to hang the subject of ridicule. These Pharisees mocked him and ridiculed his teaching with respect to the use of money.

is exalted among men is an abomination in the sight of God. 16 The law and the prophets *were* until John: from that time the [10]gospel of the kingdom of God is preached, and every man entereth violently into it. 17 But it is

[10]Or, *good tidings:* comp. ch. 3.18

15 **And he said unto them, Ye are they**—The Pharisees made great professions of righteousness and holiness before men, while their hearts were full of wickedness and covetousness. Jesus knew their hearts; he exposed the hypocrisy and covetousness of the Pharisees. He reminded them that "God knoweth your hearts." They might deceive men, but they could not deceive God; Jesus let them know that he knew what was in their heart; they were an abomination in the sight of God. These Pharisees were past masters at justifying themselves; Jesus rebuked their scoffing hearts with a withering scorn. They could deride his teaching and mock him personally, but he could show what the end would be with them. Luke has introduced some other matters before Jesus spoke his parable of the rich man and Lazarus.

16 **The law and the prophets were until John:**—Jesus here introduces the idea of a new dispensation which was drawing nigh. "The law and the prophets" belonged to the old dispensation. The entire testimony under the old dispensation is sometimes expressed more fully by "the law of Moses, and the prophets, and the psalms." (Luke 24: 44.) The law and the prophets were the sole fountains of religious truth down to John the Baptist; then the kingdom of God began to be preached, first by John, next by Jesus, and then by his disciples. The Pharisees boasted of being righteous according to the law and the prophets; they were in reality not so faithful to the law as they were faithful to their traditions of the law Jesus did not set aside the law, but fulfilled it. "Every man entereth violently into it." This is similar to Matt. 11: 12. This seems to mean that everyone was striving to enter the preparatory state of the kingdom; people were attempting to force their way into the kingdom of God; they did not understand its nature, and were doing violence to the kingdom that Jesus preached by perverting and misapplying his teachings with respect to it.

easier for heaven and earth to pass away, than for one tittle of the law to fall.

18 Every one that putteth away his wife, and marrieth another, committeth adultery: and he that marrieth one that is put away from a husband committeth adultery.

19 Now there was a certain rich man, and he was clothed in purple and

---

17 **But it is easier for heaven and earth to pass away,**—Jesus did not destroy the law; he did not set the law aside; he came to fulfill the law, and to take it away by fulfilling it or "nailing it to the cross." (Col. 2: 14.) The Pharisees had implied that he was destroying the law, but in reality he was establishing the law and giving the principles of righteousness by which all should be judged. Heaven and earth will pass away sooner than the law should fail; not the least part of the law, not "one tittle of the law" should fail. Matthew uses "one jot or one tittle" (Matt. 5: 18), while Luke uses only "one tittle." "Tittle" is from the Latin "titulus," and means a term signified by a small point or line of the Hebrew letter. I indicates that the smallest requirements of the law must be fulfilled before it is taken out of the way.

18 **Every one that putteth away his wife,**—For other statements of Christ on this subject see Matt. 5: 32; 19: 9; Mark 10: 11, 12. The connection of this verse with what precedes or what follows is obscure. Jesus simply teaches the sanctity and binding force of the marriage bond; marriage with either of the separated parties involves the crime of adultery. It is adultery to marry the wife who is put away by her husband or to marry the husband who is put away by the wife. It seems that there is one exception to the rule here laid down, given by Jesus in Matt. 5: 32 and perhaps another by Paul in 1 Cor. 7: 15. Here Paul says that there may be grounds for separation other than that of fornication, but this does not grant the party the privilege to marry another. Many hold that, even when the one cause for separation exists, the innocent party may marry another.

19 **Now there was a certain rich man,**—Some have thought that this is not a parable, but a record from real life; they say that the name of one of the principal characters is given, which is not done in any of the parables of Jesus. Others

fine linen, [19]faring sumptuously every day: 20 and a certain beggar named

[19]Or, *living in mirth and splendor every day*

claim that it is a parable; commentators generally have treated it as a parable. It does not matter whether it is regarded as a parable or not; the lesson taught by Jesus remains the same. There is no change in the points or in the lesson taught by regarding it as a parable or regarding it as a simple narration in real life. It is treated here as a parable. Luke records this, and he is the only one who does; he places it in his record in close connection with what Christ had taught with respect to the proper use of riches and the ridicule and scoffing of the covetous Pharisees against his teaching; it may be regarded as a further reply to the scoffing of the Pharisees. At least, it exposes their sin and folly and points out to them their future and appalling doom.

A "certain rich man" is given as one of the principal characters of the parable; he is mentioned first. Some have thought that "Dives" is the name of this character in the parable; however, "Dives" is the Latin word for "rich man." He is described as being "clothed in purple"; this is one of the marks of wealth. "Purple" is a term used by the ancients to include three distinct colors—namely, a deep violet, with a black or dusky tinge; a deep scarlet or crimson, the Tyrian purple; and the deep blue of the Mediterranean. The dye of the purple was fadeless and retained its freshness of color. Purple is also an emblem of royalty. "Fine linen" was a yellowish flax and the linen made from it was considered to be of the finest quality. It was used in making the tabernacle. (Ex. 25: 4; 28: 5; 35: 6.) Some of the Egyptian linen was so fine that it was called "woven air." Later this term was applied to cotton and silken goods. He fared "sumptuously every day." Literally he made "merry in splendor each day"; some have translated it "he ate each day shiningly." He was a Jew, a descendant of Abraham whom he addressed as "Father Abraham" (verses 24, 30) and to whom Abraham responded, "Son" (verse 25). He is described, as many Pharisees lived and thought, as thinking he was entitled to every blessing because of his "father Abraham."

Lazarus was laid at his gate, full of sores, 21 and desiring to be fed with the *crumbs* that fell from the rich man's table; yea, even the dogs came and licked his sores. 22 And it came to pass, that the beggar died, and that he

---

20, 21 and a certain beggar named Lazarus—This is the only parable of our Lord where a character has received a proper name. "A certain beggar" sets him apart from many beggars of that day. The term "beggar" designates his destitution of the necessary things of life; he was dependent upon charity for food. The original indicates deep poverty. "Lazarus" is an abbreviated form of "Eleazar" and means "God a help." This was a common name among the Jews. He "was laid" at the rich man's gate; literally, "was thrown," or cast carelessly down by his bearers and left there; he did not place himself there; he was unable to handle himself. He was placed at the rich man's "gate," or "gateway"; sometimes it is rendered "porch." To make the description more vivid and pathetic, Lazarus is described as being "full of sores."

and desiring to be fed with the crumbs—He was not fed from the crumbs, but "desired" to be fed with the crumbs that fell from the rich man's table. He was humble and was asking only for the bare necessities of life. He asked only for the crumbs from so much abundance of the rich man. Eagerly he desired the things that fell from the table, but he did not receive what he desired. The same thing is implied in the record of the prodigal son, where the same word is used, "he would fain" have been filled (15: 16), but the pods did not satisfy his hunger. Moreover, "even the dogs came and licked his sores." This description reaches the climax in the dogs licking his sores. The only medical attention that this poor, helpless, hopeless man had was that from the dogs which came and licked his sores. It is not clear whether the licking of the dogs increased his misery or whether he received momentary relief by it. His very existence was a scramble with the dogs.

22 And it came to pass, that the beggar died,—Death was the first and the last relief that came to such a sufferer as Lazarus; the grace receives all alike. We do not know how long

was carried away by the angels into Abraham's bosom: and the rich man
also died, and was buried. 23 And in Hades he lifted up his eyes, being in tor-

---

the suffering had continued; nothing is said of his burial, for
that was of no moment in comparison to what immediately
occurred to his soul at death. If he had a burial, it was so
brief, obscure that no one knew of it. However, "he was carried away by the angels into Abraham's bosom." The angels
took him in charge and bore his soul away. "Abraham's
bosom" is equivalent to being with Abraham in paradise.
Abraham, to the Jew, seems to be the personal center and
meeting point of paradise. Some think that "Abraham's
bosom" was a name given to that part of the unseen world, or
place of departed spirits, where the patriarchs and the righteous were in happiness. It is similar to the expression used
by Jesus in Matt. 8: 11. This description fully met the view
of the pharisaic Jew with respect to the future blessedness of
the good. Abraham was the father of the faithful and the
head of the whole Jewish family, and to be with him after
death implied happiness. "And the rich man also died, and
was buried."

23 **And in Hades he lifted up his eyes,**—Finally they both
died; the rich and poor meet in death; there is the meeting
place for all. Death brings the rich and poor, the high and
the low, the good and the bad, the wise and the foolish, all to
a common level. They did not both dwell together here, and
they are separated in their death. "In Hades" the rich man
lifted up his eyes. "Hades," in the New Testament, is a broad
and general conception, with an idea of *locality* bound up with
it. It is the condition following death, which is blessed or the
contrary, according to the moral character of the dead, and is
divided into different realms, represented by "paradise" or
"Abraham's bosom," and "Gehenna." It simply means the
unseen world, or the underworld. "Hades" in the Greek has
the same meaning as "Sheol" in the Hebrew, both representing the region of the departed. "Hades" occurs ten times in
the New Testament. (Matt. 11: 23; 16: 18; Luke 10: 15; 16:
23; Acts 2: 27, 31; Rev. 1: 18; 6: 8; 20: 13, 14.) The story

ments, and seeth Abraham afar off, and Lazarus in his bosom. 24 And he
cried and said, Father Abraham, have mercy on me, and send Lazarus, that
he may dip the tip of his finger in water, and cool my tongue; for I am in
anguish in this flame. 25 But Abraham said, [1]Son, remember that thou in

[1]Gr. *Child*

here needs no comment, nor rhetoric to make it awfully impressive. "Being in torments" designates the place to which
the rich man had gone; "in torments" is put in contrast to
"Abraham's bosom"; Jesus puts this case in such terms as to
make the great facts clear and unmistakable; he shows that
the rich man is in misery, and that Lazarus is among the
blessed and happy. The rich man was buried; it is natural to
suppose that he was buried with the usual ceremonies that belong to the rich. "In Hades" he lifted up his eyes and saw
"Abraham afar off, and Lazarus in his bosom." "He lifted up
his eyes" shows that the rich man is conceived as being in the
abyss, in the lower region of Hades, and looking up toward
paradise. "Afar off" represents the distance, or a bridgeless
gulf that separated him from Lazarus. He saw Lazarus in
Abraham's "bosom." Lazarus was reclining in honor at the
banquet of bliss, while the rich man was agonizing in the misery of eternal punishment.

24 **And he cried and said, Father Abraham,**—Jesus represents the rich man as a Jew, as he addresses Abraham as
"Father." He longs for relief from his sufferings and begs for
at least a moment of relief from his anguish. He asks that
Lazarus be sent with the smallest means of comfort; he even
pleads for Abraham to have mercy on him in giving him a
moment's relief from his anguish. He wishes water to cool
his tongue and says that he is "in anguish in this flame." He
is continually and eternally tormented. We have here material and physical imagery of spiritual anguish, soul misery. It
matters not what may be our views on the nature of this suffering, we must admit that it is terrible beyond anything we
can imagine. The mind shrinks back aghast from the horrible
torment which is here described.

25 **But Abraham said, Son, remember**—Abraham is represented as answering the rich man; he addressed him as "Son."

thy lifetime receivedst thy good things, and Lazarus in like manner evil things: but now here he is comforted, and thou art in anguish. 26 And ²besides all this, between us and you there is a great gulf fixed, that they that

²Or, *in all these things*

This word literally means "child." The answer of Abraham is in great kindness, yet it was frank and severe, calm and firm. The rich man had addressed him as "Father Abraham," and Abraham does not deny the relationship. Joshua spoke to Achan and addressed him as "my son." (Josh. 7: 19.) "Remember" is a fearful word at this time; there was nothing that the rich man could remember that would be a satisfaction to him now. Memory keeps alive the unpleasant as well as the pleasant things of life. The rich man had only to be reminded of the past to understand the reason of his present misery. The rich man is told plainly that retribution has come. He has to remember that in his "lifetime" or earthly life he received his "good things," and that "Lazarus in like manner evil things." This is another contrast; he had in life exhausted his store of happiness; he had no more claim on the good things which were for him, and which he made the sole object of life. He had enjoyed to the fullest not only the necessities of life, but the rich abundance of luxuries; Lazarus had not enjoyed the meager necessities of life, and had none of the luxuries; the rich man had reveled in his wealth and Lazarus had suffered in his poverty. In this way Lazarus had received his "evil things." Abraham did not say "his" evil things, but just "evil things."

26 **And besides all this, between us and you**—In addition to all these things Abraham calls attention to a second reason why the request of the rich man could not be granted. It was literally impossible to comply with the request. "Between us and you there is a great gulf fixed." "Gulf" is the original word for "yawn," "or chasm," a "gaping opening." In medical language, which Luke frequently employed, it meant the cavities in a wound or ulcer. This "great gulf" separated the rich man and Lazarus; the separation was greater in their destinies than it could possibly have been in their lives on

would pass from hence to you may not be able and that none may cross over
from thence to us. 27 And he said, I pray thee therefore, father, that thou
wouldest send him to my father's house; 28 for I have five brethren; that he

---

earth. It was a "great gulf," and was too deep to be filled up,
too wide to be bridged over, too great for any passage from
one side to the other. It was "fixed"; it could not be changed.
The word in the original conveys the idea of fixedness. It
was unchangeable in nature, unalterable in condition, and
eternal in its establishment.

they that would pass from hence to you—It is not meant
that any would want to cross from the side where Lazarus
and Abraham were to the side where the rich man was if they
knew the conditions on that side; it is not implied that they
were ignorant of the conditions on the side of the rich man.
Abraham simply means that there can be no passing from one
side to the other. It might be that all who were on the side of
the rich man would like to pass to the side where Lazarus
was; but no one can do that. At death the destinies are determined; there can be no further preparation made, as there can
be no passage from one side to the other. It simply means
that when one goes to hell there is no way to get out.

27 And he said, I pray thee therefore, father,—This is the
second request that the rich man makes of Abraham. The
rich man now understood that his case was desperate, his destiny and doom sealed. There is no chance for repentance and
salvation in the "intermediate state." In fact, the Bible is not
clear as to whether there is an "intermediate state." The rich
man had prayed first for himslf to Abraham, and his second
prayer is for others. He remembered his brethren and the example that he had set them; he seems to have thought that
they might come to that place of torment through his influence, and this added more to his misery and anguish. Their
presence would give them an opportunity to reproach him and
thus increase his own torment. Hell will be the more miserable because those who have influenced others to go there will
forever be reproaching them and adding to their misery if possible. This time he asks Abraham to send Lazarus to his

may testify unto them, lest they also come into this place of torment. 29 But Abraham saith, They have Moses and the prophets; let them hear them. 30 And he said, Nay, father Abraham: but if one go to them from the dead,

---

father's house. He had nothing in common with Lazarus while on earth, but now he is pleading for Lazarus to render service to him. He knew that he could not escape from his place to go and warn his brethren, but he relied on the mercy of Abraham to send Lazarus to them.

28 **for I have five brethren;**—Perhaps these were five Pharisees who were following in the footsteps of the departed brother. Nothing can be inferred further than that they were headed in the direction of the rich man. His five brethren were still living. It has been argued by some that the rich man's anxiety about his five brethren was a sign of improvement in him, and that his punishment had already purified his heart, and made him love his brethren; hence, the notion of "purgatory" has some endorsement in the Bible. However, such an idea is destitute of any truth. He did not want his five brethren to come to his doom. He thought perhaps they would turn if they were warned.

29 **But Abraham saith, They have Moses and the prophets;** —Abraham's answer here is also decisive. The law of Moses was still in force. The expression, "Moses and the prophets," has reference to the Old Testament scriptures, and since they were still under the law, they should hear and do what the law required. "Let them hear them"; the verb "hear" is often used in the sense of "obey." They should take heed to follow Moses and the prophets. We have here one of the many testimonies of Jesus, including that of Abraham from the heavenly world, that the Old Testament scriptures are the word of God.

30 **And he said, Nay, father Abraham:**—The rich man argues the question with Abraham; he pleads for his brethren more than he pleaded for himself. He seemed to think that if one should return from the spirit world his brothers would surely listen to the message. Hence, he said: "If one go to them from the dead, they will repent." The meaning here seems to be that if one should come "from within," they

they will repent. 31 And he said unto him, If they hear not Moses and the prophets, neither will they be persuaded, if one rise from the dead.

---

would come nearer repenting than if one should go to them "from the outside." Arising from among the dead was more than a messenger going "from" the dead. The rich man was ignorant of the results from miraculous visions and messages; he had false views of repentance, supposing that something sudden and miraculous would produce it.

31 **And he said unto him, If they hear not Moses and the prophets,**—The answer of Abraham is positive and final; the rich man had affirmed that "they will repent" if one should go to them from among the dead. Abraham tells him that they would not. If they would not hear God at one time, they would not hear him at another time. He had spoken to them through "Moses and the prophets"; if they would not hear them they would not "be persuaded, if one rise from the dead." As proof of this, Jesus was crucified, buried, and arose from the dead, yet the Jewish leaders still rejected him. The truth of God brought to the heart is necessary to repentance; and if it fails vain will be the efforts of men, living or dead, however miraculous. No stronger inducement now can be presented to men for repentance than that which God has presented.

23. WARNINGS TO HIS DISCIPLES
17: 1-10

1 And he said unto his disciples, It is impossible but that occasions of stumbling should come, but woe unto him, through whom they come! 2 It

---

1 **And he said unto his disciples,**—This chapter was probably spoken while Jesus was still in Perea, or on his way from Perea to Jerusalem; some, however, think that he was in Galilee. It does not matter, as we cannot trace the steps of Jesus with accuracy; it is not necessary to do this. This was spoken to his disciples; some of them had proved unfaithful; this may have called up the warnings given to the disciples at this time. The wickedness of men is such that it cannot well be otherwise than that "occasions of stumbling should come."

were well for him if a millstone were hanged about his neck, and he were
thrown into the sea, rather than that he should cause one of these little ones
to stumble. 3 Take heed to yourselves: if thy brother sin, rebuke him; and if
he repent, forgive him. 4 And if he sin against thee seven time in the day,

---

The original from which "impossible" comes is only found
here in the New Testament. The wickedness of men, the
snares and temptations of the devil, give rise or produce the
occasion to cause people to stumble. (Rom. 14: 13.) A condemnation is placed upon the one "through whom they come."

2 It were well for him if a millstone—"Millstone" here
means a common hand stone, not a large millstone which was
turned by an ass, as in Matt. 18: 6. Meal was ground in ancient times by taking one stone in the hand and pounding the
grain on another stone which was firmly fixed on the ground
or pavement; this was a hand mill. However, the stone was
large enough to hold one down in the water. It was better
then and is now that one suffer physical death rather than to
cause any of God's children to stumble, even the least one of
them. Hence, it is a fearful thing to cause any of God's people to stumble.

3, 4 Take heed to yourselves:—Here the warning comes
with great force. They are to "take heed" to themselves; it is
well to watch the conduct of others that one does not stumble,
yet it is better to take heed to ourselves. Christians may be
the occasion of other's stumbling. Jesus had just spoken of
the causes of stumbling and the fearful consequences that
await the one who causes stumbling; he now warns his disciples that they need not look so far away from themselves;
that they will find these occasions among themselves. "If thy
brother sin, rebuke him." The word "rebuke" is the same
here in the original as in Luke 9: 21; it implies an emphatic
and solemn charge; strictly, it means to "lay a penalty upon
one" or "to charge under penalty." This rebuke should be administered in such a way as to bring about repentance. "If he
repent, forgive him."

And if he sin against thee seven times—"Seven" is a term
that must be taken indefinitely; it means "very frequently,"

and seven times turn again to thee, saying, I repent; thou shalt forgive him. 5 And the apostles said unto the Lord, Increase our faith. 6 And the Lord said, If ye had faith as a grain of mustard seed, ye would say unto this sycamine tree, Be thou rooted up, and be thou planted in the sea; and it

---

"very often." (Matt. 12: 45; 18: 22; Luke 11: 26.) "Seven" is often used to denote a complete number; it is called a sacred number and is closely connected in the scriptures with forgiveness and retribution. (Lev. 4: 6; 16: 14; 26: 18, 21, 24, 28; Psalm 79: 12; Dan. 4: 16; Rev. 15: 1.) The meaning is that as often as one sins and repents and asks forgiveness, so often shall forgiveness be extended. The disciples of Jesus should exercise forbearance and forgiveness at all times; by keeping in this frame of mind, one will not be caused to stumble by others sinning against him. Mutual concessions and mutual forgiveness are generally needed. It is well to compare this precept for the private intercourse of Christians. (See Matt. 18: 15-18.)

5 **And the apostles said unto the Lord,**—The apostles felt that they were deficient in this spirit of forgiveness, which Jesus had enjoined upon them; this has been pointed out as the only instance that we have of "the apostles" as a body saying anything to our Lord, or making any request. Doubtless they did make requests "as a body"; Matt. 17: 19 and Acts 1: 6 seem to be other instances when they made requests of Jesus. Their request here is that their faith be increased. It is a prayer: "Lord, increase our faith." Jesus had frequently rebuked the lack of faith. (Matt. 8: 26; 14: 31; 17: 19-21.) This is a prayer that all should pray; the literal meaning of the Greek seems to be "add to us faith"; that is, "give us more faith." Possibly these disciples could have answered their own prayer.

6 **And the Lord said, If ye had faith**—Jesus now shows what faith would do; this was his way of answering their prayer. If they could see what faith could do, they could see how they could increase their faith. Jesus does not deny that they have faith, but said, "If ye had faith as a grain of mustard seed, ye would say unto this sycamine tree, Be thou

would obey you. 7 But who is there of you, having a ³servant plowing or
keeping sheep, that will say unto him, when he is come in from the field,
Come straightway and sit down to meat; 8 and will not rather say unto him,
Make ready wherewith I may sup, and gird thyself, and serve me, till I have

³Gr. *bondservant*

plucked up, and it would be rooted up. "Grain of mustard
seed" was a term used to indicate a very small degree of faith.
(Mark 11: 23; Luke 13: 19.) "Sycamine tree" was similar to
the mulberry tree; it was different from the "sycomore tree"
in Luke 19: 4; however, the names are sometimes confused,
but a physician, as Luke was, would make a distinction, as
both were used medically. In Matt. 17: 20 we have "mountain" in place of "sycamine tree." This faith manifestly has
reference to that special fatih which was necessary to work
miracles. It seems that the least degree of this faith was sufficient to perform such a miracle.

7 But who is there of you, having a servant plowing—It is
difficult to see the relation of these verses with that which
precedes. However, it is introduced with "but" which insti-
tutes a contrast. Yet as it is brought by Jesus in this connection, we may see that it comes in close connection. Even if
the disciples should have such faith as to perform miracles,
they should not be elated over such achievements and filled
with pride. In exercising such faith and such an unselfish
spirit as to forgive a penitent brother, though he should sin
against one seven times a day, and one should think that he
did not merit anything, yet one has only done his duty when
forgiveness is extended. So in exercising miraculous faith,
one has only done one's duty and merits no reward and should
not be puffed up. A servant is supposed to obey his master,
and when he is commanded to do anything when he has come
into the house from the field, and is told to do something
else, it is only his duty to do that.

8 and will not rather say unto him,—The plowing and feeding the sheep were common duties of servants; serving the
master in the house may be considered extra duties imposed
on those who have served in the field; yet it is the duty of the
servant to serve his master in the house. The additional ser-

eaten and drunken; and afterward thou shalt eat and drink? 9 Doth he thank the ³servant because he did the things that were commanded? 10 Even so ye also, when ye shall have done all the things that are commanded you, say, We are unprofitable ⁴servants; we have done that which it was our duty to do.

⁴Gr. *bondservants*

vice to the laborers of the field illustrates the patience and untiring obedience of the servants. The field labor was ordinary service; the preparation for the evening feast demanded of them, when they returned weary with toil, tested the principles of their zeal and fidelity to their master. We are to take this parable or illustration in the sense which lies on its surface, of the obligations strictly implied in the relation of a servant to a master. A faithful servant will obey promptly every command of the master.

9 **Doth he thank the servant**—No special thanks are to be extended the servant for doing his duty. Being a faithful servant, he gladly gave the extra time and the larger measure of service, expecting nothing except the good will of the master. The servant will provide his master's meal and serve him while eating it, and then consider that he has done only his well-understood duty, but nothing that calls for special gratitude from his master.

10 **Even so ye also, when ye shall have done all the things**— Jesus makes his own application. His disciples are to serve him faithfully; it matters not what the service may be; some services will be delightful—such as worshipping God and praising him; other services will be unpleasant—such as bearing burdens, suffering persecutions in his name, and ministering to the afflicted. With the apostles there were services of the ordinary disciple of Jesus; then there were the special works of the apostles, and miraculous gifts and other work of the Holy Spirit. However, after they had done everything, they were to say: "We are unprofitable servants; we have done that which it was our duty to do." "Unprofitable" does not mean "useless," but having rendered no service beyond what was due.

24. THE SAMARITAN LEPER
17: 11-19

11 And it came to pass, ⁵as they were on the way to Jerusalem, that he
was passing ⁶along the borders of Samaria and Galilee. 12 And as he entered into a certain village, there met him ten men that were lepers, who

⁵Or, *as he was*
⁶Or, *through the midst of &c.*

---

11 **And it came to pass, as they were on the way to Jerusalem,**—It seems that Jesus was on the border between Samaria
and Galilee; others think that these things occurred as Jesus
went through Galilee and Samaria. Some think that Jesus at
this time traveled a more unfrequented route to avoid the conflicts that he might have when traveling the routes that the
Jews usually traveled. Jesus was going from Ephraim north
through the midst of Samaria and Galilee so as to cross
over the Jordan near Bethshean and join the Galilean caravan
down through Perea to Jerusalem. (John 11: 54.) The Samaritans did not object to people going north away from Jerusalem, but did not like to see them going south toward the
city. (Luke 9: 51-56.) It is thought that Jesus was on his
way to Jerusalem to attend the feast of the tabernacles, which
occurred in the seventh month of the Jewish year.

12, 13 **And as he entered into a certain village,**—We are not
told what village this was; it is designated with the indefinite
phrase "a certain village." Lepers were considered unclean
by the law; they were not allowed to enter towns and villages,
but were often found near the gates begging of the travelers
who passed by. (Lev. 13: 46; Num. 5: 2, 3.) Oftentimes
lepers went together; they were bound by common interests
and sympathetic cords. There were ten lepers at the gates of
this village as Jesus entered; they "stood afar off." They
were required by law to keep themselves from others so that
others would not be defiled by them. They stood far off from
the highway in order not to pollute anyone by contact with
him. The law for this separation is found in Lev. 13: 45, 46
and Num. 5: 2. We have an illustration of it in 2 Kings 15: 5.

and they lifted up their voices,—Being afar off they would
have to lift "up their voices," or speak loud enough or shout

stood afar off : 13 and they lifted up their voices, saying Jesus, Master, have
mercy on us. 14 And when he saw them, he said unto them, Go and show
yourselves unto the priests. And it came to pass, as they went, they were
cleansed. 15 And one of them, when he saw that he was healed, turned back,
with a loud voice glorifying God; 16 and he fell upon his face at his feet,

---

to those who pass by. They cried for mercy; they wanted
help; this time they were not asking for alms. They said:
"Master, have mercy on us." At another time a leper came to
Jesus and asked to be healed. (Matt. 8: 2, 3.) Bartimaeus
called Jesus "son of David," and asked for mercy. (Mark 10:
47.) They asked Jesus to take pity on them, which included
his healing them; while their prayer was gentle, the particular
thing they wanted was to be healed.

14 **And when he saw them, he said unto them,**—They got
the attention of Jesus by their loud cry for mercy. The eyes
and ears of Jesus were ever open to the cry of the distressed.
They asked with a certain degree of faith; Jesus tested their
faith by commanding them to go and show themselves "unto
the priests." A leper, according to the law, when cured, was
to show himself to the priest, who would admit him into the
congregation, giving him a testimony or certificate of his cure.
(Lev. 13: 1-6; 14: 1-32; Luke 5: 14.) As they went their way,
"they were cleansed." This was a severe test of their faith;
they were not cleansed the moment Jesus spoke to them; they
heard his command, and they began to obey him; they had
started to the priest and were cleansed as they were thus
obeying the command of Jesus. When they arrived at the
house of the priest, they were ready for him to pronounce
them healed.

15, 16 **And one of them, when he saw**—We are not told how
far they had gone before they discovered that they were
healed. It was sufficient distance to test their faith; possibly
they had gone some distance from Jesus before one of them
turned back, and "with a loud voice" glorified God. This one
was so overwhelmed with joy and gratitude that he wanted to
give God the glory for his cleansing. The other nine did not
return. The one who did return to give thanks was "a Samaritan." It was least expected that the Samaritan would praise

giving him thanks: and he was a Samaritan. 17 And Jesus answering said,
Were not the ten cleansed? but where are the nine? 18 [7]Were there none
found that returned to give glory to God, save this [1]stranger? 19 And he
said unto him, Arise, and go thy way: thy faith hath [2]made thee whole.

[7]Or, *There were none found . . . save this stranger*
[1]Or, *alien*
[2]Or, *saved thee*

God and thank Jesus; however, from the one from whom it
was least expected came the greatest gratitude and praise.
He not only gave open and loud expression of his praise to
God, but "he fell upon his face" at the feet of Jesus. It is remembered that the Jews and Samaritans had no dealings with
each other. (John 4: 9.) The one man who felt grateful
enough to return and thank Jesus and praise God for his
cleansing was a despised Samaritan.

17 **And Jesus answering said,**—Only ten per cent of those
who received the blessings here showed gratitude. There is
something pathetic in the question that Jesus asked: "But
where are the nine?" Ten had been cleansed; one had returned to praise God and thank him; this one was a Samaritan
—the least expected of the number. Jesus remembered everyone whom he blessed; he did not forget that he had cleansed
ten, and he noticed that only one had returned. All were
ready to receive a blessing; all cried for mercy; but nine were
not as anxious to give praise and thanksgiving. Many today
are far too much like the nine lepers.

18, 19 **Were there none found that returned**—This verse
continues the thought introduced in the preceding verse.
Some have thought that this Samaritan returned because he
was not permitted to approach the priest and worship with the
other nine. Jesus received no answer to his query, and he
thus asks another one in this verse. "Were there none found
that returned to give glory to God, save this stranger?"
"Stranger" here means an alien, foreigner, belonging to another nation. This "stranger" probably had stronger faith
than the other nine, or he would not have appealed to a
prophet of the Jews, who were his enemies. After receiving
no answer to his question Jesus said to the Samaritan who was
prostrate at his feet (verse 16): "Arise, and go thy way: thy

faith hath made thee whole." The Samaritan who had been
cleansed was humble, grateful, and full of faith; it was according to his faith that he was made whole. It has been argued
that Jesus cleansed the leper both in body and soul.

25. THE COMING OF THE KINGDOM
17: 20-37

20 And being asked by the Pharisees, when the kingdom of God cometh,
he answered them and said, The kingdom of God cometh not with observation: 21 neither shall they say, Lo, here! or, There! for lo, the kingdom of
God is ³within you.

³Or, *in the midst of you*

20, 21 And being asked by the Pharisees,—Jesus had
preached, as did John, that the kingdom of God "was at
hand"; he had taught his disciples to preach the same message. Now the Pharisees come to him and ask him particularly "when the kingdom of God cometh." "The kingdom of
God" is equivalent to "kingdom of heaven" in Matt. 3: 2. "The
kingdom of God," as a phrase, may have special reference to
the owner of the kingdom, while "kingdom of heaven" has
special reference to its central locality. It is the same as
"kingdom of Christ," or simply "kingdom." (Eph. 5: 5; Heb.
12: 28.) The prophets had foretold of a spiritual kingdom,
but the Jews had misunderstood the nature of the kingdom
and perverted the meaning of the prophecy so they were expecting an earthly and temporal kingdom. This kingdom of
which Jesus taught was the same as his reign or administration, and was spiritual in its nature. (John 18: 36; Rom. 14:
17.) We do not know what prompted the Pharisees to ask
this question at this time; we are persuaded that they had no
good motive in asking it.

The kingdom of God cometh not with observation:—The
original Greek from whence we get "observation" is used only
here in the New Testament. There is some measure of rebuke to the Pharisees in this statement; the progress of the
kingdom could not be determined by visible marks like that of
an earthly kingdom; its approach could not be observed by

22 And he said unto the disciples, The days will come, when ye shall
desire to see one of the days of the Son of man, and ye shall not see it. 23
And they shall say to you, Lo, there! Lo, here! go not away, nor follow

the senses, or its progress watched by its outward manifestations. This spiritual kingdom is not to be judged by outward
show, political and military triumphs, or the glory of an external and conquering kingdom. This kingdom is not of such a
nature that they could, with the fleshly senses, locate it either
here or there. This kingdom "is within you." Some translations put it "among you," but "within you" seems to be a better translation. Some think that "within you" means that the
kingdom was not within the Pharisees, and that Jesus is not
speaking of the "inwardness" of the kingdom, but of its "presence."

22 **And he said unto the disciples,**—Jesus now turns from
the Pharisees and speaks to his disciples. He said that the
day would come when they should "desire to see one of the
days of the Son of man, and ye shall not see it." It is difficult
to determine just what Jesus means here; to what special
event or clutter of events does Jesus here refer? It is thought
that he had reference to the severe trials and struggles and
progress that his kingdom would have; the time would come
when they should "desire to see one of the days of the Son of
God." "One of the days" that they should desire to see may
refer to one of the days that was then passing when mercy
was offered by Jesus. During the life of Jesus the fate of the
nation hung in the balance. If the disciples in times of dis-
couragement and despondency should wish again the earthly
presence of their Lord, how much more would this be true of
the Pharisees and the unbelieving Jews in the days of their
dreadful calamities, when they shall discern and acknowledge
too late the character and claim of the Messiah whom they rejected.

23, 24 **And they shall say to you, Lo, there!**—Jesus knew
that after his departure from earth there would arise many
false Christs whom his disciples would be urged to recognize
and follow; he plainly warns them to give no attention to

after *them*: 24 for as the lightning, when it lighteneth out of the one part under the heaven, shineth unto the other part under heaven; so shall the Son of man be 'in his day. 25 But first must he suffer many things and be rejected of his generation. 26 And as it came to pass in the days of Noah,

'Some ancient authorities omit *in his day*

these false claims, nor endeavor to satisfy their longing desire for the personal presence of the Messiah by giving heed to those pretenders, who would throng the land, as the time of the righteous retribution of the nation drew near.

for as the lightning,—The coming of the Messiah would not be from the earth, but from heaven; it would not be manifested only in a certain place, but everywhere conspicuous, like the lightning, which "shineth unto the other part under heaven." The earthly presence of Christ while on earth was as clear and manifest as the lightning which flashes over and illuminates the whole heaven; so also his second coming will be manifest so that no one need be mistaken. (Matt. 24: 30, 31; 25: 31.) No doubt or uncertainty will accompany his coming. The second advent of Christ will be so sudden, so clearly marked, and so unmistakable that true believers shall at once recognize it as the coming of their King; all should be ready for his coming. Some have thought that Jesus meant nothing more than the march of the Roman armies to destroy Jerusalem. This is entirely unsatisfactory as an explanation.

25 But first must he suffer many things—The second advent must come after the cross. Here Jesus predicts his further persecution, his suffering, his crucifixion, his burial, his resurrection, and his ascension back to heaven. Since his coming is "from" heaven, he must of necessity ascend back to heaven. He would be "rejected of this generation"; in his condemnation to death and demanding his crucifixion he emphasized their rejection of the gospel and his kingdom. (Luke 23: 18-21; John 19: 15; Acts 3: 13-15; 7: 51, 52; 13: 46; 28: 25-28.) This rejection of Jesus was foretold by the prophets and fulfilled by the generation among whom Jesus moved at that time. In this rejection there was also implied the necessary sufferings of his disciples. (Matt. 10: 24, 25; Rom. 8: 17; 1 Pet. 4: 13.)

even so shall it be also in the days of the Son of man. 27 They ate, they
drank, they married, they were given in marriage, until the day that Noah
entered into the ark, and the flood came, and destroyed them all. 28 Likewise even as it came to pass in the days of Lot; they ate, they drank, they
bought, they sold, they planted, they builded; 29 but in the day that Lot went
out from Sodom it rained fire and brimstone from heaven, and destroyed

---

26, 27 **And as it came to pass in the days of Noah,**—The
parallel record of this is found in Matt. 24: 37-41. It has been
argued by some that this has reference only to the second advent of Christ, while others have argued that it has reference
to the establishment of his kingdom and the destruction of Jerusalem by the Roman army. A similarity exists between the
condition of the people during the days of Noah and the condition that will exist when Christ comes again. Noah warned
the people and told them of the impending flood; they refused
to heed his warnings and went along in the daily affairs of
their sinful life; they gave no heed to his warnings; "they ate,
they drank, they married, they were given in marriage, until
the day that Noah entered into the ark." They followed their
sinful ways without giving any heed to his warning and were
all destroyed. They ridiculed the idea of a flood and their
own destruction. So their destruction came upon them when
they least expected it.

28, 29 **Likewise even as it came to pass in the days of Lot;**
—Luke records two comparisons between the conditions at
the second coming of Christ and former times; first he brings
in contrast the manner of living just before the flood, and then
the manner of living during the days of Lot. Lot was a so-
journer of Sodom; the people were very wicked at that time.
(2 Pet. 2: 5, 6; Jude 7, 14, 15.) The suddenness of the doom
of Sodom is recorded in Gen. 19: 1-29. The people were eating, drinking, buying, selling, sowing, reaping, and building
when the sudden destruction came upon the Sodomites. The
suddenness of the destruction is indicated by its raining "fire
and brimstone from heaven." Burning brimstone and sulphu-
rous flames came from heaven; God controls the elements as
he wills. The account of the destruction of Sodom is given in

them all: 30 after the same manner shall it be in the day that the Son of
man is revealed. 31 In that day, he that shall be on the housetop, and his
goods in the house, let him not go down to take them away: and let him that
is in the field likewise not return back. 32 Remember Lot's wife. 33 Who-

---

Gen. 19: 24: "Then Jehovah rained upon Sodom and upon Go-
morrah brimstone and fire from Jehovah out of heaven."

30 after the same manner shall it be in the day—With the
same suddenness and unexpectedness shall the Son of man be
revealed; when he shall appear the second time with all of his
power and glory manifested, it will be with such suddenness
that no one will have time to make further preparation; hence,
the importance of watching and being ready. Many refer this
to the destruction of Jerusalem; they claim that in such a
manner will the sudden, unexpected, and tragical destruction
of Jerusalem come. It seems that the destruction of Jerusalem is first and typical of the coming of Christ and the destruction of all earthly things.

31 In that day, he that shall be on the housetop,—A parallel
of this may be found in Matt. 24: 17, 18. "In that day" evidently means the day when "the Son of man is revealed"; this
would appear to refer primarily to his second coming, but may
also be applied to its type, the destruction of Jerusalem, when
the power of Christ, the King of kings, was revealed in judgment upon a wicked and unbelieving people. "Housetop" literally means "upon the house." The houses in Palestine were
built with flat roofs, and were close enough together that one
who was on the housetop could travel from one house to another and finally reach the walls of the city and escape without
coming down into the street. Many dwelt on the housetop as
we now occupy "the living room." The admonition is not
against "coming down," but against coming down "to take"
away "his goods in the house." There would be no use in
attempting to save what household goods one had, when the
sudden destruction came upon them.

32 Remember Lot's wife.—Jesus again refers to the destruction of Sodom and reminds us that in addition to the destruction of the Sodomites Lot's wife was destroyed. She began to
flee through the urgency of the angels, but she hesitated,

soever shall seek to gain his life shall lose it: but whosoever shall lose *his*
life shall ⁵preserve it. 34 I say unto you, In that night there shall be two
men on one bed; the one shall be taken, and the other shall be left.   35
There shall be two women grinding together; the one shall be taken, and the

⁵Gr. *save it alive*

looked back with longing desire, and even turned her face toward the doomed city, and perished in its destruction.
Instead of following closely the steps of her husband, she
turned her face toward the home she was unwillingly leaving
and was destroyed. She became "a pillar of salt." (Gen. 19:
26.)   Thus she became a monument of the fearful consequences of delaying or refusing to obey God.

33 **Whosoever shall seek to gain his life shall lose it:**—Here
Jesus still further warns against any effort to save material
things, or even one's life; when the destruction comes,
whether it be that of Jerusalem or the destruction at the second coming of Christ, one should not give so much concern to
earthly life or the material things that sustain it. Jesus here
uses a proverbial saying that he frequently repeated. (Matt.
10: 39; 16: 25; Mark 8: 35; Luke 9: 24; John 12: 25.) "But
whosoever shall lose his life shall preserve it." The one who
seeks to preserve his life by neglecting or refusing to do God's
will shall lose his life; but the one who is willing to sacrifice
his own life for the sake of Christ shall gain eternal life. He
shall not, if he is faithful to God, perish among those who are
wicked at the second coming of Christ.

34, 35 **I say unto you, In that night**—"In that night" or "on
this night" when Christ comes. It is equivalent to "in that
day." (Verse 31.) In representing the close and intimate fellowship denoted by two occupying the same bed, it would be
natural to say "in that night" being the time when persons
were accustomed to being in bed. Christ is represented as
coming "as a thief in the night" (1 Thess. 5: 2) and at a time
when no one is expecting him (Matt. 24: 44). "Two men on
one bed," may be a "dining couch," so some think. One of
them shall be taken and the other forsaken; one may be faithful to the Lord and the other unfaithful. Another illustration
is given—"two women grinding together"—one of them

other shall be left.⁶ 37 And they answering say unto him, Where, Lord?
And he said unto them, Where the body *is*, thither will the ⁷eagles also be
gathered together.

⁶Some ancient authorities add ver. 36 *There shall be two men in the field; the one
shall be taken, and the other shall be left.* Mt. 24.40
⁷Or, *vultures*

should be taken and the other left. Grain was ground by a
hand mill, and as women generally prepared the meal, the
grinding was done by women.

Some ancient authorities add verse 36: "There shall be two
men in the field; the one shall be taken, and the other shall be
left." This verse is recorded in Matt. 24: 40. The Revised
Version omits verse 36 on good authority. It carries with it
the same force as the other two illustrations, and does not add
anything to the teachings. Some think that it is an interpola-
tion from Matthew since the oldest manuscripts do not contain it; it is omitted by the highest and best critical authorities.

37 **And they answering say unto him, Where, Lord?**—The
question here asked by his disciples is: "Where shall this take
place?" Where shall this separation for life and death take
place? The disciples could not appreciate the spiritual truths
of their Master's teaching. They did not understand the nature of his kingdom, or the nature of his first advent; they
could not comprehend his teaching on his second advent.
Jesus replied that where there is a carcass there will be the
eagles to devour it; wherever there may be these great sins,
crying to God for retribution, there the agents of God's retribution will come down and pour their vials upon the place.
Luke, more than Matthew or Mark, notices the questions
which gave rise to the teachings presented here. The disciples seem to have been excited with mingled surprise and
fear; their question gave Jesus an opportunity to declare that
punishment will not be confined to any one spot, but will be
inflicted where sin may be found. The simple meaning seems
to be that as surely as the eagles gather around a lifeless
body, so surely will the Son of man come to judgment.

26. THE UNRIGHTEOUS JUDGE
18: 1-8

1 And he spake a parable unto them to the end that they ought always to pray, and not to faint; 2 saying, There was in a city a judge, who feared not God, and regarded not man: 3 and there was a widow in that city; and she came oft unto him, saying, °Avenge me of mine adversary. 4 And he would

°Or, *Do me justice of:* and so in ver. 5, 7, 8

1 **And he spake a parable unto them**—Luke is the only writer that records this parable. It is thought that Jesus was still in Perea when he gave this parable, and that it grew out of the preceding conversation. It was given "to the end that they ought always to pray, and not to faint." It is observed that Luke, more than any of the other writers, notices Jesus at prayer; he relates several parables of Jesus on prayer. (Luke 11: 5-10; 18: 9-14.) The disciples of Jesus can pray at all times; they should pray at regular and stated times; there is no time when they may not pray. The spirit of prayer should be kept constant and alive by exercise. (1 Thess. 5: 17.) They should pray and faint not; they should not languish and fail and become discouraged because of opposition. It does not mean that one should be incessantly performing the act of prayer.

2 **There was in a city a judge,**—In a certain city there was a certain judge. According to the law of Moses, all the cities of Israel were to have their judges who were to administer justice without partiality. (Ex. 18: 21; Deut. 16: 18; 2 Chron. 19: 6, 7.) Jesus gave a very vivid picture of this judge; he "feared not God, and regarded not man." He was an unprincipled man and reckless in his depravity; he stood in no awe of God—had no reverence and respect for God, neither did he have any mercy or respect for man. He acted contrary to all of the requirements of the law. (Ex. 23: 6-9; Lev. 19: 15; Deut. 1: 16, 17.) To disregard and disrespect the law that God had given was to disrespect God.

3 **and there was a widow in that city;**—This parable brings the unrighteous judge into sharp contrast with the widow. The condition of widows was indeed desolate, helpless, and friendless; God has legislated in favor of the widow because

not for a while: but afterward he said within himself, Though I fear not God, nor regard man; 5 yet because this widow troubleth me, I will avenge her, [9]lest she [10]wear me out by her continual coming. 6 And the Lord said, Hear what [11]the unrighteous judge saith. 7 And shall not God avenge his elect, that cry to him day and night, [12]and yet he is longsuffering over them?

[9]Or, *lest at last by her coming she wear me out*
[10]Gr. *bruise*
[11]Gr. *the judge of unrighteousness*
[12]Or, *and is he slow to punish on their behalf?*

man has been prone to impose upon them. (Ex. 22: 22; Deut. 10: 17; 24: 17; 27: 19; 1 Kings 17: 9, 12; Mal. 3: 5; Mark 12: 40.) This widow was without influence and unable to bribe; she had little to hope for from this wicked judge. She lived in the same city with him, and "came oft unto him" begging him to avenge her of her adversary; she was asking justice against those who had mistreated her; she was asking to be delivered from the oppression of her adversary.

4, 5 **And he would not for a while:**—The judge was unwilling to give her justice and put her off from time to time and refused to hear her petition. He finally came to a decision "within himself" that though he feared not God, nor regarded man, nevertheless, because the widow continued to trouble him, he decided that he would give her justice, "lest she wear me out by her continual coming." He decided to give her justice because he did not want to be troubled longer with her; his reasoning was entirely selfish; not for her sake, nor for the sake of right, but in order to get rid of her, he would grant her petition. Even in doing right from such a motive, he loses by his selfishness the praise of a sense of justice. (Gal. 6: 9.) The judge feared lest her continued importunity might finally culminate in personal violence.

6, 7 **And the Lord said, Hear what the unrighteous judge saith**—It seems that Jesus paused in his discourse a moment so that due attention would be given to what he said. He asked them to reflect upon what the "unrighteous judge" had concluded to do; this includes his motive, his selfishness, and his final actions. They should note the power of importunity even upon an unrighteous and faithless man, when applied by a weak and defenseless widow. Jesus then asks a question which carries the force of the truth that he wished to teach:

8 I say unto you, that he will avenge them speedily. Nevertheless, when the Son of man cometh, shall he find ¹ᵃfaith on the earth?

¹ᵃOr, *the faith*

"Shall not God avenge his elect, that cry to him day and night, and yet he is longsuffering over them?" God is just, and it is impossible for him to reject or neglect his chosen people. The argument is "a fortiori," which is establishing a stronger conclusion even than ordinary premises need to warrant us. If so wicked a judge would grant justice, how much more will the Judge of all the earth do right?

8 **I say unto you, that he will avenge them speedily.**—Jesus here, as he frequently does, draws his own lesson from his parable, and makes the proper application of it. "Nevertheless, when the Son of man cometh, shall he find faith on the earth?" It has been frequently argued as to whether this coming of the Son of man is to be understood to have reference to his final coming to judgment; or whether it may mean only that whenever he shall come among men to look for faith, he will find a lack of faith upon the earth. Some think that Jesus asked this question, meaning to convey that there would be little faith among men during the Christian age; others seem to think that he means to say that there will be but little faith on the earth when he comes the second time.

27. THE PHARISEE AND THE PUBLICAN
18: 9-14

9 And he spake also this parable unto certain who trusted in themselves that they were righteous, and set ¹⁴all others at nought: 10 Two men went

¹⁴Gr. *the rest*

9 **And he spake also this parable**—Luke is the only writer that records this parable. There are two principal characters in this parable also; another contrast between two characters is brought out here. In this parable we have a comprehensive account of two representative characters who are praying; we have their prayers that we may see the manner of their worship. This parable was addressed to "certain who trusted in themselves that they were righteous, and set all others at

up into the temple to pray; the one a Pharisee, and the other a [15]publican. 11 The Pharisee stood and prayed thus with himself, God, I thank thee, that

[15]See marginal note on ch. 3.12

nought." It seems to have been spoken, not so much to the disciples, but to the Pharisees. The Pharisees thought that they were righteous before God, and that they could by their righteousness merit an answer to their prayers. This man "set all others at nought," or considered all others as amounting to nothing. He looked down on all others as being sinners and outcasts. He has the wrong attitude toward others and toward God.

10 **Two men went up into the temple to pray;**—Both of these men had access to the temple worship; they were both in covenant relation with God; presumably both were Jews. They do not represent an alien sinner and a Christian; the parable was not given to teach the difference between the prayers of an alien and a Christian; such an application does violence to the teachings of our Lord. The Jews attended daily the services at the temple; these two went up for that purpose, and met in the court of the Israelites, near the sanctuary. They are types of opposite classes of worshipers. The temple was the place of prayer as well as the place of sacrifice. "A Pharisee" was one of the two principal sects of the Jews at that time; the Pharisees originated about one hundred fifty years before Christ; they were noted for their rigid observance of the letter of the law and of their traditions; among their leading characteristics were formality, self-righteousness, and hypocrisy. "A publican" was one of the collectors of revenue and taxes under the Roman government. Publicans were classed with the outcasts or sinners. These two men thus classified are now presented individually by their prayers.

11, 12 **The Pharisee stood and prayed thus with himself,**— "Stood," in the original, means that he struck a pose, or assumed an attitude where he could be seen; the condemnation is not so much upon the standing in prayer as it is upon the posture assumed merely to be seen of men; he manifested no

I am not as the rest of men, extortioners, unjust, adulterers, or even as this
[15]publican. 12 I fast twice in the week; I give tithes of all that I get. 13
But the [15]publican, standing afar off, would not lift up so much as his eyes
unto heaven, but smote his breast, saying, God, [1]be thou merciful to me [2]a

[1]Or, *be thou propitiated*
[2]Or, *the sinner*

humility, piety, or reverence. He prayed "thus with himself";
some think that this means that he only prayed mentally or in
silence; others think that it means that the Pharisee standing
by himself prayed these things. He first gave thanks, which
was an important part of his communication with God. He
thanked God that he was "not as the rest of men, extortioners,
unjust, adulterers, or even as this publican." He thanked God
that he was made separate from sinners, as he thought; he did
not feel any need of God's pardon, for he counted himself as
being righteous; he trusted in himself that he was sufficiently
righteous to merit God's favors. "Extortioners"—the original
means a robber and plunderer, grafters, like the publicans.
"Unjust" means one who deals unfairly with his fellows; one
who is unjust in feelings and attitude toward others.
"Adulterers"—those who have transgressed the law in relation to others; those who have violated the law that requires a
pure life. He seemed to reach the climax when he thanked God
that he was not "even as this publican." There is no evidence
that he knew anything about the man except that he was a
publican. He sustained an attitude of contempt toward the
publican. After looking at himself negatively, and feeling
that he was righteous, he then began to tell the Lord about
his good deeds. He said: "I fast twice in the week; I give
tithes of all that I get." In his egotism and self-righteousness
he has used the pronoun "I" five times in this short prayer.
The only fast positively enjoined was on the day of atonement, the tenth day of the seventh month. (Lev. 23: 27.)

13 **But the publican, standing afar off,**—What a contrast between the two! The Pharisee struck a pose so that everyone
could see him and know that he was praying, while the publican "standing afar off" made his prayer. In his humility he
"would not lift up so much as his eyes unto heaven." He
stood at a distance from the Pharisee, not from the sanctuary;

sinner. 14 I say unto you, This man went down to his house justified rather
than the other : for every one that exalteth himself shall be humbled ; but he
that humbleth himself shall be exalted.

---

he was not wanting to be seen of men; he was contrite in
heart and humble in life. He was timid in attitude; merely
standing afar off, while the Pharisee was posing to be seen of
men. He "smote his breast," a natural gesture, which the
heart dictates to all men; it was a proof of the sincerity of his
grief and an open confession of his sins. He prayed: "God, be
thou merciful to me a sinner." We have here a full confession
and an anxious cry for mercy; he not only makes a general
confession, but singles himself out as "a sinner." He seems to
acknowledge himself as the sinner that the Pharisee charged
him of being. He simply pleads for God to be merciful to
him. The Pharisee thought of others as sinners; the publican
thinks of himself only as the sinner, not of others as did the
Pharisee. It is a matter of dispute among critics as to
whether it should be "a sinner" or "the sinner"; there is but
little difference, as the publican acknowledged himself to be a
sinner in the sight of God and in the sight of men; whether he
was the particular sinner that the Pharisee accused him to be
is of little consequence.

14 **I say unto you, This man went down to his house**—Here,
again, Jesus draws his own lesson from the parable. He com-
mented briefly on the parable and said that the publican
"went down to his house justified rather than" the Pharisee.
The word "rather" here is to be explained by such scriptures
as Eph. 4: 28; 5: 4, 11; Heb. 11: 25; the word excludes comparison and includes contrast. The Pharisee was not justified
at all; he offered no petition and requested no blessing. The
publican was conscious of his sins and confessed them. To
him belonged the promise: "But to this man will I look, even
to him that is poor and of a contrite spirit, and that trembleth
at my word." (Isa. 66: 2.)

Jesus makes his own application here and emphasizes a fun-
damental truth: "For every one that exalteth himself shall be
humbled; but he that humbleth himself shall be exalted."

This maxim which Jesus here announced has been repeated by him often. (Prov. 16: 18; Luke 14: 11.)

28. JESUS BLESSING LITTLE CHILDREN
18: 15-17

15 And they were bringing unto him also their babes, that he should touch them: but when the disciples saw it, they rebuked them. 16 But Jesus called them unto him, saying, Suffer the little children to come unto me, and

15 **And they were bringing unto him also their babes,**—It is thought that Jesus was still in Perea when this was spoken. Parallel records of this event are found in Matt. 19: 13-15; Mark 10: 13-16. Mark gives a fuller record of this event than do the other writers. Matthew and Mark say that they brought to him "little children," while Luke says "their babes"; the word that Luke uses means "babe" or "an infant." They were evidently little children of tender age; they were too small to "come" to Jesus and were "brought" to him; they were carried in their arms, or were led to Jesus. We are not told who brought them; probably the fathers and mothers or those who had them in charge. Some think that Jesus was about to depart from the place where he was, and hence the parents may have sought his blessings on their children before he left. They wanted Jesus to "touch them," according to Luke; "that he should lay his hands on them, and pray," according to Matthew. The disciples of Jesus rebuked those who brought the children. The disciples probably felt that the various duties of Jesus were too urgent for him to turn aside to bless little children.

16 **But Jesus called them unto him,**—Some think that Jesus called the parents with the children to him and addressed them, while others think that he addressed the disciples who had rebuked them. The context seems to indicate that he called the parents with the children to come closer to him and then rebuked his disciples for rebuking the parents. "Suffer the little children to come unto me." The plea of Jesus is that the children be allowed to come to him and receive his blessings. No one has a right to forbid anyone's coming to Jesus. "For to such belongeth the kingdom of God." The thought

forbid them not: for ³to such belongeth the kingdom of God. 17 Verily I say unto you, Whosoever shall not receive the kingdom of God as a little child, he shall in no wise enter therein.

³Or, *of such is*

seems to be from that which follows this statement, and the parable which precedes it, that Jesus was teaching the beauty of a humble and childlike spirit, and to commend such a spirit to his disciples for imitation. Evidently he does not say that the kingdom of heaven belongs to children, but "to such" does the kingdom of heaven belong. This idea is strengthened by the record given by Mark: "For to such belongeth the kingdom of God." (Mark 10: 14.)

17 **Verily I say unto you, Whosoever shall not receive**— This makes it clear that Jesus is here speaking of those who have the characteristics of a little child are the ones to whom the kingdom of God belongeth. If one does not have these characteristics "he shall in no wise enter therein." No one can be saved without these characteristics; one can enter the church or the kingdom of God on earth only by receiving Christ. The meek, humble, and childlike disposition is characteristic of a citizen in the kingdom of God. Jesus here describes the spirit and frame of mind which are absolutely necessary to salvation; pride, self-righteousness, and self-exaltation must be laid aside; all must be converted and become as little children to enter the kingdom of God. (Matt. 18: 3.)

29. THE RICH RULER
18: 18-30

18 And a certain ruler asked him, saying, Good Teacher, what shall I do

18 **And a certain ruler asked him,**—Matthew and Mark give parallel records of this event. (Matt. 19: 16-26; Mark 10: 17-27.) In both Matthew and Mark we have the same setting with what precedes and with what follows; the salient points of the case are the same in all the records. Mark adds a new feature by saying that "there ran one to him, and kneeled to him"; Mark also records the fact that Jesus "was going forth into the way" when this "certain ruler" came to him. (Mark

to inherit eternal life? 19 And Jesus said unto him, Why callest thou me good? none is good, save one, *even* God. 20 Thou knowest the commandments, 'Do not commit adultery, Do not kill, Do not steal, Do not bear false witness, Honor thy father and mother. 21 And he said, All these things

'Ex. 20.12-16; Dt. 5.16-20

10: 17.) Mark also records that "Jesus looking upon him loved him" (Mark 10: 21), and that the disciples were astonished at his word. He addressed Jesus as "Good Teacher," or "Master," as some translations have it. He came with a very important question: "What shall I do to inherit eternal life?" This is the same way that Mark records the question, but Matthew records it, "What good thing shall I do, that I may have eternal life?" (Matt. 19: 16.) We do not know how much he knew about "eternal life." Sometimes the word "archon" means a chief, sometimes a magistrate, sometimes prince, counselor. (Matt. 20: 25; Luke 12: 58; John 14: 30; Acts 7: 27; 16: 19.) "Inherit" means possess or enjoy; "eternal life" may have been borrowed from Dan. 12: 2, the only place where it occurs in the Old Testament. It implies everlasting happiness.

19 And Jesus said unto him,—Jesus promptly replied to the young ruler to teach him something of God. He asked: "Why callest thou me good?" And then he said there is none good "save one, even God." Matt. 19: 17 represents Jesus as saying: "Why askest thou me concerning that which is good?" It is a matter of controversy as to what Jesus meant by this question. Some think that he meant to say that no one except God is originally, essentially, infinitely, and independently good. Here Jesus makes no reference to his own divinity, but shows the young ruler how vain are his thoughts of doing an absolutely good thing; this was the first blow to his self-righteousness.

20, 21 Thou knowest the commandments,—Matthew records Jesus as saying: "Keep the commandments," and the ruler asked, "Which?" Mark's record is the same as that of Luke. Jesus proceeded to enumerate some of the commandments as found in Ex. 20: 12-16 and Deut. 5: 16-20. The rich young ruler was a Jew and was instructed in the law. Jesus

have I observed from my youth up. 22 And when Jesus heard it, he said
unto him, One thing thou lackest yet: sell all that thou hast, and distribute
unto the poor, and thou shalt have treasure in heaven: and come, follow me.
23 But when he heard these things, he became exceeding sorrowful; for he

enumerated five of the six commandments of the Decalogue,
which regulated man's duty to his fellow man. "Thou shalt
not covet" is the one omitted here by Jesus. Mark records the
six commandments and gives the one that Matthew and Luke
omit as "do not defraud." (Mark 10: 19.) The commandments are not given in their order as found in Exodus. The
seventh commandment is put first, then the sixth, then the
eighth, then the ninth, and last of all the fifth. Matthew gives
the sixth first and then the seventh, but Mark the same as
Luke. Some think that the fifth is placed last because it is a
positive command. Matthew adds, "Thou shalt love thy
neighbor as thyself," a positive summary of the second table.
Mark adds "defraud not" by covetousness or any dishonest
act, which appears to be a brief summary of the tenth commandment. (Ex. 20: 17.) The young man replied that he had
observed all these commandments "from my youth up."

22 **And when Jesus heard it,**—Jesus heard the young man's
reply and answered his question: "What lack I yet?" Mark
tells us that Jesus loved the young man and said: "One thing
thou lackest yet." If the young man desired to have moral
completeness and lack nothing, if he would "be perfect and
entire, lacking in nothing" (James 1: 4) he should "sell all
that thou hast, and distribute unto the poor," in order that he
should "have treasure in heaven"; then he should "come, follow me." Jesus touched the weak point in the young man's
character; he placed before him a perfect standard; he must
deny himself, sell his goods, distribute them to the poor, take
up his cross and follow Jesus. This was the answer that
Jesus gave to his question as to what he should do to inherit
eternal life.

23 **But when he heard these things,**—The young man had
honestly inquired as to what he should do; Jesus plainly and
simply told him what he should do. There was pointed out

was very rich. 24 And Jesus seeing him said, How hardly shall they that
have riches enter into the kingdom of God! 25 For it is easier for a camel
to enter in through a needle's eye, than for a rich man to enter into the

---

only one way for him to inherit eternal life; no alternative was
offered him; it was do what Jesus commanded him to do or
refuse and be lost. The young man "became exceeding sorrowful" when he heard what Jesus had told him. Matthew
says that "he went away sorrowful" (Matt. 19: 22), while
Mark says that "his countenance fell at the saying, and he
went away sorrowful" (Mark 10: 22). The record adds an explanation to his sorrow: "For he was very rich." Matthew
says that he "had great possessions"; Mark makes about the
same statement. The test of his faith was now put to him; he
must part with his possessions or with Jesus; he chose to remain with his earthly possessions.

24 **And Jesus seeing him said,**—Jesus saw the young man
turn to his riches and go away from him; he saw the struggle
that the young man had and he saw the decision that the
young ruler had made. Jesus "looked round about, and saith
unto his disciples": "How hardly shall they that have riches
enter into the kingdom of God!" Matthew records Jesus as
saying, "It is hard for a rich man to enter into the kingdom of
heaven," while Mark uses about the same words. Jesus says
that it is exceedingly difficult for a rich man to become the
subject and attain the blessings and honors of the new dispensation.

25 **For it is easier for a camel to enter in through a needle's
eye,**—Some consider this as a current proverb for the impossible; the Talmud speaks twice of an elephant passing through
the eye of a needle as being impossible. It is similar to the
statement in Jer. 13: 23; it expresses the greatest conceivable
difficulties, the greatest human impossibility of a rich man entering the kingdom of God. A needle's eye being very small
and the camel being very large, the proverb well expresses an
impossibility. (See Matt. 23: 24.) Some think that there is
an allusion here to the low gateways through which camels
were forced on their knees; and it is said that an opening of
this sort is called the eye of a needle. The simple teaching of

kingdom of God. 26 And they that heard it said, Then who can be saved? 27 But he said, The things which are impossible with men are possible with God. 28 And Peter said, Lo, we have left ⁵our own, and followed thee. 29

⁵Or, *our own* homes. See Jn. 19.27

Jesus is that it is as impossible for a rich man who trusts in his riches to go to heaven as it is for a camel to go through a needle's eye.

26 **And they that heard it said,**—The disciples of Jesus and others who were present asked the question: "Then who can be saved?" The disciples were poor men themselves and thoroughly familiar with the ills of poverty and accustomed to look at the bright side only of the rich man's case; it was simply amazing to them and unaccountable that salvation should come so hard to the rich man; what can the poor man do if the rich man cannot go to heaven? If the way of life was so difficult, they asked, who can be saved? It was usually considered that the rich men acquired merit by their deeds of charity and gifts to the temple.

27 **But he said, The things which are impossible with men** —It is a human impossibility for one to save himself in the absolute; he can do so only by doing what God teaches him to do. It is God who saves. It is beyond human power for any to be saved, and especially those who are surrounded with the dangers and difficulties of wealth. The truth of God can break the spirit of covetousness, purify the heart by faith in the truth, and make the rich humble. In this way, that which is impossible with man is possible with God. Jesus has in mind the illustration that he has just given; the human impossibility of the camel going through the needle's eye has become possible with God.

28 **And Peter said, Lo, we have left our own,**—Matthew records Peter as saying that "we have left all, and followed thee; what then shall we have?" (Matt. 19: 27.) When the apostles were called they left all, their property and business, and followed Jesus as personal attendants. (Mark 1: 16-20; 2: 14.) This may have been suggested to Peter by what Jesus had commanded the rich young ruler to do: "Sell that which

And he said unto them, Verily I say unto you, There is no man that hath left house, or wife, or brethren, or parents, or children, for the kingdom of God's sake, 30 who shall not receive manifold more in this time, and in the *world to come eternal life.

*Or, *age*

thou hast" and come and follow me. Peter was not boasting; if he had been boasting he would have received a different answer from Jesus. Peter was always quick to see and to speak and apply a new thought.

29, 30 And he said unto them, Verily I say unto you,—Jesus kindly answered Peter's question. "There is no man that hath left house, or wife, or brethren, or parents, or children, for the kingdom of God's sake" but that will receive his reward. The enumeration of various family ties indicates that the self-denial must be complete, that consecration to the kingdom of God must be supreme. The one who does this has been promised blessings here, in self-denial for Christ, and in his kingdom. He shall receive "manifold more in this time" than the things which he leaves behind, and "in the world to come eternal life." Life here means not merely existence, but existence in its right relation to God and truth, hence holy and happy existence. Physical life consists in certain connections of soul and body; so spiritual life consists in certain connections of the soul with God. The reward for leaving all and following Christ begins in this world, but has its greatest realization in the life to come.

30. FORETELLING HIS DEATH AGAIN
18: 31-34

31 And he took unto him the twelve, and said unto them, Behold, we go up to Jerusalem, and all the things that are written through the prophets

31 And he took unto him the twelve,—Matthew and Mark record Jesus' prediction of his sufferings and death repeatedly; the first instance we have is in the regions of Caesarea Philippi (Matt. 16: 13-21), and then again while they abode in Galilee (Matt. 17: 22, 23). Matthew and Mark give records of this prediction. (Matt. 20: 17-19; Mark 10: 32-34.) Jesus and his disciples were still in Perea on their way to Jerusalem.

shall be accomplished unto the Son of man. 32 For he shall be [7]delivered up unto the Gentiles, and shall be mocked, and shamefully treated, and spit upon: 33 and they shall scourge and kill him: and the third day he shall rise again. 34 And they understood none of these things; and this saying was hid from them, and they perceived not the things that were said.

---

[7]Or, betrayed

Jesus said: "We go up to Jerusalem, and all the things that are written through the prophets shall be accompoished unto the Son of man." It seems that Jesus took the "twelve" apart from the other followers. We should note that Jesus said: "We go up to Jerusalem." Jerusalem is about four thousand feet higher than the Jordan valley. (Psalm 122: 3, 4.) The prophets had testified beforehand of the crucifixion of Jesus. (Read Isa. 53.) Everything that was spoken by the prophets must be fulfilled in Jesus.

32, 33 **For he shall be delivered up unto the Gentiles,**—Jesus, by the treachery of Judas and by the Sanhedrin, should be delivered to the Gentiles. "Gentiles," the Greek word, here means "nations"; that is, "all nations" except the Jews, hence it is equivalent to our use of the word "heathen." In particular it refers here to the Romans, to Pilate, and to the Roman soldiers. He should "be mocked and shamefully treated, and spit upon." The Romans, who bore rule in Judea, executed Jesus; he was delivered by the Jews into the hands of the Romans. The Jews would have executed him if they could have done so; their mode of punishment to death was stoning, while the Roman mode of execution was crucifixion. Jesus knew that they would mock him, treat him with insolence, and spit upon him; this was considered the grossest insult. They would "scourge and kill him." After whipping him and punishing him severely, they would put him to death. "Scourging" usually preceded crucifixion. On "the third day he shall rise again." On the third day after his death he would be raised from the dead.

34 **And they understood none of these things;**—It seems strange that his disciples would not understand him. His language is plain and simple; it is not adorned with figures of speech; yet they fail to understand him. The crucifixion and

resurrection of Jesus did not fit into their scheme of the establishment of his kingdom; they would not understand that
which did not fit into their conception. It may be that they
did not attempt to understand him; they did not desire to understand him here. Under such circumstances we are slow to
understand that which we do not want to understand. It
seems that they received the facts into their minds, but did
not understand them.

31. THE BLIND MAN AT JERICHO
18: 35-43

35 And it came to pass as he drew nigh unto Jericho, a certain blind man
sat by the way side begging: 36 and hearing a multitude going by, he in-

35 **And it came to pass, as he drew nigh unto Jericho,—**
Matthew and Mark record this event. (Matt. 20: 29-34; Mark
10: 46-52.) Mark gives the fullest record of this event, but
Luke is the only one that records the effect of the miracle on
the people. (Verse 43.) Matthew says: "And behold, two
blind men sitting by the way side." Hence, Matthew mentions two blind men, while Mark and Luke describe one;
probably they describe the more conspicuous one. It seems
that the one named Bartimaeus by Mark was the principal
one and that he had a companion; hence, Matthew mentions
Bartimaeus and his companion, while Mark and Luke mention
only Bartimaeus. Matthew and Mark record the event as
"they went out from Jericho," while Luke records the incident
as taking place when "he drew nigh unto Jericho." The
seeming discrepancy may be explained by the fact that they
came to the blind man and his companion as they went into
Jericho, and the healing occurred after they left the old Jericho and approached the new Jericho which Herod the Great
had built at some distance away. History gives a record of
the two Jerichos. Some have offered a possible explanation of
this apparent discrepancy by the fact that the blind men made
application for help when Jesus approached the city, but were
not then healed until after they left the city. Compare Matt.
15: 23ff. and Mark 8: 22f. "Jericho" means "the fragrant
place," and was a city of Benjamin (Josh. 18: 21), situated

quired what this meant. 37 And they told him, that Jesus of Nazareth passeth by. 38 And he cried, saying, Jesus, thou son of David, have mercy on

about eighteen miles northeast of Jerusalem, and seven miles
west of the Jordan; it was situated on the highway. It is also
called "the city of palm-trees." (Deut. 34: 3.) Jericho has
quite a lengthy history in the Old Testament. This blind man
was a beggar; probably his blindness accounted for his poverty.

36, 37 **and hearing a multitude going by,**—While he could
not see, yet he was blessed with the faculty of hearing. He
heard the multitude going by, and made inquiry as to the
cause of the tumult. Jericho at this time of the season, being
on the highway, would be full of people who were going up to
Jerusalem to attend the Feast of the Passover. The number
would be greatly increased by those coming from Galilee by
the way of Perea to avoid passing through Samaria. In answer to his inquiry as to the cause of the great confusion, he
was told "that Jesus of Nazareth passeth by." Jesus of Nazareth" had become famous now as a prophet. Nazareth was
about midway between the Sea of Galilee and the Mediterranean Sea; it was about seventy miles from Jerusalem. Here
Jesus lived with his parents for about twenty-eight years; he
early acquired the title of "Jesus of Nazareth" to distinguish
him from others of the same name and to show his lowly life.

38 **And he cried, saying, Jesus,**—Some of the multitude had
told the blind man that "Jesus of Nazareth" passed by, but
the blind man addressed him as "Jesus, thou son of David."
Jesus was a descendant of David; he was a successor to the
throne of David. The angel of the Lord had previously applied this title to Joseph. (Matt. 1: 20.) This title was a
common designation of the Messiah (Matt. 22: 42), and by
the use of it this blind man acknowledged the Messiahship of
Jesus. Jesus did not apply this title to himself. The titles,
"the Son of man," "the Son of God," and others were of
deeper significance and less liable to be perverted. He cried
for the Messiah, or "son of David," to have mercy on him.

me. 39 And they that went before rebuked him, that he should hold his
peace: but he cried out the more a great deal, Thou son of David, have
mercy on me. 40 And Jesus stood, and commanded him to be brought unto
him: and when he was come near, he asked him, 41 What wilt thou that I
should do unto thee? And he said, Lord, that I may receive my sight. 42

---

39 **and they that went before rebuked him,**—Those who accompanied Jesus and who led the procession did not wish to
be disturbed and interrupted on the journey; hence, they rebuked the beggar and asked him to hold his peace. But, as
Luke gives an account of only one, "he cried out the more a
great deal." The more they tried to quiet him the louder became his cry for mercy; the rebuke of the multitude only
aroused his earnestness, for he believed that Jesus would be
willing to heal him. It was a trial of his faith, and he continued to cry: "Thou son of David, have mercy on me." The
poor man understood the difficulty of the situation and the
ability of Jesus to help him, hence his more earnest plea for
help. He was determined to surmount every barrier and to
get the attention of Jesus; he was not to be outdone, even by
the multitude.

40, 41 **And Jesus stood, and commanded him to be brought**
—Jesus "stood"; Matthew says that he "stood still," as also
does Mark; Jesus stopped the procession. This would arrest
the attention of the multitude that was accompanying him; all
eyes would be fixed on the cause of the halting of the procession. Jesus then "commanded him to be brought unto him."
Jesus recognized the title by which he was called and stopped
to hear further particulars of the request. Jesus commanded
those who led the blind man to bring him to him, or commanded those who were in the way to move so that the blind
man could approach him. Mark is more graphic in his description. He represents the multitude as calling to the blind
man and saying: "Be of good cheer: rise, he calleth thee."
(Mark 10: 49.) When the blind man heard this, he cast away
his outer garment, "sprang up, and came to Jesus." When he
came near Jesus asked him: "What wilt thou that I should do
unto thee?" The blind man immediately replied: "That I
may receive my sight." Luke being a physician records most

And Jesus said unto him, Receive thy sight: thy faith hath [8]made thee whole. 43 And immediately he received his sight, and followed him, glorifying God: and all the people, when they saw it, gave praise unto God.

[8]Or, *saved thee*

of the salient points in a practical way; he shows the intense earnestness of the blind man, the warm compassion of Jesus, and his promptness in meeting the request.

42 And Jesus said unto him, Receive thy sight:—It was a beautiful and impressive scene to see Jesus stop the dense crowd in order that the case of this beggar, smitten with unfortunate blindness, should be ministered to. With swift promptness Jesus said: "Receive thy sight." He then added: "Thy faith hath made thee whole." The faith of the blind man was such that he cried the more earnestly for mercy, believing that Jesus had the power to heal and would exercise his power in healing him. His eyes were opened because of his strong faith.

43 And immediately he received his sight—There was no delay; the promptness with which Jesus granted the request showed his interest in this unfortunate man. The multitude who winessed this could know just what was done; they knew that the man was blind, and now they knew that he had received his sight. The man not only received his sight, but he "followed him, glorifying God." The multitude who at first rebuked the man now joined in his praising God for his great goodness and power in giving him his sight. At the very word of Jesus the man received his sight; he wished to be with Jesus, and mingle in the joyous procession as it moved on toward Jerusalem.

32. ZACCHAEUS AND THE PARABLE OF THE POUNDS
19: 1-28

1 And he entered and was passing through Jericho. 2 And behold, a man

1 And he entered and was passing through Jericho.—Luke is the only one that records the events connected with Zacchaeus. As Jesus was passing through Jericho, this event occurred. The apparent discrepancy between Luke and the

called by name Zacchæus; and he was a chief publican, and he was rich. 3
And he sought to see Jesus who he was; and could not for the crowd, because he was little of stature. 4 And he ran on before, and climbed up into a
sycomore tree to see him: for he was to pass that way. 5 And when Jesus

---

other writers was removed by the explanation that Jesus entered the old part of the town, and passed through and entered
the new part of the town; as the road passed through the city
or some suburb of the city, Jesus came in contact with Zacchaeus.

2 And behold, a man called by name Zacchaeus;—"Behold"
is a term used to call attention to the incident about to be related. "A man," the Greek word here interpreted as "man"
means "a man indeed," which shows clearly that Zacchaeus
was a person of importance and great consideration. He was
a Jew as is seen from his name, which is the same as "Zaccai."
(Ezra 2: 9; Neh. 7: 14.) "Zacchaeus" means "pure," just, or
innocent; he was a Jew and a son of Abraham. He was "a
chief publican"; Jericho was close to the fords of the Jordan
and was therefore an appropriate seat for an officer of superior
rank to preside over the collection of revenues. Zacchaeus
had superior wealth and was able to receive the highest offices
of his trade. He was a chief collector of taxes, and was despised as the publicans were by the Jews; there was nothing
wrong in his occupation; taxes were necessary, and someone
had to collect them.

3, 4 And he sought to see Jesus who he was;—He "sought";
that is, he continued to get a view of Jesus; probably he
had heard much about Jesus and now, since he was passing
that way, he desired earnestly to see Jesus. He not only
desired to see him, but he was determined to see him. We
do not know whether it was through curiosity or from some
other motive; we do know that he was determined to see
Jesus. He could not see Jesus because of the crowd; Zacchaeus was "little of stature," and could not look over the
heads of the crowd and see Jesus; hence "he ran on before,
and climbed up into a sycomore tree to see him." The words
"ran" and "climbed" showed that Zacchaeus was not to be
outdone; he was a man of energy, forethought, and determi-

came to the place, he looked up, and said unto him, Zacchæus, make haste, and come down; for to-day I must abide at thy house. 6 And he made haste, and came down, and received him joyfully. 7 And when they saw it, they all murmured, saying, He is gone in to lodge with a man that is a sin-

---

nation. "Sycomore" was similar to "fig tree" or mulberry; the fig-mulberry resembled the fig in fruit and mulberry in foliage. It grows with its large branches down and open so that Zacchaeus could easily have climbed into it. Jesus was to pass along by this tree so Zacchaeus took advantage of it to see Jesus.

5, 6 **And when Jesus came to the place,**—It may be that Zacchaeus thought that he could see Jesus, but that Jesus could not see him; but as Jesus came to the place, "he looked up, and said unto him, Zacchaeus, make haste, and come down." Perhaps Zacchaeus was surprised when Jesus spoke to him. Jesus not only saw Zacchaeus, but he saw the secret history of his heart, and the desire which had brought him to this place of prominence where he could see Jesus; Jesus saw his soul and saw what it needed. If Zacchaeus was surprised when Jesus saw him and spoke to him, how much greater was his astonishment when Jesus told him that he would abide at his house. Although Zacchaeus was a man of authority, prominence, and wealth, yet Jesus commanded him to come down from the tree, and imposed himself upon Zacchaeus as a self-invited guest. This was enough to impress Zacchaeus with the fact that Jesus could and did speak with commanding authority.

7 **And when they saw it, they all murmured,**—When the Pharisees and others of the multitude saw what Jesus had done and heard what he had said, they "all murmured"; some think that the word "all" included the disciples of Jesus. They did not think that it was becoming in a teacher, prophet, or one who claimed to be the Messiah, to go into the house as a guest of a publican. It seems that they kept murmuring; they were haters of the publicans and murmured because Jesus turned aside to become a guest that day of such a man as Zacchaeus. They said among other things that Jesus had gone "in to lodge with a man that is a sinner." It seems that those

ner. 8 And Zacchaeus stood, and said unto the Lord, Behold, Lord, the half of my goods I give to the poor; and if I have wrongfully exacted aught of any man, I restore fourfold. 9 And Jesus said unto him, To-day is salvation come to this house, forasmuch as he also is a son of Abraham. 10 For the Son of man came to seek and to save that which was lost.

who murmured here had no enmity against Jesus, but that they doubted the propriety of his being a guest of so notorious a publican as Zacchaeus. Some, however, have classed these murmurers with the Pharisees who seem to have attended Jesus to watch his words and actions to discover some ground of accusation against him. Others think that the murmuring came only from his friends.

8 **And Zacchaeus stood,**—Probably Zacchaeus heard the murmurings, and bethought himself and the reputation that publicans had, so he at once began to make confession. Zacchaeus "stood"; that is, he took a posture as of one who is about to make a solemn declaration; he was like the Pharisee in attitude, but different in spirit, though the same word describing the Pharisee's posture is used of the publican. Zacchaeus, noting the murmuring of the people, seeks to justify Jesus in entering his house. He denies being an extortioner or unjust, and declares that he has given half of his goods to help the poor; that is, he had given half of his income to help the poor. Some think that Zacchaeus had not been so liberal, but that he now declares his liberality by saying that he would give half of his goods to feed the poor. It seems that he was expressing what he had done and that what he purposed to continue to do. He was willing to restore according to the law anything that he had "wrongfully exacted" of anyone, and restore "fourfold." The law of Moses required only the addition of one-fifth to the amount of which the person had been defrauded. (Num. 5: 7.) Zacchaeus was willing to observe the extreme requirements of the law. (Ex. 22: 1.)

9, 10 **And Jesus said unto him,**—Jesus saw his heart and knew his penitence and his faith. He said: "To-day is salvation come to this house." Salvation had come to this house because Jesus was present as a welcomed guest; it had come

11 And as they heard these things, he added and spake a parable, because he was nigh to Jerusalem, and *because* they supposed that the kingdom of God was immediately to appear. 12 He said therefore, A certain nobleman went into a far country, to receive for himself a kingdom, and to return. 13

to Zacchaeus in that he was penitent and willing to receive instruction from Jesus. Zacchaeus, Joseph of Arimathaea, Nicodemus, and others remained in the situation in which Jesus found them for the time being. Probably other members of his household became disciples of Jesus. Zacchaeus was a descendant of Abraham and thus entitled to the blessings of the ministry of Jesus. Jesus then announces to Zacchaeus and all others the purpose of his mission: "For the Son of man came to seek and to save that which was lost." Zacchaeus was one of the lost sheep of the house of Israel; hence, Jesus came to save him. (Matt. 10: 6; 15: 24; Luke 15: 1-6.)

11 **And as they heard these things, he added and spake a parable,**—It seems that this parable was the conclusion of his discourse in the house of Zacchaeus, or as he left the house and went along the way toward Jerusalem. "He added and spake a parable" to what had already been said; this form of expression is equivalent to saying that he continued his discourse. There are two reasons assigned here for giving this parable: (1) "because he was nigh to Jerusalem"; (2) "because they supposed that the kingdom of God was immediately to appear." Jesus and his disciples were on the way to Jerusalem, followed with great throngs of excited people; everything betokened the approach of great and stirring events; the nearer the approach to Jerusalem, the more crowded the thoroughfare with excited people. They thought that the kingdom of God was to be announced as set up when Jesus arrived in Jerusalem.

12, 13 **He said therefore, A certain nobleman**—Some have confused this parable of the pounds with the parable of talents recorded in Matt. 25: 14-30. They are two different parables spoken at different times and different places. The parable of the pounds was spoken in Jericho or on the way from Jericho to Jerusalem; the parable of the talents was spoken on the

And he called ten ¹servants of his, and gave them ten ²pounds, and said unto them, Trade ye *herewith* till I come. 14 But his citizens hated him, and sent

¹Gr. *bondservants*
²*Mina*, here translated a pound, is equal to one hundred drachmas. See ch. 15.8

Mount of Olives near Jerusalem; the parable of the pounds was spoken before Jesus made his triumphal entry into Jerusalem, while the parable of the talents was·spoken about the third day after his entrance into the city. The parable of the pounds was spoken to the multitudes as well as his disciples, while that of the talents was spoken to the innermost circle of his trusted followers. The scope of the parable of the pounds is wider and more complex than that of the talents. They differ in every essential and important point.

"A certain nobleman went into a far country" to receive a kingdom; this was customary; it is said that Archelaus had done this very thing; hence there was historical basis for this parable. The nobleman called "ten servants of his" and gave to each of them a "pound," or ten pounds to ten servants; they were to trade with these pounds and get gain for their master. The original Greek for pound is "mimas," and was equal to about one hundred drachmas, or between sixteen and eighteen, dollars. This was rather a small amount to be committed to the servants, and is small compared to a "talent." A "talent" was equal to 6,000 denarii, or about a thousand dollars, or 240 pounds. In the parable of the talents the Lord is transferring to his servants his entire property, while in the parable of the pounds he is putting into the hands of his servants only a small amount to test their faithfulness. All prominent men in Rome had many servants; sometimes they had a servant to do each particular task. This nobleman called "ten" of his servants to him and committed to them this trust.

14 **But his citizens hated him,**—This actually occurred with Archelaus; when Herod died he was followed by his son, Archelaus; he had no right to the throne until he obtained the sanction of Caesar. He took ship with certain attendants and went to Rome that he might receive the kingdom and return;

an ambassage after him, saying, We will not that this man reign over us. 15 And it came to pass, when he was come back again, having received the kingdom, that he commanded these ¹servants, unto whom he had given the money, to be called to him, that he might know what they had gained by trading. 16 And the first came before him, saying, Lord, thy pound hath made ten pounds more. 17 And he said unto him, Well done, thou good

---

the people were tired of the Herods; while he was on the way, his citizens who hated him sent an ambassage after him with the message that they would not submit to the reign of Archelaus. Jesus here could recite history with which the people were familiar. It is worthy of note to observe that this declaration was twice made by the Jews: "We have no king but Caesar," and "Write not, The King of the Jews." (John 19: 15, 21.)

15 **And it came to pass, when he was come back again,—** This nobleman had gone to the proper authority to receive sanction for his reigning over a certain province or kingdom; while he was gone, the people of that kingdom sent to the authority from whence the nobleman was to receive sanction, and prejudiced him against the nobleman; however, the nobleman received "the kingdom," and returned. He then "commanded these servants, unto whom he had given the money," to come before him and give an account of their stewardship. The day of reckoning had come for them. He first took account of his servants and afterward inflicted judgment on his enemies. Judgment is to "begin at the house of God." (1 Pet. 4: 17.) The reckoning was made to determine who had gained by trading and how much was gained. There is suggested here the stern character of justice.

16, 17 **And the first came before him,—**We know not the order in which he called these servants; we do not know which one ranked first. The first one who had been summoned to give an account to his lord had a very favorable report to make. He reported that "thy pound hath made ten pounds more." He had so used what was entrusted to him that it had gained ten other pounds; literally, this means that the one pound had "worked out" ten other pounds, which was a tenfold increase; this was accomplished because of the wise and energetic management of the servant. This was a splen-

³servant: because thou wast found faithful in a very little have thou authority over ten cities. 18 And the second came, saying, Thy pound, Lord, hath made five pounds. 19 And he said unto him also, Be thou also over five cities. 20 And ⁴another came, saying, Lord, behold, *here is* thy pound, which I kept laid up in a napkin: 21 for I feared thee, because thou art an austere man: thou takest up that which thou layedst not down, and reapest that

³Gr. *bondservant*
⁴Gr. *the other*

---

did report for this servant to make; he was not boasting, but modestly gave a faithful report. The master pronounced a blessing upon his servant and said: "Because thou wast found faithful in a very little" he would give him "authority over ten cities."

18, 19 And the second came,—The second servant that reported had gained five pounds. The verb "came" is different in the original and signifies a less intimacy and a less nearness of approach. The same personal merit is recognized in this servant as that one who had gained ten pounds. The implication is that he had been as faithful as the other, but his ability was not as great as that of the first servant. People with different abilities may be equal in faithfulness or the one with less ability may be even greater in faithfulness. He had gained fivefold, and his reward was in proportion to his faithfulness. He was placed "over five cities" because he had been faithful. His ability showed that he was qualified to manage five cities.

20, 21 And another came,—This one was unfaithful; he was either indolent and did not use his pound to gain for his master, or he was dishonest with his gain, or used bad judgment. His report was that he "laid up in a napkin" the pound and kept it until his master returned. "Napkin" as here used means a cloth for wiping off the sweat; this servant had been indolent and did not need a napkin for that purpose, hence he used it to wrap around his money. He gave as his reason for not using his pound that he feared his master, "because thou art an austere man." It seems that he feared his master unwisely, for he should have been afraid of punishment if he did not use the pound as directed. "Austere' comes from the Greek which means "to dry," hence "dry," and thence "hard";

which thou didst not sow. 22 He saith unto him, Out of thine own mouth
will I judge thee, thou wicked ⁵servant. Thou knewest that I am an austere
man, taking up that which I laid not down, and reaping that which I did not
sow; 23 then wherefore gavest thou not my money into the bank, and ⁵I at
my coming should have required it with interest? 24 And he said unto them
that stood by, Take away from him the pound, and give it unto him that
hath the ten pounds. 25 And they said unto him, Lord, he hath ten pounds.

⁵Or, *I should have gone and required*

it means here harsh, stern, unforgiving; in Matthew the word
"hard" is used. The servant proceeded to give some characteristics of his master; he said that he took up that which he
did not lay down, and that he reaped where he did not sow.

22, 23 **He saith unto him, Out of thine own mouth**—"Out of
thine own mouth"; that is, on the very principle of the excuse
that the idle servant offered for his unfaithfulness, he should
be judged. The master will judge this servant according to
the principle that he attributed to his master. This is not an
acknowledgment on the part of the nobleman that the servant's description was correct. The master then told him
how he could have handled the matter, since he was too indolent to use the pound in a way to gain; he could have put the
"money into the bank" so that the master would have had interest on it when he came. "Bank" as used here means the
"table" of the money-changers. The exchangers were the
bankers of that day, who sat at the counter or table to trans-
act the necessary business.

24 **And he said unto them that stood by,**—"Them that stood
by" means his officers of justice, or other servants whose duties were to execute the will of the lord; the day of reckoning
had come; it always comes. The master commanded that
they take the pound from this unfaithful servant and give it to
"him that hath the ten pounds." No mention is here made of
positive punishment inflicted on the unfaithful servant, such
as we find inflicted on the man who buried his talent in the
parable of the talents. The privation of all privileges and taking away of all gifts and subjecting the servant to such humiliation is punishment to him. The servant that should make
good use of his master's property should be entrusted with
greater honors; this one pound was taken away from the idle

26 I say unto you, that unto every one that hath shall be given; but from
him that hath not, even that which he hath shall be taken away from him.
27 But these mine enemies, that would not that I should reign over them,

servant and given to the one who had ten pounds, because he
had proved himself able to manage a larger share of his master's goods.

25, 26 **And they said unto him, Lord, he hath ten pounds.**—
They were surprised that the one who had gained ten pounds
should be given more; this was expressed as implying a doubt
in the fairness of the distribution. This verse seems to be
parenthetical; some think that it was spoken by those who
heard the parable, and hence, it was a criticism against Jesus
for his unfairness in distributing affairs. Still others think
that his verse forms a part of the parable itself and was spoken by Jesus. In either case the lesson is the same; it shows
that the honor placed on faithfulness is in proportion to the
trust and responsibility.

I say unto you, that unto every one that hath—Jesus here
gives point to his parable. He who has neglected to use the
trust, however small, committed to him, shall lose it, but he
who has diligently used that which was entrusted to him and
has thus increased it, to him more shall be entrusted. Fidelity
and ability, as shown in the use of the trusts or events, are the
tests according to which Christ will bestow trusts in his spiritual kingdom. Here Jesus assigns the reason for the principle; it furnishes a reply to the wondering exclamation of the
bystanders; some consider this language as an admonition to
the disciples. Those who have acquired by industry and
economy shall have more; they are worthy and capable of
handling more; but the one who does not have the ability and
faithfulness to handle shall lose even that which he has. Even
that which was originally entrusted to one, and which he
failed to improve, shall be taken from him. Jesus repeated
this frequently. (Luke 8: 18.)

27 **But these mine enemies,**—Jesus here reverts to his enemies (verse 14). The unprofitable servant represents those
Jews who persisted in unbelief when Christ came among

bring hither, and slay them before me.

28 And when he had thus spoken, he went on before, going up to Jerusalem.

---

them. When this King comes into power the enemies who resisted his claim must be treated as rebels. They assumed this risk when they put themselves in hostile attitude against Jesus; now they must meet their doom; the day of retribution will come and final judgment will be meted out to them. There seems to be three classes of people as represented in the parable; first, those who were open opposers of Christ and the gospel; second, those who were faithful disciples; and third, those who were unfaithful disciples.

28 And when he had thus spoken, he went on before,—Jesus now resumes his journey toward Jerusalem. "He went on before." Jesus led the way with determination to meet his enemies in Jerusalem; we cannot think of Jesus trailing behind anyone. He knew what awaited him at Jerusalem, but steadily marched, leading the way on to Jerusalem; he did not falter in his purpose, although he knew the suffering that awaited him. Again, he went "up to Jerusalem." The road from Jericho leads "up" to Jerusalem. Jerusalem was geographically several thousand feet above the Jordan plain where Jericho was located.

SECTION FIVE

THE MINISTRY OF JESUS IN JERUSALEM; LAST DAYS OF PUBLIC TEACHING
19: 29 to 21: 38

1. TRIUMPHAL ENTRY
19: 29-48

29 And it came to pass, when he drew nigh unto Bethphage and Bethany, at the mount that is called Olivet, he sent two of the disciples, 30 saying, Go your way into the village over against *you;* in which as ye enter ye shall find a colt tied, whereon no man ever yet sat: loose him, and bring him. 31

29 **And it came to pass, when he drew nigh**—Parallel records are found in Matt. 21: 1-11; Mark 11: 1-11; John 12: 12-19. We come to the last movements and teachings of Jesus; the close of his public ministry, except the little that he said during the Jewish and Roman trials, is brought within the scope of the last week. His final teachings are given to his disciples. There is a close verbal resemblance between all the writers of this remarkable portion of our Lord's history, yet there is enough diversity of expression to establish their claims to independent authorship. Between this triumphal entry into the city and the visit at the house of Zacchaeus, many place the visit of Jesus at Bethany. (John 12: 1, 9-11.)

"Bethphage and Bethany." These places are mentioned together and may have designated different parts of the same village. "Bethphage" means "place of figs," while "Bethany" means "the place of dates"; the first place denotes a fig orchard, while the other denotes a palm grove. Bethany was about a mile and a half from Jerusalem, corresponding to the "fifteen furlongs" of John 11: 18. "Mount that is called Olivet" is the well-known eminence facing Jerusalem on the east and separated from it by the narrow, deep valley of the Kidron.

30 **saying, Go your way into the village**—Jesus sent two of his disciples and commanded them to "go into the village that is over against you," and that they should find "an ass tied and a colt with her"; they should "loose them and bring

And if any one ask you, Why do ye loose him? thus shall ye say, The Lord
hath need of him. 32 And they that were sent went away, and found even as
he had said unto them. 33 And as they were loosing the colt, the owners
thereof said unto them, Why loose ye the colt? 34 And they said, The Lord
hath need of him. 35 And they brought him to Jesus: and they threw their

them" to him. (Matt. 21: 2.) The dam was probably
brought because they would go better in company. Jesus further describes the colt as one "whereon no man ever yet sat."
Neither the Jews nor heathen employed in sacred use animals
that had been employed for secular purposes. (Num. 19: 2;
Deut. 21 : 3 ; 1 Sam. 6: 7.)

31, 32 **And if any one ask you,**—If anyone should inquire
why they were thus taking the animal, they were to reply:
"The Lord hath need of him." Matthew has "the Lord hath
need of them." Mark gives the same answer that Luke recorded. Jesus who knew that the colt was there also knew
that the owner would send him for his use; the man may have
been a disciple of Jesus, and would gladly send the colt to
him. The disciples "found even as he had said unto them."
This showed that Jesus had divine wisdom. This must have
strengthened the faith of these two disciples in the divinity of
Jesus.

33, 34 **And as they were loosing the colt,**—The owner or
some of his servants or someone else standing by asked why
they should loose the colt; Luke represents the owner of it as
asking this question, while Mark represents those "that stood
there" (Mark 11: 5) asking the question. They promptly replied that "the Lord hath need of him." This was exactly
what Jesus had told them to answer. It is very probable that
the owner with the others understood this as referring to
Jesus. Mark represents them as saying that Jesus commanded
them to take it. (Mark 11: 6.) The faith of the two disciples
should have been strengthened because the owner or others
asked the very question that Jesus had predicted.

35, 36 **And they brought him to Jesus:**—Matthew tells us
that they "brought the ass, and the colt" (Matt. 21: 7), while
Mark and Luke mention only the colt. They put their "gar-

garments upon the colt, and set Jesus thereon. 36 And as he went, they spread their garments in the way. 37 And as he was now drawing nigh, *even* at the descent of the mount of Olives, the whole multitude of the disciples began to rejoice and praise God with a loud voice for all the [1]mighty works which they had seen; 38 saying, Blessed *is* the King that cometh in the name of the Lord: peace in heaven, and glory in the highest. 39 And

[1]Gr. *powers*

ments," or mantles upon the colt as .a saddle; the disciples seem to have put their mantles upon the colt, while the multitude spread their garments on the highway or along the way. "And set Jesus thereon." This is the only case on record in which Jesus "rode" any animal; it is presumed that he always walked on his tours throughout Galilee, Perea, and Judea. The ancients were accustomed to placing their clothes, branches of tree, flowers, and other objects of adornment along the way before kings and conquerors in their trumphant marches. (2 Kings 9: 13.)

37 **And as he was now drawing nigh,**—The procession was moving from Bethany westward toward Jerusalem; there was a valley between the Mount of Olives and Jerusalem; they had passed down the western slope of the Mount of Olives, and had crossed the narrow valley and were ready to proceed on into Jerusalem. At this point the multitude raised a shout and "began to rejoice and praise God with a loud voice for all the mighty works which they had seen." Some describe the descent from the Mount of Olives as going down the southern slope and then making a turn. As they turned down to the city the view of Jerusalem stirred the crowd to rapturous enthusiasm; this was the first sight of the city on this route which is soon obscured in the descent. The second view burst upon them. (Verse 41.) This praise was a long pent-up enthusiasm which had gathered all along the way from Jericho; now it was unrestrained.

38 **Blessed is the King that cometh in the name of the Lord:**—Matthew records their saying: "Hosanna to the son of David: Blessed is he that cometh in the name of the Lord; Hosanna in the highest." (Matt. 21: 9.) Mark records their saying: "Hosanna, Blessed is he that cometh in the name of the Lord: Blessed is the kingdom that cometh, the kingdom

some of the Pharisees from the multitude said unto him, Teacher, rebuke thy disciples. 40 And he answered and said, I tell you that, if these shall hold their peace, the stones will cry out.

---

of our father David: Hosanna in the highest." (Mark 11: 9, 10.) Here the praise is a quotation from Psalm 118: 25, 26. John represents a multitude coming out of Jerusalem and meeting the procession and joining in the praise as they continued the march into Jerusalem. "For this cause also the multitude went and met him, for that they heard that he had done this sign." (John 12: 18.) The chorus of praise started by the procession that accompanied Jesus was swelled by the multitude that came out of the city and joined them. The leaders in this movement were his disciples, yet many who were not so closely associated with him joined in the movement; this served to bring his claims prominently before the people of Jerusalem, and in this respect it was of supreme importance at the closing stage of his public ministry. Matt. 21: 10, 11 suggests this: "When he was come into Jerusalem, all the city was stirred, saying, Who is this? And the multitudes said, This is the prophet, Jesus, from Nazareth of Galilee."

39, 40 **And some of the Pharisees**—The enemies of Jesus were on hand watching his movements, and they caught some word or expression, which they made the ground of accusation. They took offense at the application to Jesus of the prophetic words which could be used only of the Messiah. They were not willing for the people to ascribe to him the honors of the Messiah. In the same spirit of unbelief the chief priests and scribes rebuked Jesus after he came into the temple for permitting the application to himself of such ascriptions of praise. Some think that these Pharisees had hypocritically disguised their enmity to Jesus and had followed him from Jericho as his friends. They asked Jesus to rebuke his disciples for ascribing to him the praise. Jesus promptly answered them and said: "I tell you that, if these shall hold their peace, the stones will cry out." Luke is the only one that records this.

41 And when he drew nigh, he saw the city and wept over it, 42 saying,
²If thou hadst known in ³this day, even thou, the things which belong unto
⁴peace! but now they are hid from thine eyes. 43 For the days shall come
upon thee, when thine enemies shall cast up a ⁵bank about thee, and compass
thee round, and keep thee in on every side, 44 and shall dash thee to the
ground, and thy children within thee; and they shall not leave in thee one

²Or, *O that thou hadst known*
³Some ancient authorities read *this thy day*
⁴Some ancient authorities read *thy peace*
⁵Gr. *palisade*

41, 42 **And when he drew nigh,**—The procession led by
Jesus descended the slope of Olivet, and when the city appeared in view the guilt and future ruin of Jerusalem gave the
occasion for the mingled weeping and lamentation over the
city; in pathetic sympathy Jesus said: "If thou hadst known
in this day, even thou, the things which belong unto peace!
but now they are hid from thine eyes." Jesus seems to mean
that if Jerusalem and the multitude even who were acclaiming
him King had known that he was the Christ, they could have
saved the city and themselves from much misery and destruction. Jerusalem had rejected God's messengers, the prophets
in former times; from the time of their departure from Egypt,
they had been a rebellious people; yet if they had at least
known in his day they could have done something to avoid
the impending destruction. Their prejudice, their ignorance,
their unbelief had blinded their eyes to the truth. Truly their
hearts had "waxed gross, and their ears are dull of hearing,
and their eyes they have closed; lest haply they should perceive with their eyes, and hear with their ears, and understand
with their heart, and should turn again, and I should heal
them." (Matt. 13: 15.)

43, 44 **For the days shall come upon thee,**—Jesus now points
out clearly the doom that awaited the city. Their enemies
should "cast up a bank about thee." "Bank" here means
stake, palisade, rampart; the ancient mound raised against cities was constructed of earth thrown up and set with sharp
stakes or a palisade; the excavation made by the earth thus
removed was called the "trench," and was on the side of the
rampart next to the city. The enemy should "compass thee
round, and keep thee in on every side." The city was to be

stone upon another; because thou knewest not the time of thy visitation.
45 And he entered into the temple, and began to cast out them that sold,

completely surrounded, there was no hope of escape. Those
who are familiar with the description of the siege of Jerusalem as given by Josephus know how effectively the city was
besieged. The manner of destruction was also described by
Jesus; the enemies would dash them upon the ground; destroy their children; should not leave one stone upon another
because they were ignorant of the time "of thy visitation."
The erection of the temple was described as the laying of
stone upon stone (Hag. 2: 15), hence the destruction of it is
described as not leaving "one stone upon another." The utter
ruin of the city and temple was predicted; this vivid description and prophecy of Jesus of the destruction of Jerusalem
was so completely fulfilled that critics have denied the predic-
tive prophecy, and said that Luke wrote after the destruction
of Jerusalem.

45, 46 **And he entered into the temple,**—Jesus after this descriptive destruction of Jerusalem entered into the temple.
We have parallel records of this in Matt. 21: 12, 13 and Mark
11: 15-18. "Temple," as used here, means the sacred place, including all the enclosure, as well as the temple proper. It is
not to be understood that Jesus went into the temple as did
the priests; they went into the holy place and the high priest
into the most holy, but Jesus did not go into these places.
When he went in he "cast out them that sold"; according to
Mark (11: 11-15) this was not done the first day, for he says
that Jesus looked round upon all in the temple, and then retired to Bethany as the evening had come. Those who
bought and sold animal sacrifices were present and Jesus drove
them out and overthrew "the tables of the moneychangers."
It is probable that they obeyed Jesus here, not only because
the multitude were on his side, which does not appear to have
been the case when he first came to the temple (John 2: 13-
22) and cleansed it the first time. This cleansing is the second cleansing of the temple; he cleansed it at the first of his
public ministry and now again at the close.

46 saying unto them, It is written, °And my house shall be a house of prayer: but ye have made it a den of robbers.

47 And he was teaching daily in the temple. But the chief priests and the scribes and the principal men of the people sought to destroy him: 48 and they could not find what they might do; for the people all hung upon him, listening.

°Is. 56.7
⁷Jer. 7.11

And my house shall be a house of prayer:—This is a quotation from Isa. 56: 7; Luke gives the meaning of the quotation, but not the words; Mark gives more nearly an exact quotation. The Jews had violated the sanctity of the temple by bringing these animal sacrifices into the courts and porches of the temple; they were not so much interested in the sacrifices that the people made as they were the profit that they would gain by selling the animals as sacrifices. This vigorous cleansing of the temple was an assertion of the prerogative of Jesus as the temple of God. Jesus so quotes the prophet. It seems that Jesus here quoted Jer. 7: 11 and applied the epithet of "a den of robbers" to these money-changers. Their disregard for the sacredness of the temple and their lack of interest in the welfare of the worship, together with their dishonesty, made them "a den of robbers."

47, 48 **And he was teaching daily in the temple.**—This is the last week of the earthly life of Jesus; it appears that he spent each night in Bethany, returning to the city and teaching through the day, and then returning to Bethany at night during the last week of his ministry. He continued his teaching every day of that week up to the time of his arrest; it appears from Matt. 21: 14 that he worked miracles also; he occupied the outer court of the temple. "Chief priests" were those at the head of the twenty-four courses, and probably included the high priest. (2 Chron. 36: 14; Ezra 8: 24; Neh. 12: 7.) David had divided the priests into twenty-four courses, and had appointed a head of each course called a "chief priest." (1 Chron. 24:1-31; 2 Chron. 22: 8.) "Scribes" were those who transcribed the law; after the Jews were carried into Babylonian captivity, they began to build synagogues, and each synagogue needed a copy of the law; this required some-

body to write copies of the law; these men were called
"scribes." They were also teachers of the law; as they transcribed the law they were supposed to know the law, hence
became teachers. "The principal men of the people" included
the elders and rulers of the people; all the dignitaries were
thus determined to destroy Jesus. They sought to find a way
that they might destroy him. They were afraid of the people,
as the people believed in Jesus and "all hung upon him, listening."

2. JESUS EXERCISING AUTHORITY
20: 1-8

1 And it came to pass, on one of the days, as he was teaching the people
in the temple, and preaching the ⁸gospel, there came upon him the chief
priests and the scribes with the elders; 2 and they spake, saying unto him,
Tell us: By what authority doest thou these things? or who is he that gave

⁸Or, *good tidings:* comp. ch. 3.18

1 **And it came to pass, on one of the days,**—We are now in
the last week of the earthly life of Jesus; it is not necessary to
attempt to outline what he taught each day of this week;
some have attempted to classify what he did and what he
taught according to each day of the week. "He was teaching
the people in the temple." Parallel records of this are found
in Matt. 21: 23-27 and Mark 11: 27-33. This was a day of
controversy; the chief priests and scribes and elders drew him
into controversy at many points; this as many think was the
last day of the temple teaching. The leaders had determined
to attack Jesus on this morning, both Sadducees, from whom
came most of the chief priests, and the scribes who were for
the most part Pharisees. Jesus "was teaching" and "preaching the gospel"; the "teaching" the people included the
"preaching the gospel." To "teach" means to instruct, while
to "preach" means to proclaim; however, this distinction is
not kept throughout the New Testament.

2 **and they spake, saying unto him,**—These chief men, who
were now becoming bolder enemies of Jesus, asked him "by
what authority doest thou these things?" They are attempting to get Jesus to make some declaration by which they can

thee this authority? 3 And he answered and said unto them, I also will ask you a ⁹question; and tell me: 4 The baptism of John, was it from heaven, or from men? 5 And they reasoned with themselves, saying, If we shall say, From heaven; he will say, Why did ye not believe him? 6 But if we shall

⁹Gr. *word*

condemn him; they are not wanting the truth. They had rejected the evidence that Jesus had given them; they had ignored the miracles that he worked, even the one of raising Lazarus from the dead; they now ask for the authority under which he acted. Jesus had given the highest authority and had presented the strongest proofs. He had been with them for more than three years, and in the face of the three years, during which he had taught and worked miracles, they still asked for proof and authority for what he was doing. Their question was double; they wanted to know where he got this authority, or the source of his power.

3, 4 **And he answered and said unto them,**—There is a dignity and authority in his reply; he does not quibble with them; his answer showed that they had not disturbed or disconcerted him by their question. He proposed to answer their question on the condition that they would answer a question which he asked them. He answered by giving them a question as to the authority of John the Baptist. He asked: "Was it from heaven, or from men?" That is, was John's authority to baptize from men or was it from God? John had called upon them to repent and to believe on the Messiah who was to come; where did he get his authority to demand repentance and baptism? This question put them in a dilemma. This question threw the responsibility back on them as to the source of authority; John had testified of Jesus; he had pointed him out to the people; what can they do now with respect to this question?

5, 7 **And they reasoned with themselves,**—They saw the dilemma and felt the clutches of it. It seems that they went aside and reasoned "with themselves." The original for "reasoned" is used only here in the New Testament, and it not only means "with themselves," or "together," but denotes a very close conference. If they, they said, should say that

say, From men; all the people will stone us: for they are persuaded that John was a prophet. 7 And they answered, that they knew not whence it *was*. 8 And Jesus said unto them, Neither tell I you by what authority I do these things.

John's baptism was "from heaven," then he would reply: "Why did ye not believe him?" They had rejected John's baptism, and to admit that John's baptism was from heaven would be to admit that they had rejected the authority of God. On the other hand, if they should deny God as the authority of John's baptism, they would be antagonizing the people for "they are persuaded that John was a prophet." They were anxious to retain the favor of the people; they must seek some way to get the people to turn against Jesus. These leaders had resorted to mob violence and had encouraged the people in acts of violence when argument and reason had failed them. Later they practiced this in the death of Stephen (Acts 7: 54-60), and at a still later period with respect to Paul (Acts 21: 27-36). At this time they feared the people; if they deny to John, whom the whole nation honored as a holy man, the claim of being a teacher sent from God, the people might turn with violence upon them.

8 **And Jesus said unto them, Neither tell I**—They had convicted themselves of moral dishonesty; they had shown that they did not want the truth. They were not wanting to know by what authority Jesus taught, preached the gospel, cleansed the temple, and worked miracles; they must have known, but would not acknowledge. It was useless for Jesus to give them further evidence. If they rejected John, they would reject Jesus; if they would not believe John's testimony in his favor (John 1: 15, 29-36; 5: 33-36), they would not believe that which Jesus would offer for himself.

3. PARABLE OF THE HUSBANDMEN
20: 9-18

9 And he began to speak unto the people this parable: A man planted a

---

9 **And he began to speak unto the people this parable:—** Parallel records of this parable are found in Matt. 21: 23-46 and Mark 12: 1-12. This parable is similar to the parable in

vineyard, and let it out to husbandmen, and went into another country for a long time. 10 And at the season he sent unto the husbandmen a [10]servant, that they should give him of the fruit of the vineyard: but the husbandmen beat him, and sent him away empty. 11 And he sent yet another [10]servant: and him also they beat, and handled him shamefully, and sent him away empty. 12 And he sent yet a third: and him also they wounded, and cast him

[10]Gr. *bondservant*

Isa. 5: 1-7. "He began to speak unto the people this parable"; this cannot mean that he spoke only at this time in parable, neither can it mean that he "began" to speak this parable at this time, but finished it later. Luke has all of the essential features of the parable but his record contains fewer of the particulars, especially the description of the vineyard. Luke is the only writer of the parable that mentions the time in which the lord of the vineyard was absent. The details of the parable are simple enough; a man planted a vineyard and rented it to others called husbandmen; the man then went into another country and remained there "for a long time." The vineyard is planted, rented to others, a body of laborers, who are to pay their rental out of the products.

10 **And at the season he sent unto the husbandmen a servant,**—It was customary then to rent vineyards and collect the rent. "At the season" means the vintage time or the time when the fruit ripened and the harvest gathered. The harvest of the vineyard was converted into wine. The landlord sent his servant to receive his share of the product. Those who had rented the vineyard "beat him" and "sent him away empty." They scourged the servants to intimidate him so that he would not come back; he was sent away without any part of that which belonged to the landlord. Evidently they thought that they would get to keep the rent which should have been given to the owner.

11, 12 **And he sent yet another servant:**—It is not known whether the first servant returned to the master and reported all that had been done; but the landlord sent another servant, and instead of honestly paying over all that was due the owner, they abused him shamefully, and beat him as they had the other servant, and sent him away empty. They treated this servant even worse than they treated the first one; finally

forth. 13 And the lord of the vineyard said, What shall I do? I will send my
beloved son; it may be they will reverence him. 14 But when the husbandmen saw him, they reasoned one with another, saying, This is the heir; let
us kill him, that the inheritance may be ours. 15 And they cast him forth
out of the vineyard, and killed him. What therefore will the lord of the
vineyard do unto them? 16 He will come and destroy these husbandmen,
and will give the vineyard unto others. And when they heard it, they said,

---

a third servant was sent "and him also they wounded, and
cast him forth." Matthew records that they "took his servants, and beat one, and killed another, and stoned another."
(Matt. 21 : 35.)

13 **And the lord of the vineyard said,**—The owner of the
vineyard saw that the wicked men to whom he had rented his
vineyard cared nothing for his servants; they had shamefully
treated them, beating and killing some of them; so the owner
thought that they would surely respect his son. He was an
only son, and is described as "my beloved son." If there was
left in them any respect for the master, they surely would respect his only son. The owner of the vineyard dearly loved his
son and felt that others ought to respect and love him; but he
was to be disappointed in this.

14 **But when the husbandmen saw him,**—When the husbandmen saw the son coming, they reasoned among themselves and said: "This is the heir; come, let us kill him, and
the inheritance shall be ours." (Mark 12: 7.) They thought
that by destroying the heir they would then claim the vineyard. These wicked husbandmen reached the climax of their
crime by murdering the son. They thought they would own
the vineyard instead of being tenants. Jesus thus outlines
clearly and emphatically the conduct of these Jews; they were
planning to do just as Jesus here describes these tenants of
doing.

15, 16 **And they cast him forth out of the vineyard,**—They
killed the son. Their crime grew worse; they began by beating and shamefully treating the servants, but have ended in
killing the son and the heir; they began by withholding the
rent of the vineyard from its proper owner and ended by an
attempt to seize the vineyard; they began by robbing the
owner of the vineyard and they ended in an attempt to take

[1]God forbid. 17 But he looked upon them, and said, What then is this that
is written,

          [2]The stone which the builders rejected,
          The same was made the head of the corner?
    18 Every one that falleth on that stone shall be broken to pieces; but on
whomsoever it shall fall, it will scatter him as dust.

[1]Gr. *Be it not so*
[2]Ps. 118.22

---

the vineyard from him. "What therefore will the lord of the
vineyard do unto them?" Jesus answered this question; there
could be but one answer to it; he would destroy them and
take the vineyard away from them and give it to others who
were more worthy. Jesus had asked the question to give
point to his parable, and, according to Matthew, those who
heard him answered his question. "They say unto him, He
will miserably destroy those miserable men, and will let out
the vineyard unto other husbandmen, who shall render him
the fruits in their seasons." (Matt. 21:41.)

    17 **But he looked upon them, and said,**—Here Jesus quotes
Psalm 118:22. They had said that his parable could not be
true, or that it was impossible, and Jesus referred them to this
scripture, and asked to what then does it refer? Peter quotes
the same psalm in 1 Pet. 2:4-7. "The stone," a stone, one
which the builders had cast aside as not fit to go into the
building, was later found to be "the head of the corner." This
has been applied to Christ in prophecy and in fulfillment.
(Isa. 28:16; Eph. 2:20.) It is strange that these leaders
could have always referred this scripture to the Messiah, yet
did not see that it was fulfilled in the case of Jesus who was
rejected by the scribes and priests. (Acts 4:11.) Though
the Jews rejected Jesus, yet God has made him the headstone
of his spiritual temple, uniting both Jews and Gentiles in himself. (Gal. 3:28.)

    18 **Every one that falleth on that stone**—Jesus added an-
other word of warning to them by still using and applying the
figure of a stone. Everyone that shall stumble "on that stone
shall be broken to pieces." This signifies that everyone who
stumbles at Christ and his gospel, and refuses to accept him,
such a one will be "broken" or destroyed. On the other hand,

everyone "on whomsoever it shall fall," or shall be found unbelieving when Christ appears, shall be destroyed. The first seems to describe the doom of all those who are offended in Jesus and will not accept him; while the last part of the statement describes a more sudden extermination of those upon whom the awful retributions of justice must fall for their sins against the Son of God. It seems that Jesus has here presented himself in four aspects under the figure of the stone: (1) a rejected or disallowed stone; (2) the headstone of the corner; (3) a stumbling stone; (4) the stone of retribution.

4. QUESTION AS TO PAYING TRIBUTE
20 : 19-26

19 And the scribes and the chief priests sought to lay hands on him in that very hour; and they feared the people: for they perceived that he spake this parable against them. 20 And they watched him, and sent forth spies, who feigned themselves to be righteous, that they might take hold of his speech, so as to deliver him up to the ³rule and to the authority of the gov-

³Or, *ruling power*

19 **And the scribes and the chief priests**—The scribes and chief priests are more determined to bring the issue to a climax. They have two major tasks: first, to get some charges against Jesus; second, to get the people on their side. They attempt to accomplish these two purposes by forcing Jesus to make some decision against the people. They are maddened into rage at the plain application of the parable that he has just announced. "In that very hour" they would have taken him, for they saw that the parable was leveled against them, but their fear of the people compelled them to defer their actions.

20 **And they watched him, and sent forth spies,**—Parallel records of this are found in Matt. 22: 15-22 and Mark 12: 13-17. Matthew tells us that the Pharisees went and "took counsel how they might ensnare him in his talk." (Matt. 22: 15.) Mark states that the "Herodians" joined the Pharisees in this attempt to "catch him in talk." (Mark 12: 13.) It is probable that the Pharisees took the lead in this. Though the Pharisees and Herodians hated each other, yet they hated Jesus so much more that they could unite in their

ernor. 21 And they asked him, saying, Teacher, we know that thou sayest and teachest rightly, and acceptest not the person of *any*, but of a truth teachest the way of God: 2. Is it lawful for us to give tribute unto Cæsar, or not? 23 But he perceived their craftiness, and said unto them, 24 Show

opposition to him. They "sent forth spies," who hypocritically acted as though they were friends of Jesus; they desired in pretense to have a great regard for the law and to know how to reconcile their duties to it with respect to the Roman government. They sought by the expression of a single word to get something against Jesus that they might involve him in trouble with the Roman authorities.

21, 22 **And they asked him, saying, Teacher,**—They affirm here what is true, but they do so hypocritically. Nicodemus used about the same speech, but he was sincere. They came to Jesus not as Pharisees, or Herodians, but just as honest searchers for the truth, hoping by their words to hide their character and purpose, and by flattering Jesus to put him off his guard and lead him into a snare that they had set for him. They pretended to believe him to be all that he claimed and to be ready to abide by his decisions, since they would be absolutely true and just, independent of the influence and authority of men. They hypocritically acknowledged his doctrine to be true and righteous; to encourage him, as they thought, to give a decision that would incriminate him before the Roman authorities, that he would render such a decision without respect of persons; they thus attempted to encourage him to give the very decision that they wanted him to give, which they thought would incriminate him before the Roman authorities. Their question was artfully, skillfully, and adroitly framed: "Is it lawful for us to give tribute unto Caesar, or not?" Mark adds: "Shall we give, or shall we not give?" (Mark 12: 14.)

23 **But he perceived their craftiness,**—They thought that they had Jesus in a dilemma; it matters not which horn of it he should take; they thought they would condemn him. If he said that they should pay tribute to Caesar, he would render himself unpopular with the people. This was what the Jews

me a ⁴denarius. Whose image and superscription hath it? And they said,
Cæsar's. 25 And he said unto them, Then render unto Cæsar the things
that are Cæsar's, and unto God the things that are God's. 26 And they

---

⁴See marginal note on ch. 7.41

---

wanted; they wanted to turn the people against him so that it
would be easier for them to condemn him. If he said that
they should not pay tribute to Caesar, they would condemn
him for being in rebellion against the Roman authorities; and
they were anxious to have the Roman authorities condemn
him and put him to death. Jesus perceived their "craftiness."
He knew the thoughts and intentions of their hearts. The
original for "craftiness" means "any deed done in wickedness." The Greek, so translated, is found only five times in
the New Testament; it is the same word that is used in describing Satan's "subtlety" in tempting Eve. (2 Cor.11 : 3.)

24 **Show me a denarius.**—This was a Roman silver coin,
worth about fifteen to seventeen cents. The Jews had a
maxim that "wherever a king's coin is current, there his sovereignty is acknowledged." This coin was evidence of the
Roman dominion over the land, and by using it the Jews acknowledged their subjection to the Roman power. When he
received the "denarius" he asked: "Whose image and superscription hath it?" The "image" was probably the likeness of
the Roman emperor, Tiberius Caesar; the "superscription"
was the motto of the coin, the title of the emperor declarative
of his sovereignty. The image showed that it was not a Jewish coin, for the Jews put no images on their coins; they did
put inscriptions on them.

25 **And he said unto them, Then render unto Caesar the
things**—They had correctly answered his question about the
image and the superscription on the denarius. He then made
this reply to them. "Render unto Caesar" means "pay off," or
"render a gift," or "render what is due." If they had Caesar's
coin in circulation, they should render unto Caesar that which
belonged to him. No one could dispute what he had said; everyone should give to the government under which he serves
that which is justly due it. Sometimes governments claim of

were not able to take hold of the saying before the people: and they marvelled at his answer, and held their peace.

their citizens that which is not right; in such a case as this,
the citizen does not owe the government that which is wrong.
It is a common principle of honesty to give all their dues and
no one can dispute this; so they should give unto Caesar the
things which are Caesar's. This principle was expanded in
Rom. 13: 1-7. The Jews even taught that a king ought to
have his dues. The second part of the answer was that they
should render unto "God the things that are God's."

26 **And they were not able to take hold**—They were unable
to pervert his language and do damage against him at any
time. They were astonished and "marvelled at his answer,"
but they held their peace. His reply was so unexpected, so
apt, so true, and so wise that they were caught in a snare—the
one that they had thought to impose upon Jesus. He completely put them to silence; they "held their peace" and "left
him, and went away." (Matt. 22: 22.)

5. QUESTION AS TO THE RESURRECTION
20: 27-40

27 And there came to him certain of the Sadducees, they that say that

27 **And there came to him certain of the Sadducees,**—Parallel records of this are found in Matt. 22: 23-33 and Mark 12:
18-27. There is but little difference in the three records of
this event. The Pharisees and Herodians had tried their hand
to ensnare Jesus, but had been defeated and humiliated before
the public. We should not lose sight of the fact that we are
now in the midst of the last week of the earthly life of Jesus.
The Sadducees now make an attack on him. The Sadducees
were a Jewish sect, and were so called either from "righteousness," the meaning of the name "Zadok," or from their great
zeal for righteousness. This sect originated about 260 B.C.
They were opposed to the Pharisees and rejected the traditions which the Pharisees promoted; they denied the resurrection and the existence of angels or spirits. (Acts 23: 8.)

there is no resurrection; 28 and they asked him, saying, Teacher, ⁵Moses
wrote unto us, that if a man's brother die, having a wife, and he be childless,
his brother should take the wife, and raise up seed unto his brother. 29
There were therefore seven brethren: and the first took a wife, and died
childless; 30 and the second: 31 and the third took her; and likewise the
seven also left no children, and died. 32 Afterward the woman also died. 33

⁵Dt. 25.5

They laid stress on the freedom of the will. As a sect they
disappeared from history after the first century; they were
men of rank, wealth, and education; the priestly families in
the days of Jesus belonged to the Sadducees. They had one
great argument with which they had frequently defeated the
Pharisees; it was a stock conundrum with which they had
often gotten a laugh on the Pharisees. They volunteered to
try it on Jesus.

28 **and they asked him, saying,**—They approached Jesus
with an apparent regard as a prophet or religious teacher;
they also approached him with an air of great respect for the
law of Moses. They presented him their problem based on
Deut. 25: 5-10. The case that they cited required a brother to
take his deceased brother's wife and raise a son unto his
brother that his brother's name might not perish in the genealogy. The Sadducees thought to show from the law the
manifest absurdity of the doctrine of the resurrection, because
they presumed that the present relations of life must continue
in the future state.

29-31 **There were therefore seven brethren:**—It is very
likely that this was a fictitious case; it was a favorite argument of the Pharisees with the Sadducees, and illustrates the
manner of their opposition to the resurrection. The first born
of the wife of the deceased brother was to perpetuate the
name, provided the first born was a son. The Sadducees present this case as an actual fact, for they said: "Now there
were with us seven brethren" (Matt. 22: 25), which presents
the case as an actual fact. The number of brethren who had
the same woman as a wife presented a very complex problem
so the Sadducees thought; the Pharisees were not able to
meet the argument. While it may have been a fictitious case,

In the resurrection therefore whose wife of them shall she be? for the seven
had her to wife. 34 And Jesus said unto them, The sons of this [a]world
marry, and are given in marriage: 35 but they that are accounted worthy to
attain to that [a]world, and the resurrection from the dead, neither marry, nor
are given in marriage: 36 for neither can they die any more: for they are

[a]Or, *age*

all grant the possibility of such a thing happening, but the im-
probability of it is very evident.

32, 33 **Afterward the woman also died.**—There was no sur-
viving husband and the wife died. The woman had married,
according to supposition, successively to seven brothers, from
each of whom she was separated by death. The Sadducees
thought that Jesus would either deny the belief as to the resurrection, or that he would make some statement contrary to
the law of Moses. If he denied the resurrection, he would
incur the enmity of the Pharisees, who believe in the resurrection; if he denied the law of Moses or contradicted it, he
would be condemned for perverting the holy law. They did
not care which Jesus did; they were only seeking an opportunity to condemn him. Whose wife would she be in the resurrection? The problem was squarely put to Jesus, and from
their point of view, there was no escape for him. But they
did not know Jesus of Nazareth.

34, 35 **And Jesus said unto them,**—Both Matthew and Mark
preface Jesus' reply by: "Ye do err, not knowing the scriptures, nor the power of God." (Matt. 22: 29.) "The sons of
this world" marry and are given in marriage; "sons of this
world" simply means the present state of being as confined to
mortals; the expression simply means that in this life the marriage relation obtains. In the future life, or life after death,
there are no regulations of sex. Sex belongs to this fleshly
state, and ceases when the fleshly state ceases. Sex belongs
to this physical body and was ordained to perpetuate the
physical existence. Marriage belongs to the physical existence, or to the physical body for the procreation of the animal
part of man; but when the earthly existence and the fleshly
body shall have ceased, marriage will have ceased as all the
physical elements of marriage have ceased. In the future ex-

equal unto the angels; and are sons of God, being sons of the resurrection.
37 But that the dead are raised, even Moses showed, in '*the place concerning*
the Bush, when he calleth the Lord the God of Abraham, and the God of
Isaac, and the God of Jacob. 38 Now he is not the God of the dead, but of
the liviig: for all live unto him. 39 And certain of the scribes answering

7Ex. 3.6

istence those who have attained unto the resurrection of the
dead "neither marry, nor are given in marriage"—there is no
such thing as marriage after death.

36 **for neither can they die any more:**—After the resurrection there is no death, hence no need of procreation. Here we
die physically, and the human race would soon become extinct
if there was no generation going on to perpetuate the race;
but in the future state where there is no death there is no
need of marriage to perpetuate the beings there. "They are
equal unto the angels"; that is, angels do not die; they have
an eternal existence; so after the resurrection we have an
eternal existence, and in that sense, we are equal to the angels.
The existence, relations, and state are equal to that of the angels. In the resurrection there is not an earthly state which is
sensual and mortal, but heavenly, spiritual, and immortal.
They are "sons of God," which means that they share in the
resurrection of the just, and are in possession of a new life. It
is evident here that Jesus is speaking only of the resurrection
of the just; the resurrection of the wicked does not come into
view here.

37, 38 **But that the dead are raised,**—Jesus gives an invinci-
ble argument for the resurrection; he holds that the words
spoken to Moses concerning the burning bush (Ex. 3:6) prove
the fact of a resurrection. Jesus meets the error of the Sadducees fundamentally; he strikes at the very mistake on which
their error is founded. These Sadducees were "materialists";
they held that man was no more than an animal; that death
ended all of men. They based their argument against the resurrection on the ground that man has no spirit, and, therefore,
no life after the death of his body. Matthew puts this argument in an interrogative form: "Have ye not read that which
was spoken unto you by God, saying, I am the God of Abra-

said, Teacher, thou hast well said. 40 For they durst not any more ask him
any question.

---

ham, and the God of Isaac, and the God of Jacob?"
(Matt. 22: 31, 32.) Jesus in commenting on this says that
God is not "the God of the dead, but of the living." This
shows that Abraham, Isaac, and Jacob were still in existence;
they were dead physically, but their personality and identity
continued; hence there is a life after death, and if a life after
death, there is a resurrection.

39, 40 And certain of the scribes answering said,—The
scribes belonged to the Pharisees; they enjoyed seeing Jesus
put the Sadducees to silence, for they had often encountered
their error, and apparently had never been able to refute it so
successfully. They complimented Jesus for having answered
well, and thought it wise for themselves to ask him no more
questions. The courage of the Pharisees, Herodians, and Sadducees now vanished; they will now have to follow some
other course in order to destroy Jesus.

6. A QUESTION AND A WARNING
20: 41-47

41 And he said unto them, How say they that the Christ is David's son?

---

41 **And he said unto them, How say they**—Parallel records
of this are found in Matt. 22: 41-46; 23: 1-13; Mark 12: 35-40.
The Pharisees, Herodians, and Sadducees had been plying
questions to Jesus, attempting to ensnare him; they had been
unsuccessful. Jesus had put them to silence and they thought
it wise not to ask him any more questions. Jesus now puts a
question to them; he turns the tables on them. He asked
them: "How say they that the Christ is David's son?" Matthew
gives a fuller record and says: "What think ye of the Christ?
whose son is he?" (Matt. 22: 42.) They answered that he
was "the son of David." And Jesus then put another question
to them and asked how then could David call him Lord, if he
was the son of David. They were not able to answer him.

42 For David himself saith in the book of Psalms,
  ⁸The Lord said unto my Lord,
  Sit thou on my right hand,
  Till I make thine enemies the footstool of thy feet.
44 David therefore calleth him Lord, and how is he his son?
45 And in the hearing of all the people he said unto his disciples, 46 Beware of the scribes, who desire to walk in long robes, and love salutations in the marketplaces, and chief seats in the synagogues, and chief places at

⁸Ps. 110.1

42, 44 **For David himself saith**—Jesus now quotes Psalm 110: 1 and makes three points in his argument. First, all the prophets hold that the Messiah is to be in the line of David. (2 Sam. 7: 12-29; Isa. 11: 1-10; 55: 3, 4; Jer. 30: 9; Ezek. 34: 23, 24; 37: 24; Hos. 3: 5; Luke 1: 69; Rev. 22: 16.) Second, David himself calls this Messiah "Lord" in the passage here quoted from Psalm 110: 1. Third, "Lord" is a title of dignity, superiority, used appropriately by a son of his father, but never by the father of his son. How then is this enigma to be solved—that a father speaks of his son as his Lord? What sort of son must this be? All Jews held David in high honor, but what of this yet greater Son? The Jews referred this quotation to the Messiah, yet they could not tell how he could be a descendant of David, and yet be his Lord, not knowing that beside his human nature, which descended from David (Rev. 22: 16), he possessed a divine nature as the Son of God (Rom. 1: 3, 4). The deity and humanity of Jesus disturbed the Jews at that time and is still a matter of much discussion by critics today.

45, 46 **And in the hearing of all the people**—In the presence of all, while the people were listening, Jesus gave a warning to his disciples, saying: "Beware of the scribes." Matthew adds "and the Pharisees." (Matt. 23: 2.) Jesus then describes these scribes and Pharisees; he states their ruling passion, which was the love of display and honor "to be seen of men." (Matt. 23: 5.) The seven woes pronounced upon them, recorded in Matt. 23: 13-25, are among the most scathing denunciations that Jesus pronounced upon any class. They desired "to walk in long robes"; that is, to go about in long, flowing robes such as were worn by priests and kings and by persons of high rank and distinction. They loved "sal-

feasts; **47** who devour widows' houses, and for a pretence make long prayers: these shall receive greater condemnation.

utations in the marketplaces." They loved the complimentary salutations which were performed in a formal and ceremonious way. "The marketplaces" were the places to which people were accustomed to resort. They loved these public greetings in the public place; they were vain and haughty. "Chief seats in the synagogues" means the first seats nearest the reading desk where the sacred books were kept; and they occupied "chief places at feasts."

47 who devour widows' houses,—They were like cunning, ferocious beasts; they devoured the substance of widows who were the most defenseless of the poor and the most deserving of sympathy and kindness. They influenced widows to give them of their property as an act of piety, or to bequeath it to them. As spiritual advisers of men, and sometimes as the executors of their wills and the guardians of their children, they had special opportunities to rob widows of their property. "For a pretence make long prayers" is another characteristic of their hypocritical conduct. They made religion a mask in order to gain the confidence and property of even the most helpless. It is said that some of the rabbis would spend nine hours in prayer in a day. Jesus stated that "these shall receive greater condemnations."

7. THE WIDOW'S MITES
21: 1-4

1 And he looked up, and ⁿsaw the rich men that were casting their gifts

ⁿOr, *and saw them that . . . treasury, and they were rich*

1 And he looked up, and saw the rich men—A parallel record of this is found in Mark 12: 41-44. It seems that Jesus had taken his seat after the debate was over and his enemies had retreated; even his disciples were not very close to him. He had taken a position near the treasury, "over against the treasury." (Mark 12: 41.) The word for "treasury" is a compound in the original and means guard or protection. Jesus

into the treasury. 2 And he saw a certain poor widow casting in thither two mites. 3 And he said, Of a truth I say unto you, This poor widow cast in more than they all : ⁴for all these did of their superfluity cast in unto the gifts ; but she of her want did cast in all the living that she had.

---

was observing, according to Mark, the rich who put in their gifts. This was the last occurrence in the public ministry of Jesus except the trial and crucifixion; this is his last appearance in the temple. His public teaching is over except the few sentences of his defense in his trial and the seven statements that he uttered on the cross. The Pharisees and Sadducees had been defeated and had withdrawn from the scene, and even the disciples were at some distance as Jesus sat alone by the treasury.

2 And he saw a certain poor widow—As Jesus sat there and observed the rich "cast money into the treasury," there came a "certain poor widow casting in thither two mites." "Mite" was the smallest coin in circulation during the ministry of Jesus; its value has been variously estimated from one-eighth to one-fifth of a cent. Mark says: "There came a poor widow, and she cast in two mites, which make a farthing." (Mark 12: 42.) The value of the "two mites" was estimated at less than half a cent in our money. The coin was bronze.

3, 4 And he said, Of a truth I say unto you,—Mark records that Jesus "called unto him his disciples" (Mark 12: 43), and said: "This poor widow cast in more than they all." He compares or contrasts what the widow cast in with, not what one rich man cast in, but with what all the rich men cast in. Her contribution is thus contrasted with the sum total of the contributions of all who contributed on that occasion. Jesus knew how to evaluate gifts and he evaluated her gift as being "more than all they that are casting into the treasury." He tells the ground or basis of his evaluation; they cast in "of their superfluity," but "she of her want did cast in all the living that she had." Of their abundance they contributed a little, but of her meager and scant supply, she gave all. Hers was real self-denial; she felt what she gave; in love she devoted *all* to God, and trusted in his providential care.

8. DESTRUCTION OF JERUSALEM; THE COMING
OF CHRIST
21 : 5-38

5 And as some spake of the temple, how it was adorned with goodly
stones and offerings, he said, 6 As for these things which ye behold, the

Jesus foretells the destruction of Jerusalem, the persecution
of his disciples, and his second coming. Parallel records are
found in Matt. 24: 1-51 and Mark 13: 1-37. We have here a
remarkable prophetic discourse of Jesus, which has been variously interpreted and explained; it has been considered one of
the most important and difficult discourses recorded of Jesus.
It is given most fully in Matthew; verses 5 and 6 were spoken
as he was leaving the temple; the remainder of the discourse
was spoken as he sat upon the Mount of Olives over against
the city and temple. Between the incident of the widow's
casting in her two mites, and his leaving the temple, we are to
place what is related in John 12: 20-50. This discourse is the
background of the death of Jesus; the destruction of Jerusalem is recorded as punishment in part of the crucifixion of
Christ. This catastrophe is itself a symbol of the punishment
of the world at the second coming of Christ. Jesus predicts
his own second coming. The various aspects of this discourse
should be noticed as it is studied.

5, 6 **And as some spake of the temple,**—These verses were
spoken as Jesus left the temple. Some of the disciples observed the adornment of the temple "with goodly stones and
offerings." Mark tells us that this remark was made by one
of his disciples as Jesus went out of the temple. (Mark 13:
1.) "Goodly stones" has reference to the arches of the bridge
which spanned the valley of Tyropoeon, and connected the ancient city of David with the royal porch of the temple, and
measured twenty-four feet in length by six in thickness; these
were not the largest in the masonry of the temple; both the
southeastern and southwestern angle stones have been found
measuring from twenty to forty feet long and weighing more
than one hundred tons. Jesus replied that the days would
come when "there shall not be left here one stone upon an-

days will come, in which there shall not be left here one stone upon another, that shall not be thrown down. 7 And they asked him, saying, Teacher, when therefore shall these things be? and what *shall be* the sign when these things are about to come to pass? 8 And he said, Take heed that ye be not

other, that shall not be thrown down." This prediction of Jesus was literally fulfilled about forty years afterward, A.D. 70, when Titus, a Roman officer, destroyed Jerusalem. Josephus relates that Titus gave orders to demolish the entire city and temple except three towers and part of the western wall. The rest of the wall was laid so completely even with the ground by those who dug it up from the foundation that there was nothing left to make those believe that came thither that it had ever been inhabited. It is recorded that after the destruction by Titus, Terentius Rufus, an officer in the army of Titus, ordered the site of the temple to be furrowed with a plowshare, thus nothing was left but parts of the massive foundations which still remained. (Jer. 26: 18; Mic. 3: 12.)

7 **And they asked him, saying, Teacher,**—There are two questions asked here by the disciples, namely: "When therefore shall these things be?" and "What shall be the sign when these things are about to come to pass?" The first question is the same in all three of the records, but the second question is different in Matthew's record. Matthew records the second as: "What shall be the sign of thy coming, and of the end of the world?" Evidently Luke and Mark mean the same thing as the question recorded by Matthew; hence, the second coming of Christ and the destruction or "end of the world" mean the same thing. Mark records that Peter, James, John, and Andrew "asked him privately" (Mark 13: 3, 4) about these things. Obviously the rest of the twelve came after them and heard the discourse; or it may be that these four disciples asked for themselves and the rest of the apostles. "These things" mean the destruction of the temple, the judgment of God upon Jerusalem, and upon the Jews. "What shall be the sign?" If the temple was to be destroyed, they should naturally expect his coming immediately when, after destroyng his enemies, he should establish his kingdom. (Matt. 24: 21; Acts 1: 6.) such terrible events as Jesus predicted naturally

led astray: for many shall come in my name, saying, I am *he;* and, The time
is at hand: go ye not after them. 9 And when ye shall hear of wars and
tumults, be not terrified: for these things must needs come to pass first; but
the end is not immediately.

10 Then said he unto them, Nation shall rise against nation, and kingdom

---

aroused their desire to know definitely more about it; hence,
they ask for the *time* and the *sign* of "all these things." The
two questions should be kept in mind as the discourse is studied and the answer to each question should be clear to the stu-
dent.

8, 9 **And he said, Take heed that ye be not led astray:**—At
first Jesus gives a warning to his disciples; they should "take
heed" that they be not led astray. There would arise different
ones claiming to be the Messiah or representing the Messiah
who would lead them astray. There were many such; Josephus, a Jewish historian, not converted to Christianity, but an
eyewitness of the calamities of the destruction of Jerusalem,
gives in minute detail the wonderful fulfillment of this prediction. He speaks of the country being overrun with magicians,
seducers, and impostors, who drew the people after them into
the wilderness, promising to show them signs and wonders;
thus Theudas, not the one mentioned in Acts 5: 36, but a later
one, persuaded a large body of people to follow him to the
Jordan, promising to divide the river as Elijah and Elisha had
done. However, he was captured and taken prisoner before
he arrived at the Jordan and was beheaded. An Egyptian also
pretended to be a prophet (Acts 21: 38) and deluded thirty
thousand men. After the destruction of Jerusalem Bar-
Cocheba and Jonathan appeared; in almost every age there
have been false Christs. Jesus further warns them that when
they heard "of wars and tumults," they should not be de-
ceived or terrified; all these things must come to pass, "but
the end is not immediately." Every generation has known of
wars and rumors of wars; some have been terrified by them
and some have supposed that these wars were signs of the
second coming of Christ.

10, 11 **Then said he unto them, Nation shall rise**—It seems
that the prophecy beginning with verse 10 and concluding

against kingdom; 11 and there shall be great earthquakes, and in divers places famines and pestilences; and there shall be terrors and great signs from heaven. 12 But before all these things, they shall lay their hands on you, and shall persecute you, delivering you up to the synagogues and prisons, ¹bringing you before kings and governors for my name's sake. 13 It

¹Gr. you *being brought*

with verse 19 admits of a double interpretation; primarily it applies to the wars connected with the destruction of Jerusalem, and the afflictions of Christians after the death of Jesus; secondarily; it applies to the times immediately preceding the destruction of the world. "Nation shall rise against nation"; that is, race against race and kingdom against kingdom. In verse 9 Jesus had said: "Ye shall hear of wars," but now he states what will actually take place—a difference between the rumors that they shall hear and what shall occur. National struggles and political upheavals and revolutions shall take place. These shall be accompanied with physical catastrophes; "great earthquakes," "famines," and "pestilences" shall afflict the earth and its inhabitants. Historians speak of several famines in different parts of the world, one of which was very severe in Judea about A.D. 44 to 47. (Acts 11: 28.) "Pestilences" were common attendants of famines then as now. History records one at Rome in the autumn of A.D. 65, which carried off thirty thousand persons.

12 **But before all these things,**—Before the things predicted in verses 10 and 11 occur, Jesus tells what will be done to his disciples. "They shall lay their hands on you," "shall persecute you," "delivering you up to the synagogues," and bringing them into the civil courts because of their faithfulness to their Lord. They should be persecuted in the ecclesiastical courts of the Jews and the civil courts of the Romans. All of these persecutions should be prompted and encouraged by the Jews, and the motive that prompted the persecutions would be because of Christ. The context seems to limit the persecutions mentioned here between the ascension of Christ and the destruction of Jerusalem. The Acts of the Apostles records a number of these persecutions. (Acts 4: 3; 5: 27; 22: 19, 25: 23; 26: 10.)

shall turn out unto you for a testimony. 14 Settle it therefore in your hearts, not to meditate beforehand how to answer: 15 for I will give you a mouth and wisdom, which all your adversaries shall not be able to withstand or to gainsay. 16 But ye shall be [2]delivered up even by parents, and brethren, and kinsfolk, and friends: and *some* of you [3]shall they cause to be put to

[2]Or, *betrayed*
[3]Or, *shall they put to death*

---

13 **It shall turn out unto you**—It will come off, turn out for you, seems to be the meaning here. It would give an opportunity for them to bear testimony of Jesus; an opportunity would be given them to preach the gospel to persons who would not otherwise listen to them. Paul before Agrippa and other Roman officials is an example of this. Jesus means here that the harm which the enemies would seek to do his disciples should be overruled and prove to be an advantage to his cause and kingdom; they would prove the sincerity of his disciples, purify their lives, and make of them more efficient witnesses for him.

14, 15 **Settle it therefore in your hearts,**—This was spoken to encourage Christians while they are persecuted; the disciples were to resolve to endure the persecution without faltering. They need not "meditate beforehand" how they should answer their enemies; they need not give attention to their defense; they need not be concerned about the outcome of the persecution. All these things would be taken care of in due time. The very answer which they should make would be given them. "I will give you a mouth and wisdom" is the promise that Jesus made to his disciples at this time. Their answer when given would be complete, and would be such that their adversaries would not be able to "withstand or to gainsay" it. This should be a great encouragement to his disciples; it was demonstrated in the case of Stephen, who so reputed his enemies that "they were not able to withstand the wisdom and the Spirit by which he spake." (Acts 6: 10.)

16 **But ye shall be delivered up even by parents,**—We have no case on record in the Acts illustrating this; however, the early Christians suffered all sorts of betrayals and persecution. There were cases of betrayal in families; Tacitus reports that in the persecution under Nero many were convicted by testi-

death. 17 And ye shall be hated of all men for my name's sake. 18 And not
a hair of your head shall perish. 19 In your ⁴patience ye shall win your
⁵souls.

⁴Or, *stedfastness*
⁵Or, *lives*

money of persons from among themselves. Jesus had said:
"Think not that I came to send peace on the earth: I came not
to send peace, but a sword."

17, 18 And ye shall be hated of all men—The disciples of
Jesus were not popular with the world; they were to be hated
by the world. Jesus said of his disciples: "I have given them
thy word; and the world hated them, because they are not of
the world, even as I am not of the world." (John 17: 14.)
Again he had said: "If the world hateth you, ye know that it
hath hated me before it hated you." (John 15: 18.) The
early history of the church as given in the Acts bears witness
that the disciples of Jesus were "hated of all men." "For as
concerning this sect, it is known to us that everywhere it is
spoken against." (Acts 28: 22.) Christians have been persecuted and hated far beyond the persecution heaped against
any other religion. (1 Pet. 2: 12; 3: 16; 4: 14.) They were to
be hated "for my name's sake." We see here the reason of
Christians being so universally hated, not only in every age,
but also in the apostolic age. God is a jealous God, and
Christ is a jealous Savior; all other religions are wrong;
Christianity opposes all sects and parties in religion; hence, it
incurs the enmity of all these. Christianity will not share
with any other religion; other religions will share with each
other, and at times persecute each other, but finally they will
all unite in their opposition to Christianity. "And not a hair
of your head shall perish."

19 In your patience ye shall win your souls.—Even if death
should come, or if they should be put to death, in their patience they would sin their souls. The word "patience" may
be rendered "perseverance." It is expressed by Matthew and
Mark in this way: "But he that endureth to the end, the same
shall be saved." (Matt. 24: 13; Mark 13: 13.) By their endurance they should preserve their souls; it has been applied

20 But when ye see Jerusalem compassed with armies, then know that her desolation is at hand. 21 Then let them that are in Judæa flee unto the mountains; and let them that are in the midst of her depart out; and let not them that are in the country enter therein. 2. For these are days of vengeance, that all things which are written may be fulfilled. 23 Woe unto them that are with child and to them that give suck in those days! for there

to Christians during the destruction of Jerusalem, for it is claimed that no Christian perished at that time.

20 **But when ye see Jerusalem compassed**—It is reported that Christians fled from Jerusalem to Pella before it was too late; they followed the instructions of Jesus as here recorded. Here is a sign for them as they had requested in verse 7. Just so sure as Jerusalem would be encompassed with armies, just so sure would she be destroyed. It is a matter of history that the Roman army first under Cestius Gallus besieged Jerusalem about A.D 66, and then withdrew from it; again, the city was besieged by Vespasian about A.D. 68; the devastation continued until the final overthrow and destruction by Titus in A.D. 70. The disciples were to know that when the city was compassed with armies that meant that it would be destroyed; hence, as they believed the words of the Savior, Christians were prepared and escaped from the city.

21 **Then let them that are in Judaea flee**—Palestine during the personal ministry of Christ was divided into three divisions—Judea on the south, Samaria just north of Judea, and Galilee north of Samaria. When the disciples were to know that the destruction of Jerusalem was at hand, those in the country, towns, and cities of Judea were to flee to the "mountains," where there were caves affording a safe retreat. For some cause unknown now to historians, the Roman general, Cestius Gallus, after taking a portion of Jerusalem, withdrew without capturing the entire city; this gave the Christians an opportunity to escape; the same warning was given to those who were in the country—they were not to go into the city.

23 **Woe unto them that are with child**—There is an exclamation of pity expressed for mothers and prospective mothers; these would not be in condition to flee or to endure the hardships of the siege. Josephus relates that the houses at the siege of Jerusalem were full of women and children

shall be great distress upon the ⁰land, and wrath unto this people. 24 And they shall fall by the edge of the sword, and shall be led captive into all the nations : and Jerusalem shall be trodden down of the Gentiles, until the times of the Gentiles be fulfilled.

⁰Or, *earth*

who perished in the famine; mothers snatch the food out of their infants' mouths; and Mary, daughter of Eleazer, of a rich and illustrious family, boiled her child and ate him. The miseries of women in the siege of Jerusalem are probably foretold in Deut. 28: 56, 57. Vengeance and wrath referred to here is the divine vindication which had been foretold.

24 And they shall fall by the edge of the sword,—The fearful punishment inflicted by the enemy on the inhababitants of Jerusalem is here minutely described. According to Josephus eleven hundred thousand perished during the siege at Jerusalem by the sword, pestilence, and famine. The city was full of people attending the Passover festival when the last siege of Titus commenced; thousands had come from remote parts of the earth, not only to attend the festival, but to assist in the defense of their religion, country, liberties, city and temple; ninety thousand were taken prisoners and sold into perpetual bondage; during this time nearly three hundred thousand Jews perished elsewhere, in addition to a vast multitude who died in caves, woods, common sewers, banishment, and various ways, of whom no computation could be made. Some suppose that Josephus greatly exaggerated the number of sufferers; Tacitus gives six hundred thousand as the number within the city at the time of the siege.

"Jerusalem shall be trodden down of the Gentiles." Jerusalem was captured again about A.D. 135 in consequence of an insurrection, which brought most terrible sufferings upon the Jews, who were utterly driven out from the land of their fathers. Judea was sold by Vespasian, and Jerusalem has been successively under the dominions of the Romans, Saracens, Franks, Mamelukes, and Turks. A temple of Jupiter was erected on the site of the temple; afterwards, A.D 635, the mosque of Omar was built upon the same site. The distress of the Jews still continues, and Jerusalem is still

25 And there shall be signs in sun and moon and stars; and upon the
earth distress of nations, in perplexity for the roaring of the sea and the bil-
lows; 26 men ⁷fainting for fear, and for expectation of the things which are
coming on ⁸the world: for the powers of the heavens shall be shaken. 27

⁷Or, *expiring*
⁸Gr. *the inhabited earth*

---

trodden under foot by the Gentiles. "Until the times of the
Gentiles be fulfilled" has been variously interpreted. Some
think that Jerusalem will be desolate until it is rescued from
the Gentiles by the Jews; others think that it will continue as
it now is until all the Jews are converted; still others think
that it means that the Gentiles will control it until Christ
comes again. It is observed here that the learned and pious
have differed widely in their views, and perhaps it is wise not
to speak too positively about the fulfillment of obscure prophecies. Those who find here a plain prophecy that Jerusalem will be rebuilt during a millennium, and then be reoccu-
pied by the Jews, and have Christ come and occupy the literal
throne and reign over the Jews in Jerusalem, have great difficulty in proving their interpretation to be the correct one.

25, 26 **And there shall be signs in sun and moon and stars;**
—As here observed this great prophetic discourse of Jesus is
adorned with figurative language and symbolic terms.
Whatever else the language may teach, we do know that it
means that great calamities and revolutions among the nations of earth will occur. It is difficult to determine how
much of this may be taken literally; it is best to take this language of Jesus literally unless there is some just grounds for
regarding it figuratively. There are to be terrific phenomena
and changes in nature; just when these would take place is
not clear. Some think that they occurred immediately after the
Jewish people were destroyed at the destruction of Jerusalem;
there were, during the crucifixion of Jesus, some great catastrophes; the powers and forces of nature, the elements of the
heavens, were agitated and convulsed like the waves of the
sea. It seems there will be a repetition of these at the end of
the world when Christ shall appear in his glory. (2 Pet. 3:
12; Rev. 21: 1.) Fear and distress and trembling shall take

And then shall they see the Son of man coming in a cloud with power and great glory. 28 But when these things begin to come to pass, look up, and lift up your heads; because your redemption draweth nigh.

29 And he spake to them a parable: Behold the fig tree, and all the trees: 30 when they now shoot forth, ye see it and know of your own selves that

possession of the stoutest as they realize the symptoms of approaching dissolutions. The powers and the forces of nature, the elements of the heavens, shall be shaken, agitated, and convulsed. (Heb. 12: 26.)

27, 28 And then shall they see the Son of man coming—It seems clear that Jesus here has reference to his second coming. The coming of Christ is frequently spoken of as actual and visible. (Acts 1: 9, 11; 1 Thess. 4: 16; 2 Thess. 1: 8; 2 Pet. 3: 10, 12; Jude 14; Rev. 1: 7.) Jesus is frequently represented as coming in a cloud and great glory; he ascended back to heaven in a cloud (Acts 1: 9), and he will return in a cloud with power and great glory. At this time when others will be terrified the disciples should "look up" and not be disturbed, but be encouraged; the disciples of the Lord should turn themselves to face the Lord and greet him as a Friend and Deliverer. The disciples should know at that time that their "redemption draweth nigh." Their redemption and complete deliverance is just at hand; they will have waited long and patiently; now they are to greet the glorified Lord as he comes to elevate them to glory unspeakable. "Redemption" is here used in the same sense as in Rom. 8: 23; Eph. 1: 14; 4: 30. It signifies that full and complete redemption of the believer which will be accomplished at the resurrection.

29, 30 And he spake to them a parable:—Matthew and Mark say: "Now from the fig tree learn her parable." (Matt. 24: 32; Mark 13: 28.) Jesus means to say that they can learn what he has said from the fig tree; that it represents or illustrates the circumstances and signs preceding these great events; he simply says learn the illustration which the fig tree affords. Jesus and his disciples were on the Mount of Olives, where there were many fig trees; it was convenient and apt for Jesus to point to the fig tree and illustrate what he was saying. They knew enough about nature to know that when

the summer is now nigh. 31 Even so ye also, when ye see these things coming to pass, know ye that the kingdom of God is nigh. 32 Verily I say unto you, This generation shall not pass away, till all things be accomplished. 33 Heaven and earth shall pass away : but my words shall not pass away.

34 But take heed to yourselves, lest haply your hearts be overcharged with surfeiting, and drunkenness, and cares of this life, and that day come on you

---

this tree put forth its buds and foliage summer was near; this was a simple and direct prophecy and pledge of summer; so when they saw these signs that he had mentioned, they would know that the end was near.

31 **Even so ye also, when ye see these things**—Jesus makes his own application of the parable; as they know that summer is nigh by observing the leaves on the fig tree, so they know that the "kingdom of God is nigh" when they see the signs which he has mentioned.

32, 33 **Verily I say unto you, This generation shall not pass** —Many of the things which Jesus had mentioned would occur before that generation should pass. This shows that much that he had said belonged to the destruction of Jerusalem. The word of God as expressed by the prophets and by Jesus himself must be fulfilled; "all things" must be accomplished; the word of God should not pass away until everything has been accomplished. The heavens and the earth were generally regarded as firm and unchangeable (Psalm 89: 37; Jer. 33: 25), but these should pass away before the word of God should pass; this was another way of saying that the word of God would not pass or fail in anything. The word of God is more certain than the established order of nature. (Isa. 40: 8; 51 : 6; 1 Pet. 1 : 24, 25.)

34, 35 **lest haply your hearts be overcharged**—Jesus now warns his disciples that they be found faithful; their salvation, as does our salvation, depended upon their remaining faithful. The important thing that Jesus makes clear here is that his disciples be on their guard when the fulfillment of his prediction takes place. They should not eat to gluttony, drink to drunkenness, and sleep to stupidity; the cares of this life should not so engross their attention that they would not be ready. Jerusalem would be besieged and a great number

suddenly as a snare: 35 for *so* shall it come upon all them that dwell on the face of all the earth. 36 But watch ye at every season, making supplication, that ye may prevail to escape all these things that shall come to pass, and to stand before the Son of man.

---

would be destroyed; drunkenness would prevent their being watchful and being ready; they are to be alert to all dangers. The Lord has promised to take care of his own, but they must do their part in avoiding all unnecessary things and be alert to detect quickly any danger. The suddenness of that time would come upon them like a snare. "Surfeiting" is a word common in the vocabulary of medical writers for the nausea that follows a debauch. "Drunkenness" in the original is from the word "methu," which means wine, and is used in the New Testament only here and Rom. 13: 13 and Gal. 5: 21. "Cares of this life" means the anxieties of life, while "as a snare" means to make fast as a net or trap; Paul uses this word several times in speaking of the devil's snares. (1 Tim. 3: 7; 2 Tim. 2: 26.) God's judgment comes unlooked for, "suddenly," as a trap or "snare" upon the careless.

36 But watch ye at every season,—In wisdom and mercy Jesus exhorts his disciples to "watch." "Watch" in the original means "to hunt"; the picture is of one in pursuit of sleep, and therefore wakeful, restless. Some translate it: "See! Wake ye and pray ye!" Keep awake and be ready is the admonition given by Jesus. "Making supplication" means to be praying; watchfulness without prayer is not sufficient; neither praying without watchfulness is sufficient. They are to watch and pray that they "may prevail to escape all these things that shall come to pass, and to stand before the Son of man." If the disciples of Jesus are watching and praying, they will be ready and will be able to stand with no fear before the Son of man. Those who were watching and praying escaped the destruction that came upon Jerusalem and were ready for service in the name of the Lord, and were approved by him for the most valiant service. Those who retained their faithfulness throughout the troublesome times were honored with exalted positions in the kingdom of God, which was established

37 And every day he was teaching in the temple; and every night he
went out, and lodged in the mount that is called Olivet. 38 And all the
people came early in the morning to him in the temple, to hear him.

---

on Pentecost, while the overthrow of the Jewish state met its
doom.

37, 38 **And every day he was teaching in the temple;**—This
does not mean that Jesus taught in the temple after the delivery of this discourse; it simply means that up till this time
that week, he had been teaching in the temple during the day
and retiring to the Mount of Olives at night. Luke sums up
the teaching of this day with the general statement of the pro-
gram that he followed. After teaching during the day he
went for rest at Bethany, which was less than two miles from
Jerusalem on the Mount of Olives. Matthew tells us that he
went to Bethany. (Matt. 21: 17.) Mark also records that he
went to Bethany. On the other days, Mark says: "Every evening," or whenever evening came, "he went forth out of the
city." (Mark 11: 19.) Some think that the Greek word for
"abode" or "lodged" here means primarily "lodge" in the open
air; hence the three nights of this week, Tuesday, Wednesday,
and Thursday, Jesus and his disciples may have "lodged" in
some place on the slope of Olivet, possibly in the Garden of
Gethsemane. Hence, Judas would know where to find him on
the night of the betrayal, for John says: "Jesus oft-times resorted thither with his disciples. " (John 18: 2.) It was not
unusual for people at that season of the year in that climate to
sleep out of doors wrapped in an outer cloak, as Jerusalem
and the villages near were crowded with people who had
come to attend the Feast of the Passover.

No satisfactory exposition of this great prophetic discourse
of Jesus as recorded by Luke can be given without a very
careful and thorough comparison of it with Matt. 24 and Mark
13; these chapters are essentially parallel with Luke 21, and
evidently are the same discourse, spoken on the same occasion,
and having the same questions calling forth the discourse.
The chief points of the report of the discourse given by Matthew, Mark, and Luke which are common may be summed up
as follows: (1) The occasion was the calling of Jesus' atten-

tion to the magnificent stones and gifts of the temple; (2) the reply of Jesus that the day would come when not one stone would be left upon another; (3) the earnest and prompt questions, involving two main points—*when?* and what are to be the *foregoing signs?* (4) All agree that this discourse was spoken *after* they had retired to the Mount of Olives, where they were in full view of the city and temple. (5) The three statements agree substantially in making up the first class of foregoing events—"Be not decieved," false Christs shall rise, rumors of war, actual wars, persecution of Christians. (6) A special sign is given, namely, Jerusalem encompassed and destroyed. (7) Each of the writers reports the parable of the fig tree to show that the signs were very soon to follow. (8) All three give admonition of constant watchfulness and being ready.

It seems clear that a correct interpretation of this discourse makes Jesus predict the fall of Jerusalem before the Roman army; this was consummated in A.D. 70. That event meets all the conditions of this prophecy most fully, entirely, and unquestionably unless it be the brief passages in Matt. 24: 29-31; Mark 13: 24-27; and Luke 21: 25-28. The difficulty here is pointed by these questions: Do these brief passages relate to the fall of Jerusalem or must they be referred to the coming of Christ and the final judgment? The language seems to clearly indicate that they refer to the second advent of Christ; they seem to say more than can be legitimately applied to the destruction of Jerusalem; their symbolic language is too emphatic and the points made are too far reaching to be exhausted in the scenes connected with the fall of Jerusalem. However, many commentators make them refer primarily to the destruction of Jerusalem. The reasons that they assign for this are as follows: (1) These passages stand precisely where we naturally look for an outbreak of vengeance upon the doomed city; (2) it is definitely said by Matthew (24: 29) that the scenes of these three verses follow *immediately after* the "tribulation" described in the previous verses; (3) all these events, not only those of the previous verses, but those portrayed in these identical verses (Matt. 24: 29-31). brought within the lifetime of *that generation*: (4) all is described as coming within the personal experience of the disciples of whom Jesus was then speaking; (5) all is illustrated by the parable of the fig tree, in which leaves and blossoms fore-shadow fruitage near at hand, showing that not merely some, but *all* of these events were to follow closely after the foregoing signs which he had fully described; (6) emphatic and strong as these symbols in this contested passage are, yet they present a very different scene from that of the final judgment; (7) the passage under special discussion in each of these three accounts is quite too closely connected both with what precedes and what immediately follows, to be wrested out of its context and referred to the final judgment, when all that precedes and what immediately follows must so manifestly and certainly refer to the fall of Jerusalem; (8) that two events so unlike as the fall of Jerusalem on the one hand and the final judgment on the other, and with all so remote from each other in time, should be purposely de-scribed by the same symbols and in the same words, cannot well be supposed rational or even possible.

SECTION SIX

BETRAYAL, ARREST, TRIALS, CRUCIFIXION
OF JESUS
22: 1 to 23: 56

1. THE TREACHERY OF JUDAS
22: 1-6

1 Now the feast of unleavened bread drew nigh, which is called the Passover. 2 And the chief priests and the scribes sought how they might put him to death; for they feared the people.

1 **Now the feast of unleavened bread drew high,**—Parallel records are found in Matt. 26: 1-5 and Mark 14: 1, 2. Luke states "'the feast of unleavened bread drew nigh"; Matthew and Mark record the fact that "after two days" the Passover cometh. Matthew does not speak of the "feast of unleavened bread," but only of the "passover"; Mark speaks of "the feast of the passover" and "the unleavened bread." The difference between Mark and Luke is that Luke makes the "feast of unleavened bread" "the passover," while Mark speaks of "the feast of the passover" and "the unleavened bread." In the Old Testament there were two feasts: the Passover, which came on the fourteenth day of the first month, and "the feast of unleavened bread," which began immediately after the Feast of the Passover and continued seven days. (Lev. 23: 5, 6; Num. 28: 16, 17.) Josephus made a distinction between these two feasts; but in later times they were regarded as one feast. The Passover came on the fourteenth day of the first month; at this feast they were to put away all leaven. The feast of unleavened bread began on the fifteenth day of the first month; hence one followed the other and later one name was applied to both feasts; sometimes "the feast of unleavened bread" included the Passover and sometimes "the passover" included the feast of unleavened bread.

2 **And the chief priests and the scribes**—Luke and Mark mention "the chief priests and the scribes," while Matthew mentions "the chief priests, and the elders of the people." (Matt. 26: 3.) Matthew states that they "were gathered to-

3 And Satan entered into Judas who was called Iscariot, being of the number of the twelve.

gether" "unto the court of the high priest, who was called Caiaphas." They took counsel "together that they might take Jesus by subtlety, and kill him." (Matt. 26: 4.) Jesus had predicted that "the Son of man must suffer many things, and be rejected of the elders and chief priests and scribes, and be killed, and the third day be raised up." (Luke 9: 22.) Since, according to Matthew, they assembled at the palace of the high priest, it seems very probable that the Sanhedrin held a brief session to determine what should be done. They had purposed to put him to death, but "they feared the people." Their problem was to put him to death without incurring the condemnation of the people; they did not want to put him to death on the feast day, for the popular feeling strongly supported Jesus, and the rulers feared a tumult of the people. They "sought"; that is, they were seeking the ways and means of destroying Jesus. "Sought" in the original is in the imperfect tense, "were seeking," and means contemporaneously with the approach of the feast. At this stage they planned to "take Jesus by subtlety, and kill him."

3 **And Satan entered into Judas**—Frequently "Satan" is called "the devil." This statement is peculiar to Luke. As the rulers were seeking an opportunity to destroy Jesus, it soon presented itself; it comes from Judas, who was one of the chosen apostles. He is called "Judas Iscariot" to distinguish him from other men of that name. Some think that he was a native of Karioth, a small town in the tribe of Judah. "Satan" means "adversary," the Old Testament name of the chief of fallen spirits; "devil" means "slanderer." Both names are descriptive of his character and work. He is known by the name Beelzebub, "prince of the demons" (Matt. 12: 24), "the prince of the powers of the air" (Eph. 2: 2), and "the old serpent, he that is called the Devil and Satan, the deceiver of the whole world" (Rev. 12: 9). It seems that Judas had taken offense at the rebuke of Jesus (John 12: 4-8), and he yielded to the temptation of the devil, who worked upon his avaricious disposition (John 12: 4-8). Judas being one of the

4 And he went away, and communed with the chief priests and captains, how he might ¹deliver him unto them. 5 And they were glad, and covenanted to give him money. 6 And he consented, and sought opportunity to ¹deliver him unto them ²in the absence of the multitude.

¹Or, betray
²Or, without tumult

---

twelve aggravates his crime and fulfills the prophecy in Psalm 41: 9.

4 And he went away, and communed with the chief priests and captains,—Judas went off under the impulse of Satan and after the indignation over the rebuke of Jesus at the feast in Simon's house to confer "with the chief priests and captains." It is thought that between this and the preceding section the supper at Bethany (Matt. 26: 6-13; Mark 14: 3-9; John 12: 2-8) occurred; this is the supper at which Judas with others murmured against the use of the expensive ointment and Jesus' rebuke to Judas and others. "The captains" were in charge of the temple. (Verse 52; Acts 4: 1.) It was the duty of the captains to maintain order in the temple; they were especially busy during the feasts when crowds would be present. Judas sought the captains and the chief priests to propose his plan for betraying Jesus secretly into their hands.

5 And they were glad,—The chief priests and captains were glad that one of the twelve had offered to betray Jesus into their hands. "Glad" with a hellish glee; they were pleased to know that one would assist them who could be of real help, but they must have had no respect for the traitor; they lost no time in completing the arrangements. They "covenanted to give him money"; Matthew says: "They weighed unto him thirty pieces of silver." (Matt. 26: 15.) Thirty shekels was the price of a slave (Ex. 21: 32); some think that this was a fulfillment of Zech. 11: 12. The "thirty pieces" was equal to about fifteen dollars in our money. If this was all that was paid, it shows the contempt of the chief priests for Jesus as well as the sordid meanness of Judas who betrayed his Lord for so small a sum.

6 And he consented, and sought opportunity—Judas agreed to the price that the chief priests offered. There were five steps in the corrupt bargain: (1) Judas sought the chief priests; (2) he offered to betray Jesus; (3) they gladly made a bargain with him for money; (4) Judas agreed to the bargain; (5) he sought to fulfill his wicked pledge. He knew, as did the chief priests, the popularity of Jesus, and he adroitly sought an occasion when the multitude could not be used to defend him against assault. Judas sought to keep his betrayal a secret, and the chief priests sought to do their dastardly deed "in the absence of the multitude"; they desired that a tumult of the people be avoided. It seems to have been a part of the bargain to work "under cover" or secretly.

2. THE LAST SUPPER
22: 7-23

7 And the day of unleavened bread came, on which the passover must be sacrificed. 8 And he sent Peter and John, saying, Go and make ready for us

7 **And the day of unleavened bread came,**—Parallel records of this are found in Matt. 26: 17-19 and Mark 14: 12-16. Some think that Jesus anticipated the Passover; that is, ate it the day before the regular time for it; however, Luke seems to make it clear that Jesus and his disciples ate the Passover at the regular time. The law required the sacrifice to be made upon that day "between the evenings" (Deut. 16: 5, 6) or "at the even." The Passover came on the fourteenth day of the first month, Nisan or Abib. (Ex. 12: 2; 13: 4.) This Jewish month corresponded to the last half of March and the first half of April. All leaven had to be removed from every Jewish house. The lamb was known as the paschal lamb; it had to be slain by the head of the family. (Ex. 12: 6.) The controversy about the day when Christ ate the last Passover meal has given much concern to many; however, there is no valid reason for concluding that there were any irregularities with Jesus and his disciples.

8 **And he sent Peter and John,**—Luke is the only one who names the disciples who prepared the Passover; they were to get the room, the lamb, the bitter herbs, the wine, and whatever else would be required. Mark 14: 13 has only "two" disciples, while Matt. 26: 17 makes the disciples take

the passover, that we may eat. 9 And they said unto him, Where wilt thou
that we make ready? 10 And he said unto them, Behold, when ye are entered into the city, there shall meet you a man bearing a pitcher of water;
follow him into the house whereinto he goeth. 11 And ye shall say unto the
master of the house, The Teacher saith unto thee, Where is the
guest-chamber, where I shall eat the passover with my disciples? 12 And he

---

the initiative. "The passover" as used here means either the
meal, the feast day, or the whole period of time, while "eat
the passover" refers to the meal as here or to the whole period
of celebration in John 18: 28. The task of making ready the
Passover was an important one; hence, Peter and John were
entrusted with that responsibility. They had to select the
room, search diligently and remove all leaven, kill and roast
the paschal lamb, and make such other arrangements as were
necessary

9, 10 **And they said unto him,**—The disciples asked him
where they should make the preparation; this was an intelligent question for them to ask; they wished to please their
Lord. Jesus then told them that when they entered Jerusalem they would meet a man "bearing a pitcher of water," and
that they should follow him. The specific direction that Jesus
gave Peter and John would enable them to find the exact
place where the Master wanted to eat the Passover. It was
the custom in the East for women to bring water; hence this
sign was a peculiar one; this man would have a "pitcher" of
water; the original for "pitcher" here means an earthen vessel.
Water was usually carried in leathern vessels, or vessels made
of the skins of animals; but this was another peculiar thing,
this "man," not a woman, should have an "earthen" pitcher,
not a leathern pitcher. This man was probably a slave and
Peter and John were to follow him into the house, or central
court, and then make their wishes known. An entrance thus
far into an eastern house was not an intrusion.

11, 12 **And ye shall say unto the master of the house,**—
Many think that this man was one of the disciples of Jesus,
and that he would recognize Jesus as the "Teacher"; however,
it is not necessary to suppose that any previous arrangements
had been made between Jesus and the master of the house.

will show you a large upper room furnished: there make ready. 13 And
they went, and found as he had said unto them: and they made ready the
passover.

14 And when the hour was come, he sat down, and the apostles with him.

They were to ask him: "Where is the guest-chamber" that
Jesus and his disciples could eat the Passover. Peter and
John, having followed the man bearing the pitcher of water
into the house, would ask the master of the house for the
guest-chamber. It was customary for Jews to be very hos-
pitable, and, according to the Talmud, they would not let
rooms for hire at the Passover Feast. Jesus shows his divinity by telling them in detail what the master of the house
would say to them. They were told by Jesus that he would
show them "a large upper room furnished." They were to
make ready the Passover to be eaten in that "upper room."
They were to ask for the "guest-chamber," or small lodging
room, but the master of the house will offer them "a large
upper room"; they were to make ready the room, but the master of the house would show them a room that was already
"furnished"; that is, prepared for the Passover.

13 **And they went, and found**—Peter and John found everything as Jesus had predicted; this should have strengthened
their faith in him. "They made ready the passover"; that is,
the paschal supper was prepared. They slew the lamb, or had
it slain, in the temple; its blood was sprinkled at the foot of
the altar, and its fat burned thereon, the bitter herbs, the unleavened bread, and the wine were prepared.

14 **And when the hour was come,**—What hour? The usual
time of eating the paschal supper, on Thursday evening, after
sundown. This showed that there was no irregularity in the
time of their eating the Passover. "He sat down"; the usual
posture was to "fall back" or recline. They did not sit on
chairs or benches, as the celebrated painting of Leonardo da
Vinci represents them as doing. The early custom was to
stand, but this had been long departed from, and they now reclined. According to Ex. 12: 11 the Passover was to be eaten
standing with loins girded, as if they were going on a journey; but the Jewish doctors introduced reclining, the usual

15 And he said unto them, With desire I have desired to eat this passover
with you before I suffer: 16 for I say unto you, I shall not eat it, until it be
fulfilled in the kingdom of God. 17 And he received a cup, and when he had
given thanks, he said, Take this, and divide it among yourselves: 18 for I
say unto you, I shall not drink from henceforth of the fruit of the vine, until

posture at meals, as it symbolized the rest which they sought
in leaving Egypt and found in Canaan. It may be that the
first Passover eaten in Egypt should have been eaten standing
as they were to march out of Egypt that night, but no stress
was placed on the posture as they kept the feast; the law
given upon Mount Sinai did not require any particular posture.

15, 16 **And he said unto them, With desire**—Here Jesus expresses a very strong desire, an intense desire, "to eat this
passover" with them before his crucifixion. The expression
"with desire I have desired" is similar to rejoiceth with joy
(John 3: 29) and threatened with threatening (Acts 4: 17) in
the original. This was to be his last Passover with them, the
time when he should institute the Lord's Supper. He would
not eat again the Passover in its literal use any more, but in a
spiritual sense he would eat it "in the kingdom of God." The
law with all of its types and shadows found their fulfillment in
Christ and his kingdom; hence he would not eat it "until it be
fulfilled in the kingdom of God." The "until" does not mean
that he would again eat the Passover after the establishment
of the kingdom; but it does mean that the type was to vanish
in the presence of the antitype; the type should be superseded
by the antitype, by the sacrifice of the true paschal Lamb.
Christ is declared to be our Passover. (1 Cor. 5: 6-8.)

17, 18 **And he received a cup,**—There has been some controversy as to whether Luke departs from the order of Matthew
and Mark and mentions the institution of the supper earlier in
the evening; many think that Luke brings the supper before
Judas left the company, while others think that the supper
was not instituted until after Judas left. The wine used at the
Passover was generally mixed with water in the proportion of
one part wine to two of water. "A cup" was given him and
he gave thanks. The "cup" here named was probably the last
cup that was passed; it was called the "cup of blessing." This

the kingdom of God shall come. 19 And he took ³bread, and when he had
given thanks, he brake it, and gave to them, saying, This is my body ⁴which
is given for you: this do in remembrance of me. 20 And the cup in like
manner after supper, saying, This cup is the new covenant in my blood, *even
that which is poured out for you.* 21 But behold, the hand of him that

³Or, *a loaf*
⁴Some ancient authorities omit *which is given for you . . . which is poured out
for you*

was drunk after the lamb was eaten. A cup was passed at different intervals; they would eat for a while, then pass the
large cup or vessel that contained the wine, and each one
would fill his own cup, and as they drank, different scriptures
would be recited.

19 **And he took bread,**—The original means "a loaf"; hence,
he took a loaf of the bread that they used at the Passover,
which was unleavened bread; he gave thanks, broke the loaf,
and gave unto the disciples, saying: "This is my body which is
given for you: this do in remembrance of me." There has
been much discussion as to the meaning of this: "This is my
body." This is similar to the expression, "the seven good
kine are seven years" (Gen. 41: 26), and "the good seed, these
are the sons of the kingdom" (Matt. 13: 38), the rock was
Christ (1 Cor. 10: 4), "this Hagar is mount Sinai" (Gal.
4: 25). In all of these expressions it is clear that the word
"signify" is to be understood; so when Christ said of the loaf
that it was his body, he meant that it represented or signified
his body. "This do in remembrance of me" means that they
were to remember him in the eating of this loaf; this is repeated by Paul in 1 Cor. 11: 24. Matthew and Mark omit
this command.

20 **And the cup in like manner after supper,**—Having offered
thanks to God for it as he did for the bread, he gave instruction to his disciples. This signified a covenant or promise on
the part of God to his people sanctioned with the blood of victims. (Ex. 24: 3-12; Deut. 5: 2.) The same wine or fruit of
the vine that was used at the Passover was used here; as the
unleavened bread was used at the Passover, so that kind of
bread was used here. However, the Lord's Supper is a New
Testament ordinance, and nowhere in the New Testament do

⁵betrayeth me is with me on the table. 22 For the Son of man indeed goeth, as it hath been determined: but woe unto that man through whom he is ⁵betrayed! 23 And they began to question among themselves, which of them it was that should do this thing.

⁵See ver. 4

we find the definite kind of bread or wine specified to be used; hence, the controversy as to the kind does not come within the scope of revealed things. It is left to the good judgment and pious conviction of those who are to use these in commemorating the death and sufferings of our Lord. "This cup is the new covenant in my blood." The old covenant that was sanctified by the blood of animals was fulfilled, and now a new covenant is given which is sealed and sanctified by the blood of Christ.

21 **But behold, the hand of him that betrayeth me**—Some think that verses 21-23 are transposed; in order of time these verses should be placed before verses 19 and 20. However, no violence was done to the truth if we consider them transposed, or if we consider them in their consecutive order. Luke merely refers to the traitor after relating the institution of the Lord's Supper, which makes a central point in his narrative, and which the mention of the first cup at the Passover may have led him to introduce. In John 13: 30 we are told that Judas went out immediately after receiving the sop. So if this fact is here recorded in its true order by Luke, we must surely conclude that Judas was present at the institution of the Lord's Supper, as well as at the beginning of the Passover; many hold this view. At that time Jesus said to Judas: "What thou doest, do quickly." (John 13: 27.) If Judas was pointed out before the supper, we must place his departure before it. This was the first announcement that Jesus had made to his disciples that one of them would betray him at that time.

22, 23 **For the Son of man indeed goeth,**—The Messiah was to go in the path of humiliation, suffering, and death; this was according to the prophecies. (Isa. 53: 4-12; Dan. 9: 26; Zech. 12: 10; 13: 7.) "But woe unto that man through whom he is betrayed!" In the original we have the present participle form—"is now engaged in betraying." It was "determined" that Jesus should go this way, but the purpose of God in no way released those who participated in his crucifixion of the guilt of those who put Jesus to death.

This statement greatly excited the disciples and "they began to question among themselves, which of them it was that should do this thing." The anxious, surprised, and troubled faces of his disciples showed their anguish of soul. It seems that they had not suspected Judas; this brief reference to the traitor warrants the inference that Luke adds these facts here to his account to complete his sketch of these events, but without intending to place them in chronological order. The woe upon the traitor points him out as an object both of pity and of wrath; God's purpose was foretold by the prophet, yet the murderers and betrayer were without excuse. (Acts 2: 22-24.)

3. STRIFE ABOUT RANK
22: 24-30

24 And there arose also a contention among them, which of them was

24 **And there arose also a contention**—It is strange that this contention should be renewed at this time; it had frequently been raised among the apostles as to who should be the greatest in the kingdom. (Matt. 18: 1-4; 20: 20-28; Luke 9: 46-48.) They were still at the Passover supper; Jesus had announced that one of them should betray him; yet at this late hour the apostles raised the question and argued among themselves as to who would be the greatest. Jesus had mentioned his kingdom in connection with the institution of the Lord's Supper; this mention of the kingdom gave the occasion for the old question to be raised. It shows that the disciples were still laboring under an erroneous conception of the kingdom; they thought that it would be an earthly kingdom, and there were still ambitious for positions of honor in that earthly kingdom. They were thinking of royalty, high positions, worldly states, and ranks in an earthly kingdom. At the supper John appears to have had a place next to Jesus; Peter was not very far from him; we do not know how the

accounted to be [6]greatest. 25 And he said unto them, The kings of the Gentiles have lordship over them; and they that have authority over them are called Benefactors. 26 But ye *shall* not *be* so: but he that is the greater among you, let him become as the younger and he that is chief, as he that doth serve. 27 For which is greater, he that [7]sitteth at meat, or he that serveth? is not he that [7]sitteth at meat? but I am in the midst of you as he

[6]Gr. *greater*
[7]Gr. *reclineth*

others were arranged. Possibly the arrangement at the supper renewed the old question and gave rise to the contention among them.

25 **And he said unto them,**—It seems that their contention was in the presence of Jesus; he gives them further instructions as to the nature of his kingdom. He calls attention to the fact that "the kings of the Gentiles have lordship over them"; this is the spirit of all human governments. Those who exercise the lordship over their subjects are puffed up by flattering titles such as "Benefactors." Jesus had given a similar rebuke in Matt. 20: 25- 26. The title "Benefactor" as used here means a "doer of good," or one who had brought a blessing to them. Rulers like for the people to think that they are "benefactors" to them.

26, 27 **But ye shall not be so:**—The "shall" is not in the original, and Jesus simply says: You are not to be as these Gentile kings; though they are distinguished by grace, yet they are not to love and seek superiority. On the contrary, the "greater among" them is the one who renders the greatest service to them. They should avoid the appearance of lordship; each one should be ready to do anything that will accommodate and serve a disciple. Jesus illustrates this principle by simply calling their attention to a common custom and courtesy among them. The one that sits at the table is honored by the one who serves; and since greatness is to be determined by service, the one who serves the most is greatest among them. He further emphasized this truth by stating: "I am in the midst of you as he that serveth." Evidently they ascribed greatness to Jesus; he was greater, in their own conception, than all the others; yet he was serving them in a way that others had not served them.

that serveth. 28 But ye are they that have continued with me in my temptations; 29 and 'I appoint unto you a kingdom, even as my Father appointed unto me, 30 that ye may eat and drink at my table in my kingdom; and ye shall sit on thrones judging the twelve tribes of Israel.

¹Or, *I appoint unto you, even as my Father appointed unto me a kingdom, that ye may eat and drink &c.*

28, 29 But ye are they that have continued—His disciples had now been following him for many months; they had witnessed his many temptations, and had continued with him in his temptation. "Continued" here means "have remained through" his temptation. The life of Jesus was full of temptation. His temptation had begun soon after his baptism, and he was never free from temptation; he was tempted in all points as we are, yet without sin. (Heb. 4: 15.) When Satan tempted Jesus, "he departed from him for a season" only. (Luke 4: 13.) "I appoint unto you a kingdom" means that they should come into possession of the kingdom from the Father; they should attain through trials and service, even as Jesus had experienced, unto his kingdom. Jesus bequeathed as by will or testament to them the kingdom that he came to establish. This shows that they were not at this time in his kingdom, neither were they in full possession of the blessings of that kingdom; but they should through trials and sufferings attain unto it. The new dispensation was inaugurated on the first Pentecost after the ascension of Jesus; at that time the kingdom was established and these apostles became the charter members of it.

30 that ye may eat and drink at my table—Jesus has said to his disciples that since they had been with him through all of his earthly toils he would give to them high places in his kingdom of service. In the blessings and blessedness of such service, they would be pre-eminent, sitting upon thrones, as it were, and administering judgment. This seems to be the same thought as expressed in Matt. 19: 28. Eating and drinking "at my table" in this kingdom does not merely refer to the Lord's Supper, but the promise is that they may partake of the kingly feast upon the merits of the Redeemer, and enjoy the pleasures of the table prepared for the supply of all spiritual blessings in Christ. They should "sit on thrones judging

the twelve tribes of Israel." There have been various interpretations given to this. Some think that it means that all
would be judged by the teachings of the apostles; others
think that the apostles will condemn the Jews, as the Ninevites and the queen of Sheba did in former days (Luke 11 : 31,
32) ; again others think that it means that the apostles should
be cojudges with Christ in the judgment; still others think
that it means that the apostles should be preeminent after the
second coming of Christ. Paul expressed a similar thought:
"Know ye not that the saints shall judge the world?" And
"angels?" (1 Cor. 6: 2, 3.) There may be some truth in all of
these positions; the apostles were invested with authority
over the true spiritual Israel, and by their teachings all will be
judged; through their teachings they continue to exercise
their authority. In the final judgment they will virtually
judge, for all are to be judged by the will of God expressed
through the writers of the New Testament.

4. PETER'S DENIAL FORETOLD
22: 31-34

31 Simon, Simon, behold, Satan ²asked to have you, that he might sift you

²Or, *obtained you by asking*

31 **Simon, Simon, behold, Satan asked to have you,**—Parallel records of this event are found in Matt. 26: 31-35; Mark
14: 27-31; John 13: 36-38. This is one of the few events recorded by all four of the writers of the gospel. This prediction to Peter was a forewarning that he would deny the Lord.
Matthew and Mark, with Luke, locate it after the institution
of the Lord's Supper and immediately before the agony in the
Garden of Gethsemane. Some think that the record in John
13: 31-38 was a prediction before this one, and that Jesus here
foretells the second time the denial of Peter and the dispersion
of the disciples. Jesus calls Peter "Simon" and repeats his
name to emphasize that which he is predicting; he does not
use the name "Peter" which signifies a more stable character.
"Satan" had asked to have Peter; he had demanded Peter as
he had demanded Job. (Job 1: 6-12; 2: 1-6.) "To have you"

as wheat: 32 but I made supplication for thee, that thy faith fail not; and do
thou, when once thou hast turned again, establish thy brethren. 33 And he
said unto him, Lord, with thee I am ready to go both to prison and to death.
34 And he said, I tell thee, Peter, the cock shall not crow this day, until
thou shalt thrice deny that thou knowest me.

---

is in the plural, and means "you all," or includes all the disciples.

32 but I made supplication for thee,—In the Greek the word
for "you" is plural in fact as well as form, and may apply to
all the disciples; but Simon is solemnly addressed and
warned, since he was foremost in the strife. Jesus did not in-
vest in Peter any pre-eminence or sanctity, as is claimed by
those who worship the pope at Rome; Peter is regarded as
being fallible. When he had "turned again," or when he had
recovered from his fall, then his work would be to "establish"
or "strengthen" his brethren. The act of returning is Peter's;
he should correct his wrong, and then teach and encourage
others to do likewise. He should confirm others in the faith,
especially those who might be influenced by his own fall.
Jesus had prayed for him that his faith should not fail; that
his trust and conviction that Jesus was the Son of God should
not falter.

33 And he said unto him, Lord,—Peter was still full of self-
confidence; he little knew his own heart, neither did he know
the wiles and snares of the devil. He could now face prison
and death for Jesus; a few hours later he could not face the
taunts of a housemaid without denying the Lord.
Oftentimes, we boast about what we will do or will not do,
but when faced with the realities of the situation, we act differently. Peter needed to learn the lesson of depending on
God, and not on himself.

34 And he said, I tell thee, Peter,—It is strange as we read
this distinct and terrible warning that Peter was off his guard
in less than twenty-four hours after this. It has been affirmed
that the Jews around Jerusalem were forbidden fowls because
they scratched up unclean worms; hence, it is said that this
statement was out of harmony with the facts in the case.
However, the Roman residents, over whom the Jews had no

authority, might keep fowls. Mark says: "Before the cock crow twice, thou shalt deny me thrice" (Mark 14: 72), and Matthew says, "Before the cock crow, thou shalt deny me thrice" (Matt. 26: 34). The first crowing was about midnight, and the second about three o'clock in the morning; the second crowing more generally marked time, and was the one meant when only one "cockcrowing," as here, was mentioned. Peter would deny or disown Christ three times. Jesus simply says that before a single cock shall be heard, early in the night, Peter would deny him. There was a wide contrast in what Jesus predicted and what the self-confident Peter thought he would do.

5. FURTHER PREPARATION
22: 35-38

35 And he said unto them, When I sent you forth without purse, and wallet, and shoes, lacked ye anything? And they said, Nothing. 36 And he said unto them, But now, he that hath a purse, let him take it, and likewise a

35 And he said unto them, When I sent you forth—Jesus had sent out his apostles on their "limited commission" (Matt. 10: 5; Mark 6: 7; Luke 9: 2); they were to go not in the way of the Gentiles nor among the Samaritans, but rather to the lost sheep of the house of Israel. The instructions there given are compared with those he now mentions; the circumstances have changed. At that time they were to go "without purse, and wallet, and shoes." They were to be wholly dependent on those with whom they labored; they were to make no provision whatever for their wants, but throw themselves for support upon such friends in every place where they went. Jesus asked them if they lacked anything. They answered, "Nothing." Their wants were fully supplied. Their answer to his question was frank and sincere; they had no complaint to make; they had gone forth with no means of support, and yet there was not a single need which was not fully supplied. Conditions have changed and new requirements are to be met.

36 And he said unto them,—Since conditions and circumstances have changed, Jesus now tells them that they are to

wallet; ³and he that hath none, let him sell his cloak, and buy a sword. 37
For I say unto you, that this which is written must be fulfilled in me, ⁴And
he was reckoned with transgressors: for that which concerneth me hath
⁵fulfilment. 38 And they said, Lord, behold, here are two swords. And he
said unto them, It is enough.

³Or, *and he that hath no sword, let him sell his cloak, and buy one*
⁴Is. 53.12
⁵Gr. *end*

take their purse and wallet, and if they have not these things
they should sell their cloak "and buy a sword." This verse
has given much difficulty to commentators. Does Jesus command his disciples to arm themselves? Is he speaking only
with reference to danger that night? It seems that Jesus here
is impressing upon them the impending crisis; that there will
be need of every resource because of the peculiar dangers.
We are not to infer that Jesus commanded his disciples to
arm themselves against the perils just of that night; it is better to consider this as a proverbial expression conveying the
idea of imminent danger from enemies; they must be prepared
for the worst. The time was swiftly approaching when his
disciples would have to defend themselves without the visible
presence and leadership of Jesus. We cannot allow that Jesus
meant for each of his disciples to sell his garment and buy a
sword. This idea is utterly precluded by the universal doctrine which Jesus taught—"resist not evil."

37 **For I say unto you, that this which is written**—Luke
quotes Isa. 53: 12. The predictions of his sufferings and
death are now to be fulfilled; he was ready to be brought to
the cross, and his disciples would be involved in trouble; so
they should be prepared for it. Jesus was crucified between
two malefactors, which was a fulfillment of the prophecy concerning him. The things which were predicted of Jesus had an
end; this is true about the predictions of his kingdom; all
prophecies must be fulfilled. Jesus died the death of one who
had been convicted of crime, and was crucified between two
malefactors to heap ignominy upon him; all this was in
fulfillment of the prophecies.

38 **And they said, Lord,**—The disciples understood Jesus to
mean that they should be prepared to fight in his kingdom
with carnal weapons. We do not know when his disciples ob-

tained these swords. If they had been obliged to depend on swords for their defense, not a hundred would have been sufficient; but for the lesson of that awful night two swords were enough. It may be observed that the impetuous Peter had one of these. It seems that his disciples failed to understand his prediction of his death in the fulfillment of prophecy; although he had made the announcement several times to them. It is difficult to understand just what he meant by "It is enough."

6. THE AGONY IN GETHSEMANE
22 : 39-46

39 And he came out, and went, as his custom was, unto the mount of Olives; and the disciples also followed him. 40 And when he was at the place, he said unto them, Pray that ye enter not into temptation. 41 And he

39 **And he came out, and went, as his custom**—Parallel records of this event are found in Matt. 26: 30-46; Mark 14: 26-42; John 18: 1. Matthew, Mark, and Luke do not give the record of the discourse and prayer of Jesus found in John 14 to 17; the Synoptics record only the fact of Jesus' leaving the upper room and going to Gethsemane after the institution of the supper. We know not how long they tarried in the upper room before they sang the hymn. Jesus was now entering into the greatest conflict that has ever been known to man; it was the awful contest of the powers of hell with the powers of heaven; by prayer Jesus would put himself into direct communion with the Father as the best preparation for the conflict; hence, he sought his accustomed place of retirement in the field or Garden of Gethsemane. "Mount of Olives" literally means "the mount of the olives," being descriptive of the olive trees which grew there. Olive trees still grow there, but not so many as did anciently. This mount is frequently mentioned in the Bible. (2 Sam. 15: 30; Neh. 8: 15; Ezek. 11: 23; Zech. 14: 4.) This mount is also called "Olivet" (Acts 1: 12), a place set with olives, an olive yard.

40 **And when he was at the place,**—"The place" means the Garden of Gethsemane; "Gethsemane" means "olive press," a name prophetic of the agony of Jesus, where he trod the wine

was parted from them about a stone's cast; and he kneeled down and prayed, 42 saying, Father, if thou be willing, remove this cup from me: nevertheless not my will, but thine, be done. 43 [6]And there appeared unto him an angel

[6]Many ancient authorities omit ver. 43, 44

press alone (Isa. 63: 3), without the city (Rev. 14: 20). The eleven disciples were present; Judas had gone to betray him. Eight of the apostles were left near the entrance of the garden, and three of them, Peter, James, and John, were taken further into the garden with him. The eight were directed to remain where they were and pray for deliverance from temptation. Jesus left Peter, James, and John and went still further into the garden; they were also instructed to watch and pray. A great test was just before them and they needed prayer.

41, 42 **And he was parted from them about a stone's cast;**— He retired of his own will from Peter, James, and John "about a stone's cast." "Stone's cast," "arrow's flight," with the ancients, were in common usage, as we now have "within gunshot" and "within a stone's throw." "He kneeled down and prayed." Matthew says: "He went forward a little, and fell on his face, and prayed" (Matt. 26: 39) and Mark says: "He went forward a little, and fell on the ground, and prayed" (Mark 14: 35). It is very likely that he first knelt, and as his agony increased he fell forward as Matthew says "on his face." This posture was indicative of his extreme humiliation and anguish. The different postures that he assumed can be true at different stages of his experience; one writer recording one posture and another recording another posture.

His prayer was: "Father, if thou be willing, remove this cup from me: nevertheless not my will, but thine, be done." "This cup" means the bitter cup of anguish. "Cup" is a common figure of scripture, sometimes representing joy (Psalms 16: 5; 23: 5; 116: 13), and sometimes sorrow (Psalms 11: 6; 75: 8; Isa. 51: 17; Jer. 25: 15; Rev. 16: 19.) This cup with Jesus signified his great sorrow and anguish and death. Some think that it did not include his death, but just his great anguish of soul. This prayer uttered in deep humility and reverence shows that the will of Jesus was in harmony with the

from heaven, strengthening him. 44 And being in an agony he prayed more earnestly; and his sweat became as it were great drops of blood falling down upon the ground. 45 And when he rose up from his prayer, he came unto the disciples, and found them sleeping for sorrow, 46 and said unto them,

---

will of God; his human nature naturally shrank from the terrible pain and death; Jesus willingly submitted to God's will in this awful hour. "Nevertheless not my will, but thine, be done." The resignation of Jesus to the will of God both as priest and victim is swallowed up in the divine will.

43 **And there appeared unto him an angel**—This was in keeping with the prediction: "For he will give his angels charge over thee, to keep thee in all thy ways." (Psalm 91: 11.) The anguish was not removed, but Jesus was strengthened to bear it; he was made "lower than the angels." (Heb. 2: 7.) We do not know how angels ministered to him, whether by sympathy, words of cheer, wiping away the sweat, or by worshiping him to signify recognition of his lordship. His human nature must be upheld so that a full atonement may be made; this angel assisted in doing this. "Mine arm also shall strengthen him" (Psalm 89: 21); the Father sent this angel to sustain him. Angels visited Jesus at the close of the three temptations at the beginning of his ministry. (Matt. 4: 11.)

44 **And being in an agony he prayed**—Luke is the only writer that records this fact; only Luke records the visit of the angel. The original here denotes progressive agony; he progressed from the first prayer into an intense struggle of prayer and sorrow. "Agony" is only found here; it is used by medical writers, and the fact of a "sweat" accompanying an agony is also mentioned by medical writers; this is another evidence peculiar to Luke, the physician. Cases of great mental anguish, causing drops of blood to ooze from the body like sweat, are known to medical authorities.

45, 46 **And when he rose up from his prayer,**—Luke does not record, as do Matthew and Mark, that he prayed three times, "saying the same words," and that he returned to his disciples three times for sympathy, but found them asleep. Luke tells why they were asleep; they were found "sleeping

Why sleep ye? rise and pray, that ye enter not into temptation.

---

for sorrow." This seems to be common among those who
have sustained great and prolonged grief; no excuse is given
for the apostles' being asleep on this eventful occasion; but an
explanation is given for their being found asleep. The strongest will be overcome, and fall asleep, under the strain of great
grief. Jesus was in sympathy with them and said: "Why
sleep ye? rise and pray, that ye enter not into temptation."
Jesus, who was alert, may have heard the approach of Judas
and his company. He enjoins prayer with special reference to
themselves that they might not fall under the power of "temptation." The hour of trial was at hand, and they needed both
to watch and to pray. Jesus commands that his disciples
arouse from their sleepy posture and pray, as their only safe-
guard at this crisis was in prayer; and if they neglected this
means of defense against the adversary, they were lost.

7. THE ARREST OF JESUS
22: 47-53

47 While he yet spake, behold, a multitude, and he that was called Judas,
one of the twelve, went before them; and he drew near unto Jesus to kiss

---

47 **While he yet spake,**—A "multitude" led by Judas at this
hour of the night came into the garden. This "multitude"
consisted, first, of "the band" (John 18: 3, 12), or Roman co-
hort, which consisted of from three to six hundred armed
men; they were kept in the tower of Antonia, overlooking the
temple, and were kept ready to put down any tumult or arrest
any disturber. It is not known whether the entire band was
present. Then there were the "captains of the temple" (verse
52) with their men who guarded the temple and kept order; it
is not known how many of these were present. Also there
were some of the chief priests and elders (verse 52), and finally some servants, such as Malchus and others (John 18: 10),
who had been commissioned by the Jewish authorities.
"Judas, one of the twelve," led the company; he had agreed to
betray Jesus into their hands; it is an ugly picture to see this
apostolic criminal leading this mob at night into the garden of

him. 48 But Jesus said unto him, Judas, [7]betrayest thou the Son of man
with a kiss? 49 And when they that were about him saw what would follow,
they said, Lord, shall we smite with the sword? 50 And a certain one of

[7]See ver. 4

sorrow to arrest Jesus. Judas "went before them" as their
guide and leader. (John 18: 3.) When they arrived, Judas
"drew near unto Jesus to kiss him."

48 **But Jesus said unto him, Judas,**—This verse is found
only in Luke; the kiss of Judas is here placed in strong contrast with the betrayal which it subserved, in order to show
how devoid of all noble and generous feeling was the traitor,
who could prostitute to so vile a purpose, that which among
all nations was regarded as the pledge and token of intimate
friendship. There seems to be sympathy with the rebuke
which Jesus used when he said: "Judas, betrayest thou the
Son of man with a kiss?" Do you dare to bring those pol-
luted lips in contact with mine and play the hypocrite? Away
with your hypocrisy! Do your fiendish work! (John 18: 4-
9.)

49, 50 **And when they that were about him saw**—Those who
were "about him" were his disciples; they now seem to sense
the danger; they thought that Jesus would enable them to de-
feat the mob and vindicate him by means of the "two swords"
which they had. How little did they understand the situation! They asked: "Lord, shall we smite with the sword?"
They had not learned the lesson at this time. After the agony
had passed, Jesus with Peter, James, and John whom he had
chosen to accompany him (Matt. 26: 37; Mark 14: 33), returned to the eight disciples, whom he had left at the entrance
of the garden. It seems that immediately after he had joined
them the band sent to take him with Judas as their guide, and
probably a little in advance of the main body, was discovered
approaching. It was at this time that the disciples asked if
they should use the sword; and "a certain one of them smote
the servant of the high priest, and struck off his right ear." It
seems that Judas was stung by the words of Jesus, and understood that his treachery was known; he seems to have fallen
back again to his band (John 18: 5) so that when they came

them smote the [8]servant of the high priest, and struck off his right ear. 51
But Jesus answered and said, Suffer ye *them* thus far.   And he touched his
ear, and healed him.   52 And Jesus said unto the chief priests, and captains

[8]Gr. *bondservant*

to Jesus they were somewhat at a loss to identify him (John
18: 4-9).   This shows that Judas so cowered beneath the
searching glance and calm, severe language of Jesus that he
retreated from his side, where he had probably intended to remain until the band came fully up, in order that there might
be no possible mistake in regard to the apprehension of the
right person.   In the midst of this confusion, the disciples
may have asked whether they should smite with the sword;
they stood ready against such fearful odds to defend their
Lord.   Peter, still impetuous, rushed forward and smote off
the right ear of Malchus, a servant of the high priest.
Peter struck at his head, and miss his aim, and cut off his ear.
Matthew, Mark, and Luke record the incident without naming
Peter; John alone says that the disciple that cut off Malchus'
ear was Peter.   Some think that when the first three wrote,
perhaps it would have unduly exposed Peter to have named
him, but when John wrote, Peter had probably already suffered death, so that no harm would follow from giving the
name.

51 **But Jesus answered and said,**—There has been some controversy as to whom Jesus addressed this language; some
think that it was addressed to the captors, and meant that
they should allow his disciples to go away, and he would heal
the man.   Others think that it was addressed to his disciples
to restrain them, and meant that his disciples should permit,
without defense, the band to take him.   It seems from the full
account as given by Matthew and John that Jesus addressed
this to his disciples.   Jesus "touched his ear, and healed him."
Of course, Jesus could have healed the ear without the touch,
and the decided reproof of the disciples for the rashness of
this act closely follows the act, and indicates that all his conversation was addressed to them.

52 **And Jesus said unto the chief priests, and captains**—
"The chief priests" were so eager to take Jesus that they had

of the temple, and elders, that were come against him, Are ye come out, as against a robber, with swords and staves? 53 When I was daily with you in the temple, ye stretched not forth your hands against me: but this is your hour, and the power of darkness.

---

accompanied Judas and the band of Roman soldiers. Jesus now rebuked them and the Jewish officers for their cowardice and wickedness; they had come secretly and were basely hounding his footsteps to arrest him by night as though he were a common robber or desperate character. If they really believed that he was a bad man, why did they not take him in the daylight while he was in the temple? They had come out against him "as against a robber, with swords and staves." It was an indignation that Jesus with such peaceful habits should be surrounded with a band of soldiers and others with an array of weapons of all sorts, as though he were a robber to be hunted down and captured like a wild beast. They were armed with "swords and staves"; that is, they were armed with all sorts of sticks and cudgels.

53 **When I was daily with you in the temple,**—The last week had been spent by Jesus in the temple teaching; at night he would retire to Bethany or to the Mount of Olives. This was a rebuke to them for coming secretly by night, when they could have come to him while he was in the temple teaching daily; this was an indictment against them for their cowardice. They made no attempt to arrest him while he was in the temple; they feared the multitude. "But this is your hour, and the power of darkness." The time predicted had arrived; it was now permitted of God that the powers of evil should vent their rage against Jesus, and for a time triumph in the apparent success of their plans to crush Jesus and his disciples. Some think that Jesus had reference to the time of night, but this inference does not justify the statement.

8. PETER'S DENIAL
22 : 54-62

54 And they seized him, and led him *away,* and brought him into the high

---

54 **And they seized him, and led him away,**—Parallel accounts of Peter's denial are found in Matt. 26: 57-75; Mark

priest's house. But Peter followed afar off. 55 And when they had kindled
a fire in the midst of the court, and had sat down together, Peter sat in the

---

14: 53-72; John 18: 15-17. Jesus was arrested in the Garden
of Gethsemane and they "led him away." He was "seized"
and bound and brought "into the high priest's house."
Literally it means that after seizing Jesus in the garden by
ruthless force, they took him to the house of the high priest;
we have no way to determine the hour of night that he arrived
at the "house of the high priest." It has been a matter of discussion as to who the high priest was. Some think that he
was Caiaphas; others think that he was Annas. John relates
that they led him first to Annas, and then "Annas therefore
sent him bound unto Caiaphas the high priest." (John 18:
24.) Annas had been high priest for several years and had
been deposed by Roman authorities; he was still the legiti-
mate high priest according to the law of Moses since the high
priest was to serve during life. (Num. 20: 28; 35: 25.) Jesus
was examined in an informal way before Annas (John 18: 12-
14), and then, in order to have him officially tried and condemned in the eye of the Roman law, he sent him to Caiaphas.
Peter is the only one mentioned here as following Jesus, and
he followed him "afar off"; he was near enough to see what
became of Jesus, but far enough away from him to be out of
danger; he seemed to show more courage than any of the
eleven except John.

55 **And when they had kindled a fire**—Luke does not mention an earlier examination or trial, but at once describes the
conditions upon which Peter denied his Lord. The high
priest's palace was between the upper city and the temple; it
was to this place that Peter followed "afar off," while John
went into the palace with Jesus and the guards, as he knew
the high priest; Peter lingered without, but John spoke to the
maid at the door and Peter was admitted. (John 18: 15, 16.)
The usual meeting place of the Sanhedrin was the "court," or
an apartment in one of the courts of the temple; some have
described it as being at the southeast corner of the court of
Israel. In cases of emergency, or in this case, where great se-

midst of them. 56 And a certain maid seeing him as he sat in the light *of the fire*, and looking stedfastly upon him, said, This man also was with him. 57 But he denied, saying, Woman, I know him not. 58 And after a little while another saw him, and said, Thou also art *one* of them. But Peter said,

---

crecy was desired, it was at the house of the high priest, who generally presided over the court. The nights at Jerusalem at this season were frequently cold; John states that the fire was made because "it was cold." (John 18: 18.) John also states that Peter stood with them around the fire, but Luke says, they "sat down together, Peter sat in the midst of them." There is no contradiction, since John could describe their *standing* around the fire at one time and Luke having in mind another time would describe them as *sitting*.

56, 57 **And a certain maid seeing him**—This maid appears to have been the one who let him in. (John 18: 17.) Mark tells us that this maid was a servant of the high priest. (Mark 14: 66.) John speaks of her as the one who kept the door of the porch; she seems to have observed Peter as he came in, and afterward, when he was seated with the servants of the high priest she recognized him; something about his appearance or manner excited her suspicion; again she thinks that she remembered seeing him with Jesus. She approached him and looked intently upon him and said: "This man was also with him." Matthew and Mark both record that she told Peter that she recognized him as one of the disciples of Jesus, while John records that she asked Peter if he were not one of the disciples of Jesus. (John 18: 17.) Peter very bluntly denied and said: "Woman, I know him not." This was Peter's first denial.

58 **And after a little while another saw him,**—This is Peter's second denial. At this time a man identifies Peter. Matthew and Mark mention a maid who charged Peter with being one of the disciples of Jesus, while John says: "They said." At this time Peter had gone from the light to the gate or entrance. (Matt. 26: 71.) It is easy to understand the harmony of all of the writers; that a maid, a man, and others of the crowd in the palace court joined in the charge almost simultaneously; this would be a natural thing at such a time. Peter's

Man, I am not. 59 And after the space of about one hour another confidently affirmed, saying, Of a truth this man also was with him; for he is a
Galilæan. 60 But Peter said, Man, I know not what thou sayest. And
immediately, while he yet spake, the cock crew. 61 And the Lord turned,
and looked upon Peter. And Peter remembered the word of the Lord, how

denial is emphatic: "Man, I am not." Peter denies as though
he was just one of the company who had come through curiosity to learn the cause of the excitement. This denial is
stronger than the first, and is a step in advance of the first denial. At the first Peter was probably surprised and possibly
somewhat confused; but now he had reflected somewhat and
his denial is more emphatic. Possibly the number of those
who accused him prompted him to make this denial more emphatic.

59, 60 **And after the space of about one hour**—Matthew
says, "After a little while" (Matt. 26: 73), so also Mark
(Mark 14: 70); Matthew and Mark both state that "they that
stood by" accused Peter of being one of the disciples of Jesus;
but Luke says "another confidently affirmed" that Peter was
with Jesus, "for he is a Galilæan." John states that a servant
who was a kinsman "of him whose ear Peter cut off" made
the charge. (John 18: 26.) This is the third charge made
against Peter, and it was "about an hour" after the other
charge; someone recognized that Peter was a Galilean; they
said that his speech betrayed him. The peculiarities of the
Galilean dialect are shown and example given by Peter; these
help to identify Peter as one of the disciples. He could not
hide his speech if he talked. This time Peter's denial was still
the more emphatic. He said: "Man, I know not what thou
sayest." He meant: "What are you talking about?" He
claimed to be totally ignorant of the man and the matter.
Peter not only denied and thus lied, but began to curse and to
swear, saying: "I know not this man of whom ye speak."
(Mark 14: 71.) Peter solemnly invoked curses on himself,
taking solemn oaths in confirmation of his previous assertions
that he did not know who the prisoner was.

61, 62 **And the Lord turned, and looked upon Peter.**—What
a look of sorrow and pain it must have been! Who can repro-

that he said unto him, Before the cock crow this day thou shalt deny me thrice. 62 And he went out, and wept bitterly.

---

duce or describe that look? Was it an angry, disdainful, indignant look? Was it a look of pity and regret? Jesus could not stretch forth his manacled hands to Peter and save him as he did when Peter was sinking while walking on the water, but he did give him a look of tender sympathy for his weakness and a look of love that saved Peter. Peter never forgot that look; it has its desired effect at this time on him, for it called to his mind what Jesus had said to him. How that look must have pierced the heart of Peter, when he remembered the terrible warning which Jesus had given him; he also remembered that he had stoutly affirmed that others might forsake him, but that he was willing to die for him. Peter rushed from the place "and wept bitterly." He could stand no longer the look of Jesus, and he needed to get out and give expression to his sorrow. The bitterness of his penitence knew no relief until the assurance of forgiveness came.

9. JESUS BEFORE THE SANHEDRIN
22 : 63-71

63 And the men that held ¹Jesus mocked him, and beat him. 64 And they

¹Gr. him

---

63 **And the men that held Jesus mocked him,**—The officers and soldiers treated Jesus as they would treat a common slave who had committed some heinous crime and was worthy of death with all the cruelties that they could impose upon him. They "mocked him" with insulting language and accusations. While Peter was shamefully denying his Lord in the courtyard, the night examination and trial of Jesus before the high priest went on, and the guards were permitted to heap all sorts of cruelties upon the prisoner. Judas had "received the band of soldiers, and officers from the chief priests and the Pharisees" (John 18: 3), when he betrayed Jesus in the Garden of Gethsemane; hence, these officers were the ones who helped to mock Jesus. They "beat him" with their fists and with other things they smote him severely. The guards per-

blindfolded him, and asked him, saying, Prophesy: who is he that struck
thee? 65 And many other things spake they against him, reviling him.
66 And as soon as it was day, the assembly of the elders of the people
was gathered together, both chief priests and scribes; and they led him away

---

mitted others to mock, beat, blindfold, smite, and revile the
Son of God. Matthew and Mark record these insults before
the account of Peter's denial; Luke records the three denials
of Peter together, while the other writers record what occurred between the denials. While Peter was denying his
Lord, the enemies reviled him and smote him. Possibly no
common slave received worse treatment than did our Lord.

64, 65 **And they blindfolded him,**—Matthew records that
some smote him with their fists, and Mark records that the
servants struck him. They made sport of him by imitating
the children's play of "blindman's bluff." After he was blindfolded they struck him and asked him to "prophesy" or tell
them who hit him; this was a mockery on his claim to be a
prophet. Little did they know how much he knew, but he chose
not to gratify their curiosity; he permitted them to do what
they would with him. They smote him on the face; they spit
in his face and buffeted him. (Matt. 26: 67; Mark 14: 65.)
"And many other things spake they against him, reviling
him." Luke is the only writer that records this verse; it
shows that their hatred found outlet not only in acts of violence and insult, but in the most abusive language. They had
pronounced condemnation on him for blasphemy, yet they
were the only ones who spoke blasphemous words, and that
too of the most appalling nature. Strange that they were
guilty of the very things with which they charged Jesus.

66 **And as soon as it was day,**—Matthew and Mark say:
"Now when morning was come" (Matt. 27: 1; Mark 15: 1)
they led Jesus away to the Sanhedrin. The trials before
Annas and Caiaphas that night were not legal; the Jewish
Sanhedrin did not meet at night for legal procedures; so after
daylight the Sanhedrin assembled in formal meeting to confirm what had already been determined. There had been a
smaller meeting in the night; the Sanhedrin formerly met in
the hall Gazith, the hall of square stone, in the temple area,

into their council, saying, 67 If thou art the Christ, tell us. But he said unto them, If I tell you, ye will not believe: 68 and if I ask *you*, ye will not answer. 69 But from henceforth shall the Son of man be seated at the right

but its meeting had been removed to another, the hall of Purchase, on the east side of the temple court. However, some think that this meeting was held in the palace of the high priest. This meeting was to pass in a formal way the sentence on Jesus. Luke gives very brief details of this meeting. At this meeting they conferred together as to the best means of putting Jesus to death, and formulating the twofold charge of blasphemy and treason; the Sanhedrin could condemn to death, but could not put the sentence into execution without the sanction of the Roman governor. (John 18: 31.) The Jews lost the power to execute the penalty of death when Archelaus was deposed, about A.D. 6.

67, 68 **If thou art the Christ, tell us.**—They were fully prepared to condemn him; this question was asked in a very malicious and cunning way; whatever answer he might give would be used against him. The question was designed to force him to incriminate himself in their judgment. They would not believe any answer that he would give, as they were ready to condemn him for blasphemy. Hence, Jesus said: "If I tell you, ye will not believe: and if I ask you, ye will not answer." Jesus says that if he should tell them plainly and emphatically that he was the Christ, they would not believe his statement; neither if he would ask them a question, or propose a question in support of his claims that they would not answer him; if he convinced them that he was the Christ, they would not release him. They had already seen convincing proof of his Messiahship and had rejected it; if he should present convincing proof now, they would not release him, for they were bent on his death.

69 **But from henceforth shall the Son of man**—This is a Messianic prediction from Psalm 110: 1 and Dan. 7: 9-14. The Jewish rulers should have understood this reference, but it is very likely that they did not. It was a claim to be the Messiah, as he was fulfilling these claims. Jesus meant that soon after his resurrection he would ascend to the Father and

hand of the power of God. 70 And they all said, Art thou then the Son of God? And he said unto them, [2]Ye say that I am. 71 And they said, What further need have we of witness? for we ourselves have heard from his own mouth.

[2]Or, *Ye say* it, *because I am*

would claim the title that belonged to him as the Son of God and would be exercising the authority granted unto him. The attribute of power is referred to by Christ in the time of his flesh as "seated at the right hand of the power of God." To sit on the right hand of God implies elevation to supreme power, honor, and favor. He was not *standing* as a prisoner and a criminal, but then he would *sit* in his glory as Lord of lords and King of kings at the right hand of God, sharing and exercising supreme power.

70 **And they all said, Art thou then the Son of God?**—This question was asked by the Sanhedrin; they all joined in this question. "The Son of man" was the same as "Son of God." Jesus had thus declared that "the Son of man" would be seated at the right hand of God; Jesus claimed to be "the Son of man"; now if Jesus be the "Son of man," and "the Son of man" is "the Son of God," this was equivalent to his claiming to be the Son of God; hence the Sanhedrin asked him plainly if he were "the Son of God." Jesus answered: "Ye say that I am." This was an affirmative answer; it was a Jewish idiom, meaning, it is as ye say, or a Greek idiom for "Yes." It is similar to "Thou hast said" in Matt. 26: 64 and "I am" in Mark 14: 62.

71 **And they said, What further need**—They now had an admission from Jesus or a declaration from him that he was the Son of God. Matthew (26: 65) says that at this stage the high priest "rent his garments," his ordinary dress; his high priestly robe was worn only in the temple. This was an expression from the high priest of condemnation of a speech or act; the high priest rent his garments standing from the neck straight downward about nine inches in length. The high priest was forbidden to rend his clothes (Lev. 21: 10); yet it seems to have been allowable in extraordinary cases of blasphemy and public calamity. The practice of rending clothes

for blasphemy was based on 2 Kings 18: 37. The unexpected answer of Jesus, declaring his divine glory and judgeship, aroused the hatred, rage, and horror of the high priest to the utmost bounds, and he rends his garments as if too narrow to contain his exasperated emotion; he does this as if in holy indignation and horror; terribly excited feelings and hypocrisy were mingled. He accused Jesus of blasphemy.

10. JESUS BEFORE PILATE AND HEROD
23: 1-25

1 And the whole company of them rose up, and brought him before Pilate. 2 And they began to accuse him, saying, We found this man perverting

1 **And the whole company of them rose up,**—Parallel accounts of this event are found in Matt. 27: 2, 11-14; Mark 15: 1-5; John 18: 28-38. Jesus had been subjected to a threefold trial before the Jews—first, before Annas, next before Caiaphas with a few members of the Sanhedrin present, and last before the entire Sanhedrin after daylight. They condemned Jesus as a blasphemer, but as they could not put him to death without the permission of the Roman authorities, they brought him before Pilate. The Roman trial also comprised three stages: (1) the first appearance before the Roman governor, Pilate; (2) the appearance before Herod Antipas, the native ruler of Galilee appointed by the Romans; and (3) the final appearance before Pilate. "The whole company" means "the assembly of the elders of the people" which composed "their council." (Luke 22: 66.) The Sanhedrin had held its session "as soon as it was day" that morning in order to ratify the previous decision; it was probably held at the palace of Caiaphas as John says: "They lead Jesus therefore from Caiaphas into the Praetorium: and it was early; and they themselves entered not into the Praetorium, that they might not be defiled, but might eat the passover." (John 18: 28.) Pilate was the Roman procurator, or governor. Matthew speaks of him as "the governor." (Matt. 27: 2.) Matthew often speaks of him simply as the governor, but Mark never so speaks of him; Luke speaks of him only once as the governor. (Luke 3: 1.) It is very probable that Nicodemus and Joseph of Ari-

our nation, and forbidding to give tribute to Cæsar, and saying that he himself is Christ a king. 3 And Pilate asked him, saying, Art thou the King of the Jews? And he answered him and said, Thou sayest. 4 And Pilate said

---

mathaea, members of the Sanhedrin, were not present. When Pilate became governor his first act was to bring the silver eagles of the Roman legion to Jerusalem, and to use money from the temple treasury for secular purposes; this greatly enraged the Jews.

2 **And they began to accuse him,**—The account of the charges against Jesus is recorded by Matthew, Mark, and John as well as by Luke. Matthew and Mark record about the same facts that are given by Luke, while John gives a much fuller record. The Sanhedrin would not enter into the praetorium, but made their charges to Pilate who came out to them. They simply wanted Pilate to ratify their decision; this he refused to do without knowing their accusation and the evidence that they had to give. The Jews felt that this was an insult to their high tribunal, the Sanhedrin. It is to be noticed that the charges they preferred against Jesus before Pilate were different from the ones they preferred against him in their own court; before the Sanhedrin he was charged with the crime of blasphemy, but before the Roman governor he is charged with "perverting our nation, and forbidding to give tribute to Caesar, and saying that he himself is Christ a king." These three charges before Pilate were false; Jesus had neither perverted the Jewish nation, nor had he forbidden to pay tribute to Caesar, neither was he a "King" aspiring to an earthly throne.

3 **And Pilate asked him,**—Pilate simply asked Jesus if the charges were true, and especially if he was "the King of the Jews." Before Jesus answered Pilate, he brought out clearly the distinction between a civil and a spiritual kingdom, declaring that his kingdom was "not of this world." (John 18: 36.) Jesus answered: "Thou sayest." This was an affirmative answer. (See Luke 22: 70.) All four of the writers of the gospel record Pilate's question to Jesus in the same language. (Matt. 27: 11; Mark 15: 2; Luke 23: 3; John 18: 33.)

unto the chief priests and the multitudes, I find no fault in this man. 5 But
they were the more urgent, saying, He stirreth up the people, teaching
throughout all Judæa, and beginning from Galilee even unto this place. 6
But when Pilate heard it, he asked whether the man was a Galilæan. 7

Matthew, Mark, and Luke record Jesus' answer in the same
language, while John gives a fuller answer.

4 **And Pilate said unto the chief priests**—Here Pilate declares the innocence of Jesus; his judgment was not pronounced until after the private interview Pilate had with Jesus.
Only John relates this interview. (John 18: 33-38.) It seems
that thus early in the day a multitude had now assembled, and
was present with the Sanhedrin. This is the first mention of
"the multitude"; it was now after daybreak; the procession of
the Sanhedrin would naturally draw a crowd; some of them
may have come to ask for the release of Jesus. (Mark 15: 8.)
There was need of haste if the condemnation went through
before friends of Jesus came.

5 **But they were the more urgent,**—The Jews kept insisting
that Pilate pass judgment on Jesus; it seems that they
thought that Pilate had taken the matter too lightly; hence,
they were more vigorous in repeating the charge that he perverted the nation or stirred up the people. Pilate had been
convinced that Jesus had committed no crime of treason
against the Roman government; he was not concerned about
their being aroused over any religious teaching. In fact, Pilate did not like the Jews, and he did not care who disturbed
their peace of mind so long as they remained peaceful citizens
of Rome. The Jews had found that their charge against Jesus
as a king did not disturb Pilate, hence they emphasized the
charge that he was an insurrectionist.

6, 7 **But when Pilate heard it,**—The Jews had mentioned the
fact that Jesus had disturbed their nation "throughout all Judaea, and beginning from Galilee," hence Pilate is prompted
to ask if Jesus "were a Galilaean." It is probable that the
Jews intended to excite prejudice against Jesus by mentioning
Galilee, knowing that Pilate had no love for Herod or the Galileans. If they thought that they would excite prejudice
against Jesus by speaking of Jesus as a Galilean, they were

And when he knew that he was of Herod's jurisdiction, he sent him unto Herod, who himself also was at Jerusalem in these days.

8 Now when Herod saw Jesus, he was exceeding glad; for he was of a long time desirous to see him, because he had heard concerning him; and he hoped to see some ³miracle done by him. 9 And he questioned him in many words; but he answered him nothing. 10 And the chief priests and the scribes stood, vehemently accusing him. 11 And Herod with his soldiers set him at nought, and mocked him, and arraying him in gorgeous apparel sent

³Gr. *sign*

again disappointed. So soon as Pilate learned that Jesus was a Galilean, he sought to evade any responsibility by referring Jesus to Herod. Herod was in Jerusalem at that time. Some think that Pilate was not seeking to get rid of a troublesome case, but that he was seeking for an occasion to become reconciled to Herod. At any rate, Pilate sent Jesus to Herod. It was easy for Pilate to do this, as Herod was in Jerusalem at that time, probably to attend the feast.

8 **Now when Herod saw Jesus,**—Herod had longed to see Jesus; he had recovered from his fright that Jesus was John the Baptist raised from the dead. (Matt. 14: 1, 2.) Herod was still selfish; he wanted to witness some miracle; he was not interested in Jesus as the Messiah or as a Savior; he was weak and sensual and cunning, but superstitious and cruel; he was revengeful. (Matt. 14: 9; Luke 3: 19; 9: 9; 13: 32.) Herod's curiosity had been excited greatly by the reports that he had heard of the miracles of Jesus; he wanted to be entertained by Jesus' working miracles; he had no further interest than to gratify his vain curiosity.

9-11 **And he questioned him in many words;**—Jesus had no desire to satisfy the wicked curiosity of Herod; he asked Jesus questions; we know not what the questions were, save than to know that he was not searching for the truth. Doubtless they were weak and frivolous questions, corresponding to the character of Herod. Jesus made no reply to Herod; he knew Herod's motive, and he had no intention of satisfying his curiosity. When Herod propounded his questions to Jesus the "chief priests and the scribes stood, vehemently accusing him." These Jews were afraid that Herod would not render a verdict in their favor; hence they loudly

him back to Pilate. 12 And Herod and Pilate became friends with each other
that very day: for before they were at enmity between themselves.

13 And Pilate called together the chief priests and the rulers and the people, 14 and said unto them, Ye brought unto me this man, as one that perverted the people: and behold, I having examined him before you, found no
fault in this man touching those things whereof ye accuse him: 15 no, nor
yet Herod: for ⁴he sent him back unto us; and behold, nothing worthy of

⁴Many ancient authorities read *I sent you to him*

---

and piously accused Jesus; what they lacked in facts they attempted to make up in their vehement charges. Herod and
his soldiers "mocked him, and arraying him in gorgeous apparel sent him back to Pilate." Herod was greatly disappointed, and he is willing to let his bodyguard join with the
Jews in reviling him. The Son of God stood before them, but
they could see in him only an object of contempt and derision!

12 And Herod and Pilate became friends—Luke does not
state why enmity existed between Herod and Pilate; neither
does profane history record the cause of enmity between them.
Some have thought it arose from some encroachment of Pilate
upon the jurisdiction of Herod. Herod seems to have regarded the case of Jesus as beneath his judicial notice, and Pilate wished to escape judging the case; yet it becomes the occasion of the reconciliation between Herod and Pilate. Pilate
had performed an act of courtesy toward Herod, which gave
him an opportunity to become friendly with Pilate We find
that Luke is the only writer that records the part that Herod
had to do with this transaction. We notice that before Herod,
Jesus maintained persistent silence, having not the least respect for his character, and being by no means disposed either
to gratify his curiosity or recognize his authority in the matter. It is a strange affair for two Gentile rulers at enmity
with each other to become reconciled in the trial of Jesus. It
is probable that they both agreed in despising Jesus, and in insulting him; it is common today to see the enemies of Jesus
agreeing in their opposition to the church.

13-15 And Pilate called together the chief priests—Herod
sent Jesus back to Pilate, and Pilate called "the chief priests
and the rulers and the people" together; we are not told why
he called "the people" with the rulers; perhaps he thought

death hath been done by him. 16 I will therefore chastise him, and release

---

Jesus might have some friends among the people who would help him plead for Jesus. Pilate was about to deliver his decree or judgment, hence if the people were present and in sympathy with Jesus, it would make it easier for Pilate to release Jesus. When they were assembled Pilate plainly told them that they had brought "this man" to him and had preferred certain charges against him, but that he had examined him in their presence and had "found no fault in this man"; he told them that their accusations against Jesus had not been sustained. Furthermore, he told them that he had sent Jesus to Herod, and that Herod had examined him, and had returned him without any charges proved against him. Pilate thus strengthens his own decree by the official judgment of Herod. He was not worthy of death; he had done nothing which seemed to be a violation of Roman law. Pilate delivers his judgment with emphatic words which imply that the Jews themselves could see that there was nothing to the charges which they made.

16 **I will therefore chastise him,**—Pilate was convinced that Jesus had done nothing worthy of death, or even worthy of any punishment; but in order to satisfy the Jews, he offers to "chastise" Jesus and release him. "Chastise" in the original means "to bring up a child," hence "to instruct," "to discipline or correct." This word is not synonymous with "punish," but since it always inplies an infliction, it gradually took the meaning of "punishment." "chasten" is derived from this word and properly means to "purify." Instead of punishing Jesus with death, Pilate thought to "chastise" him in order to teach him better. The chastisement that Pilate suggested here was that of scourging. It was a Roman custom to inflict upon criminals before crucifixion such punishment; sometimes during the trial of a prisoner, the Romans inflicted scourging in order to make the prisoner confess to the crime. The Roman scourging was more severe than the Jewish; the number of lashes was not limited to forty among the Romans. The whips were fitted with bones or lead to render the blow

him.⁵ 18 But they cried out all together, saying, Away with this man, and release unto us Barabbas:—19 one who for a certain insurrection made in the city, and for murder, was cast into prison. 20 And Pilate spake unto

⁵Many ancient authorities insert ver. 17 *Now he must needs release unto them at the feast one* prisoner. Comp. Mt. 27.15; Mk. 15.6; Jn. 18.39. Others add the same words after ver. 19

more fearful and to tear or lacerate the flesh. The criminal was generally bound to a low block, in a stooping posture, and received the fearful blows upon the naked back. The scourging before crucifixion was generally exceedingly cruel, and victims frequently died while being scourged.

The American Revised Version omits verse 17; it seems not to occur in the best manuscripts now available. In the King James Version it is inserted and inclosed in parentheses. It is found in Matt. 27: 15; Mark 15: 6; John 18: 39. "Now he must needs release unto them at the feast one prisoner." Though this verse is omitted from Luke, yet the other writers and history fully establish the custom established by the Romans of releasing a prisoner at the feast; the custom was established to conciliate the Jews and make them more submissive to Roman law at their feast; the Jews gathered from all countries at Jerusalem to keep their feast, and oftentimes they were rebellious. Many insurrections among the Jews occurred at their feasts.

18, 19 **But they cried out all together,**—Matthew and Mark particularly describe the character of Barabbas; Matthew records the dream and message of Pilate's wife. (Matt. 27: 19.) "They" include the chief priests, the rulers, and the people; the rulers had "persuaded the multitudes that they should ask for Barabbas, and destroy Jesus." (Matt. 27: 20.) Mark mentions only the "chief priests" as being the ones who stirred up the multitude to ask the release of Barabbas. (Mark 15: 11.) From Matthew we learn that Pilate himself had suggested the release of Barabbas. (Matt. 27: 17.) The Jews who claimed to be sticklers for the law deliberately violate their own law in preferring to release a murderer and put to death the Messiah. (Lev. 24: 17; Num. 35: 16-24.) Peter said later in accusing the Jews of the death of Jesus that they had delivered him up, "and denied before the face of Pilate,

them again, desiring to release Jesus; 21 but they shouted, saying, Crucify, crucify him. 22 And he said unto them the third time, Why, what evil hath this man done? I have found no cause of death in him: I will therefore

when he had determined to release him." He further charges them that they had denied "the Holy and Righteous One, and asked for a murderer to be granted" unto them. (Acts 3: 13, 14.) The multitude was made up of those who had come together during the arrest and trial of Jesus, and those who had gathered from the streets as they marched Jesus as a prisoner to Pilate's court.

20, 21 **And Pilate spake unto them again,**—Pilate, like most weak men, was evidently superstitious, as the tone of his wife's message implies. (Matt. 27: 19, 24.) He desired to release Jesus because he knew that he was innocent and that the Jews were envious of him. The people had made their choice; it was opposed to the judgment of Pilate; Pilate asked them what he should do with Jesus. Pilate had hoped that they would choose to release Jesus; he had put up one of the worst criminals that was held in prison at that time, thinking that surely they would choose to release Jesus rather than Barabbas; but now when they chose to release Barabbas, Pilate seeks another way of releasing Jesus. Hence, according to Matthew and Mark, he asks what he should do with Jesus. They, in answer to this query, "shouted, saying, Crucify, crucify him." Their clamor was so loud and so persistent that Pilate is swayed by their choice; however, he knows that Jesus is innocent.

22 **And he said unto them the third time,**—Pilate was persistent in his attempt to release Jesus. He asked them the third time what wrong he had done; they had proved none of their charges; Pilate had let them know that he did not accept the evidence that they gave; furthermore, he let them know that he did not believe that Jesus had done anything worthy of death. In asking them the third time the reason for their demand, Pilate was rejecting all former charges and evidence formerly given. The Jews were as persistent in demanding the death of Jesus as Pilate was in desiring to release him. Instead of acquitting Jesus, Pilate partially laid aside his

chastise him and release him. 23 But they were urgent with loud voices, asking that he might be crucified. And their voices prevailed. 24 And Pilate gave sentence that what they asked for should be done. 25 And he re-

rights as a judge and asked the decision of the people. (Mark 15: 12.) Pilate now, having heard their decision, accepts the situation, but strives to reason with them. If they insist on his death, they must show some crime meriting such a punishment. Jesus had done nothing worthy of crucifixion. Instead of stopping to reason with them, Pilate should have retraced his steps and acted the part of a righteous judge and released Jesus. However, he again offered to "chastise him" and release him. Though he had found no evil in him, yet as a matter of expediency, he again proposes to conciliate the Jews by the milder punishment of scourging. The Jews saw their advantage and made the most of it.

23, 24 **But they were urgent with loud voices,**—The Jews with loud and importunate cries demanded that Jesus be crucified. The people led by the rulers prevailed upon Pilate to comply with their wishes. "Prevailed" implies great and persistent effort before they could induce the governor to pass sentence upon him who they knew and Pilate knew was innocent. Nothing short of death by crucifixion would satisfy their rage and bitter hatred. Pilate gave his judicial sentence after the renewed efforts to release Jesus. He had tried every means and method that he knew to release Jesus; he was too weak to exercise his own good judgment; he was too wicked to uphold a righteous judgment. He had no right to pronounce what he knew to be an unrighteous condemnation, and to relieve himself of the responsibility of a judge was impossible. At this time Matthew records that Pilate took a basin of water and washed his hands before the multitude (Deut. 21: 6-9) and said: "I am innocent of the blood of this righteous man: see ye to it" (Matt. 27: 24). Pilate could not have escaped full legal and moral responsibility for his cowardly surrender to the Sanhedrin; the guilt of the Pharisees and Sadducees unites in the demand for the blood of Jesus, hence they are not free from his blood. This was a bitter mockery of justice in the sentence that Pilate passed; his sentence is not accord-

leased him that for insurrection and murder had been cast into prison, whom they asked for; but Jesus he delivered up to their will.

ing to the guilt of the prisoner, not in harmony with the testimony, but was a yielding to the hatred of the Jews toward Jesus.

25 And he released him that for insurrection and murder— The Jews had asked for the release of Barabbas instead of Jesus; they knew the character of Barabbas; they chose him, not so much because they preferred or endorsed murder, but because they hated Jesus so much. Luke omitted from his record the scourging of Jesus, the mockings of the soldiers, Pilate's appeal to the sympathy of the Jews, their declaring him worthy of death because he made himself the Son of God, Pilate's greater fear and his bringing Jesus again into the judgment hall, Jesus' speaking of Pilate's power and the greater sin of the Jews, Pilate's seeking again to release Jesus, the declaring of the Jews that Pilate is not Caesar's friend if he let Jesus go, Pilate's bringing Jesus to his judgment seat on the pavement, the Jews' answer to Pilate's final appeal.

11. THE CRUCIFIXION
23: 26-38

26 And when they led him away, they laid hold upon one Simon of Cyrene, coming from the country, and laid on him the cross, to bear it after Jesus.

26 And when they led him away,—Jesus was led away to be crucified; Pilate had given his judicial sentence; the rulers of the Jews were now satisfied; they had won a victory. Luke's account of the crucifixion is the fullest; Mark describes Simon of Cyrene more fully than do the others. Parallel records may be found in Matt. 27: 31-34; Mark 15: 20-23; John 19: 16, 17. As they led Jesus away, "they laid hold upon one Simon of Cyrene." He was led out of the city, for the crucifixion took place without the gates of the city. (Lev. 16: 27; Heb. 13: 12.) Criminals were executed outside the city, and eJsus was crucified as a criminal. (Lev. 24: 14; Num. 15: 35; 1 Kings 21: 13; Acts 7: 58.) The four soldiers (John 19: 23)

27 And there followed him a great multitude of the people, and of women
who bewailed and lamented him.   28 But Jesus turning unto them said,
Daughters of Jerusalem, weep not for me, but weep for yourselves, and for

---

under the direction of the centurion, who usually rode on
horseback, led the procession; the victim to suffer followed.
Simon of Cyrene came along as Jesus bore his cross; Matthew
and Mark record that they compelled Simon to bear the cross
of Jesus. We know nothing further of this Simon; Cyrene
was an important city in northern Africa between Egypt and
the territory of Carthage; many Jews resided there at this
time. Probably Simon with others had come to Jerusalem to
the feast; we know that some Jews attended the feast from
Cyrene. (Acts 2: 10; 6: 9.) We know not the weight of the
cross; the cross was in various forms. It was originally a
simple stake; afterwards it was made of two pieces of wood
crossed like the letter T; sometimes it was in the form of the
letter X. The transverse beam crossed the upright beam a
short distance from the top.

27 **And there followed him a great multitude**—This multitude was mingled with friends, foes, and those who were curious to see what was to be done. The women who followed
lamented; they evidently were not of the company who
shouted: "Crucify, crucify him." The original conveys the
idea that they "bewailed," literally "beat themselves," and "lamented," literally "wept aloud" for him. Luke is the only
writer that records this scene. Usually wailing was accompanied by beating the breast in token of grief. Women were the
only ones recorded as weeping for Jesus as he marched to the
place of crucifixion; women were the last at the tomb and the
first at the tomb on the morning of the resurrection.

28 **But Jesus turning unto them said,**—This shows that the
women were weeping for Jesus, and that they were not from
Galilee, but Jerusalem. Jerusalem was soon to be destroyed
and these women were to suffer untold evils themselves;
Jesus in tenderness and loving-kindness foretold these sufferings. He was going to a glorious victory through death, not
for himself, but for others, and they need not weep for him.
They should weep for themselves and their children because

your children. 29 For behold, the days are coming, in which they shall say,
Blessed are the barren, and the wombs that never bare, and the breasts that
never gave suck. 30 Then shall they begin to say to the mountains, Fall on
us; and to the hills, Cover us. 31 For if they do these things in the green
tree, what shall be done in the dry?

32 And there were also two others, malefactors, led with him to be put to
death.

---

their children would be involved in the destruction of Jerusalem. The sorrow which they were now experiencing was only
the beginning of that which would soon come upon them.

29, 30 **For behold, the days are coming,**—The prediction
here admits of application to any times of distress and calamity in the history of the Jews; but it seems to have direct reference to the sufferings that should come upon them in the
destruction of Jerusalem. "Blessed are the barren" because, if
they had children, they would have to see them suffer the destruction that awaited the doomed city. Such intense sufferings would characterize those days that those who had never
borne children would be regarded as fortunate. Among the
Jews it was considered very unfortunate for wives to be barren; but the time would come when this would be reversed.
The universal dread of barrenness was felt by every Jewish
female in ancient days, but the time would come when they
would be glad that they were barren. This language seems to
have been taken from Isa. 54: 1.

31 **For if they do these things in the green tree,**—Jesus here
uses a common proverb to convey more vividly the awfulness
of their coming sufferings. The green tree is the symbol of
the righteousness and the dry tree of the wicked. (Psalm 1:
3; Ezek. 20: 47.) If an innocent man should so suffer, what
would be the fate of the wicked? The green tree is representative of one which bears fruit, while the dry tree represents
the one that does not bear fruit, but is ready to be burned.
The Jewish people were now rejecting him and leading him
forth to the death of the cross; upon them would come fearful
judgment. They were more guilty than those who would
take no part in the crucifixion. (1 Pet. 4: 12-18.)

32 **And there were also two others, malefactors,**—"Malefactor" means evildoer; Matthew and Mark call them "robbers"

33 And when they came unto the place which is called ¹The skull, there they crucified him, and the malefactors, one on the right hand and the other on the left. 34 ²And Jesus said, Father, forgive them; for they know not

¹According to the Latin, *Calvary*, which has the same meaning
²Some ancient authorities omit *And Jesus said, Father, forgive them: for they know not what they do*

(Matt. 27: 38, 44; Mark 15: 27); they were guilty of some crime, probably that of robbing. Some think that they belonged to the band of Barabbas; however, we cannot determine this. We do not know when the malefactors were condemned; it seems that they had been condemned previous to the condemnation of Jesus, and were awaiting their execution. It was prophesied that Jesus should be numbered with the transgressors, but nowhere is he called a malefactor. (Isa. 53: 12; Luke 22: 37.) These malefactors were conducted by the soldiers to the place of execution and were compelled to bear their own cross.

33 **And when they came unto the place**—The corresponding word for "skull" in the Aramaic or Hebrew is "Golgotha," while in the Latin it is "Calvary." It is thought that it was called "skull" because the shape of the mountain or hill resembled a skull. Jesus was crucified between the two robbers and on the cross probably that Barabbas was to have suffered on. The governor was accustomed to crucify criminals at the Passover; it was a suitable time, as it would impress on the multitude the importance of submitting to the Roman law. They nailed Jesus to the cross; it is not known whether he was nailed to the cross before it was erected, or after it was erected; both methods were used at that time. Death did not ensue in most cases until many hours after the victim was thus affixed to the cross.

34 **And Jesus said, Father, forgive them;**—There are seven recorded statements that Jesus made while on the cross; this is the first one that Luke records. We do not know the chronological order of the seven recorded utterances made by Jesus on the cross; they are called "the seven words." They are as follows: "Father, forgive them; for they know not what they do" (Luke 23: 34); "To-day shalt thou be with me in Paradise" (Luke 23: 43); "Woman, behold, thy son!"

what they do. And parting his garments among them, they cast lots. 35
And the people stood beholding. And the rulers also scoffed at him, saying,
He saved others; let him save himself, if this is the Christ of God, his chosen. 36 And the soldiers also mocked him, coming to him, offering him vinegar, 37 and saying, If thou art the King of the Jews, save thyself. 38 And

---

"Behold, thy mother!" (John 19: 26, 27); "My God, my God,
why hast thou forsaken me?" (Matt. 27: 46)'; "I thirst"
(John 19: 28); "It is finished" (John 19: 30); "Father, into
thy hands I commend my spirit" (Luke 23: 46).

They were ignorant of the enormous crime that they were
committing; this ignorance, though it did not excuse.them,
may have mitigated somewhat their sin. (Acts 3: 17; 1 Cor.
2: 8.) "Parting his garments among them, they cast lots";
criminals were crucified naked; some think that a linen cloth
was bound about the loins; from John 19: 23, 24, it appears
that the four soldiers who are engaged in the crucifixion divided some of the garments among themselves, but cast lot
for his coat, as it was without a seam and woven throughout.

35 **And the people stood beholding.**—Both Matthew and
Mark speak of the people scoffing him as they pass by; Luke
does not deny this, but adds that the "rulers also scoffed at
him." Luke tells us just what they said: "He saved others; let
him save himself, if this is the Christ of God, his chosen."
The rulers could not let him die in peace; they were not willing for him to have a quiet moment in which to die. They
had been compelled to acknowledge his supernatural power in
saving others, and should have believed on him; but they now
taunt him with having lost that power when he needed it for
his own deliverance; they treated him as an impostor. They
thought that if he was what he claimed to be he would be able
to save himself; they mocked his claim as the Son of God.
They sneered at him and heaped all indignities upon him in
his dying moments. How great was their sin!

36, 37 **And the soldiers also mocked him,**—The soldiers
joined in the popular excitement and clamor. They were willing in their cruel and crude way to add to the humiliation suffering of Jesus. We are told that they brought him vinegar to
drink and derided him; they mocked him and his claims to be

there was also a superscription over him, THIS IS THE KING OF THE
JEWS.

King of the Jews. They used almost the same language that
the chief priests used. (Matt. 27: 42.) The rulers derided
Jesus as the Christ, while the soldiers jeered him as the
King of the Jews. "The Gentiles and the peoples of Israel,
were gathered together, to do whatsoever" they could against
Jesus. (Acts 4: 27, 28.) They meant that Jesus pretended to
be a king and that now was the time for him to show his authority; they did not understand the nature of his kingdom.

38 **And there was also a superscription over him,**—It was
the custom to write the crime for which the victim was dying
and place it over his head on the cross. Sometimes a public
crier announced it; he would follow the victim as he bore his
cross and announce to the people along the way the crime for
which he was to die. It seems that Pilate had written this inscription. (John 19: 22.) Sometimes the inscription was
written on a white tablet and hung about the neck of the criminal. In some instances all three methods were followed: one
would follow or lead and announce the crime, then the victim
would have a placard bound around his neck telling the crime,
and then another would be placed on the cross. This inscription was written in Greek, Latin, and Hebrew so that all
could read it. All four writers of the gospel give this inscription; they differ as to the wording of the inscription. This
difference is accounted for in the fact that it was written in
three languages: one writer would give the translation in one
of the languages, another in another language. The writers
could give only the meaning of the inscription and not the
words of it.

12. THE THIEF ON THE CROSS
23: 39-43

39 And one of the malefactors that were hanged railed on him, saying,

---

39 **And one of the malefactors**—Both Matthew and Mark
say that the "robbers" or "they that were crucified with him

Art not thou the Christ? save thyself and us. 40 But the other answered, and rebuking him said, Dost thou not even fear God, seeing thou art in the same condemnation? 41 And we indeed justly; for we receive the due reward of our deeds: but this man hath done nothing amiss. 42 And he said,

---

reproached him." (Matt. 27: 44; Mark 15: 32.) Luke speaks of only one who railed upon him, and records that only one asked him if he were "the Christ," and if he be the Christ to save himself and "us." This is harmonized by the fact that both at first may have joined in the reproaches hurled at Jesus by the rulers and people; but one of them, being afterward convinced of the Messiahship of Jesus, repented. It seems that the climax of the picture is reached in the reproaches of his fellow sufferers. The agonies of crucifixion did not suppress nor subdue the enmity toward Jesus. If he be the Christ, then he should show his power by coming down from the cross.

40, 41 **But the other answered, and rebuking him said,**— The rebuke was conveyed in the question: "Dost thou not even fear God?" The meaning seems to be that those who were railing upon Jesus among the rulers and chief priests did not fear God, and this malefactor, by railing upon Jesus, put himself in the class of those who did not fear God. The meaning is, have you no fear of divine justice, that at this awful moment you can taunt and jeer at an innocent man? This robber confessed that he and his fellow robber were suffering justly; that they, by their crimes and wickedness, merited in a judicial sense the punishment that they were suffering. "But this man hath done nothing amiss. Both were soon to appear before God; Jesus had nothing to answer for, but the other had added to his former sins the sin of reviling an innocent man in his death. Even in the mind of this malefactor the commission of one of the greatest crimes that the human mind could conceive would not justify such taunts, jeers, and insults as were being heaped upon Jesus by the rabble who had gathered around the cross.

42 **And he said, Jesus, remember me**—The penitent malefactor now turns to Jesus and pleads that he may be remembered when Jesus comes into his kingdom. He seems to pray to

Jesus, remember me when thou comest ³in thy kingdom. 43 And he said
unto him, Verily I say unto thee, To-day shalt thou be with me in Paradise.

³Some ancient authorities read *into thy kingdom*

Jesus, not for deliverance from the cross, nor for any present
good, but for a blessing which can be conferred only after his
death, which he recognized as inevitable. Some think that he
had a misconception of the nature of the kingdom that Jesus
was to establish, and that he thought, in some way, that Jesus
would come into possession of his earthly kingdom, and that
he might save him from the cross. If he understood the nature of the kingdom that Jesus was to establish he had a
deeper insight into the spiritual nature of the kingdom than
did the apostles, or anyone else, at that time. This penitent
malefactor had confessed his sins, reproved his companion, de-
fended Jesus, and now asked Jesus to remember him. We do
not know how much knowledge of Jesus and his claim this robber had. We only have Luke's record of the account. The
kingdom had not been established at this time, and this robber
lived and died under the law of Moses; he must be judged by
it.

43 **And he said unto him, Verily I say unto thee,**—The answer that Jesus gave to this penitent malefactor has received
many different interpretations. Jesus used his familiar form
of speech to preface his answer. Jesus said to him : "To-day
shalt thou be with me in Paradise." Jesus had observed the
most profound silence amidst the jeers of the rulers and multitude, but now he is ready to make reply to this penitent,
dying man. The statement that Jesus gave him can be understood when we know the general teachings of the Christ.
"To-day," not at some time in the distant future, but this
very day, you are to be associated with me in the pains and
death of the cross and are to be associated with me in "Paradise." "Paradise" originally meant "an enclosed park or plea-
sure-ground." In the Septuagint Version (Gen. 2: 8) it
means the Garden of Eden. We are told that in Jewish theol-
ogy the department of Hades where the blessed souls await
the resurrection is calld "Paradise"; it is equivalent to
"Abraham's bosom." (Luke 16: 22, 23.) It occurs three

times in the New Testament—in this passage, 2 Cor. 12: 4;
Rev. 2: 7. It always seems to mean the abode of the blessed.
Some doubt that the evidence in the scripture is strong
enough to warrant a belief in the intermediate state of the
dead. Whatever may have been the conception of the early
Hebrews with regard to the separation between the righteous
and the wicked in Sheol, those of a later period did conceive a
separation; hence to them Hades and Sheol designated the
place of the righteous and the wicked dead; Hades was the
place for the blessed and called Paradise, while the wicked
dwelt in the abyss called Tartarus. Evidently Jesus did not
mean that this robber would go with him to heaven that day,
as it seems clear from other statements that Jesus did not go
to heaven that day. His day of ascension came about forty
days after that time. After Jesus was raised from the dead
and appeared to Mary, when she recognized him he said to
her: "Touch me not; for I am not yet ascended unto the
Father." (John 20: 17.)

13. THE BURIAL OF JESUS
23: 44-56

44 And it was now about the sixth hour, and a darkness came over the

44 **And it was now about the sixth hour,**—Parallel records
of this are in Matt. 27: 45-50; Mark 15: 33-37; John 19: 28-
30. It seems that Jesus was crucified or nailed to the cross
about nine o'clock Friday morning, as Mark says that "it was
the third hour, and they cricified him." (Mark 15: 25.) The
first three hours that Jesus remained on the cross would bring
the time to twelve noon; some think that only three of the
sayings of Jesus were spoken during these hours, which seems
to be correct. "About the sixth hour" or twelve o'clock noon,
"a darkness came over the whole land until the ninth hour."
That is, darkness came over the land of Palestine from twelve
o'clock to three o'clock in the afternoon. The darkness began
at "the sixth hour"; that is, twelve o'clock, and lasted until
three o'clock in the afternoon. The heavy veil of the temple
which separated the holy from the most holy place in the

whole ⁴land until the ninth hour, 45 ⁵the sun's light failing: and the veil of the ⁶temple was rent in the midst. 46 ⁷And Jesus, crying with a loud voice, said, Father, into thy hands I commend my spirit: and having said this, he gave up the ghost. 47 And when the centurion saw what was done, he glorified God, saying, Certainly this was a righteous man. 48 And all the multi-

⁴Or, earth
⁵Gr. the sun failing
⁶Or, sanctuary
⁷Or, And when Jesus had cried with a loud voice, he said

sanctuary of the temple was rent from top to bottom; this signified that a new, "living way" was consecrated, whereby all believers might come into the presence of God. It is not claimed that this darkness was caused by an eclipse, nor was it the natural darkness that precedes an earthquake; it was a miracle; this is the only way that we can account for it.

45, 46 **the sun's light failing:**—we can only account for the physical phenomena that occurred by saying that a miracle was worked; the Son of God was dying and the physical elements were drooped in mourning of the awful occasion; after the darkening of the earth the sun and moon were obscured; during this time the veil of the temple was rent, which signified that the end of the temple service had come. This veil separated the temple into the two parts—holy and most holy. When this veil was rent, the distinction between the two places was destroyed, and that signified the services of the high priest and other priests were at an end. The high priest entered into the most holy place only once in the year to make an atonement for the people. (Ex. 30: 10; Lev. 16: 15-17; Heb. 9: 7.) So the rending of the veil destroyed the sanctity of these two divisions of the temple. Jesus, our great high priest, entered into the most holy place to make atonement through his blood for our sins. (Heb. 9: 12-14, 25, 26.)

47 **And when the centurion saw what was done,**—Matthew records that the centurion "and they that were with him watching Jesus" "feared exceedingly." (Matt. 27: 54.) We do not know how much the centurion knew of God; he is recorded as glorifying God and saying: "Certainly this was a righteous man." His conclusion was drawn from the physical phenomena which accompanied the death of Christ. Luke mentions several centurions who were good men. (Luke 7:

tudes that came together to this sight, when they beheld the things that were
done, returned smiting their breasts. 49 And all his acquaintance, and the
women that followed with him from Galilee, stood afar off, seeing these
things.
50 And behold, a man named Joseph, who was a councillor, a good and

---

2; 23: 47; Acts 10: 1; 22: 26, 27; 43.) He felt that Jesus was
a righteous man when he saw the forgiving spirit and the
earthquake and heard all that Jesus had said on the cross.

48, 49 **And all the multitudes that came together**—The people had been urged on to their course by the chief priests and
rulers; it seems that some had been held back. When they
saw the remarkable character they were troubled and left the
scene smiting their breasts as an expression of extreme grief
and deep mental anguish. Jesus had died earlier than some
die on the cross. Sometimes the victim on the cross would
not expire for one or two days; the Jews wanted to hasten the
death of Jesus and the two who were crucified with him by
breaking their bones. (John 19: 31, 32.) However, when
they came to examine Jesus' body they found that he was
dead, and they broke the bones of the two malefactors to hasten their death, so that they would not remain on the cross over
the Sabbath. It is strange that they would be so particular
about the Sabbath when they were committing the high crime
of crucifying the Son of God! They were fulfilling the statement that Jesus had made to them when he said that they
were "blind guides, that strain out the gnat, and swallow the
camel!" (Matt. 23: 24.) A study of those who were present
at the crucifixion leads us to group them into four classes.
They were as follows: (1) the centurion and his soldiers; (2)
the Jewish leaders; (3) the women who were his disciples, and
who "stood afar off"; (4) and the crowd or multitude that
gathered around the cross. This group of women who had
"followed with him from Galilee" appeared to be a different
group of women from those who followed him as he bore his
cross. (See verse 27.) This group of women included the
mother of Jesus.

50-52 **And behold, a man named Joseph,**—Parallel records
of the burial of Jesus are found in Matt. 27: 57-61; Mark 15:

righteous man 51 (he had not consented to their counsel and deed) *a man* of Arimathæa, a city of the Jews, who was looking for the kingdom of God: 52 this man went to Pilate, and asked for the body of Jesus. 53 And he took it down, and wrapped it in a linen cloth, and laid him in a tomb that was hewn

---

42-47; John 19: 31-42. All of the records recite that Joseph of Arimathea was a disciple of Jesus. John records that he was a disciple, "but secretly for fear of the Jews" was not an open disciple. However, Mark records him as going to Pilate "boldly" and asking for the body of Jesus. He was a member of the Sanhedrin, a good, just, and rich man. He had not voted with the council to condemn Jesus; he alone is named as not agreeing to the verdict of the council, but it is probable that Nicodemus, who is present, must have voted against the decision of the Sanhedrin. It is not known whether Joseph or Nicodemus were present, though it is specifically stated that Joseph "had not consented to their counsel and deed." The exact location of Arimathea is not known, but some think that it was about six miles north of Jerusalem. Luke describes the faith of Joseph by saying that he "was looking for the kingdom of God." This shows that he expected the Messiah and expected the kingdom of God to be set up. His boldness in asking Pilate for the body of Jesus is put in contrast with his being a secret disciple of Jesus; it is hard to understand why he should be so timid during the life of Jesus, yet so bold as to ask Pilate for his body. John is the only writer who informs us that Nicodemus was with Joseph in the burial of Jesus. (John 19: 38, 39.) We have only three mentions of Nicodemus in the New Testament, and John is the only writer that mentions Nicodemus. (John 3: 1-9; 7: 50; 19: 39.)

53 **And he took it down, and wrapped it**—Joseph had "asked" or made an urgent request of Pilate for the body of Jesus. He was aided by Nicodemus and perhaps by some servants, as he was a "rich man." He took the body from the cross and "wrapped it in a linen cloth." This was a "winding sheet" in which the body of the dead was wrapped; the mummies of Egypt were wrapped in "fine linen"; the body of Jesus was wrapped "in a clean linen cloth," according to Matthew. Mark records that Joseph "bought a linen cloth" (Mark 15:

in stone, where never man had yet lain. 54 And it was the day of the Preparation, and the sabbath drew on. 55 And he women, who had come with him out of Galilee, followed after, and beheld the tomb, and how his body

⁸Gr. *began to dawn*

46), and John records that Nicodemus brought "a. mixture of myrrh and aloes, about a hundred pounds" (John 19: 39), and in this way they embalmed the body of Jesus and placed it in Joseph's new tomb. Both Matthew and John state that it was a "new tomb"; this "new tomb" was hewn out of rock. The tombs of the Jews were generally cut out of solid rock; sometimes they were below the level of the ground, but often they were above the ground on the sides of hills and mountains. It seems that the tomb of Joseph was the family vault. Joseph being a rich man could give the body of Jesus such a burial. The prophecy of Isaiah was fulfilled here, "and they made his grave with the wicked, and with a rich man in his death." (Isa. 53: 9.)

54 **And it was the day of the Preparation,**—The day before the Sabbath was called the day of Preparation; hence this was the sixth day of the week, or what we call Friday. Matthew and Mark say nothing about the "day of the Preparation," but both Luke and John mention it. The Sabbath "drew on," or literally "began to dawn," meaning the evening light of the Sabbath, not the morning; it was the dawn at sunset, for the Sabbath began at sunset. The women of Galilee observed where and how the body of Jesus was placed. Luke does not here speak of the twelve-hour day which began with sunrise. but the twenty-four-hour day which began at sunset.

55 **And the women, who had come with him**—These women had followed from Galilee; they watched where the body of Jesus was placed. Evidently the Jews had also observed what Joseph and Nicodemus had done; they were little concerned now since Jesus was dead as to what would be done with his body. It seems that while Joseph and Nicodemus were burying the body the Jews had gone to Pilate and asked that a guard be placed around the tomb. Though Matthew did not speak of that day as being "the Preparation" day as did Luke and John, yet Matthew speaks of "the day after the Prepara-

was laid. 56 And they returned, and prepared spices and ointments.
And on the sabbath they rested according to the commandment.

tion." (Matt. 27: 62.) This group of women from Galilee had often ministered to Jesus; they were standing afar off during the dreadful scene of the crucifixion, and are now observing the burial of his body.

56 **And they returned, and prepared spices and ointments.** —Luke (23: 54) notes that "the sabbath drew on" after the burial on Friday afternoon; the Sabbath began at 6:00 P.M.; then Luke notes that the women rested during the Sabbath, which would be Friday night and Saturday. The spices and perfumes that they prepared would complete the proper embalming of the body; these were bought and prepared, but owing to the late hour, seemed to be laid aside until after the Sabbath. They rested on that day according to the commandment of Moses. (Ex. 12: 16; 20: 8-11; Deut. 5: 1-15.) The teachings of Jesus served to make them careful observers of the moral law as well as the law regulating the Sabbath. Some think that the two Marys remained too long at the tomb to make purchases on Friday. (Mark 15: 47.) Matthew (27: 62-66) records the sealing and guarding of the tomb, the chief priests and Pharisees asking Pilate to make the sepulchre secure, and his granting their request.

SECTION SEVEN

RESURRECTION, COMMISSION, ASCENSION OF JESUS
24: 1-53

1. THE EMPTY TOMB
24: 1-12

1 But on the first day of the week, at early dawn, they came unto the tomb, bringing the spices which they had prepared. 2 And they found the

---

1 **But on the first day of the week,**—The Jewish Sabbath had passed, which corresponds to our Saturday; "the first day of the week," or our Sunday had now arrived. Jesus arose early on the first day of the week; he was buried shortly before sunset on Friday, and at sunset the Sabbath began. His body lay in the tomb a small part of Friday, all day Saturday, and about ten or eleven hours on Sunday. This corresponds with the seven times' repeated statement that he would or did rise "on the third day," which could not possibly mean after seventy-two hours. The phrase, "after three days," naturally denoted for Jews, Greeks, and Romans a whole day and any part of a first and third, thus agreeing with the phrase, "on the third day." The "three days and three nights" (Matt. 12: 40) need not, according to Jewish usage, mean more than what is here designated. All these expressions can be reconciled with the phrase "on the third day," and with all the facts as recorded, but the phrase "on the third day" cannot mean after seventy-two hours. Luke states definitely that Jesus was buried just before the Sabbath "drew on" (our Friday evening); that the women rested during the Sabbath (our Saturday), and that Jesus was already risen early Sunday morning when the women came to the tomb. Mark names the women as "Mary Magdalene, and Mary the mother of James, and Salome." (Mark 16: 1.) Matthew mentions "Mary Magdalene and the other Mary" (Matt. 28: 1) as coming to the tomb that morning. Some versions insert the clause "certain others with them," but this is omitted in the Revised Version. Luke mentions "Mary Magdalene, and Joanna, and Mary the

stone rolled away from the tomb. 3 And they entered in, and found not the body [1]of the Lord Jesus. 4 And it came to pass, while they were perplexed thereabout, behold, two men stood by them in dazzling apparel: 5 and as they were affrighted and bowed down their faces to the earth, they said unto them, Why seek ye [2]the living among the dead? 6 [3]He is not here, but is

[1]Some ancient authorities omit *of the Lord Jesus*
[2]Gr. *him that liveth*
[3]Some ancient authorities omit *He is not here, but is risen*

---

mother of James; and the other women with them" (24: 10); they were the women who had followed him from Galilee.

2, 3 And they found the stone rolled away—The stone served as a door to the tomb (Matt. 27: 60; Mark 15: 46), or the stone was rolled against the door of the tomb. Matthew is the only writer that records the circumstances of the removal of the stone; he states that there was a great earthquake and that "an angel of the Lord descended from heaven, and came and rolled away the stone, and sat upon it." (Matt. 28: 2.) The women were deeply concerned about the stone and discussed it as they went along the way. (Mark 16: 3.) It seems the stone was heavy, as it had been described as "a great stone." (Matt. 27: 60.) It was too heavy for the women to remove, and yet they wanted to enter the tomb, but when they arrived there early that morning, the stone had been rolled away and they entered the tomb, but "found not the body of the Lord Jesus."

4, 5 And it came to pass, while they were—The vacant tomb was not expected; those who visited it were at a loss to account for what had occurred; they were "perplexed." The women saw the empty tomb and "two men stood by them in dazzling apparel." They were "men," not "women"; Mark 16: 5 speaks of a young man while Matt. 28: 5 has "the angel." There is no contradiction here, but perfect harmony. The angel looked like a man and some of them remembered seeing two. In verse 23 "angels" are mentioned. Matthew and Mark mention one angel. Angelic beings often appeared to have the power to become visible and invisible at will. Matthew and Mark represent the angel as sitting, while Luke represents them standing; no contradiction here as they could at one moment be sitting and at another be standing, or they

risen: remember how he spake unto you when he was yet in Galilee, 7 saying that the Son of man must be delivered up into the hands of sinful men,
and be crucified, and the third day rise again. 8 And they remembered his
words, 9 and returned ⁴from the tomb, and told all these things to the

⁴Some ancient authorities omit *from the tomb*

could have been sitting when the women approached and
standing while talking to them. Frightened by the sudden
appearance of the forms in shining garments, they fell upon
their faces in fear and awe; the angels spoke tenderly unto
them and asked: "Why seek ye the living among the dead?"
This was another way of saying that Jesus had risen from the
dead; Jesus' body had been placed in the grave; he had been
among the dead, but was now, and forevermore, among the
living; those who seek him today must seek him among the
living.

6, 7 **He is not here, but is risen:**—In addition to the testimony of the angels, the physical surroundings bore evidence
of his resurrection. The empty tomb, the earthquake, the soldiers on guard falling at the sight, the stone rolled away, the
orderly folded napkin which was placed in proper order, all
were added evidence of the resurrection. The evidence given
by the Holy Spirit through the different writers of the New
Testament emphasizes the resurrection of Jesus. (Acts 1: 22;
2: 31; 4: 2; 17: 18; Rom. 6: 5; 1 Cor. 15: 1-42; 1 Pet. 1: 3.)
"Alive for evermore." (Rev. 1: 18.) The message to them
was that they should "remember how he spake unto you when
he was yet in Galilee." (See Matt. 17: 23; Luke 18: 33; John
11: 25.) Jesus had predicted his death and also his resurrection. In order that they should not forget his prediction Luke
here repeats it.

8, 9 **And they remembered his words,**—For the first time it
seems that they now understood in a vague way the significance of his language repeatedly made predicting his death
and resurrection. This company returned from the tomb to
the city, which was only a short walk requiring fifteen or
twenty minutes; they reported all that had been seen and
heard at the tomb to the eleven disciples and other disciples in
Jerusalem. It seems that Mary Magdalene went from the

eleven, and to all the rest. 10 Now they were Mary Magdalene, and Joanna, and Mary the *mother* of James: and the other women with them told these things unto the apostles. 11 And these words appeared in their sight as idle talk; and they disbelieved them. 12 But Peter arose, and ran unto the tomb: and stooping and looking in, he seeth the linen cloths by themselves: and he [6]departed to his home, wondering at that which was come to pass.

[5]Some ancient authorities omit ver. 12
[6]Or, *departed, wondering with himself*

tomb before this company and told Peter of the rolling away of the stone and of the angel. (Matt. 22: 8; John 20: 2.) The company lingered, went into the tomb, and so had other facts to report besides those observed and reported by Mary Magdalene. Luke seems to omit what is related by Matthew and Mark; no discrepancy is seen, as one writer records one point and another writer records some other; putting all the records together we have the full account.

10, 11 **Now they were Mary Magdalene, and Joanna,**—This shows that Mary Magdalene was one of the company, but when she saw the stone rolled away, she ran to tell Peter, while the others remained to look into the empty tomb. It should be remembered that Mary Magdalene was at one time terribly afflicted with demons and that Jesus had cured her. (Mark 16: 9.) It seems that she was in good circumstances, and that as a disciple of Jesus, she ministered to Jesus and the disciples the temporal things for their conduct. There is no evidence that she was at one time an unchaste woman. Joanna was the wife of Chuzas who was Herod's steward; we do not know any more of her; Susanna is associated with Mary Magdalene and Joanna. The loving ministry of these women is recorded by Luke. (Luke 8: 2, 3.) This extraordinary report of the resurrection of Jesus demanded that the names of some who reported it should be given; three are mentioned, which was a sufficient number to establish legally the truth of the report. (Deut. 19: 15.)

12 **But Peter arose, and ran unto the tomb:**—The conduct of Peter is described in graphic language; he "arose," "ran" to the tomb, stooping and looking in, he saw the "linen cloths by themselves," and then "departed to his home," and "wondering" at what he had seen. The graphic mention of his succes-

sive acts are brought out in an impressive way. He ran in his eagerness to see the basis for the report that the women had brought; when he stooped down and saw everything in order in the empty tomb, he knew that the body had not been stolen and that there were deliberation and care in the leaving; he was full of surprise; his mind was confused with doubt, yet the evidence was so clear that he could not reject it; he was in this frame of mind when he returned to his home. Peter was impulsive; he and John both ran together to the tomb, and John outran Peter and arrived first, but did not go into the sepulchre, but just stooped down and looked in and saw the cloths placed in order in the empty tomb; but when Peter arrived, true to his impulsive nature, he went into the tomb and saw the things which are here described. (John 20: 3-10.) There was no necessity for them to remain at the tomb, for it was empty.

2. THE WALK TO EMMAUS
24: 13-35

13 And behold, two of them were going that very day to a village named Emmaus, which was threescore furlongs from Jerusalem. 14 And they com-

---

13 **And behold, two of them were going**—Mark (16: 12, 13) records a very brief account of these two disciples and their walk; the other writers do not mention this event. It seems that Jesus had made five appearances on the day of his resurrection. These appearances were (1) to Mary Magdalene (John and Mark); (2) to other women (Matthew); (3) to the two going to Emmaus; (4) to Simon Peter (Luke 24: 24); (5) to ten apostles and others. Emmaus was a village "threescore furlongs from Jerusalem," or about seven miles from Jerusalem. There have been many suppositions as to which of the two disciples are mentioned here; it has been supposed that these two were on the way to Galilee. The evidence seems to be clear that these two were not of the apostles, for it is said that these two disciples "returned to Jerusalem, and found the eleven gathered together." (Verse 33.) Judas had commit-

muned with each other of all these things which had happened. 15 And it
came to pass, while they communed and questioned together, that Jesus himself drew near, and went with them. 16 But their eyes were holden that
they should not know him. 17 And he said unto them, [7]What communica-

[7]Gr. *What words are these that ye exchange one with another*

---

ted suicide, hence the "eleven." This was the same day, the
first day of the week, or Sunday, that Jesus arose from the
dead. Emmaus is not located; its site is unknown.

14 **And they communed with each other**—One of these two
disciples is named Cleopas. (Verse 18.) Some have supposed the other one to have been Luke, but there is no evidence of this. They were discussing the strange incident that
had taken place that day. They "communed" or talked together in an animated conversation; one suggested one fact
and another suggested another; they compared their views
and conjectures as to the meaning of all that had taken place
that day.

15, 16 **And it came to pass, while they communed**—While
they walked along they argued the question of the resurrection of Jesus; they could not account for the facts of the
empty tomb, and they did not as yet understand the predictions that Jesus had made about his resurrection. It was such
a new and astounding thing that they were confused about it.
While they were thus discussing the matter. "Jesus himself
drew near, and went with them." They did not know Jesus;
he had joined the two as they journeyed along, but they had
not recognized him. Mary Magdalene did not recognize him,
neither did the disciples on the Sea of Galilee at first. The
reason the two disciples here did not recognize him was partly
because he appeared in another form from that which they
were accustomed to. (Mark 16: 12.) Another reason they did
not recognize Jesus was that "their eyes were holden that
they should not know him."

17 **And he said unto them, What communications**—As yet
they did not know that they were in company with the risen
Lord; he asked them, by way of getting into the conversation,
"What communications are these that ye have one with an-

tions are these that ye have one with another, as ye walk? And they stood
still, looking sad. 18 And one of them, named Cleopas, answering said unto
him, *Dost thou alone sojourn in Jerusalem and not know the things which
are come to pass there in these days? 19 And he said unto them, What
things? And they said unto him, The things concerning Jesus the Nazarene,
who was a prophet mighty in deed and word before God and all the people:
20 and how the chief priests and our rulers delivered him up to be con-

———

⁸Or, *Dost thou sojourn alone in Jerusalem, and knowest thou not the things*

———

other, as ye walk?" Literally, the word here for "communications" means "to exchange with" or "throw back and forth to
each other," as one may throw back and forth like a ball, from
one to another; it was a game of words; his question seemed
to astound them, for he betrayed, they thought, ignorance of
the great events that had just transpired. So they stopped
suddenly in the road and looked with sadness upon him for
being so ignorant of the events that had just transpired.
They looked sad. Their melancholy looks and argumentative
discussion were what one coming up might naturally notice
first. Jesus knew what was taking place, but he asked the
question to get them interested in what he was going to say
to them.

18 **And one of them, named Cleopas,**—This is not the same
name as "Cleophas," in the Greek, Clopas. (John 19: 25.)
The question is one of surprise that even a foreigner could
lodge in Jerusalem and not know what things had taken
place; it does not mean, "Have you just come to Jerusalem,"
or "Art thou only a lodger," but is more explicit—"Dost thou
alone sojourn," and knowest not these things? That is, are
you the *only* one who sojourns as a stranger in Jerusalem and
who does not know the great events that have so recently occurred?

19, 20 **And he said unto them, What things?**—Jesus at once
puts the main question as to facts, not as a confession of ignorance, nor as a necessary implication that he did not know,
but to induce the heavy heart to express its grief. The question was designed to evoke more specific statement of the
events referred to, and Jesus neither admits that he is a stranger in Jerusalem nor denies any knowledge of the events
which had taken place. They at once replied that they were

demned to death, and crucified him. 21 But we hoped that it was he who
should redeem Israel. Yea and besides all this, it is now the third day since
these things came to pass. 22 Moreover certain women of our company
amazed us, having been early at the tomb; 23 and when they found not his
body, they came, saying, that they had also seen a vision of angels, who said

discussing the "things concerning Jesus the Nazarene."
"Nazarene" here simply means that Jesus was from the city of
Nazareth; this is where Joseph and Mary made their home,
and where Jesus grew up. (Luke 1: 26; 2: 39; 18: 37.)
These two disciples think that they are informing Jesus of the
prophet who was "mighty in deed and word before God and
all the people." It should be noted that Jesus was "mighty"
in the eyes of these two disciples, both in "deed" or miracles
and "word" or teaching. He had the power of God in his
deeds and in his words. (John 12: 17.) He performed powerful miracles and delivered powerful discourses. (Acts 2: 22;
7: 22.) Jesus was "mighty" not only "before God," but before "all the people."

21 **But we hoped that it was he**—These disciples still
thought of Jesus as a temporal deliverer; they had the right
idea about Jesus as a deliverer, but they made the wrong application of it. Jesus was the deliverer of Israel from their
sins, but was not the deliverer of them from the Roman government. They speak this in despair. They added that "it is
now the third day since these things came to pass." They
speak as if something remarkable had been predicted, but had
not been understood; it looked to them that if Jesus was to be
raised from the dead, he should be doing something toward
the establishment of his kingdom, for it was now "the third
day" since he had been crucified. They were not expecting
his resurrection on that day, but that so long a time had
passed without any relief to their anxieties.

22, 23 **Moreover certain women of our company**—These two
disciples now reported to the risen Lord just what they had
heard through "certain women," who had visited the empty
tomb and had seen that it was empty and that they had "seen
a vision of angels," who reported that Jesus was alive. These
two disciples reported some of the minor points of the testi-

that he was alive. 24 And certain of them that were with us went to the
tomb, and found it even so as the women had said: but him they saw not.
25 And he said unto them, O foolish men, and slow of heart to believe ⁹in all
that the prophets have spoken! 26 Behooved it not the Christ to suffer these
things, and to enter into his glory? 27 And beginning from Moses and from

⁹Or, *after*

mony of the women, but did not report to him the main point
of the testimony of the women—namely, that Jesus had been
raised from the dead.

24 And certain of them that were with us—Luke had already recorded (verse 12) that Peter had gone to the tomb,
but here he records that "certain of them" had also gone to
the tomb and found that the report of the women was true,
but "him they saw not." They did not see Jesus as others had
reported seeing him. This explains why they were so confused; it seemed to them that their hopes were to be blasted,
for he is dead. However, they had rumors that the body had
disappeared; this they believed to be true; but what should
they believe? Some said that Jesus was alive; others that
the tomb was empty, but they had not seen him; so these two
disciples did not know what to believe.

25 And he said unto them, O foolish men,—Jesus calls these
two disciples "foolish men"; he did not call them "fools" in
the sense that we speak of people as being fools; the original
means "dull of perception." They had read what the prophets
had spoken, but had failed to make the application to Jesus;
he further represented them as "slow of heart" in believing all
that the prophets had said concerning the Messiah. They did
not see that the sufferings of Jesus, his crucifixion, and his resurrection all were predicted by the prophets. Here the risen
Lord declares that the Jesus of Nazareth was the Messiah of
prophecy; he linked the two together.

26 Behooved it not the Christ—So far they had utterly
failed to understand the prophets or what Jesus had predicted
of himself; are not these the "things" which by the necessity
of the case Christ must suffer, and then enter into his glory?
In view of what the prophets had foretold, the Messiah should
suffer all the things which Jesus of Nazareth had suffered.

all the prophets, he interpreted to them in all the scriptures the things concerning himself. 28 And they drew nigh unto the village, whither they were going: and he made as though he would go further. 29 And they constrained him, saying, Abide with us; for it is toward evening, and the day is now far spent. And he went in to abide with them. 30 And it came to pass, when he had sat down with them to meat, he took the ¹bread and blessed;

¹Or, loaf

27 **And beginning from Moses**—Jesus presented a comprehensive view of all the Messianic prophecies from the first of the series of predictions in the writings of Moses down through the prophets to the time of his appearance; then the fulfillment of these predictions in himself; Jesus thus declared that he was the heart of the Old Testament scriptures. In accepting the scriptures with the prophets, they should have understood that Jesus was their long-looked-for Messiah.

28 **And they drew nigh unto the village,**—The risen Lord suddenly appeared on the scene in company with two disciples to Emmaus; he joined in the conversation which was about himself; the two disciples did not recognize him even after he had rebuked them for their slowness to believe what the prophets had taught of the Messiah. When they came to the village of Emmaus, Jesus made as though he would not stop, but would go on.

29 **And they constrained him, saying, Abide with us;**—Jesus had not said that he would go on, but was simply passing on, as any traveler would do; yet he was willing to abide with them, if they invited him. Jesus never forces himself upon anyone; people must desire him and invite him. "Behold, I stand at the door and knock: if any man hear my voice and open the door, I will come in to him, and will sup with him, and he with me." (Rev. 3: 20.) They "constrained" or compelled with courteous words, him to sojourn with them. By their gentle pressure of hospitality, they urged him to abide there, giving the reason that the day was far spent and that evening was very near. They were grateful to him for teaching them of the Messiah, and had learned from a stranger, as they thought, much about the prophets; they were ready to show hospitality to him as a token of their gratitude toward him.

and breaking *it* he gave to them. 31 And their eyes were opened, and they knew him; and he vanished out of their sight. 32 And they said one to another, Was not our heart burning within us, while he spake to us in the way, while he opened to us the scriptures? 33 And they rose up that very

---

30, 31 **And it came to pass, when he had sat down**—They had taken a long walk together; when the simple meal was prepared, Jesus was invited to eat with them. We are not told whether they asked him to "give thanks," but when he "took the bread" and "blessed" or gave thanks for it, he gave to them to eat. They reclined on couches and did not sit at the table as is our custom. While he was in the act of distributing to them, in an instant, their eyes "were opened" and they immediately recognized their Lord. "Their eyes were opened" is put in contrast with "their eyes were holden that they should not know him." (Verse 16.) If their eyes were "holden" through some miraculous power, "their eyes were opened" by the same power; whatever had kept them from recognizing him all along had now been removed and they "knew him." It seems that so soon as they recognized him "he vanished out of their sight."

32 **And they said one to another,**—Jesus had not simply suddenly departed from them, but he had passed away from them invisibly; so after his disappearance they recalled that their hearts burned within them while he was talking to them; this strange experience could not be explained or accounted for at the time; there was a strangeness to them that they did not know its cause, but now they knew the cause of the strange feeling that they experienced in the presence of the risen Lord. They recognize now that "he opened" to them "the scriptures." They saw the deeper and true spiritual meaning of the scriptures; they had read the words of the prophets, but had not understood the meaning and application. (See 2 Cor. 3: 14-18.) Some have thought that Jesus had spent three or four hours with them on the journey from Jerusalem to Emmaus; however, we do not know just where on the way he joined them, and hence cannot estimate the time that he was with them.

hour, and returned to Jerusalem, and found the eleven gathered together, and them that were with them, 34 saying, The Lord is risen indeed, and hath appeared to Simon. 35 And they rehearsed the things *that happened* in the way, and how he was known of them in the breaking of the bread.

33, 34 **And they rose up that very hour,**—These two disciples had left Jerusalem, about seven and a half miles or "threescore furlongs" (verse 13) from Emmaus, and had walked leisurely along conversing together about the strange things that had recently occurred in Jerusalem; the risen Lord had joined them without their recognizing him, and he had expounded to them the prophecies concerning the Messiah; their eyes had been opened and they now recognized their Lord. He had suddenly vanished from their presence and sight; they lost no time in returning to Jerusalem, the scene of the strange incidents which had so stirred them. These disciples were now full of amazement and joy; "they rose up that very hour, and returned to Jerusalem"; they had intended lodging in Emmaus, but they now returned to Jerusalem with haste. It must have been nine o'clock that evening with they arrived in Jerusalem, for they did not get to Emmaus until the day was far spent. We are not told how they got through the gates at this late hour into the city, but the gates were not closed until late during the week of the Passover. They "found the eleven gathered together" and others who were with "the eleven." They at once reported: "The Lord is risen indeed, and hath appeared to Simon." John records that "the doors were shut" for fear of the Jews. (John 20: 19.) Paul mentions his appearance to Simon. (1 Cor. 15: 5.) His appearance now seems to have more deeply impressed the eleven than the other appearances on the morning of that day, as these two disciples added their testimony of the other evidences that had been manifested.

35 **And they rehearsed the things that happened in the way,**—These two disciples add their enthusiastic testimony to the resurrection; they related how he had appeared to them and had revealed himself. The evidence of these two disciples was confirmatory, not revolutionary; the testimony of the women was true and should be believed after all; they did not

recognize Jesus in his exegesis, but they did in his "breaking of the bread." Some have applied this "breaking of the bread" to the Lord's Supper; however, there is no justification for this application. The light gradually dawned on the disciples and they finally believed in the risen Lord. The minds of "the eleven" and other disciples were now ready to receive fuller light and more abundant truth—the Christ had been raised from the dead.

3. APPEARANCE OF JESUS IN JERUSALEM
24: 36-43

36 And as they spake these things, he himself stood in the midst of them, ²and saith unto them, Peace be unto you. 37 But they were terrified and affrighted, and supposed that they beheld a spirit. 38 And he said unto them, Why are ye troubled? and wherefore do questionings arise in your heart?

²Some ancient authorities omit *and saith unto them, Peace* be *unto you*

36 **And as they spake these things,**—Parallel records of this event are found in Mark 16: 14 and John 20: 19-25. John gives a fuller record than Mark, so we have three records of this appearance. Mark says that they were reclining at a meal; John adds that they had the doors shut for fear of the Jews, and that Thomas was not with "the eleven." (John 20: 19, 24.) His appearance was mysterious, for the narratives imply that no one knew how he entered. Without any intimation of his coming, he suddenly stood among them; they heard his voice, recognized his greeting. Luke gives the appearance with accuracy and clearness. The disciples were astonished, terrified, and affrighted at the sudden appearance of the risen Lord.

37 **But they were terrified**—The manner of the appearance of the risen Lord filled the disciples with awe, and caused them to withdraw, for the moment, from his presence. While they were discussing his resurrection and what they had just heard from the two disciples from Emmaus, he suddenly appeared in their midst; they had just heard of his appearance some miles away, but now he appears in their midst.

38 **And he said unto them, Why are ye troubled?**—They were perplexed and hesitated to believe that he had risen, and

39 See my hands and my feet, that it is I myself: handle me, and see; for a spirit hath not flesh and bones, as ye behold me having. 40 ªAnd when he had said this, he showed them his hands and his feet. 41 And while they still disbelieved for joy, and wondered, he said unto them, Have ye here any-

ªSome ancient authorities omit ver. 40

yet they were unable to deny the testimony of others and the evidence of their own senses; they were slow to accept the truth of his resurrection, and could not deny it. Hence, the Lord rebukes them for the doubts and hesitations which arose in their hearts. They were doubting or hesitating about a matter which their spiritual perception ought to have recognized at once. Jesus helps them to make up their mind on the question; when once convinced, they can then preach with the highest degree of certainty his resurrection.

39 **See my hands and my feet,**—The risen Lord made them look at his pierced hands and feet, and handle his flesh, using the senses both of sight and feeling; they could hear his voice and recognize him from his speech; hence three of their physical senses were called into action to convince them. Surely a look at his hands and feet would be sufficient to convince them; but to clear the matter he tells them that he is not just a spirit, for "a spirit hath not flesh and bones, as ye behold me having." There was reality present that they could not deny, neither was it possessed by a ghost or a spirit.

40 **And when he had said this,**—Jesus not only demanded that they look at his hands and feet, but he showed them his hands and his feet pierced with the cruel nails. They used the sense of sight and then they were called upon to "handle" him and thus use the sense of touch; they had used the sense of hearing; they knew his voice. The risen Lord thus offered his scarred and mangled hands and feet for particular examining to convince them that he was alive.

41 **And while they still disbelieved for joy,**—His disciples were slowly convinced; they were overjoyed and were slow to accept the facts as real. After imposing unmistakable evidence upon their sight, touch, and hearing, the risen Lord now gives another evidence of his resurrection and reality. He asked: "Have ye here anything to eat?" He called for

thing to eat? 42 And they gave him a piece of a broiled fish.⁴ 43 And he took it, and ate before them.

⁴Many ancient authorities add *and a honeycomb*

food and ate before their eyes. They were eating when he appeared in their midst at this time. (Verse 35.)

42, 43 **And they gave him a piece of a broiled fish.**—This was possibly a remnant of the meal that they had just eaten. Many ancient authorities add "and a honeycomb." Honey in the comb was a common article of food with the ancients. (Psalm 19: 10; Prov. 24: 13; 27: 7; Song of Solomon 51: 1.) Jesus took the food and ate in their presence. His eating food was additional evidence that he had been raised from the dead. They are now to believe in his resurrection; it was no

THE APPEARANCES AFTER HIS RESURRECTION

ORDER	TIME	TO WHOM	PLACE	RECORD
1	Early Sunday morning	Mary Magdalene	Near the tomb at Jerusalem	Mark 16: 9 John 20: 11-18
2	Sunday morning	Women returning from the tomb	Near Jerusalem	Matt. 28:9, 10
3	Sunday	Simon Peter alone	Near Jerusalem	Luke 24: 34
4	Sunday afternoon	Two disciples going to Emmaus	Between Jerusalem and Emmaus, and at Emmaus	Luke 24: 13-31
5	Sunday evening	Apostles, except Thomas	Jerusalem	John 20: 19-25
6	Sunday evening of next week	Apostles, Thomas being present	Jerusalem	John 20: 26-29
7	Unknown	Seven disciples fishing	Sea of Galilee	John 21: 1-13
8	Unknown	Eleven disciples on mountain	Galilee	Matt. 28:16-20
9	Unknown	About 500 brethren at once	Galilee	1 Cor. 15: 6
10	Unknown	James only	Probably Jerusalem	1 Cor. 15: 7
11	Unknown	All the apostles at ascension	Mount of Olives near Bethany	Luke 24: 50,51 Act 1: 6-12

dream, no conjuring of a worried brain, no fancy of a grieved mind, no hallucination; they must believe, although so difficult to be convinced. Having thus minutely described this bodily appearance of Jesus after his resurrection, Luke passes over the other appearances, and gives his farewell words and final appearance at his ascension.

A tabulated list of the appearances of our Lord after his resurrection is here given, together with the time, place, and record.

Three times we are told that the disciples of Jesus touched him after he.arose. (Matt. 28: 9; Luke 24: 39; John 20: 27.) Twice we are told that he ate with them after his resurrection. (Luke 24: 42; John 21: 12, 13.)

4. THE COMMISSION
24: 44-49

44 And he said unto them, These are my words which I spake unto you, while I was yet with you, that all things must needs be fulfilled, which are written in the law of Moses, and the prophets, and the psalms, concerning

44 **And he said unto them, These are my words**—Luke omits other appearances of Jesus during the forty days after his resurrection; he gives here a summary of what Jesus taught the disciples between his resurrection and ascension. The "and" here does not necessarily denote close connection, but only a general continuation of the account and a brief statement of what Jesus said; this might be at different times before his ascension; here is given the substance of his last conversation with his disciples; it includes the commission. "All things must needs be fulfilled," which had been prophesied of Jesus, or what had been "written in the law of Moses, and the prophets, and the psalms." This includes all of the Old Testament, for here is mentioned the three divisions into which the Hebrews divided the Old Testament. "The law of Moses" included the first five books, or Pentateuch; "the prophets" included the books of Joshua, Judges, First and Second Samuel, First and Second Kings, three of the major prophets (Isaiah, Jeremiah, and Ezekiel), and the twelve minor prophets; "the psalms" included the poetical and all the other

me. 45 Then opened he their mind, that they might understand the scriptures; 46 and he said unto them, Thus it is written, that the Christ should
suffer, and rise again from the dead the third day; 47 and that repentance

---

Old Testament books sometimes called "the scriptures."
(John 5: 39.) This group contained, Psalms, Job, Proverbs,
Song of Solomon, Ruth, Lamentations, Ecclesiastes, Esther,
Daniel, Ezra, Nehemiah, and First and Second Chronicles.
When Jesus declared that all things must be fulfilled which
were written of him, he included the entire Old Testament.

45 **Then opened he their mind,**—Jesus taught his disciples
that all that was written of him in the Old Testament was fulfilled; he took the different passages that referred to him and
showed how they were fulfilled in him; in this way he
"opened" "their mind," so that they could understand. Some
think that he gave them unusual power to perceive the truth
of the "scriptures"; however, it is not necessary to infer that
they needed any divine aid to understand his language. They
could easily recall the bitter experience through which they
had gone in the arrest, trials, crucifixion, and burial of Jesus;
his resurrection was so fresh in their minds that they could
now see the meaning of the Old Testament passages. They
had been slow and dull in understanding these truths, but
now their minds were clear on these things. The Holy Spirit
afterward brought these teachings to their remembrance.
The doctrine of the Old Testament scriptures with regard to
the suffering, dying, rising of the Messiah, they now understood.

46, 47 **and he said unto them, Thus it is written,**—It was according to the divine plan that Christ should die and rise
again; God in his wisdom had seen it necessary for his own
highest glory, and had so arranged the sacred plan from the
beginning. There seems to be no direct quotation given here;
but the divine plan was carried out. (See Isa. 53; Hos. 6: 2.)
"Thus it is written" is a general expression meaning that it
was written in the scripture that the things which had taken
place concerning him had been predicted; it was "written"
that it should be so, and it was necessary therefore that it
should be. If Christ had not suffered and risen again, the

[5]and remission of sins should be preached in his name unto all the [6]nations, beginning from Jerusalem. 48 Ye are witnesses of these things. 49 And

[5]Some ancient authorities read *unto*
[6]Or *nations. Beginning from Jerusalem ye are witnesses*

scriptures would not have been fulfilled. "Repentance and re-mission of sins should be preached in his name unto all the nation." These words are a brief summary of the doctrine of the gospel; they constitute the commission that Jesus gave to his disciples. The necessity of repentance and the promise of remission of sins are included in the gospel. The gospel was to be preached by the authority of Christ "unto all the nations, beginning from Jerusalem." The risen Lord here not only pointed out that the Old Testament predicted his suffer-ing, his death, and his resurrection, but he also found in the Old Testament the preaching of repentance and forgiveness of sins to all nations. Two things were taught here; first, the apostles and first proclaimers of the gospel should not shrink from offering salvation to the greatest sinner; they were not to regard even the city where Jesus was crucified as hope-lessly wicked, and too bad to be benefited by the gospel; the Jewish leaders who crucified Jesus were to have opportunity of hearing the gospel and being saved. The second lesson learned here is that the first offer of the terms of the gospel should be made to the Jews.

48, 49 **Ye are witnesses of these things.**—The apostles had been with him from the beginning, "all the time that the Lord Jesus went in and went out among us." (Acts 1: 21.) They were to go forth and testify to all men the things which they had seen and been taught; they were to commit the same to faithful men, record it in the gospels, epistles, and pass them on to others. One duty of these disciples was to be witnesses for Christ; he did not send forth orators or enthusiasts, but simply teachers who would bear faithful witness to all that they had seen. They are promised the Holy Spirit which should come to them. They are instructed to "tarry ye in the city, until ye be clothed with power from on high." God had promised in the Old Testament prophecies to send the Holy Spirit which came on the day of Pentecost. (Isa. 44: 3; Jer.

behold, I send forth the promise of my Father upon you: but tarry ye in the
city, until ye be clothed with power from on high.

31: 33, 34; Ezek. 36: 27; Joel 2: 28.) This shows the certainty
of the coming of the Holy Spirit; it should be noted that Jesus
said: "I send forth," which can refer only to a person. It
should further be noted that the risen Lord here unites himself with God the Father in sending the Holy Spirit. They
were to wait in Jerusalem until the Holy Spirit came; they
were to "be clothed" with power from God. "Clothed" literally means to be "invested with" something which one did not
naturally possess. (Rom. 13: 14; 1 Cor. 15: 53; Gal. 3: 27;
Col. 3: 9, 10.) The command for them to tarry in Jerusalem
was repeated just before his ascension. (Acts 1: 4.)

5. THE ASCENSION
24: 50-53

50 And he led them out until *they were* over against Bethany: and he

---

50 **And he led them out until**—The risen Lord "led his disciples out until they came to a point on the Mount of Olives
which was over against or opposite Bethany; Bethany was in
sight. He "led" them by going before them and their following him; he had frequently visited this place with them; he
was now on the eastern slope of the Mount of Olives. He had
recalled Lazarus to life near this place; it was here that the
prophet of old had seen him coming. (Zech. 14: 4.) Mark
16: 19, 20 gives a parallel record of this event; Luke relates
more fully here and in Acts 1: 9-12 what Mark briefly states.
Here Luke takes no account of the forty days through which
the risen Lord met frequently his disciples and spoke to them
many things concerning the kingdom of God. Luke passes
over the appearances of Jesus to the eleven, when Thomas
was present (John 20: 24-29); also his appearance in Galilee
to seven of his disciples (John 21: 1-24), and again to above
five hundred (Matt. 28: 16-20; 1 Cor. 15: 6), the appearance to
James (1 Cor. 15: 7), and then to all the apostles (Acts 1: 3-
8). As he lifted up his hands he "blessed" his disciples; and
as he was in the act of blessing them, he disappeared out of

lifted up his hands, and blessed them. 51 And it came to pass, while he blessed them, he parted from them, [7]and was carried up into heaven. 52 And they [8]worshipped him, and returned to Jerusalem with great joy: 53 and were continually in the temple, blessing God.

[7]Some ancient authorities omit *and was carried up into heaven*
[8]Some ancient authorities omit *worshipped him, and.* See marginal note on ch. 4.7

their sight. The last vision that they get of him is as he is in the act of blessing them; he came to earth to save man, and he leaves the earth as he blesses his followers.

51 **And it came to pass, while he blessed them,**—While the risen Lord was blessing his little faithful group of disciples, he parted from them, and was carried up into heaven. The simplicity and dignity with which Luke describes this great event are impressive; there is no speculation about how the body of Jesus could go up; he simply says that "he parted from them." "He parted from them" and was seen rising till a cloud received him from the view of their strained eyes; they can think of him henceforth only as having gone into the heavens.

> "Lift up your heads, O ye gates;
> And be ye lifted up, ye everlasting doors:
> And the King of glory will come in.
> Who is the King of glory?
> Jehovah strong and mighty,
> Jehovah mighty in battle.
> Lift up your heads, O ye gates;
> Yea, lift them up, ye everlasting doors:
> And the King of glory will come in.
> Who is the King of glory?
> Jehovah of hosts,
> He is the King of glory."
>
> (Psalm 24: 7-10.)

52, 53 **And they worshipped him, and returned to Jerusalem** —The risen Lord remained on earth "by the space of forty days" (Acts 1: 3), after his resurrection, before he ascended. His repeated appearances during the forty days had comforted his disciples, cleared this spiritual vision, reestablished and confirmed their faith, corrected their former views of his kingdom, and gave them an understanding of the scriptures pertaining to his mission to earth. Later Peter wrote: "Blessed be the God and Father of our Lord Jesus Christ, who according to his great mercy begat us again unto a living hope by the resurrection of Jesus Christ from the dead." (1 Pet. 1: 3.) This apostles now saw in the crucified but risen and ascended Lord, the Christ, the long-expected Messiah; hence they worhiped him and returned to Jerusalem in obedience to his command ,and waited for further developments. This is the first formal act of adoration which we ever read of the disciples' paying to our Lord; their knowledge of his Messiahship and divinity was now clear and distinct; hence, the "great joy" which they had as they returned to Jerusalem. The darkness was past and the true light was now shining upon them. (1 John 2: 8.) Their worship continued; they went to the temple as was the custom and there blessed God. The temple was a place for all pious Jews in Jerusalem; in its spacious courts all sorts of worshipers met daily without interruption, or interference with one another. Even later, when the church was established, "every day, in the temple and at home, they ceased not to teach and to preach Jesus as the Christ." (Acts 5: 42.) It seems to have been such an established custom for all pious Jews to assemble in the temple that the apostles could even preach the gospel there.

Luke began his account of the earthly life of Jesus by describing a scene in the temple when Zacharias had his vision and now he leaves us in his narrative in the temple with the disciples worshiping God—so he ends his narrative as he begins it by a scene in the temple at Jerusalem.

In concluding these comments on Luke, it may be helpful to many readers to list the principal events which are recorded by Luke alone, and are not mentioned by Matthew, Mark, and John; they are fifty-eight in number, as follows:

BIBLIOGRAPHY

Abbott, Lyman: Commentary on the Gospels.
Alford, H.: The New Testament for English Readers.
Bengal, J. A.: Gnomon of the New Testament.
Bliss, G. R.: The Gospel of Luke.
Boles, H. Leo: Elam's Notes, 1929-31.
Boles, H. Leo: International Sunday School Lessons, Adult Quarterly, 1932-38.
Boles, H. Leo: Commentary on the Gospel According to Matthew.
Broughton, Len G.: Kingdom Parables and Their Teaching.
Brown, David: Commentary on the Four Gospels.
Bruce, A: B.: The Miraculous Element of the Gospel.
Burgess, George: Gospel of Luke.
Burkitt, W.: Expository Notes on the New Testament.
Buttrick, George A.: The Parables of Jesus.
Cadoux, A. T.: Parables of Jesus.
Campbell, Colin: Critical Studies in Luke's Gospel.
Campbell, George: The Four Gospels.
Clark, G. W.: Notes on the Gospel of Luke.
Clarke, Adam: Clarke's Commentary.
Cowles, Henry: Commentary on Luke.
Dale, R. W.: The Living Christ and the Four Gospels.
Dods, Marcus: The Parables of Our Lord.
Elam, E. A.: Elam's Notes, 1922-28.
Erdman, C. R.: The Gospel of Luke.
Everest, H. W.: The Divine Demonstration.
Farrar, F. W.: The Gospel According to Luke.
Foote, J.: Lectures on the Gospel According to Luke.
Godet, F.: A Commentary on the Gospel of Luke.
Habershon, A. R.: The Study of the Parables.
Hall, C. H.: Practical and Expository Notes on the Gospels.
Hannam, W. L.: Luke the Evangelist.
Hastings, James: Dictionary of the Bible.
Henry, Matthew: Commentary on the Bible.
Hill, John L.: Outline Studies in Luke.
Jacobus, M. W.: Notes on the Gospel.
Jacobus, Nourse, and Zenos: A New Standard Bible Dictionary.
Jamieson, Fausset, Brown: A Commentary on the Old and New Testaments.
Johnson, B. W.: The People's New Testament with Notes.
Josephus, Flavius: The Works of Josephus.
Knox, R. C.: Knowing the Bible.
Laidlaw, John: The Miracles of Our Lord.
Lamar, J. S.: Commentary on Luke.
Lipscomb, David: Gospel Advocate, 1855-1915.
MacKnight, James: A Harmony of the Four Gospels.
Maclaren, A.: The Gospel of St. Luke.
Meyer, H. A. W.: Gospel of Mark and Luke.
Morgan, G. Campbell: The Parables of the Kingdom.
Morris and Smith: Popular Expositions of the Gospels.
Norwood, F. W., and Barry, F. R.: Studies in Luke.
Orr, James: The International Standard Bible Encyclopedia.
Owen, J. J.: A Commentary on the Gospel of Luke.
Papina, Giovanni: Life of Christ.
Peloubet, F. N.: Select Notes on International Lessons, 1880-1937.

Peloubet, F. N.: Bible Dictionary.
Pendleton, J. M.: Brief Notes on New Testament.
Plummer, A.: Critical and Exegetical Commentary on the Gospel of Luke.
Rice, E. W.: People's Commentary on the Gospel According to Luke.
Robertson, A. T.: Harmony of the Four Gospels.
Robertson, A. T.: A Translation of Luke's Gospel.
Robertson, A. T.: Word Pictures in the New Testament (Vol. 2, Luke).
Robertson, A. T.: Short Grammar of the Greek New Testament.
Robertson, A. T.: Epochs in the Life of Jesus.
Robertson, A. T.: Pharisees and Jesus.
Robertson, A. T.: Studies in the New Testament.
Ryle, J. C.: Expository Thoughts of the Gospels (Vols. 1 and 2, Luke).
Schaff-Herzog: Encyclopedia of Religious Knowledge.
Scott, Thomas: Commentary on the Holy Bible.
Smith, William: Dictionary of the Bible.
Speer, R. E.: Studies in the Gospel of Luke.
Stalker, James: The Life of Jesus Christ.
Stier, Rudolph: The Words of the Lord Jesus.
Streeter, D. H.: The Four Gospels.
Summers, T. O.: Commentary on the Gospels (Vol. 3, Luke).
Thayer, J. H.: Greek-English Lexicon of the New Testament.
Trench, R. C.: Notes on the Parables of Our Lord.
Trench, R. C.: Notes on the Miracles.
Trench, R. C.: Studies in the Gospels.
Trench, R. C.: Synonyms of the New Testament.
Van Doren, W. H.: A Suggestive Commentary on Luke.
Van Oosterzee, J. J.: The Gospel According to Luke (Translated by Philip Schaff).
Vincent, M. R.: Word Studies in the New Testament.
Walker, R. H.: A Study of Luke's Gospel.
Weiss, B.: A Commentary on the New Testament.
Whedon, D. D.: Commentary on the Gospels.
Wilson, Benjamin: Studies in Luke.
Wilson, Bishop: A Plain Commentary on the Four Holy Gospels.
Young, Robert: Analytical Concordance of the Bible.

TRANSLATIONS OF THE NEW TESTAMENT

A New Testament in Modern Speech, Fenton.
Centenary Translation of the New Testament, Montgomery.
Douay Version.
Emphatic Diaglott.
Greek-English New Testament.
Modern Readers' Bible, Moulton.
New Testament in Modern Speech, Weymouth.
New Testament, H. T. Anderson.
New Testament, Goodspeed.
New Testament Critically Emphasized, Rotherham.
New Testament, Latin Vulgate.
Revised Version (Standard Edition).
The Authorized Version (King James).
The Holy Bible, Moffatt.
The Holy Bible, Young.
The New Testament, American Bible Union.
The Riverside New Testament, Ballantine.
Translation of the New Testament, Godbey.
Twentieth Century New Testament.

INDEX TO SUBJECTS

CPSIA information can be obtained
at www.ICGtesting.com
Printed in the USA
LVOW08s2136160217
524567LV00002B/93/P